COOL STUFF EXPLODED

GET INSIDE MODERN TECHNOLOGY

LONDON, NEW YORK,
MELBOURNE, MUNICH, and DELHI

For Tall Tree Ltd.:
Editors Rob Colson, Jon Richards
Designer Ben Ruocco

For Dorling Kindersley:
Senior editors Victoria Heyworth-Dunne, Claire Nottage
Senior art editor Smiljka Surla
Managing editor Linda Esposito
Managing art editor Diane Thistlethwaite
Publishing manager Andrew Macintyre
Category publisher Laura Buller
Design development manager Sophia Tampakopoulos-Turner
Picture researcher Rebecca Sodergren
Senior production editor Vivianne Ridgeway
Jacket editor Mariza O'Keeffe
Jacket designer Yumiko Tahata
Production controller Pip Tinsley
US editor Margaret Parrish

Consultant Jon Woodcock
Illustrators Nikid Design Ltd.

First published in the United States in 2008 by
DK Publishing
375 Hudson Street, New York, New York 10014

Copyright © 2008 Dorling Kindersley Limited

08 09 10 11 12 10 9 8 7 6 5 4 3 2 1
CD175 – 09/08

A catalog record for this book
is available from the Library of Congress

ISBN: 978-0-7566-4028-6

Printed and bound by Hung Hing, China

**Discover more at
www.dk.com**

COOL STUFF EXPLODED

GET INSIDE MODERN TECHNOLOGY

written by
Chris Woodford

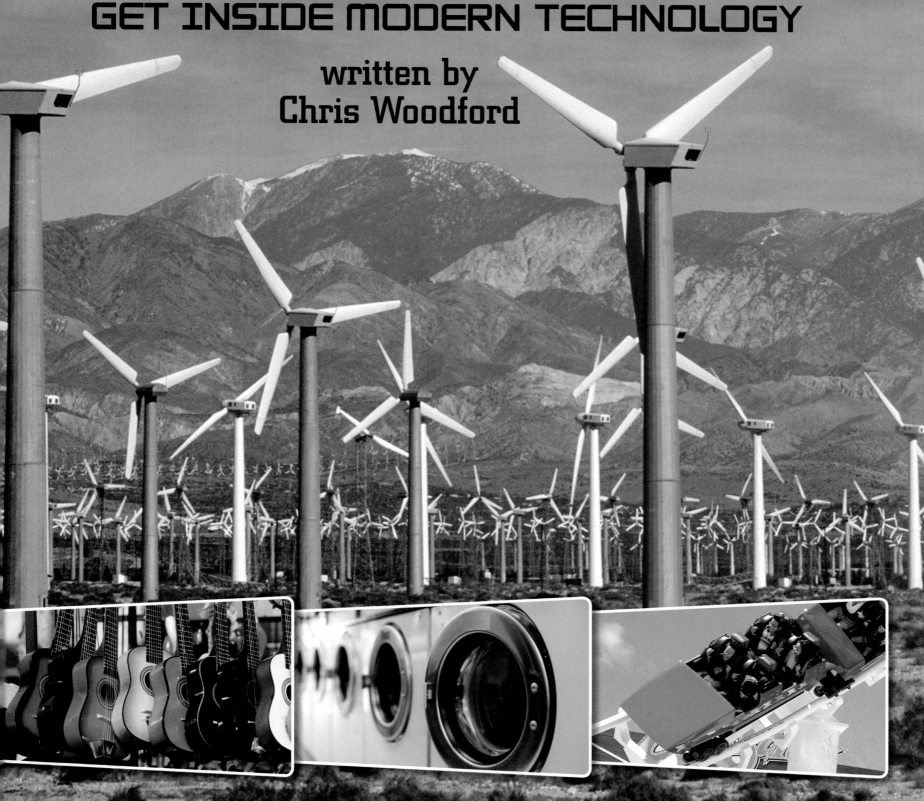

CONTENTS

ENTERTAINMENT AND LEISURE

CONTENTS

DIGITAL TECHNOLOGY

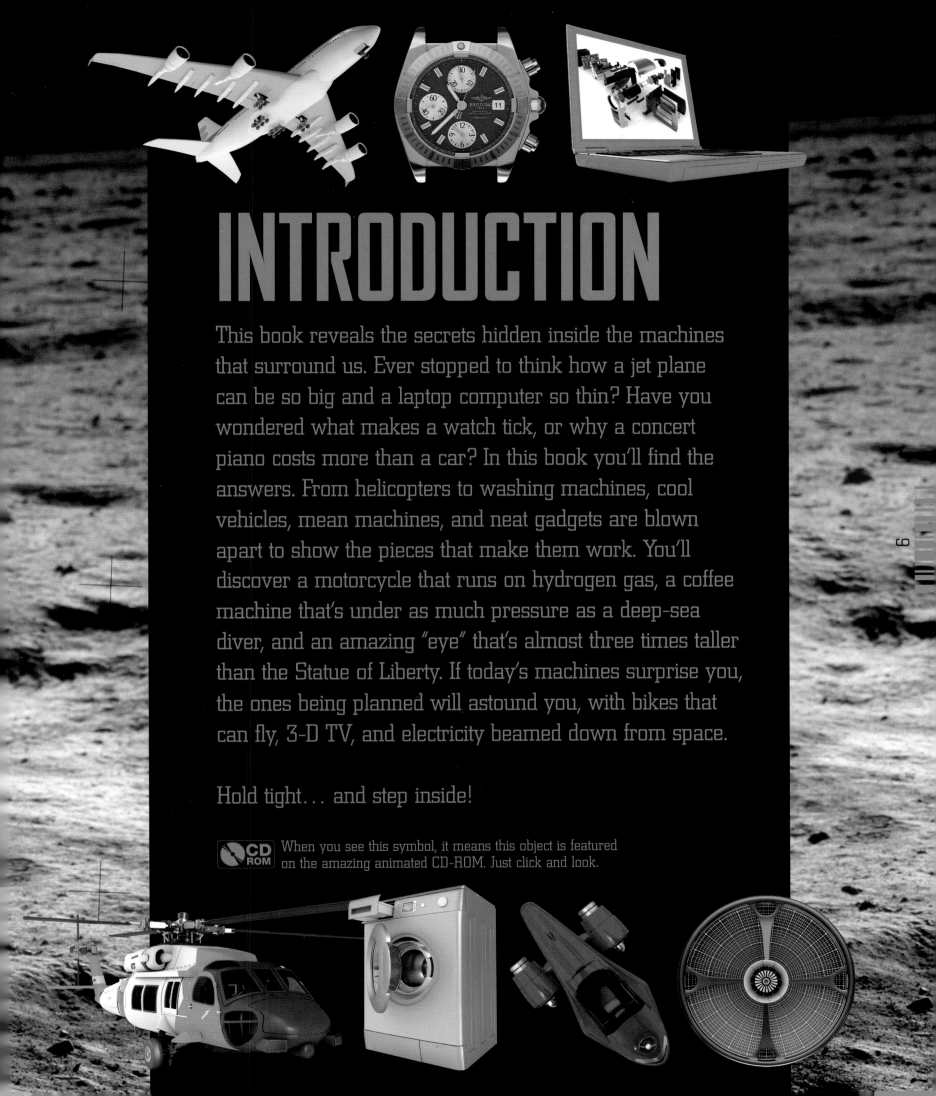

INTRODUCTION

This book reveals the secrets hidden inside the machines that surround us. Ever stopped to think how a jet plane can be so big and a laptop computer so thin? Have you wondered what makes a watch tick, or why a concert piano costs more than a car? In this book you'll find the answers. From helicopters to washing machines, cool vehicles, mean machines, and neat gadgets are blown apart to show the pieces that make them work. You'll discover a motorcycle that runs on hydrogen gas, a coffee machine that's under as much pressure as a deep-sea diver, and an amazing "eye" that's almost three times taller than the Statue of Liberty. If today's machines surprise you, the ones being planned will astound you, with bikes that can fly, 3-D TV, and electricity beamed down from space.

Hold tight... and step inside!

CD ROM When you see this symbol, it means this object is featured on the amazing animated CD-ROM. Just click and look.

Modeling

First the artist sets up the basic lighting, just as a photographer would do in a studio. Then he or she builds up the outer appearance of the model using photographs of real objects, and sketches. New parts are added and adjusted as necessary. For example, the artist added the engines to this hoverbike by starting with simple cylinders, then bending them into more complex shapes.

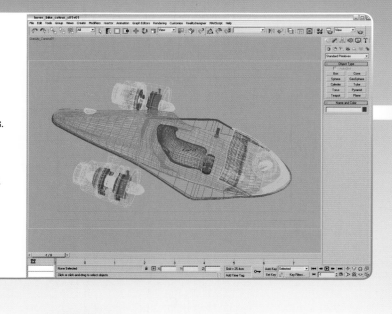

3-D MODELING

The 40 objects featured in this book may look like photos, but they are actually detailed, 3-D models produced with cutting-edge computer graphics. Each one is like a sculpture that an artist has slowly built up on the computer screen. Unlike a flat picture, an artist can rotate a 3-D model in any direction, zoom in on its details, or explode it into hundreds of pieces.

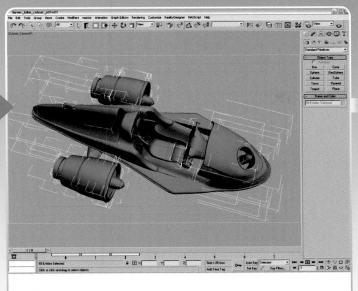

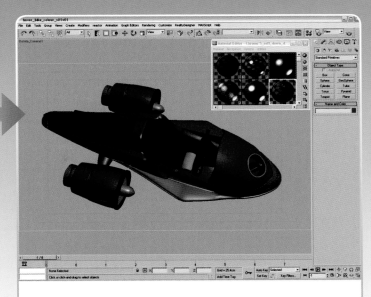

Rigging

Next, the artist "rigs" the model, specifying the object's inner structure and how the various parts connect together. Rigging is particularly important for computer animation. The end result is a "clay"—a dull-white version of the object, like an unpainted plastic model.

Texturing

In the final stage, the artist applies textures (surface finishes) and colors to the different parts of the object. The bodywork of this bike has been textured to look like shiny blue metal, while the handlebars are more like matte black plastic.

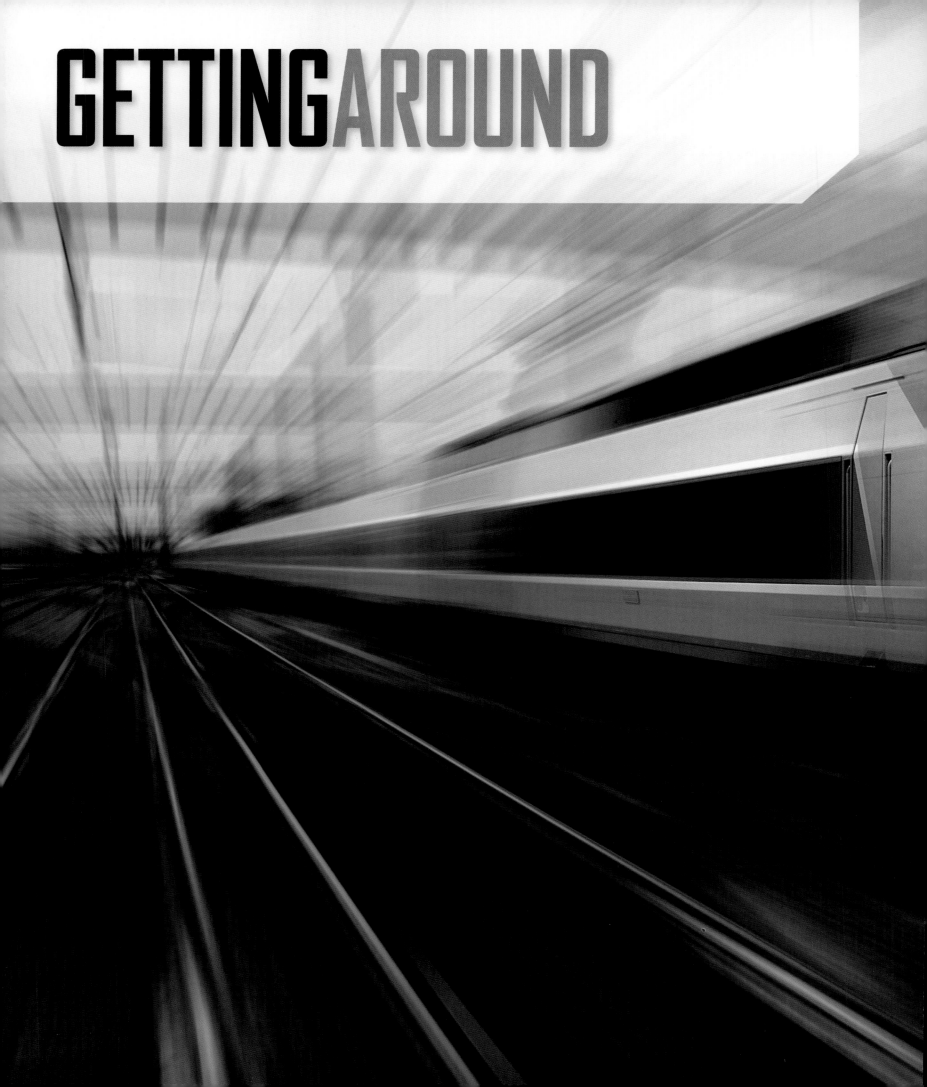

GETTINGAROUND

Trains are usually the fastest way of getting around on land—and the French TGV (*Train à Grande Vitesse*—high-speed train) is the world's fastest conventional train. A new experimental version of the TGV set a speed record of 357 mph (574.8 kph) on April 3, 2007, which is more than 100 mph (160 kph) faster than a Formula One car!

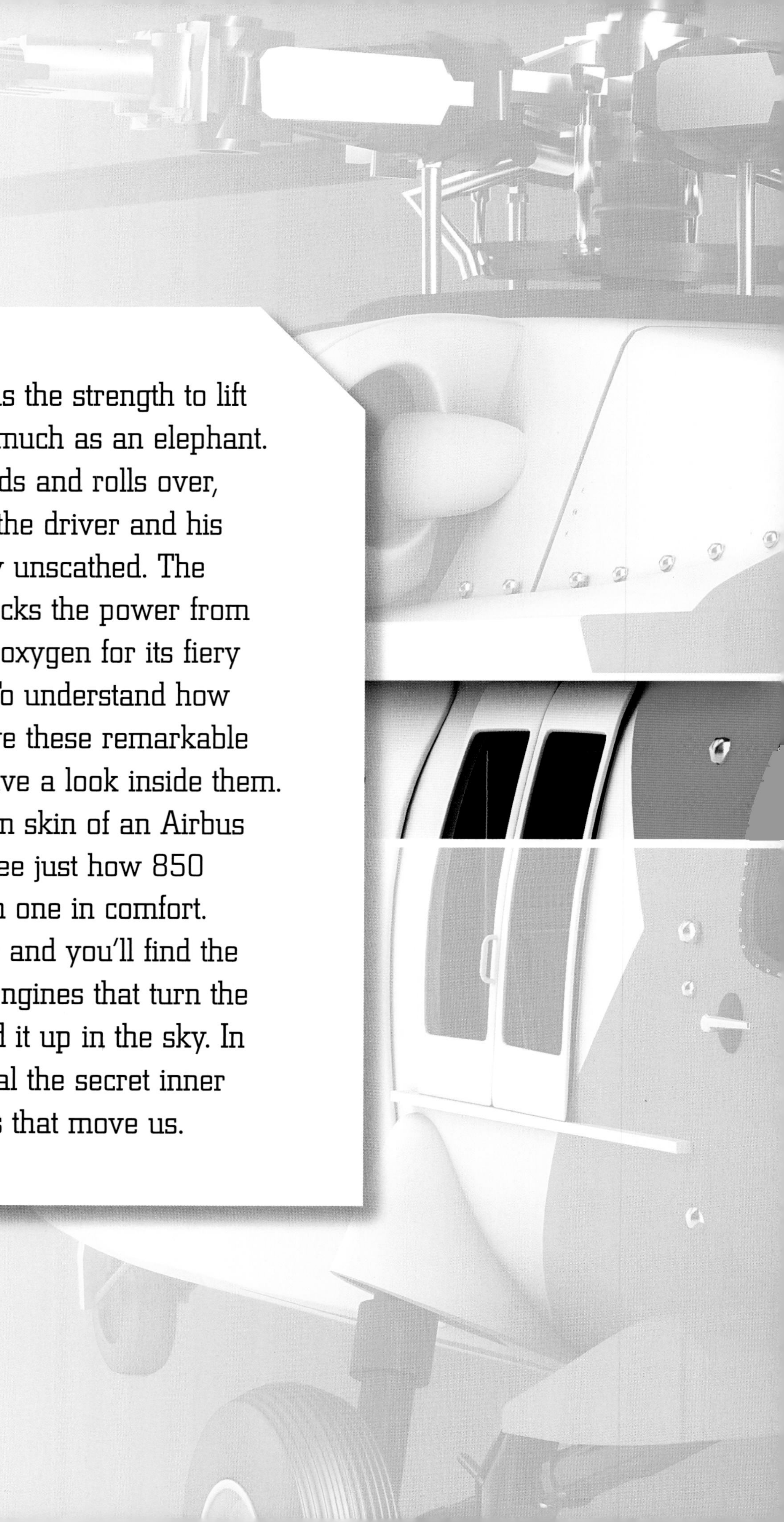

A backhoe digger has the strength to lift rocks that weigh as much as an elephant. When a rally car skids and rolls over, more often than not the driver and his navigator walk away unscathed. The *Ariane 5* rocket unlocks the power from liquid hydrogen and oxygen for its fiery escape from Earth. To understand how machines can achieve these remarkable feats, you need to have a look inside them. Peel back the titanium skin of an Airbus airplane and you'll see just how 850 passengers can fly in one in comfort. Open up a helicopter and you'll find the two powerful turbo engines that turn the rotor blades that hold it up in the sky. In this chapter we reveal the secret inner lives of the machines that move us.

RALLY CAR

This may look like an ordinary car, but appearances can be deceiving. Rally teams buy a basic factory-made car, then spend 10 times more money toughening it up so that it can thump down rough roads at high speeds. It's inevitable that rally cars will crash, so the body joints are welded more securely and a rigid inner cage is added to protect the two people inside. After it has been modified, the car's body shell is so strong that it could support the weight of 10 cars standing on its roof.

Rough ride

The wheels suffer more punishment than any other part of the car. The wheel hubs and suspension are made from strong, lightweight titanium metal to survive high-speed jolts. Rally tires last as little as 30 miles (50 km), and a single car can get through 180 tires in just one race.

FAST FACTS

Top speed	155 mph (249 kph)
Drive	4-wheel drive
Dimensions	174 in x 69 in x 56 in (441 cm x 174 cm x 143 cm)
Engine	Turbo-charged 4-cylinder

Ground hugger

Cars are shaped like aerofoils (airplane wings)—this makes the whole body lift up slightly at high speeds, which can make the car unstable and difficult to drive. Formula One racers and rally cars have spoilers (large air-deflectors) at the front and back to counteract this. By redirecting the airflow, the spoilers push the car down, increasing its grip on the road.

LOOK INSIDE

Rear spoiler increases downward force and grip on road

Roll cage protects crew if car rolls over

Rear brake light

Exhaust

Safe and sound

An ordinary car is usually strong enough to protect you if it crashes and rolls over, but this rally car has an inner safety cage that makes it two and a half times stronger. Reinforcements like this add weight and slow the car down, so all other unnecessary parts are removed. Inside, the car is little more than a skeleton—there are no luxury features or frills.

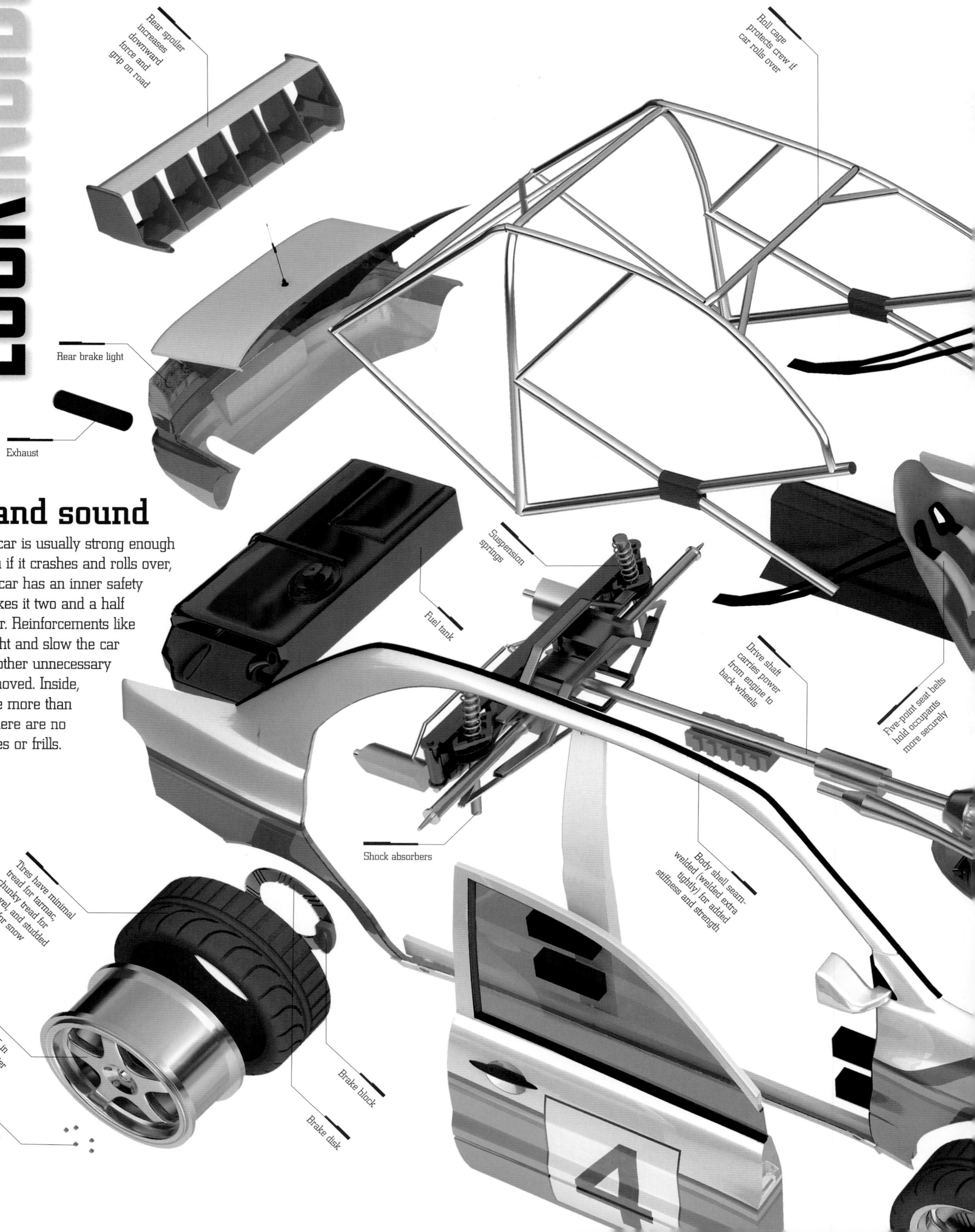

Suspension springs

Fuel tank

Drive shaft carries power from engine to back wheels

Five-point seat belts hold occupants more securely

Shock absorbers

Body shell seam-welded (welded extra tightly) for added stiffness and strength

Tires have minimal tread for tarmac, chunky tread for gravel, and studded tread for snow

Wheels are 15 in (38 cm) in diameter

Brake block

Wheel nuts bolt wheels to axles

Brake disk

4

18

Firing on all cylinders
The cylinders make power by repeating four steps over and over again. First, fuel and air enter through the valves at the top. Second, the piston moves up to squeeze the mixture. Third, a spark from the plug makes the mixture explode and this pushes the piston back down to power the car. Finally, the piston moves back up to clear out waste gases, which become the exhaust fumes.

Valve

Spark plug

Cylinder

Piston

How it works

An engine provides the energy that moves the car. This happens in metal canisters called cylinders. Pistons moving up and down the cylinders turn the crankshaft. The crankshaft drives the gearbox, which powers the drive shaft, which turns the wheels.

Crankshaft

Steering wheel has paddle control behind it for faster gear changes

Roof

Bucket seats are shaped to keep occupants in place during sharp turns

Front alloy wheel

Front brake disk

Hood

Fire extinguisher

Air intake feeds oxygen to engine cylinders

Foglights

Front bumper and spoiler made of lightweight composite material

Cylinders in engine

Gearbox

Battery

Four-cylinder engine needs to be serviced roughly every 500 miles (800 km)

Axles hold and power wheels

Radiator helps to cool engine

Global warming

Carbon dioxide gas, made by burning fuels, is smothering Earth like an invisible blanket. The planet is warming and the poles are melting. Scientists think the North Pole could be ice-free in summer by 2013, pushing polar bears toward extinction.

Pollution

You breathe about 10 million times a year. If you breathe in car exhaust fumes, your lungs are inhaling a toxic cocktail of chemicals, including some that are known to cause cancer.

CAR CRAZY

People are crazy about cars. Since 1900, the number of people on Earth has roughly quadrupled to about 6.6 billion—but over the same period, the number of cars has increased by about 10,000 times. There's now about one car for every 10 people on the planet. Cars have brought a huge benefit: the freedom to travel when and where we please. But they've challenged society, too, with environmental problems like pollution and global warming as well as major conflicts over limited supplies of oil. Will we soon have to choose between cars and our planet?

Milestones

Roman chariot
The sports cars of their day, chariots like this could reach speeds of up to 40 mph (60 kph) and were popular throughout Roman times (c. 100 BCE–400 CE).

Benz car
Karl Benz (1844–1929) made one of the first cars in 1885 by putting a gas engine onto a three-wheeled

Goodbye oil?

Oil companies are constantly discovering new reserves, but many people believe Earth's supplies of oil are limited. Nobody knows exactly how much oil is left, but some predict that most could be gone within decades. Oil will never completely run out, but it will become more expensive. People will slowly switch to other forms of energy, such as solar power or hydrogen gas, as they become cheaper.

Oil wars

Most of the world's oil is locked beneath the boundless deserts of the Middle East in such countries as Saudi Arabia, Iraq, and Iran. That is partly why this region has seen so much tension and conflict in recent decades.

Car growth

Developing nations like China and India are the fastest-growing markets for new cars. In China alone, car sales are increasing by 80 percent a year. Car makers are trying to build better cars to stop global warming, but huge growth in car numbers in developing countries will hamper their efforts.

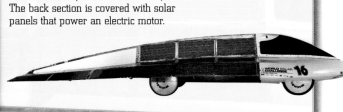

Price to pay

With a top speed of more than 250 mph (400 kph), the Bugatti Veyron is one of the world's fastest cars. It's also one of the most expensive to run—it uses up to three times as much fuel as a typical family car.

Ford Model T
American industrialist Henry Ford (1863–1947) made the first car that ordinary people could afford. He achieved this remarkable feat by building vehicles in enormous quantities. Each car was quickly assembled in a highly organized factory process called an assembly line.

VW Beetle
One of the most popular cars of the 20th century, the Volkswagen Beetle was built from 1938 until 2003. "Volkswagen" is German for "people's car."

Green cars
Future cars may be like this Sunraycer. The back section is covered with solar panels that power an electric motor.

FUTURE INTELLIGENT CAR

Future cars will be packed with sensors and satellite navigation equipment so that they'll be able to drive themselves. Future "driving" will be more like taking a taxi: you'll recline in your seat listening to music, watching a film projected onto the windshield, or reading a book—while the car does all the work!

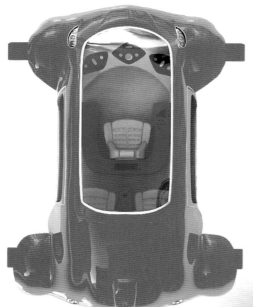

Back of windshield doubles as a widescreen TV for watching films as you travel

Driver's joystick control for manual driving

Radar-system automatically guides car at night and in bad weather

Sensors built into front and back of car guide it through traffic

Whiz wheels

This tiny future car has more room inside than a conventional car. That's because there's no engine wasting space. Instead, there are four compact electric motors built into the wheel hubs. These hub motors give four-wheel drive for better grip in bad weather. They also give four-wheel steering, which makes the car very easy to move and park. The wheels even rotate 90° so that you can drive the car sideways!

PENDOLINO TRAIN

You've probably seen motorcyclists leaning into curves as they corner at high speed, but have you ever seen trains doing the same thing? The Pendolino is an Italian-designed train with tilting carriages that can sweep around curves 30 percent more quickly than conventional trains, and just as safely. Tilting Pendolinos have slashed intercity travel times, proving hugely popular in Europe. More than 430 of these new trains are now in use in 10 different countries.

Comfort zone

Pendolinos are designed with passengers in mind. They are fully air-conditioned, and each carriage is pressurized, so passengers don't feel uncomfortable when the train enters tunnels. Large windows make the carriages feel spacious, and the electric doors are wide enough for wheelchairs.

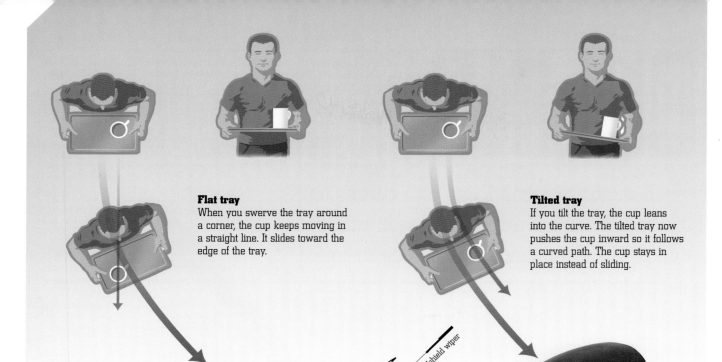

Flat tray
When you swerve the tray around a corner, the cup keeps moving in a straight line. It slides toward the edge of the tray.

Tilted tray
If you tilt the tray, the cup leans into the curve. The tilted tray now pushes the cup inward so it follows a curved path. The cup stays in place instead of sliding.

How it works

Why is it easier for a train to go around a curve at high speed, without the passengers inside being tossed around, by tilting into the curve? Suppose you are walking down a corridor quickly while carrying a cup of coffee on a tray, and you turn a corner. A basic law of physics says that objects always keep moving in the same direction and at the same speed unless another force acts on them. Unless you tilt the tray, there is no force acting on the cup to make it turn with you. It will continue in a straight line and slide across the tray as you corner.

LOOK INSIDE

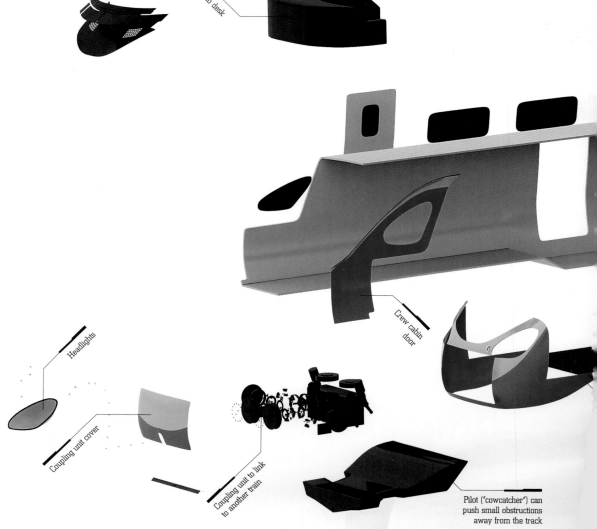

Windshield wiper

Aerodynamic front roof

Windshield

Crew seats

Driver cab desk

Crew cabin door

Headlights

Coupling unit cover

Coupling unit to link to another train

Pilot ("cowcatcher") can push small obstructions away from the track

Supersafe

Pendolinos travel faster than ordinary trains, so they need to have extra safety features. The driver is protected by a shell-like structure at the front. There are crumple zones at the ends of each car that protect passengers by absorbing most of the impact in a crash. The cars are built from a single, tube-like aluminum structure called a monocoque, which is both lightweight and very strong.

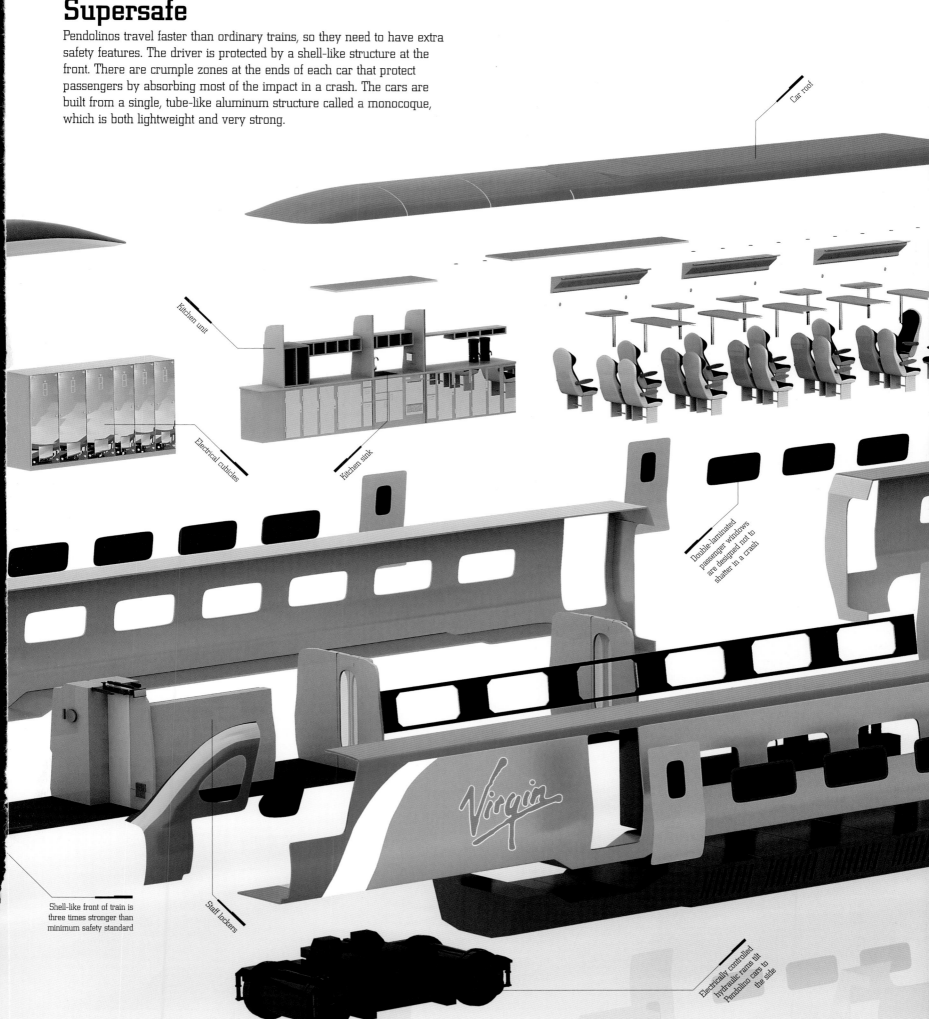

Car roof

Kitchen unit

Electrical cubicles

Kitchen sink

Double-laminated passenger windows are designed not to shatter in a crash

Shell-like front of train is three times stronger than minimum safety standard

Staff lockers

Electrically controlled hydraulic rams tilt Pendolino cars to the side

Moovie business

This futuristic concept car, the Peugeot Moovie, is how designers believe vehicles might look in 2020. The passengers sit inside a plastic bubble with two huge wheels running around it at the back. There are two more tiny wheels under the nose at the front. The car is made from lightweight materials, such as polycarbonate plastic, so it uses as little fuel as possible.

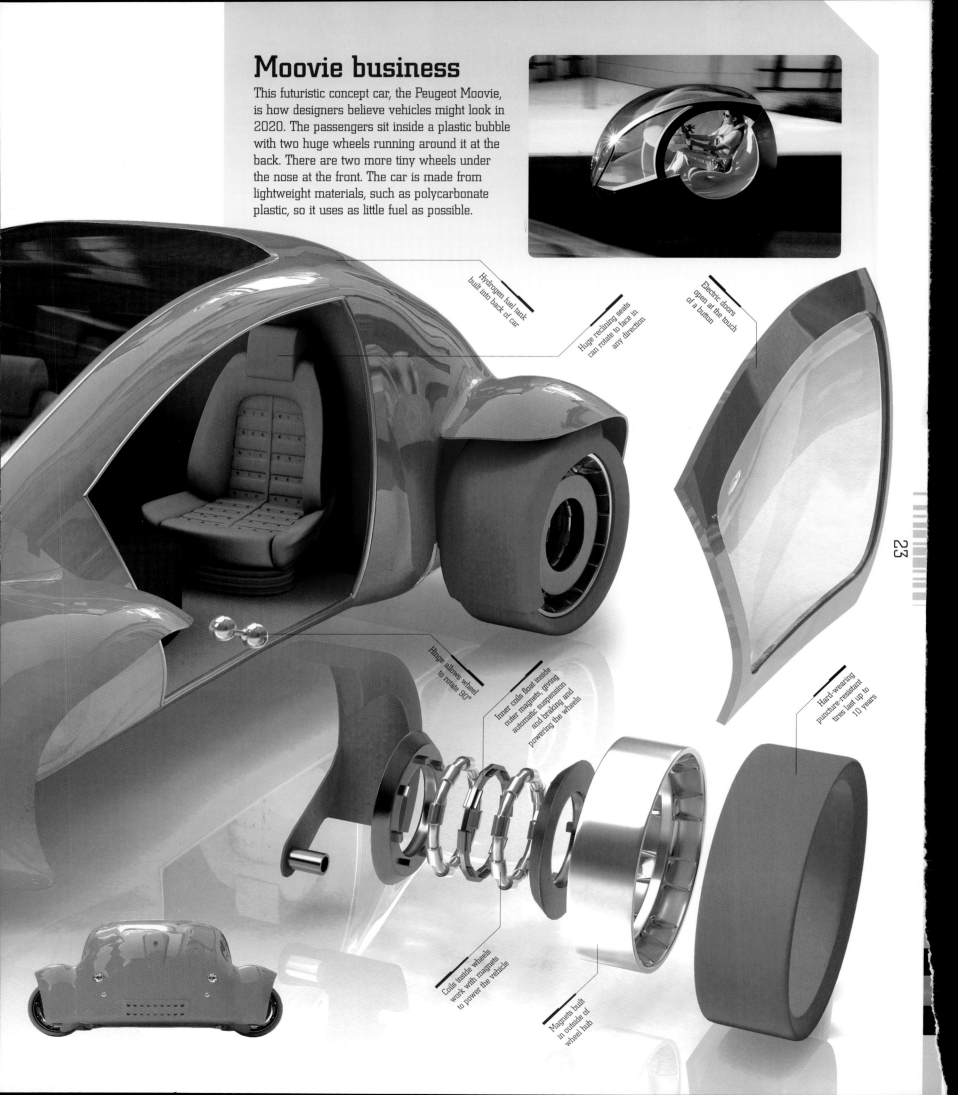

Hydrogen fuel tank built into back of car

Huge reclining seats can rotate to face in any direction

Electric doors open at the touch of a button

Hinge allows wheel to rotate 90°

Inner coils float inside outer magnets, giving automatic suspension and braking and powering the wheels

Hard-wearing puncture-resistant tires last up to 10 years

Coils inside wheels work with magnets to power the vehicle

Magnets built in outside of wheel hub

FAST FACTS

Top speed	155 mph (250 kph)
Material	Aluminum body shell
Typical configuration	7 cars (with 1 power car at each end)
Passengers	Max. 432–494
Total weight	Approx. 450 tons (including passengers)
Total train length	613 ft (187 m)

Tilting power

When a Pendolino corners at speed, hydraulic (fluid-filled) pistons tilt the top of each car up to 8° into the curve. The bogies (wheel units) underneath do not tilt, but remain safely on the track. The pantograph (overhead electricity connector) swivels so that power to the train is uninterrupted.

MAKING TRACKS

After almost a century of decline, rail travel has recently been enjoying something of a revival. Steam-powered locomotives were invented in the early 18th century. In the decades that followed, tracks were built to carry steam trains between major cities, often cutting travel times from days to hours. Rail travel then gradually fell out of favor during the 20th century. Cars replaced rail for most individual journeys, trucks carried much of the freight once moved by rail, and airplanes revolutionized long-distance travel. Now, in the early 21st century, high-speed train services are winning back business from cars, trucks, and planes. They are a fast, safe, and convenient way to travel.

Meeting in the middle

On May 10, 1869, two tracks were joined at Promontory Summit in Utah, completing a transcontinental railroad that crossed North America, connecting the east and west coasts. As more long-distance lines were laid, markets for goods became much bigger. In this way, laying railroad tracks was vital to the growth of business.

Tilting trouble

Trains can go faster around corners if they tilt. Helped by a lightweight aluminum body, this 1970s advanced passenger train (APT) could corner 40 percent faster than a conventional train. Unfortunately, it tilted so steeply around curves that it made passengers feel sick. The train was scrapped, but some of its technology was used to make the Pendolino, which was first manufactured in Italy by Fiat in 1987.

Rush hour

As train travel becomes popular again, overcrowding is a growing problem—and it's not easy to solve. Train platforms are a fixed length, so trains can't always be made longer. Running trains more often causes congestion and can delay the network as a whole.

Trains versus planes

Engines give off carbon dioxide gas, a cause of global warming. Planes give off more than trains, especially on short trips, because they need lots of fuel to take off. Taking a train instead of making a short flight cuts emissions by 90 percent.

Tight corners

Roller coasters work the opposite way from tilting trains. With wheels under the track to stop the cars from falling off, roller coasters tilt through seemingly impossible angles to make you feel excited. No one would dare go on trains that tilted like this!

Bullet train

Japanese Shinkansen trains are nicknamed "bullets" for good reason: with sloping, airplane-style fronts, they can reach speeds of up to 185 mph (300 kph). This N700 Shinkansen tilting train was introduced in July 2007.

Floating into the future

Maglev trains float on powerful magnets and can reach speeds of up to 360 mph (580 kph). Some engineers have suggested tunneling a magnetic railroad under the Atlantic Ocean. Trains would go from London to New York in just 54 minutes!

BACKHOE LOADER

CD ROM

If there's dirt to move or holes to dig, call in the backhoe loader. These amazingly versatile diggers are similar to tractors, only with hydraulic (piston-powered) digger buckets at the front and rear. Sit inside the cab and you're controlling a monster. The front bucket is strong enough to lift an elephant and big enough to move 35 cubic feet (1 cubic meter) of soil—about 60 shovelfuls—at one time. You'll get the job done in no time with a backhoe!

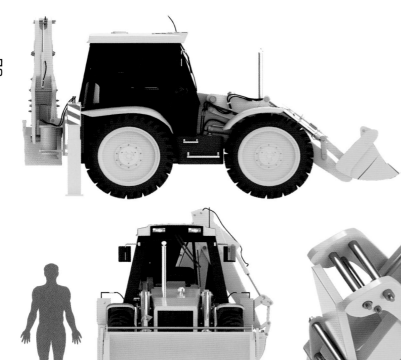

Metal muscles

Think of a backhoe as a giant extension of the driver's body. The rear digger has three separate joints similar to the shoulder, elbow, and wrist. The front bucket works like two arms outstretched and lifting together.

FAST FACTS

Dimensions	Approx. 23 ft x 6.5 ft x 10 ft (7 m x 2 m x 3 m)
Top speed	25 mph (40 kph)
Bucket swivel	Rear digger rotates through 200°
Cost	$90,000

Making tracks

Backhoe arms can dig deep below ground level: fully extended, a typical backhoe arm can go down more than 20 ft (6 m). A tracked excavator like this one (right) can dig even deeper—typically about 30 ft (9 m). The top of its body (the part above the giant caterpillar tracks) can swing through 360°, making it easy to dump spoil (waste rocks).

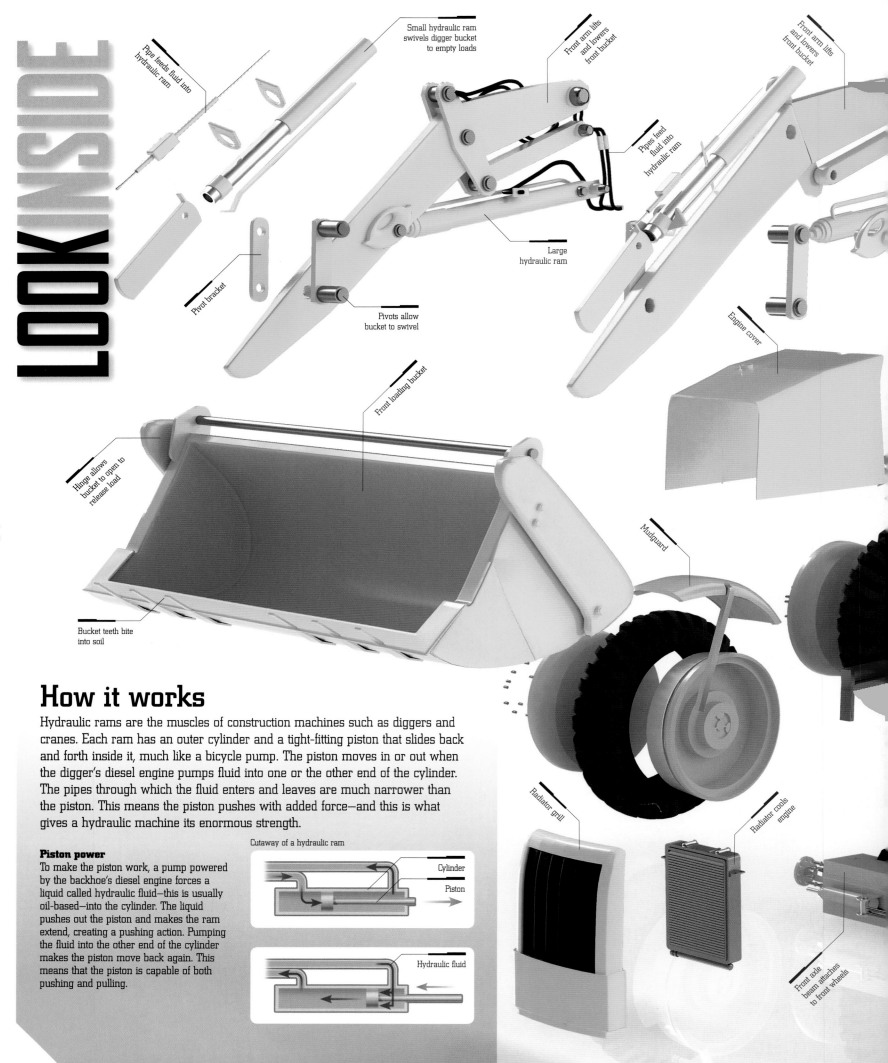

LOOK INSIDE

Pipe feeds fluid into hydraulic ram

Small hydraulic ram swivels digger bucket to empty loads

Front arm lifts and lowers front bucket

Front arm lifts and lowers front bucket

Pipes feed fluid into hydraulic ram

Large hydraulic ram

Pivot bracket

Pivots allow bucket to swivel

Engine cover

Front loading bucket

Hinge allows bucket to open to release load

Mudguard

Bucket teeth bite into soil

How it works

Hydraulic rams are the muscles of construction machines such as diggers and cranes. Each ram has an outer cylinder and a tight-fitting piston that slides back and forth inside it, much like a bicycle pump. The piston moves in or out when the digger's diesel engine pumps fluid into one or the other end of the cylinder. The pipes through which the fluid enters and leaves are much narrower than the piston. This means the piston pushes with added force—and this is what gives a hydraulic machine its enormous strength.

Piston power

To make the piston work, a pump powered by the backhoe's diesel engine forces a liquid called hydraulic fluid—this is usually oil-based—into the cylinder. The liquid pushes out the piston and makes the ram extend, creating a pushing action. Pumping the fluid into the other end of the cylinder makes the piston move back again. This means that the piston is capable of both pushing and pulling.

Cutaway of a hydraulic ram

Cylinder

Piston

Hydraulic fluid

Radiator grill

Radiator cools engine

Front axle attaches beam to front wheels

Radio antenna

Front cab lights

Roof

Rear digger arm

Digger arm struts

Pivots allow rear arm to swivel

Cab reinforced to protect driver if digger rolls over

Rear digger arm

Rear bucket

Pivots

Pivot allows rear digger bucket to swivel up and down

Rear digger hydraulics

Wing mirror

Pivot

Exhaust pipe

Warning sign

Air intake

Diesel engine and hydraulic pump

Rear digger mounting

Strong girders help to support weight of rear digger

Hydraulic pipe raises and lowers stabilizers

Stabilizers are lowered to support digger at rear

Rear axle beam

Outer part of wheel

Wheel nuts

Digging machine

Every moving part on a backhoe is powered by the diesel engine at the center. Aside from driving the wheels, it also operates the hydraulic pump, steering the digger and raising and lowering the front and rear buckets.

Engine mounting

Inner part of wheel

Big, chunky tires stop digger from sinking into mud and give grip

DIGGING DEEP

Earth is a giant rock packed full of minerals—everything from sand and coal, to silver and gold. Since prehistoric times, human ingenuity has been finding uses for practically every mineral that has ever been discovered. Digging things out of the planet is often harder than it looks, however—minerals may be locked into Earth's surface or buried miles beneath it, and getting them out can be a real challenge. In ancient times, people had no choice but to dig and scrape out the minerals they needed by hand. These days, we use giant hydraulic machines to move the dirt dozens of times faster, and far fewer people work in mines and quarries. We are also starting to recognize the harmful effects that such activity can have on our environment and the animals that live in it.

Dirty work

Mining is one of the world's most dangerous jobs. Fires and explosions are common, and mines sometimes collapse on the workers inside. Miners often have to breathe in large amounts of dust—even if this dust is not poisonous, long exposure to it can cause breathing difficulties and even death.

Ancient tools

Tools like these were the backhoes of the Stone Age. Masterpieces of design, they have stone blades attached to wooden handles by leather straps. They work scientifically, too—the long wooden handles enable the user to dig with much more force. The pointed tips concentrate the force in a smaller area, making it easier to chip through hard soil.

Mass consumption

We need giant mines because we use vast quantities of minerals. Those of us born in developed countries will consume about 1,750 tons (1,600 metric tons) of minerals during our lives—in fuel, housing, and all the products we buy and throw away.

Low tech

Despite the development of powerful machines to do the job, mining in some countries is still done by hand—and sometimes by children. The United Nations estimates that a million children as young as five work for up to eight hours a day digging and carrying heavy loads.

Big digger

This massive mechanical monster is designed to scrape coal from a strip (surface) mine using the 18 buckets on the spinning wheel at the front. The world's biggest bucket excavator, a German machine called Bagger 288, is twice as tall as the Statue of Liberty. It can dig out 260,000 tons (240,000 metric tons) of coal per day—enough to fill more than 700 very large dump trucks.

Danger signs

Construction machines are painted yellow for safety. Our eyes see yellow clearly, and it triggers warning signals in our brains—just as when we see wasps and bees.

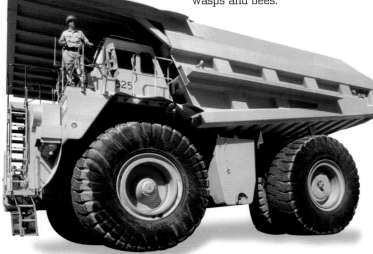

Minerals

Minerals are the nonliving materials we dig from the ground. We use them for almost everything we do. We need coal and uranium to make energy, aggregates like sand and clay to build things, and metals like iron and aluminum to make machines.

Doing damage

Mining can harm our planet. By removing vegetation, it destroys important habitats, killing the animals that live there or forcing them to flee. Many species are threatened by human activities like this.

Shipping out

It's not just people who move around the planet. Countries transport vast amounts of goods to each other, much of it in giant metal containers. The world's biggest cargo ship can carry 11,000 containers, each bigger than a family car.

Busy streets

Streets choked with traffic in the day may be totally empty at night. We could ease transportation problems if people worked from home or worked more flexible hours. Making more store deliveries at night would also help.

Ecotourism

Travel makes us appreciate the wonders of the world, but too many tourists can damage historic places and disturb wildlife. One solution is ecotourism, or green tourism. It means traveling in a more sustainable way, doing as little damage as possible to the area being visited.

PEOPLE AND PLANET

Every time you travel by car, bus, plane, or train, you hurt the planet. The engine that moves you uses oil and produces pollution. It also makes carbon dioxide gas, which causes global warming. People need to travel, but the planet is important, too. We need to get around more wisely, reducing our impact as much as we can.

Simple solutions

Saving the planet is a huge task, but people can work together to make a difference. Parents who drive children to school cause a quarter of rush-hour traffic. The "walking bus" is one simple solution to this problem. Instead of going by car, children dress up in high-visibility jackets and walk to school together two-by-two. Ideas like this cut traffic, make streets safer, and make travel more fun.

Personal change

Whose job is it to save the planet? Governments can't solve problems unless people help them. We can all make a difference by using public transportation for trips wherever possible. Better still, walk, cycle, or skate. It uses no fuel and creates no pollution. It's good for your health, and it's fun, too!

FACTOIDS

- In 1950, 25 million people traveled internationally. In 2005, that figure was 760 million.
- More than 44 million new cars roll off the production lines worldwide each year.
- Food travels 25–50 percent farther from farm to table than it did 20 years ago.

Plane truths

Flying may be the fastest way to travel, but it is usually also the noisiest and dirtiest. Roughly half of all flights are short-haul (less than three hours and only a few hundred miles). These journeys can often be made by train, which cuts the effect on global warming by 90 percent.

Rough rescue

The SEAHAWK's cabin can be changed to suit different missions. For basic troop transporting, it can hold 14 seats. For search and rescue, the seats can be removed and replaced with a winch. The winching equipment takes up almost a quarter of the cabin space, leaving enough room for the crew and the casualties they save.

When there's trouble at sea, the world's navies often have to step in. Warships can move quickly to where they're needed, carrying tough helicopters like the Sikorsky SEAHAWK. Built for the rough and tumble of life at sea, it's packed with features that help it survive in the most demanding conditions.

SEAHAWK

CD ROM

FAST FACTS

Cabin dimensions	12 ft 7 in x 6 ft 1 in x 4 ft 5 in (3.8 m x 1.9 m x 1.3 m)
Maximum load	9,070 lb (4,123 kg)
Speed	153 knots (284 kph)
Range	245 nautical miles (453 km)
Power	2 turbo-shaft engines

Space saver

The SEAHAWK can fold its rotors to save space. Normally it is 53 ft 8 in (16.4 m) wide. Folded, it is only 10 ft 8 in (3.3 m) wide.

How it works

Unlike an airplane, a helicopter does not have to move forward to fly. Its rotors work like small aerofoils that generate lift (upward force) as they spin around at high speed. The helicopter steers by tilting its rotor blades as they spin. This produces more lift on one side than the other, causing the whole craft to move in that direction.

In a spin

As the main rotor blades rotate, the whole body of the helicopter tends to turn the opposite way (red arrow). The small rotor at the tail of the helicopter pushes in the opposite direction to counteract this (blue arrow).

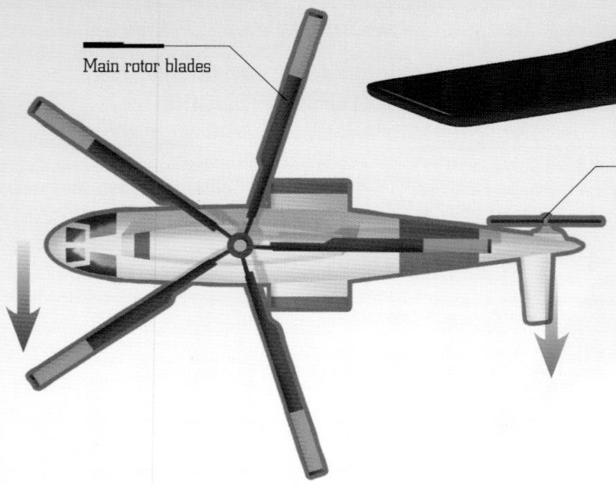

Main rotor blades

Tail rotor blades

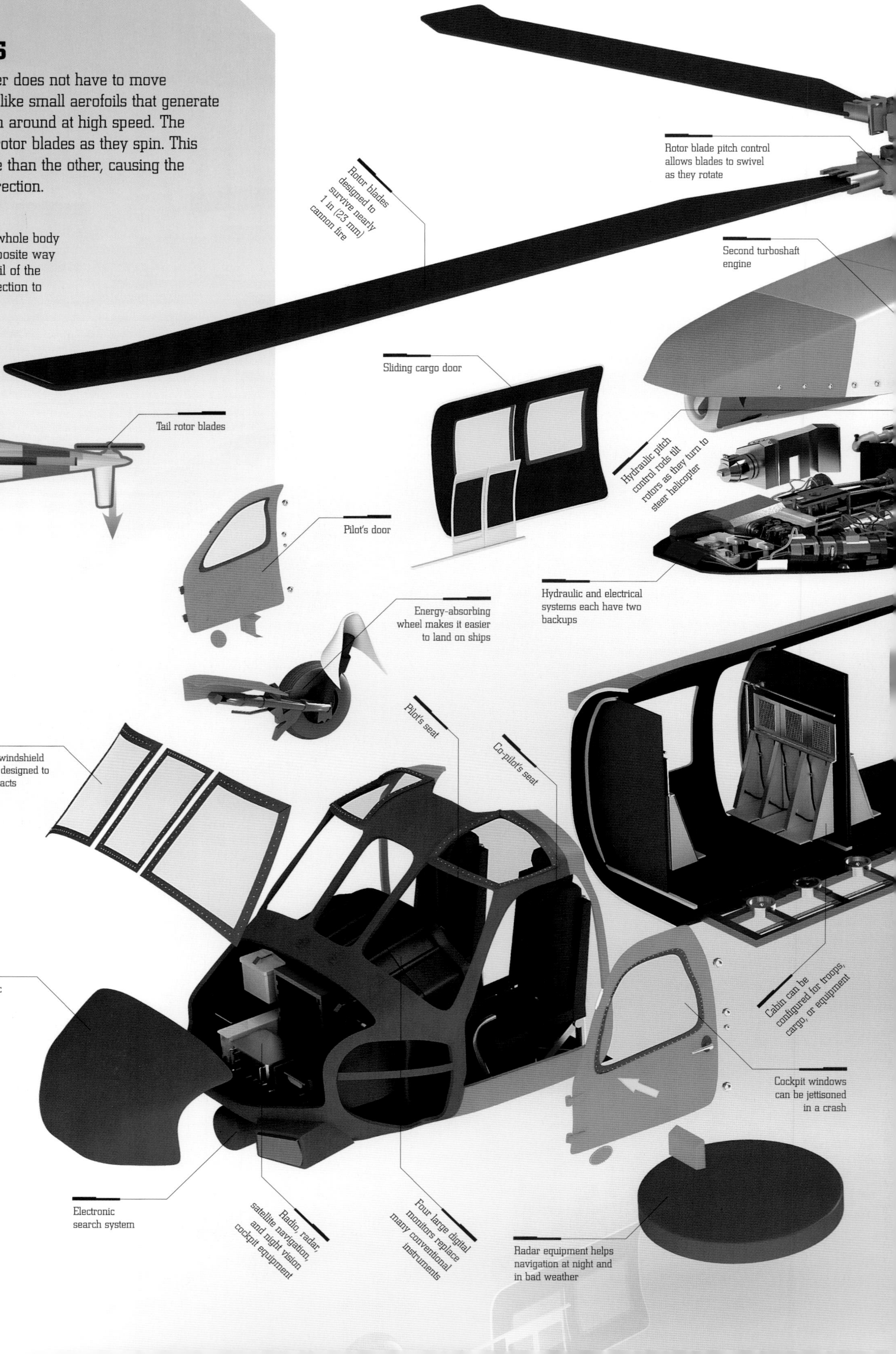

Rotor blades designed to survive nearly 1 in (23 mm) cannon fire

Rotor blade pitch control allows blades to swivel as they rotate

Second turboshaft engine

Sliding cargo door

Hydraulic pitch control rods tilt rotors as they turn to steer helicopter

Pilot's door

Hydraulic and electrical systems each have two backups

Energy-absorbing wheel makes it easier to land on ships

Toughened windshield and cockpit designed to survive impacts

Pilot's seat

Co-pilot's seat

Aerodynamic nose cone

Cabin can be configured for troops, cargo, or equipment

Cockpit windows can be jettisoned in a crash

Electronic search system

Radio, radar, satellite navigation, and night vision cockpit equipment

Four large digital monitors replace many conventional instruments

Radar equipment helps navigation at night and in bad weather

LOOK INSIDE

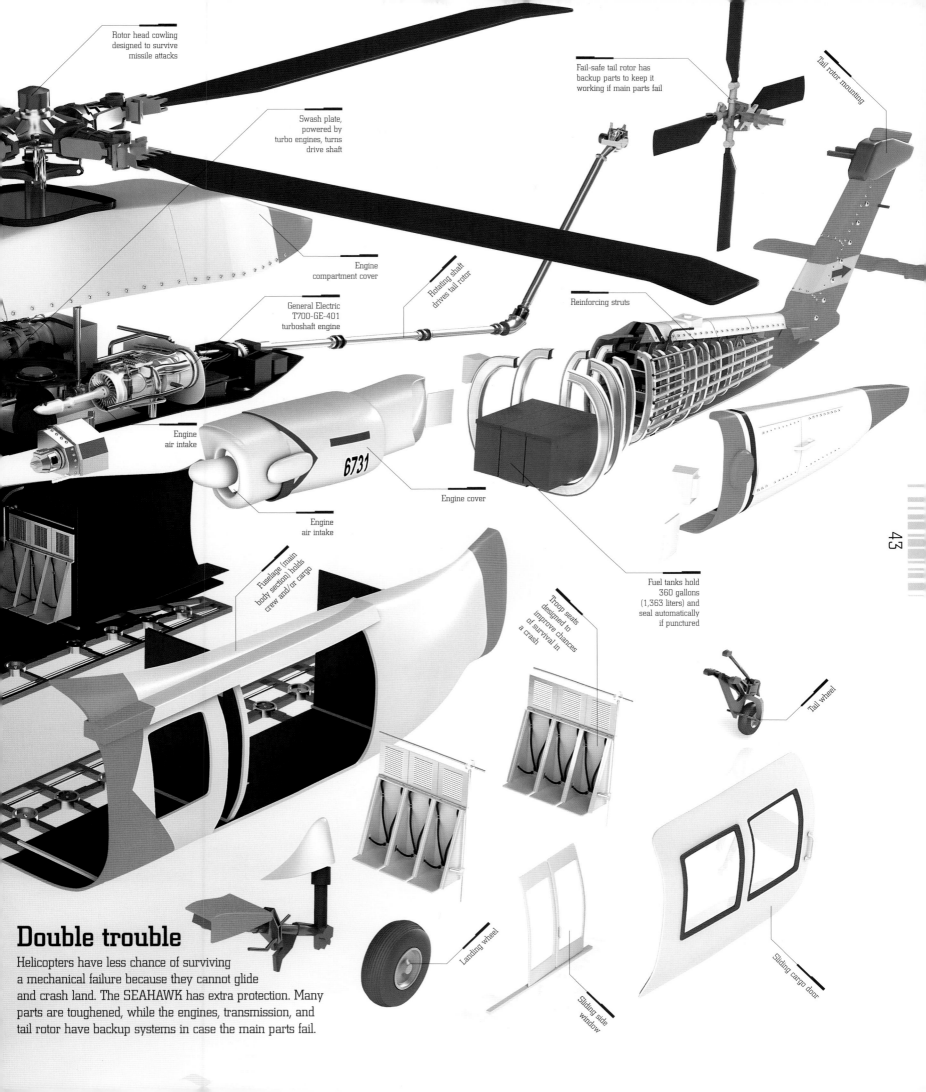

Rotor head cowling designed to survive missile attacks

Fail-safe tail rotor has backup parts to keep it working if main parts fail

Tail rotor mounting

Swash plate, powered by turbo engines, turns drive shaft

Engine compartment cover

Rotating shaft drives tail rotor

Reinforcing struts

General Electric T700-GE-401 turboshaft engine

Engine air intake

6731

Engine cover

Engine air intake

Fuselage (main body section) holds crew and/or cargo

Troop seats designed to improve chances of survival in a crash

Fuel tanks hold 360 gallons (1,363 liters) and seal automatically if punctured

Tail wheel

Double trouble

Helicopters have less chance of surviving a mechanical failure because they cannot glide and crash land. The SEAHAWK has extra protection. Many parts are toughened, while the engines, transmission, and tail rotor have backup systems in case the main parts fail.

Landing wheel

Sliding side window

Sliding cargo door

CHOPCHOP

If you're lost on a mountain or your ship's going down at sea, there's no more reassuring sound than the chop-chop of a helicopter swooping down to rescue you. Forward or backward, sideways, up, or down—a helicopter pilot can fly in any direction by tilting the rotor blades as they spin around. Helicopters can take off and land vertically, so they can reach places no airplane can go. That's why they're so useful in so many situations. When it comes to flight, helicopters really are the perfect all-arounders.

First flights?

These amazing patterns in the Nazca Desert, Peru, are visible only from the air. Some were created more than 2,000 years ago, suggesting flight may be far older than we think.

Nature's helicopter

Plants can improve their chances of reproducing by spreading their seeds. When these seeds fall from a maple tree, they spin and flutter away. Unlike helicopters, they cannot travel far because they have no onboard source of power.

Crop-dusting

Helicopters and airplanes can spray pesticides (insect-killing chemicals) onto crops more quickly than tractors. Some aircraft give the spray a static electric charge as it leaves the pipes. This makes it spread out and cover the plants more evenly.

Milestones

Leonardo's sketches

Italian inventor Leonardo da Vinci (1452–1519) sketched this mechanical helicopter in the 15th century. The screw-shaped rotor was supposed to be turned by the pilot. Sadly, scientists have calculated that it would not have had enough power to take off.

First helicopter

In 1907, four years after the Wright brothers first took to the skies, a French airman named Paul Cornu (1881–1944) made a 20-second flight in this twin-rotor helicopter.

Forest fires

Helicopters are the only way to tackle fires that break out in dense forests, far from the nearest road. This specially built firefighting helicopter uses a long dangling hose to suck up water from a lake or river, which it then drops on the fire. Its tank can hold as much water as three fire engines.

Air ambulance

Air ambulances can travel at least three times faster than road ambulances and, if accidents have happened on mountains, cliffs, or at sea, they may be the only option for a quick rescue. Most carry basic medical equipment and some even have onboard doctors.

Disaster relief

Helicopters don't need a runway or landing strip, so they are perfect for helping out after natural disasters like floods or earthquakes. The picture below shows emergency blankets arriving after a flood in Bangladesh.

Jumbo lift

The mighty Chinook is one of the world's most powerful helicopters. Its cabin is big enough to park a car inside. Using three hooks, it can lift loads up to 27 tons (25 metric tons)—the weight of three elephants!

Autogyro

This autogyro, built in 1933 by Spaniard Juan de la Cierva (1896–1936), could fly like a plane but take off or land like a helicopter. The pilot could tilt the rotors to move in any direction.

Igor Sikorsky

Always impeccably dressed, Russian engineer Igor Sikorsky (1889–1972) built the first practical, single-rotor helicopter in 1939. Aged 12, he'd built a rubber-band-powered flying machine—and he was obsessed with aircraft for the rest of his life.

Chopper plane

This US Navy Osprey has rotors on its wingtips that can point up, to fly like a helicopter, or forward, to fly like a plane.

AIRBUS A380

It's hard to believe anything so huge could actually fly. The world's biggest passenger plane, the Airbus A380, is as long as nine double-decker buses parked end to end, and is even wider from wingtip to wingtip. From the outside it looks only a little bigger than a traditional jumbo jet, but it can carry more than twice as many passengers.

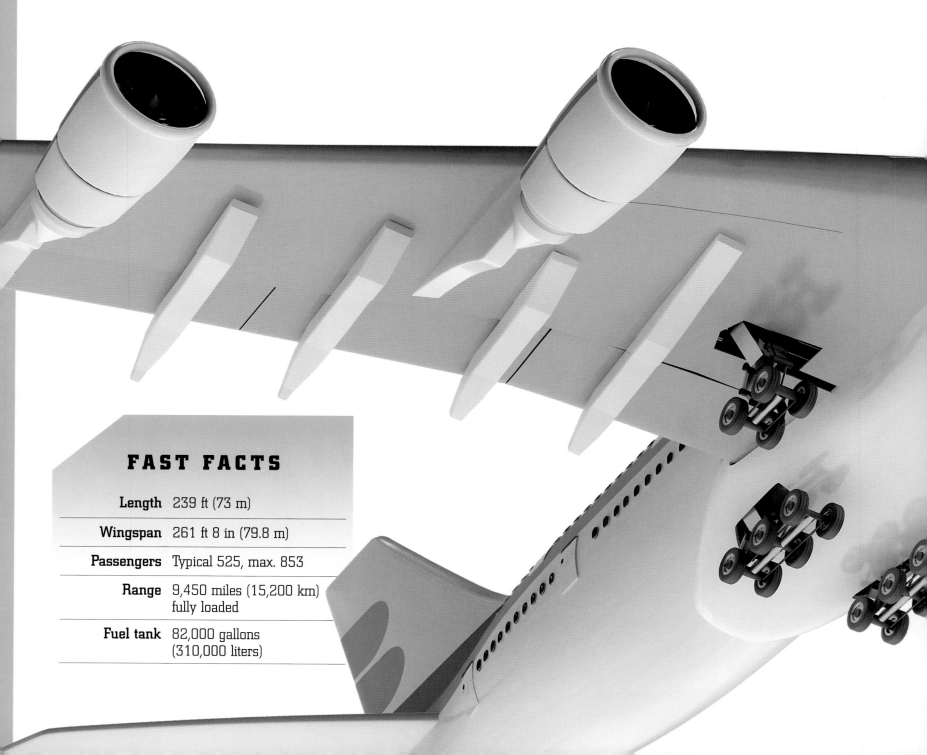

FAST FACTS

Length	239 ft (73 m)
Wingspan	261 ft 8 in (79.8 m)
Passengers	Typical 525, max. 853
Range	9,450 miles (15,200 km) fully loaded
Fuel tank	82,000 gallons (310,000 liters)

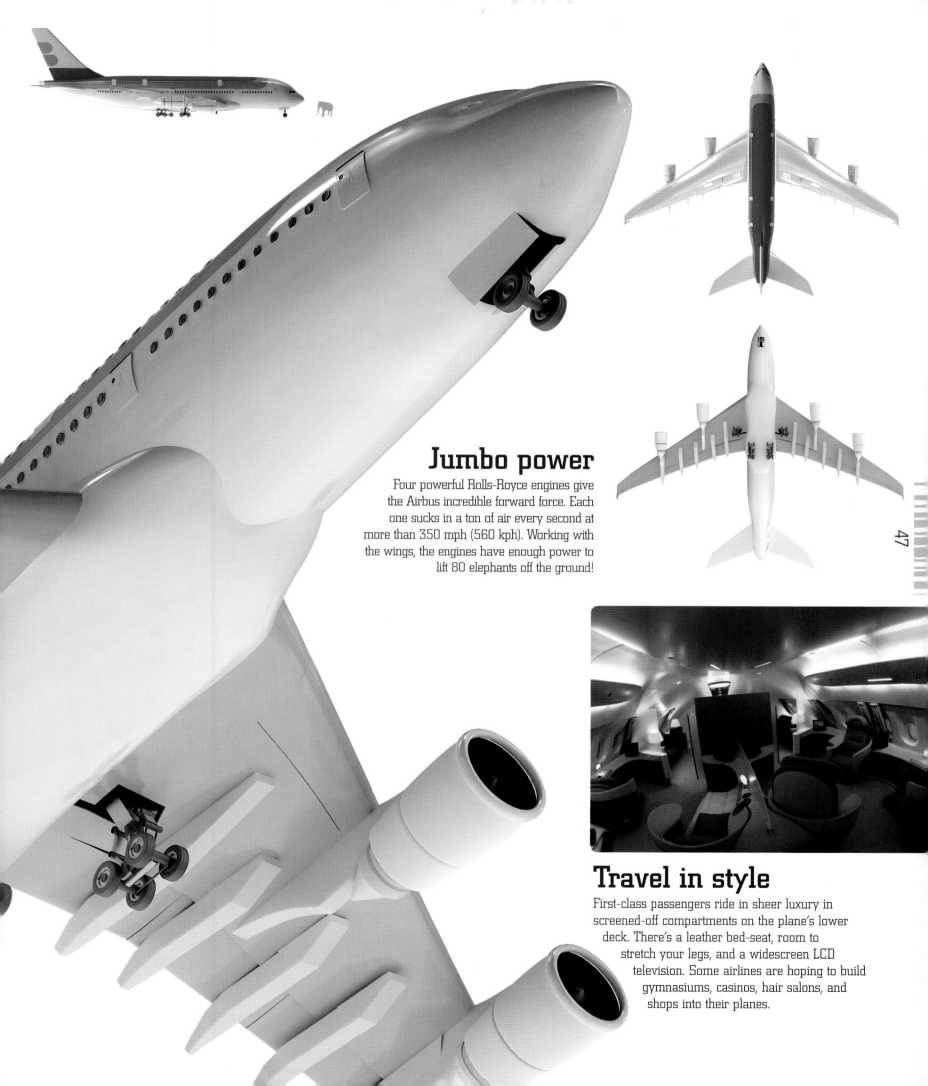

Jumbo power

Four powerful Rolls-Royce engines give the Airbus incredible forward force. Each one sucks in a ton of air every second at more than 350 mph (560 kph). Working with the wings, the engines have enough power to lift 80 elephants off the ground!

Travel in style

First-class passengers ride in sheer luxury in screened-off compartments on the plane's lower deck. There's a leather bed-seat, room to stretch your legs, and a widescreen LCD television. Some airlines are hoping to build gymnasiums, casinos, hair salons, and shops into their planes.

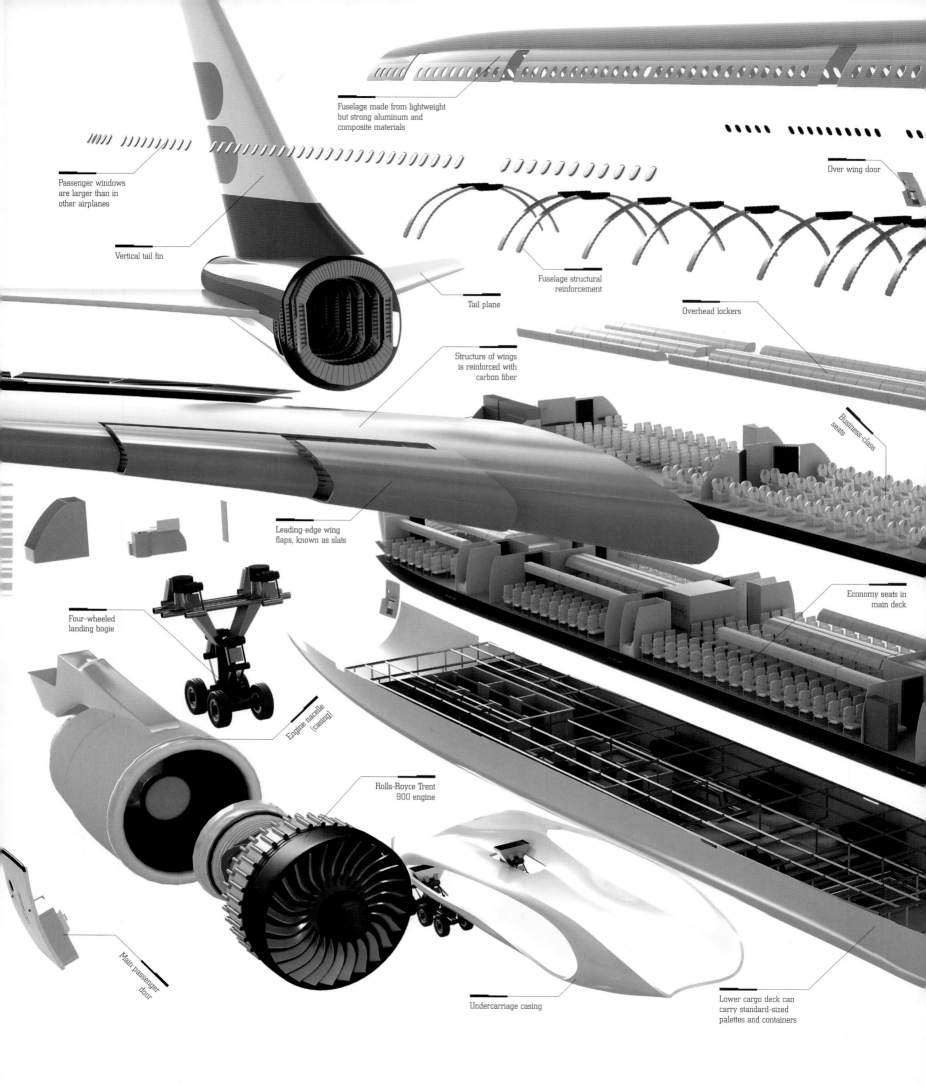

Fuselage made from lightweight but strong aluminum and composite materials

Passenger windows are larger than in other airplanes

Vertical tail fin

Over wing door

Fuselage structural reinforcement

Tail plane

Overhead lockers

Structure of wings is reinforced with carbon fiber

Business-class seats

Leading-edge wing flaps, known as slats

Economy seats in main deck

Four-wheeled landing bogie

Engine nacelle (casing)

Rolls-Royce Trent 900 engine

Main passenger door

Undercarriage casing

Lower cargo deck can carry standard-sized palettes and containers

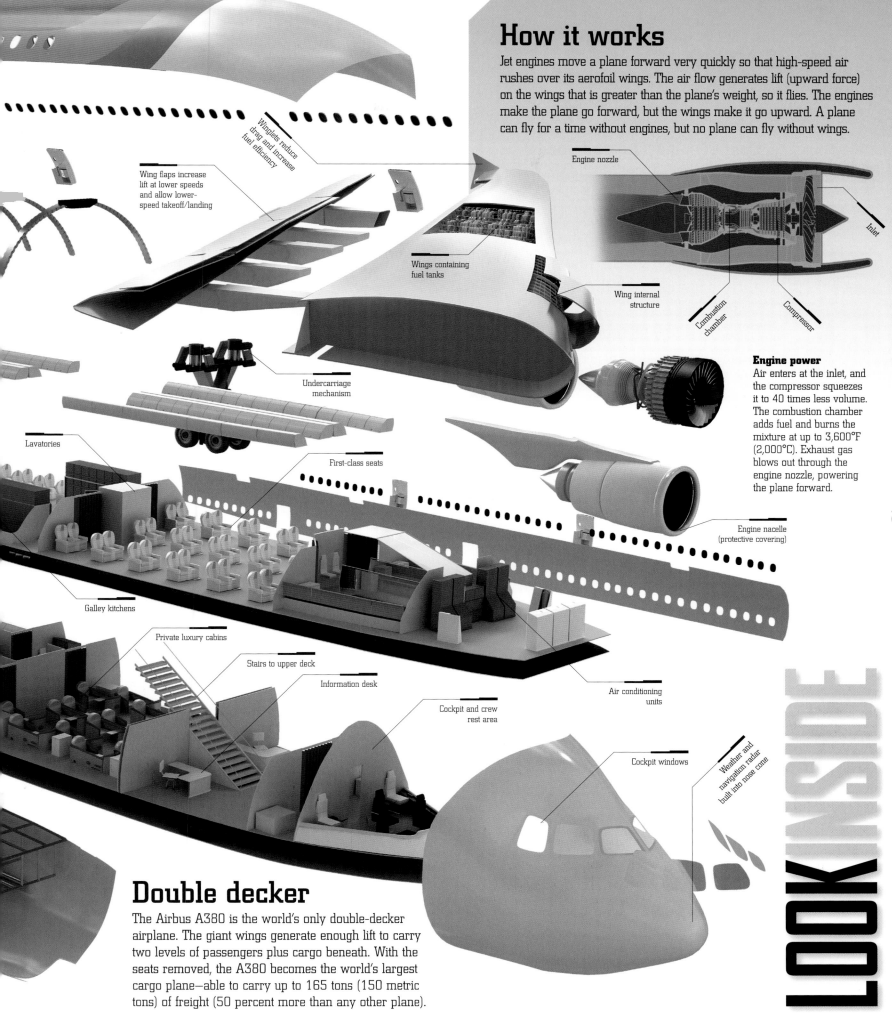

How it works

Jet engines move a plane forward very quickly so that high-speed air rushes over its aerofoil wings. The air flow generates lift (upward force) on the wings that is greater than the plane's weight, so it flies. The engines make the plane go forward, but the wings make it go upward. A plane can fly for a time without engines, but no plane can fly without wings.

Winglets reduce drag and increase fuel efficiency

Wing flaps increase lift at lower speeds and allow lower-speed takeoff/landing

Wings containing fuel tanks

Wing internal structure

Engine nozzle

Inlet

Combustion chamber

Compressor

Undercarriage mechanism

Engine power

Air enters at the inlet, and the compressor squeezes it to 40 times less volume. The combustion chamber adds fuel and burns the mixture at up to 3,600°F (2,000°C). Exhaust gas blows out through the engine nozzle, powering the plane forward.

Lavatories

First-class seats

Galley kitchens

Engine nacelle (protective covering)

Private luxury cabins

Stairs to upper deck

Information desk

Cockpit and crew rest area

Air conditioning units

Cockpit windows

Weather and navigation radar built into nose cone

Double decker

The Airbus A380 is the world's only double-decker airplane. The giant wings generate enough lift to carry two levels of passengers plus cargo beneath. With the seats removed, the A380 becomes the world's largest cargo plane—able to carry up to 165 tons (150 metric tons) of freight (50 percent more than any other plane).

LOOK INSIDE

FLYING HIGH

If you're looking for the fastest way to get around the planet, hop on a plane. There are thousands of these sleek metal "birds" soaring through our skies each day. It's easy to see why planes are so popular: roaring above mountains and soaring across oceans, jungles, and deserts, they can go almost anywhere. In the early 19th century, the fastest way to cross the Atlantic Ocean was by steamship—it took almost a month. By the late 20th century, planes could make the same journey in just three hours.

Faster than sound

With a top speed of 2,193 mph (3,529 kph), the Lockheed Martin SR-71 Blackbird (right) could travel three times faster than sound (and four times faster than an Airbus A380). It worked as a spyplane until the 1990s.

See the world

Flying opened up travel to exotic locations like Easter Island, in the Pacific Ocean off Chile (left). Few people had experienced such amazing places until air travel became popular in the 1950s.

Safer skies

You might not think it, but traveling by plane is 22 times safer than traveling by car. That's partly thanks to devices like these radar screens, which help pilots to land planes safely even in bad weather.

Milestones

Flying carpet
People were dreaming of flight long before they invented planes. In the famous Arabian Nights stories, written more than 1,000 years ago, Prince Ahmed travels on a magic carpet that flies and hovers

The Montgolfiers
Two French brothers called Montgolfier built the first practical hot-air balloons. On November 21, 1783, one of their balloons traveled 5.5 miles (9 km) across Paris in a 23-minute voyage with a two-man crew.

Food miles

Even if you've never been in a plane, you still enjoy the benefits of flying. Our supermarkets are packed with fresh fruit and vegetables flown in from around the world, so we can enjoy all kinds of food all year round. Unfortunately, it takes lots of energy to transport food, which makes groceries more expensive and harms the environment.

Jumbo load

The specially designed Airbus Beluga Super Transporter pictured below is designed to carry parts of other planes around the world. When it takes off fully fueled with a maximum load, it weighs 170 tons (155 metric tons)—as much as 22 large elephants. The cargo hold is big enough to carry more than 100,000 basketballs.

Airport ordeals

Airports are hectic places. The world's busiest airport is Hartfield-Jackson International in Atlanta, Georgia. It handles around 80 million passengers on nearly a million flights each year.

Look, no runway!

This plane has two large floats underneath it so it can take off and land on calm water near the coast. Seaplanes like this were very popular in the early 20th century, before most modern airports had been built.

The Wright brothers

Two more famous brothers, Wilbur and Orville Wright, made the first engine-powered flight in December 1903. Their flimsy wooden plane stayed in the air only 12 seconds—a short flight, but long enough to begin the age of the plane.

American hero

Millions fly across the Atlantic Ocean every year, but Charles Lindbergh (1902–1974) was the first person to make that journey alone. His 1927 solo transatlantic flight from the United States to France took a little more than 33 hours.

Jumbo jet

The Boeing 747 "jumbo jet" has been one of the world's most popular jet airplanes since it was introduced in 1970. Its wide body can carry 400–500 passengers.

FUTURE SPACE PLANE

Aerospace engineers are already designing planes that will climb 70 miles (110 km) above Earth—10 times higher than most planes go today. Those lucky enough to fly on these spaceplanes will be among the first space tourists.

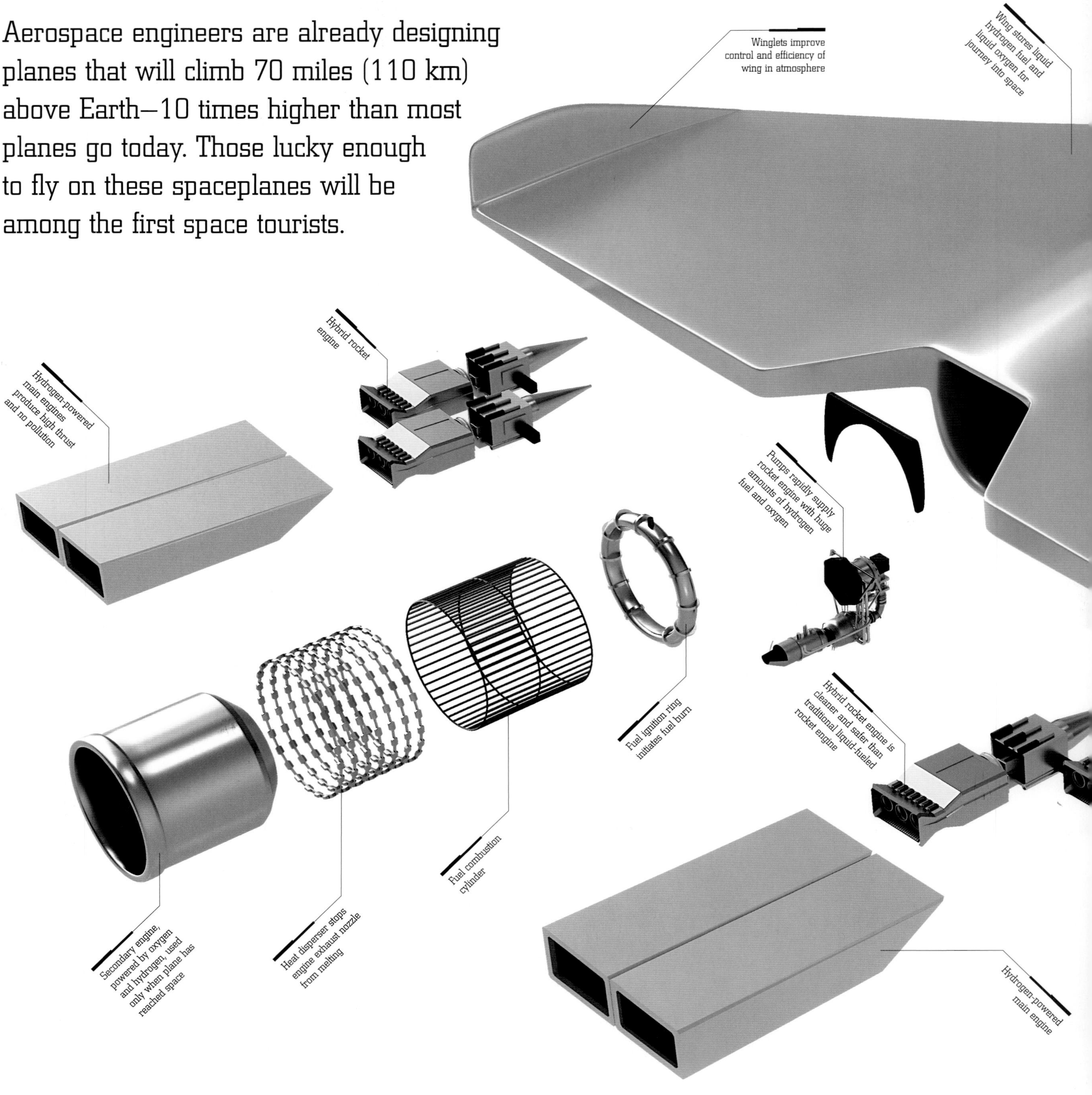

Winglets improve control and efficiency of wing in atmosphere

Wing stores liquid hydrogen fuel and liquid oxygen for journey into space

Hybrid rocket engine

Hydrogen-powered main engines produce high thrust and no pollution

Pumps rapidly supply rocket engine with huge amounts of hydrogen fuel and oxygen

Fuel ignition ring initiates fuel burn

Hybrid rocket engine is cleaner and safer than traditional liquid-fueled rocket engine

Fuel combustion cylinder

Secondary engine, powered by oxygen and hydrogen, used only when plane has reached space

Heat disperser stops engine exhaust nozzle from melting

Hydrogen-powered main engine

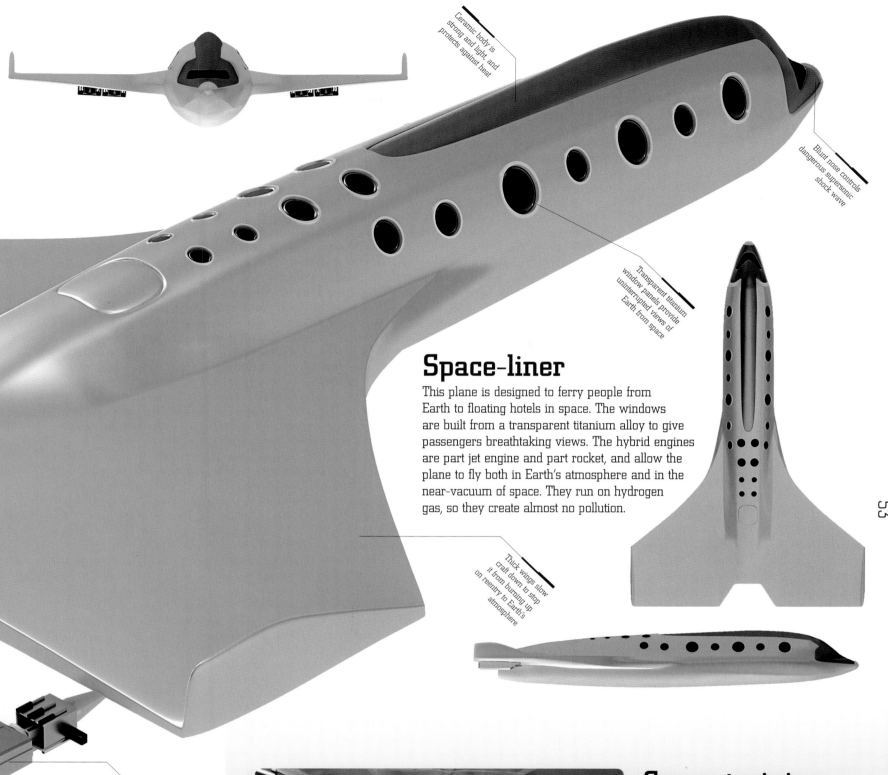

Ceramic body is strong and light and protects against heat

Blunt nose controls dangerous supersonic shock wave

Transparent titanium window panels provide uninterrupted views of Earth from space

Space-liner

This plane is designed to ferry people from Earth to floating hotels in space. The windows are built from a transparent titanium alloy to give passengers breathtaking views. The hybrid engines are part jet engine and part rocket, and allow the plane to fly both in Earth's atmosphere and in the near-vacuum of space. They run on hydrogen gas, so they create almost no pollution.

Thick wings slow craft down to stop it from burning up on reentry to Earth's atmosphere

Engine's internal shape ensures air and fuel mix efficiently to give smooth operation

Space training

English physicist Stephen Hawking (1942–) is one of the world's experts on gravity and is training to become a space tourist. He is almost completely paralyzed and normally uses a wheelchair. To celebrate his 65th birthday, in January 2007, he flew in a plane known as a "Vomit Comet." This soars to high altitudes before dropping suddenly to create periods of weightlessness for its passengers.

SPACESUIT

The human body is perfectly adapted for living on Earth, but traveling into space is something we were never designed for. Space is dark and dangerous, sometimes boiling hot, sometimes freezing cold, and there's no air to breathe. Without the help of a tough protective spacesuit—a one-person spaceship—you have no chance of survival.

Outer skin

Our bodies are machines with fleshy pipes, pumps, and all kinds of self-regulating mechanisms packed inside them to keep us alive. It's a bit like an adapter that allows the apparatus inside our bodies to keep functioning in the challenging conditions of space.

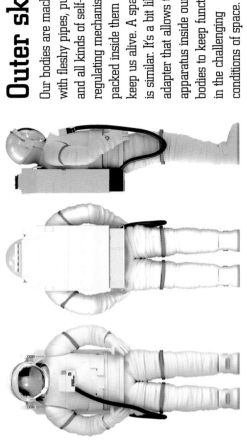

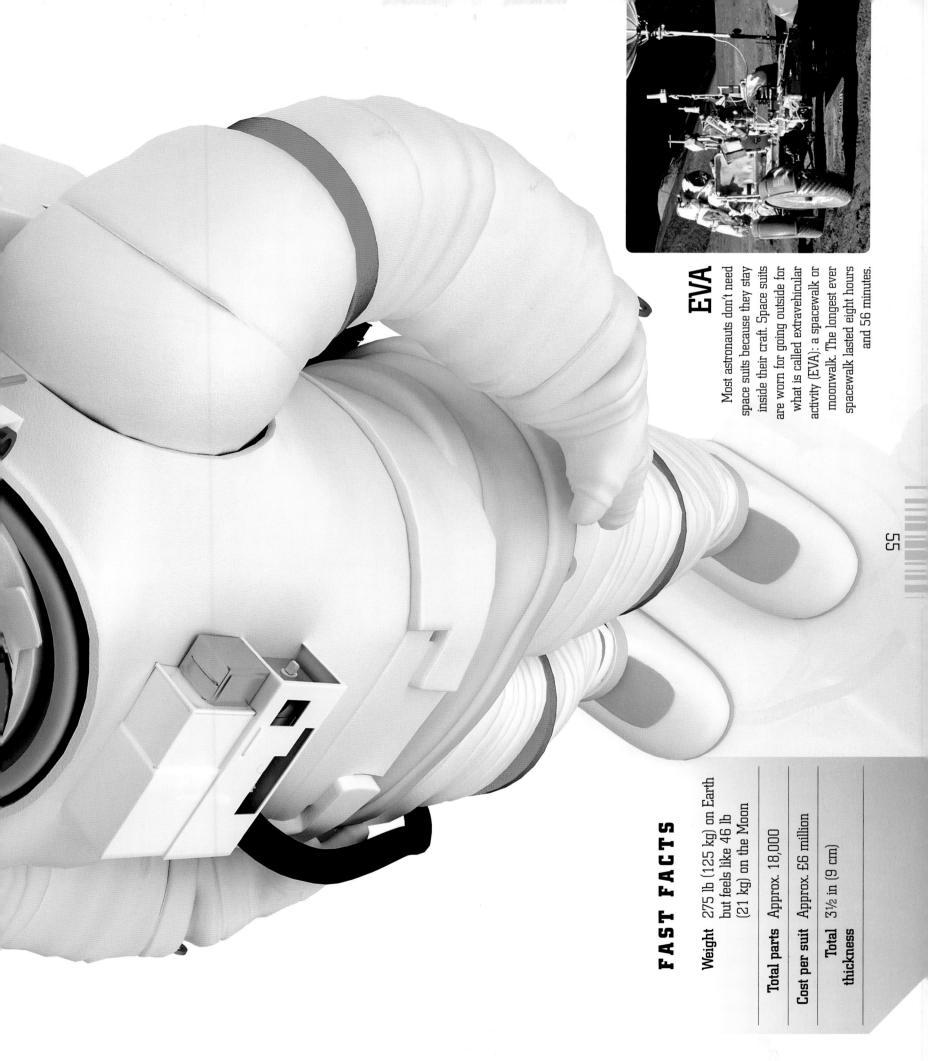

EVA

Most astronauts don't need space suits because they stay inside their craft. Space suits are worn for going outside for what is called extravehicular activity (EVA): a spacewalk or moonwalk. The longest ever spacewalk lasted eight hours and 56 minutes.

FAST FACTS

Weight	275 lb (125 kg) on Earth but feels like 46 lb (21 kg) on the Moon
Total parts	Approx. 18,000
Cost per suit	Approx. £6 million
Total thickness	3½ in (9 cm)

LOOK INSIDE

Sublimator removes water vapor from exhaled breath

Main backpack casing

Contaminant control system cleans exhaled breath

Life support system, holds oxygen tanks, battery pack, warning computer, radio, and water tank

Drink bag

Liquid cooling and ventilation garment (LCVG): double-layered bodysuit

Extravehicular visor assembly is impact-toughened and reflects light and heat

Headlights

Microphone

Inner helmet

"Snoopy" cap keeps earphones and microphones in place

Helmet

Hard upper torso: toughened inner fiberglass shell to which outer parts of suit are attached

Inner visor

Display and control module monitors life support data

Outer visor

Display and control module cover

Main oxygen tanks

Backup oxygen tanks

Electrical harness

Life support

A spacesuit has to keep an astronaut alive for several hours, so the main oxygen tanks (and backup tanks if those fail) are vitally important. Also important on a long spacewalk is the maximum absorbency garment (MAG). It's a cross between a giant diaper and a pair of underpants, and it's worn next to the skin.

Gloves thick enough to provide protection but thin enough for good finger movement

Thermal micro-meteoroid garment (TMG): eight layers of material protect against tiny space rocks

Pipes circulate water through LCVG to keep astronaut cool

Boots

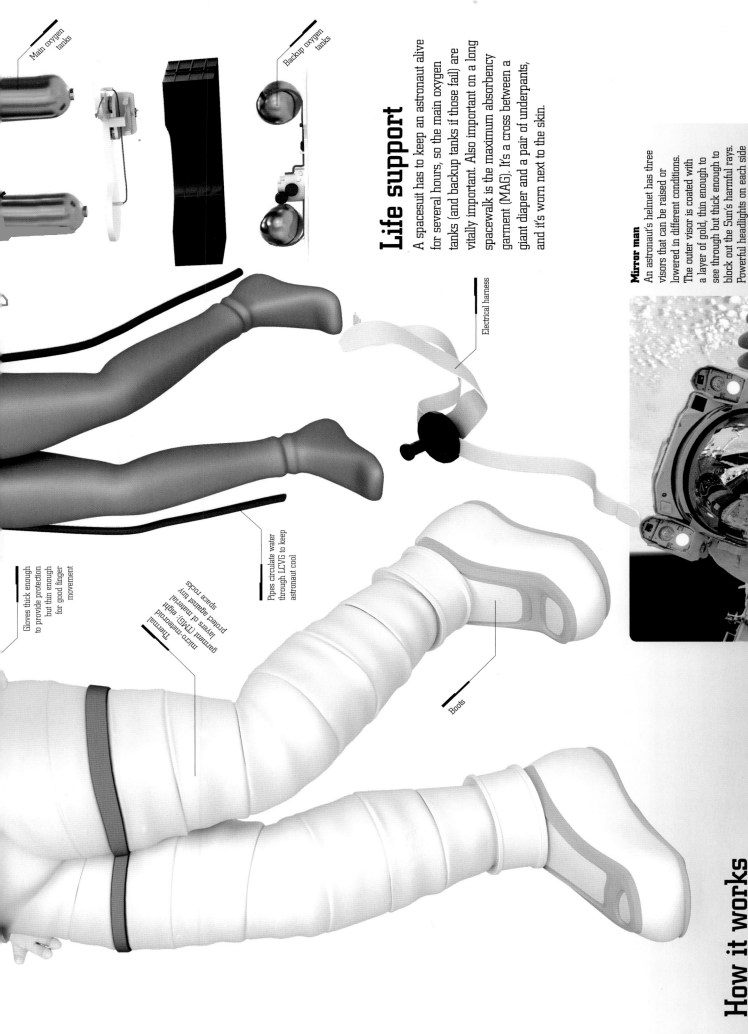

Mirror man
An astronaut's helmet has three visors that can be raised or lowered in different conditions. The outer visor is coated with a layer of gold, thin enough to see through but thick enough to block out the Sun's harmful rays. Powerful headlights on each side are for working in places where sunlight doesn't reach.

How it works

When astronauts step into space, suits like this are their only protection. A typical suit has 13–24 different layers, each of which does a specific job. The outer layer shields against micro-meteorites (tiny flying space rocks) and is fireproof, too. Inner layers protect against extreme heat (in sunlight) and cold (in shadow). The inside of the suit is pressurized like a jet plane cabin, so breathing and other body processes work much as they would back on Earth.

Sunglasses

Most sunglasses have plastic lenses. Thanks to space research, some are now coated with diamondlike carbon (DLC) that is 10 times harder to scratch. This very thin carbon film also makes the lenses smoother, so rain runs off more quickly.

Cold comfort

On the Moon, temperatures soar from a toe-tingling -250°F (-157°C) to a blood-boiling 250°F (120°C), so lunar astronauts wore suits with 24 insulating layers to protect them. Things are less extreme on Earth, but layers still help. Outer layers keep out the wind, while base (inner) layers carry moisture from your skin, trap air, and help your body retain heat.

LESSONS FROM SPACE

Skid lid

Helmets used to be hot and heavy, but not any more. The aerodynamic shape and air vents on this cycling hat were developed through aerospace research. Helmets like this have a crunch-proof polycarbonate outer layer and shock-absorbing foam inside.

You may not think of yourself as a space traveler, but that's exactly what you are. You live on a rock, spinning through space, often facing similar challenges to an astronaut. Even walking to the store, you may have to wear glasses to block out the Sun's harmful rays or insulating layers to keep out the cold. Materials developed for space travel can often prove useful here on Earth. Look around you and you'll see cyclists wearing shock-proof helmets based on NASA technology, and joggers hitting the streets in shoes developed from moon boots!

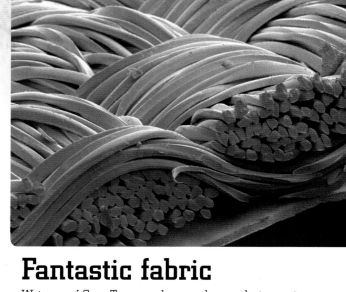

Fantastic fabric

Waterproof Gore-Tex, seen here under an electron microscope, is made from the slippery Teflon used in space suits. The fabric has microscopic holes 20,000 times smaller than a water droplet. Rain cannot get in from outside, but sweat can escape. That's why Gore-Tex is waterproof and "breathable" at the same time.

Water warmth

Water can suck heat from your body 40 times faster than air, which is why people can die in cold seas in a matter of minutes. Wetsuits are made from neoprene (synthetic rubber), with inner layers of metals like titanium or copper to reflect back heat. They fit tightly and trap water inside. The body quickly warms this water, which acts as an insulating layer. Space suits have neoprene layers, too.

Springy steps

Some shoes contain viscoelastic "memory foam" that softens and relieves pressure as it gets warmer. NASA scientists designed it in the 1970s for seats that would cushion astronauts from extreme forces during rocket blastoff. The shock-absorbing foam is also used in pain-relieving mattresses and pillows.

Fire away

Under their outer clothes, race-car drivers wear fire-resistant inner suits made from a carbon-based material called Nomex. Some space suits and boots also have layers of Nomex for fire and heat protection. You may find Nomex in your own home—hi-tech oven gloves are often made from it.

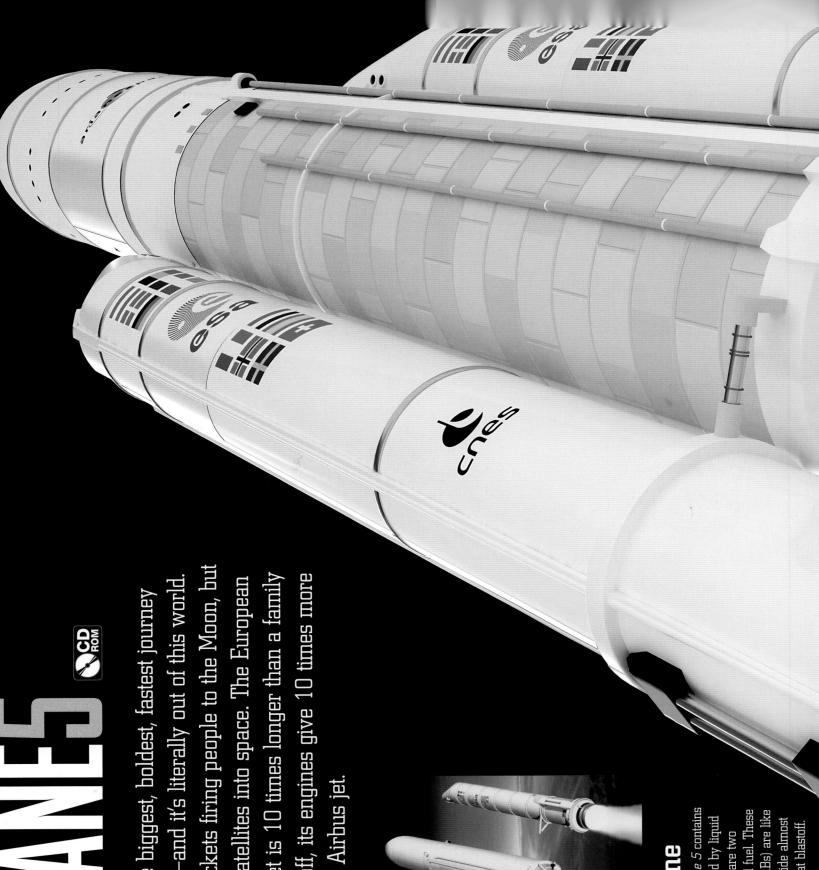

ARIANE 5

CD ROM

Blastoff! It's the biggest, boldest, fastest journey you can make—and it's literally out of this world. We think of rockets firing people to the Moon, but most just put satellites into space. The European *Ariane 5* rocket is 10 times longer than a family car and, at liftoff, its engines give 10 times more power than an Airbus jet.

Three in one

The central part of *Ariane 5* contains the main engine, powered by liquid fuel. On each side, there are two rockets powered by solid fuel. These solid rocket boosters (SRBs) are like giant fireworks that provide almost 90 percent of the thrust at blastoff.

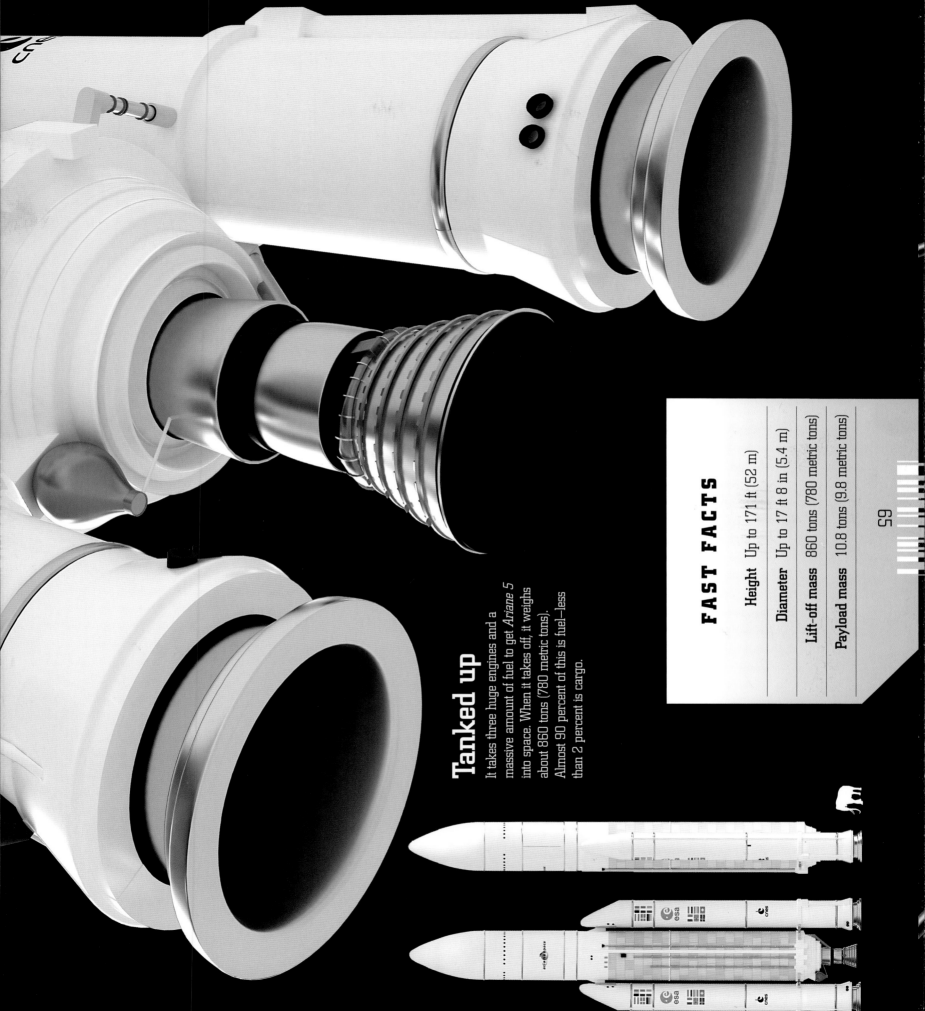

Tanked up

It takes three huge engines and a massive amount of fuel to get *Ariane 5* into space. When it takes off, it weighs about 860 tons (780 metric tons). Almost 90 percent of this is fuel—less than 2 percent is cargo.

Space first

If this strange metal ball looks like a vision of the future, imagine how it must have seemed half a century ago. This is *Sputnik 1*, the first ever artificial satellite, which the Soviet Union (Russia and her former republics) launched into space on October 4, 1957. The size of a beach ball, *Sputnik* circled the planet once every 96 minutes until early 1958.

Milestones

Chinese fireworks
The seeds of the space age were sown 1,400 years ago when the Chinese invented fireworks. By the 13th century, these had evolved into simple missiles.

Congreve rockets
In the early 19th century, William Congreve (1772–1828) made rockets out of fireworks for the British army. The rockets could travel more than 2 miles (3 km). They were first used during the Napoleonic Wars with France.

EYES IN THE SKY

Next time you're walking down the street, look up at the sky and smile: there's every chance your photograph is being taken by a space satellite! There are thousands of these unmanned electronic spacecraft spinning around Earth. Some take photographs or make scientific measurements. Some help us beam phone calls, TV pictures, and internet data from one side of the world to the other. Others tell us where we are and help us find our way around. The almost instant communication that we now take for granted is made possible by the satellites in orbit at various heights above our heads.

Always in touch

Communications satellites can transmit phone calls between any two places on Earth. Orbiting at exactly the speed Earth turns, they stay in the same spot above the planet, 22,300 miles (35,900 km) over the equator.

Before and after

Satellites that take photos orbit about 250–1,000km (150–620 miles) above our heads. These pictures (left) were taken by the *Landsat 7* satellite. They show the US city of New Orleans before (top) and after (bottom) the floods caused by Hurricane Katrina in August 2005.

Ariane crash

Ariane rockets have launched around 300 satellites, but not all of them made it into space. The very first *Ariane 5* launch on June 4, 1996, was a disaster. A software error meant the rocket crashed just after takeoff, destroying the four science satellites on board.

Konstantin Tsiolkovsky
Russian schoolteacher Konstantin Tsiolkovsky (1857–1935) was decades ahead of his time. He predicted that one day rockets would carry people into space, and even drew designs for an early space station.

Robert Hutchings Goddard
American scientist Robert Hutchings Goddard (1882–1945) built his first liquid-fueled rocket in 1926. When he suggested that rockets could take people to the Moon, he was widely ridiculed. Since his death, many of his ideas have proved correct and he is now considered the father of modern rocketry.

Werner von Braun
During World War II, German engineer Werner von Braun (1912–1977) designed long-distance rocket bombs that terrorized much of Europe. After the war, he worked for NASA, helping to put men on the Moon in 1969.

MOUNTAINBIKE

Tough stuff

Tough and lightweight, off-road mountain bikes first appeared in the 1970s. They are very different from racing bikes. Their smaller wheels produce less speed but give you more control on tricky terrain. Also, disk brakes give more stopping power than the rim brakes on a normal bike.

Brace yourself for a rough ride! If you're hurtling down a hill or churning through a field, you need a bike that's tough enough to survive. Mountain bikes have to be much stronger than racing bikes, but that can make them heavy, sluggish, and slow. This one is made from feather-light carbon fiber so you waste less energy reaching top speed. Chunky tires bite the ground beneath you, while powerful front and rear suspension smooths away the rocks and knocks.

Lighter load

The bike weighs less than a conventional steel bike because it's made from carbon fiber. This composite material is a plastic that's reinforced with microscopic, rodlike strands of carbon, a bit like millions of tiny pencils.

FAST FACTS

Weight 26 lb (11.9 kg)

Gears 27-speed Shimano

Suspension Front and rear shock absorbers

Brakes Front and rear disk

Cost Approx. $1,000

LOOKINSIDE

Lean machine

Bicycles use science to get you where you want to go. From the gears to the frame, virtually every part of a bike uses scientific principles to make riding quicker or easier. Aside from being great exercise, using a bicycle is one of the most energy-efficient forms of transportation. Bicycles are around 90 percent efficient, which means they turn virtually all the energy supplied by their power source—your legs—into kinetic energy to move you along. In contrast, a car is only 15 percent efficient overall.

Shock absorbers
This canister behind the seat makes your ride smoother. A piston inside bounces up and down in thick oil, absorbing energy when you hit a bump.

Tires
Mountain bike tires are designed for rough terrain. They're thicker and grip better than racing tires. This bike's tires are made from Kevlar, a tough, hard-wearing carbon-based fabric.

Gears
Gears increase your bike's speed along a straight path, or its climbing power up a hill. When the chain runs around one of the smaller gears, the back wheel goes faster each time you pedal, cranking up your speed. When the chain moves to a bigger gear, the back wheel slows down but turns with more force, enabling you to go uphill more easily.

Top stay (seat stay)

Rear suspension struts

Rear shock absorber

Spokes

Chain stay

Rear wheel and tire

Rear disk brake

Brake and gear cables

Freewheel and rear sprockets (gear wheels)

Rear derailleur moves chain during gear changes and keeps it tight

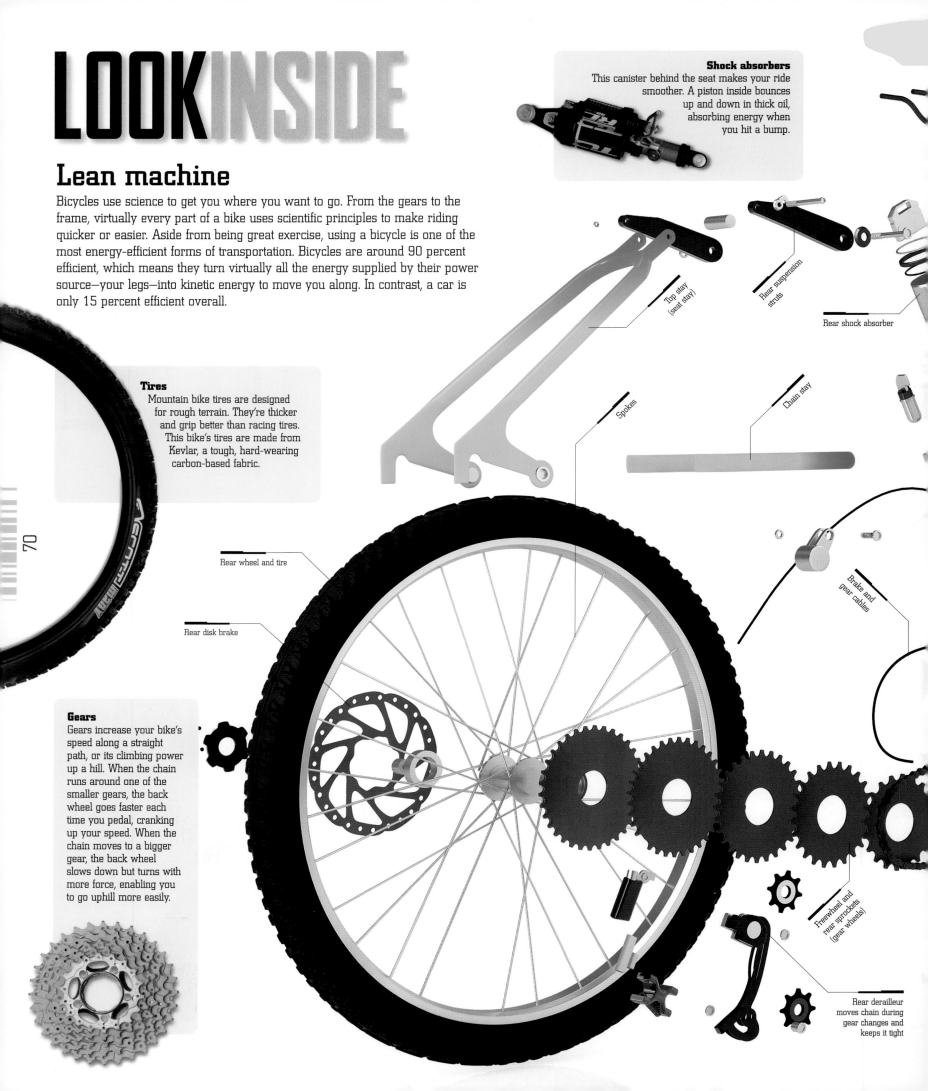

Saddle

Rear brake
lever

Front brake lever

Handlebar grips

Handlebar adjustment

Handlebar

Frame
A bike's strong
triangular frame supports
your weight and spreads it
more or less evenly between
the front and back wheels.

Seat post

Top tube (crossbar)

Front shock
absorbers

Disk brakes
When you brake, rubber
blocks press against small
perforated disks on the
wheels and slow you down.
Friction turns the bike's
energy into heat.

Seat tube

Front forks
hold front
wheel in place

Tire

Front axle
supports front
wheel

Pedal crank arm

Pedal

Down tube

Front sprockets
(gear wheels)

Front disk brake

Pneumatic inner tube

Rim of wheel

Rear axle

Chain

Wheels
Bigger wheels cover ground faster than smaller ones,
so large bike wheels help to increase your speed.
Spokes make the wheel lighter and more aerodynamic.

PEDAL POWER

Simple is often best—but simplicity is only one of the reasons why bicycles are still popular more than a century after their invention. They're very affordable, easy and lots of fun to ride, cost nothing to run, and sometimes last for decades. They're also perfect for city travel because they create no pollution and you can park them almost anywhere.

Green machines

In Paris, France, people are encouraged to leave their cars at home and use one of a new fleet of 10,000 rental bikes. You simply buy a swipe card, unlock a bike from one of 750 locations, and cycle away. The bikes clocked up four million rides in their first two months of use.

Spreading the load

Bicycles are incredibly versatile machines. In countries such as China and India, where fewer people have cars, bikes are widely used for transporting goods. In more industrialized countries, bikes can cut through heavy traffic to deliver smaller loads much faster than cars or vans.

Handcycles

This bicycle is designed for a disabled rider who cannot pedal with his legs. Instead, he powers the bike by turning hand-operated gears. The hand mechanism also controls the brakes and steering.

Milestones

Draisienne
One of the first bicycles, the Draisienne or "hobby horse," invented in 1817, was designed to help people walk more quickly. It had wooden wheels, but no gears, chain, or pedals.

High Wheeler
Before bikes had gears, they had huge front wheels, like this 1870 High Wheeler, to help them go faster. They were very hard to climb onto—and very easy to fall off!

Speed machines

Olympic cyclists try to make their bodies and bikes work together as a single machine. Special handlebars mean these riders can keep their arms in a very streamlined position. Their skin-tight clothes and pointed helmets also help to minimize drag (air resistance). The bikes themselves are made of carbon composites. These materials are as strong as metals but much lighter, giving extra speed.

Bicycles of tomorrow

Future bicycles will be better in every way. They could have aerodynamic covers like this to help them go faster, automatic gears, and tires made of puncture-proof materials. Some bikes will have solar panels and electric motors on the wheels to help you climb hills with less effort.

Rickshaws

Rickshaws (bicycle taxis) are an environmentally friendly alternative to gas-powered taxis. Originally developed in Asian countries, they are now being used as tourist taxis in Western countries to help reduce pollution and congestion.

Dunlop bike
The next big advance came in 1888, when John Boyd Dunlop (1840–1921) made more comfortable bicycles with pneumatic (air-filled) tires. Bicycles like this were much like modern ones. They had similar-sized wheels, gears, a comfortable saddle, and safety grips on the handlebars.

Folding bike
This odd-looking frame folds out to make a complete bicycle in under 10 seconds. Made of lightweight aluminum and fibreglass, it weighs just 12 lb 10 oz (5.6 kg) and is light enough to carry on a bus or train.

Future bikes
Electric bicycles could be the future of transportation. Using rechargeable batteries and lightweight electric motors, they can travel 30 miles (48 km) at speeds of up to 15 mph (24 kph).

FUEL CELL BIKE

A motorcycle might look small and efficient as it weaves in and out of stalled city traffic, but it makes up to 16 times more air pollution than a car. While cars are packed with pollution-scrubbing technologies such as catalytic converters, motorcycles pump their dirty fumes straight into the air. All that could change if bikes swapped gas power for electricity. Intelligent Energy's ENV (emissions-neutral vehicle) bike has an electric motor instead of a gas engine. It runs on clean, efficient hydrogen gas and the only waste product it makes is harmless steam.

Vroom vroom

Originally called the Cityhopper, the ENV was designed to cut the noise and pollution that traditional motorcycles make in busy streets. Its electric motor is virtually silent—but not everyone agrees this is a good thing. Silent motorcycles could be dangerous to pedestrians and other traffic, so the ENV's manufacturers are now fitting an artificial "vroom" noise, for safety, so people can hear it coming!

FAST FACTS

Weight	176 lb (80 kg)
Power source	6,000-watt, 48-volt electric motor
Top speed	50 mph (80 kph)
Acceleration	50 mph (0–80 kph) in 12.1 seconds
Range	100 miles (160 km) on 1 tank of hydrogen
Cost	Approx. $6,000

The CORE

There's no gas tank in the ENV bike. Instead, it uses a power source called the CORE: a box, the size of a desktop computer, containing a fuel cell and a tank that you fill up with hydrogen gas. The fuel cell works a bit like a battery; as long as there is hydrogen in the tank, it keeps making electricity.

How it works

All the power the ENV bike needs comes from the fuel cell inside the CORE. This takes hydrogen from its internal tank and oxygen from the air, and produces a chemical reaction between the two to make electricity. The only waste product is steam, which passes out harmlessly into the environment. It takes less than five minutes to refill the hydrogen fuel tank.

Future fuel

Fuel cells driving electric motors have many advantages over the engines we use today. They are light and compact, and are good for the environment because they are silent and pollution-free. Since they have no moving parts, they are also reliable and long-lasting.

Aerodynamic front cover improves fuel consumption

Hydrogen tank contains enough fuel for 100 miles (160 km) of travel

Brake lever

Headlights

CORE side cover

Telescopic front forks

Main chassis holds the CORE

Chunky front mountain-bike tire

LOOKINSIDE

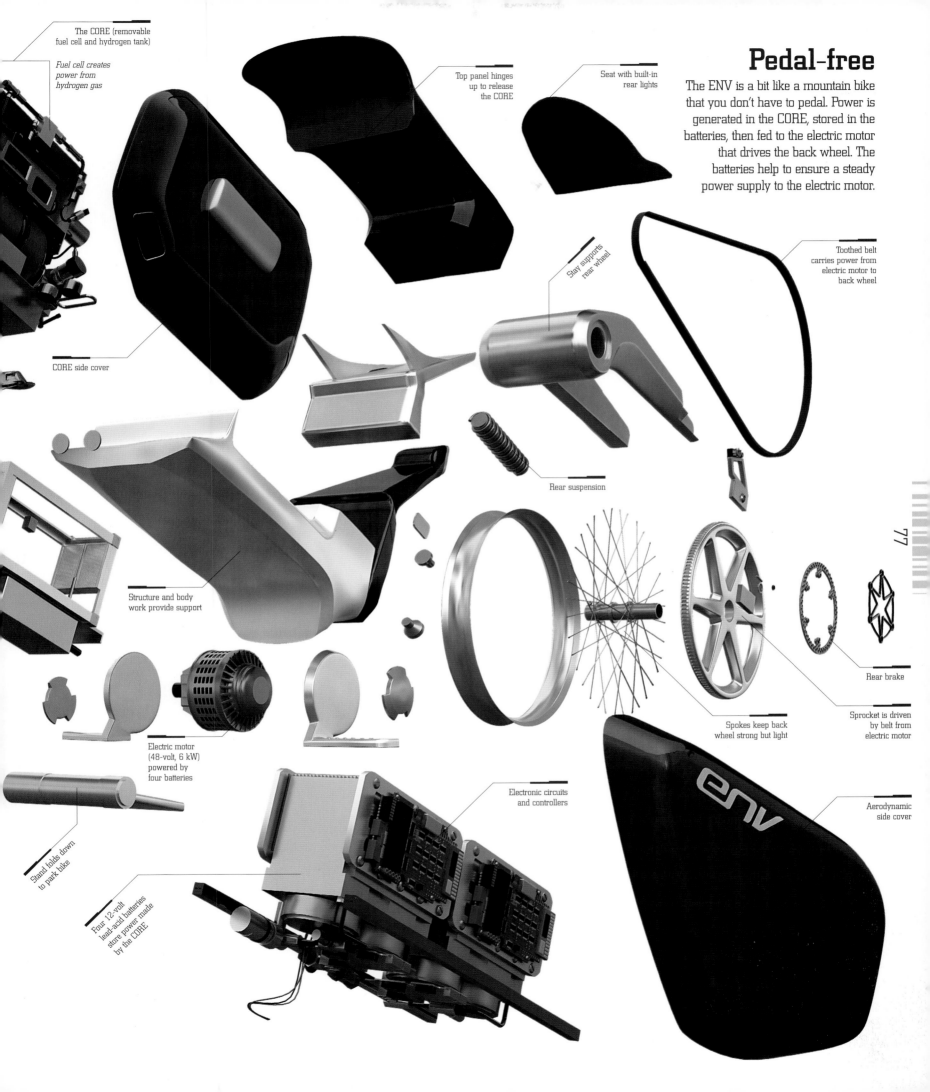

The CORE (removable fuel cell and hydrogen tank)

Fuel cell creates power from hydrogen gas

CORE side cover

Top panel hinges up to release the CORE

Seat with built-in rear lights

Pedal-free

The ENV is a bit like a mountain bike that you don't have to pedal. Power is generated in the CORE, stored in the batteries, then fed to the electric motor that drives the back wheel. The batteries help to ensure a steady power supply to the electric motor.

Toothed belt carries power from electric motor to back wheel

Stay supports rear wheel

Rear suspension

Structure and body work provide support

Electric motor (48-volt, 6 kW) powered by four batteries

Stand folds down to park bike

Four 12-volt lead-acid batteries store power made by the CORE

Electronic circuits and controllers

Rear brake

Spokes keep back wheel strong but light

Sprocket is driven by belt from electric motor

Aerodynamic side cover

env

OUTOFBREATH

Air quality has been a major problem since the Industrial Revolution. The coal-driven machines that powered us through the 18th and 19th centuries also choked our cities with smoke. Factories are now cleaner than ever, but with more than 600 million engine-powered vehicles on the planet the air is still dirtier than it needs to be, especially in cities. Pollution isn't just a nuisance: it makes lung problems like bronchitis and asthma much worse, kills trees, and even damages buildings. Fuel-cell vehicles, powered by electricity, offer one way to clear the smog.

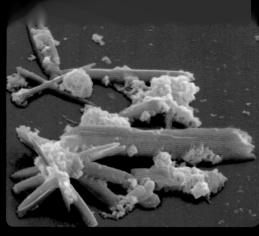

Dirty diesels

This electron microscope photo shows tiny grains of soot and unburned fuel from a car exhaust. Diesel engines use less fuel than gas engines, but produce more soot. The tiny particles they make, called PM10s, are linked to many health problems.

Monitoring pollution

This scientist (right) is studying pollution by firing a LIDAR (light detection and ranging) laser beam into the air. Different gases affect laser light in different ways, so when the beam reflects back from the sky it reveals what the pollution contains.

Smog

Mexico City is one of the world's most polluted places. Many of its factories have closed, but traffic fumes still choke the 25 million inhabitants. The filthy air over cities is called smog because it's like a cross between smoke and fog. Smog lingers when a layer of warm air above traps it like a lid.

Milestones

Fire

The basic technology inside engines is fire. Our ancestors discovered how to control fire between one and two million years ago. Nothing ever burns perfectly, so fires always make some pollution.

Steam engine

Steam engines were developed in the early 18th century, but the coal they burned made huge clouds of smoke. They powered industry but made cities really filthy.

Bad breath

This medical scan of a person's lungs shows how smoke and air pollution cause a problem called bronchitis. The patient's lungs (the blue areas on each side) become inflamed and fill with mucus (colored brown), causing shortness of breath and wheezing that can last months or even years.

Wearing away

When rain mixes with pollution from factories and power plants, it can become 1,000 times more acidic. Known as acid rain, this can kill forests, turn lakes into acid baths too toxic to support fish, and even wear away stone statues.

Gasoline engine

Gas engines were invented in the mid-19th century. Although each one is far cleaner than a steam engine, there are now hundreds of millions of them in the world—together, they produce a great deal of pollution.

Jet engine

Jet engines need to burn an enormous amount of fuel very quickly to lift a plane off the ground. They don't make much pollution at ground level, but gases from their exhausts damage Earth's atmosphere and add to global warming.

Electric motors

Electric motors are the clean engines of the future. If the electricity they use comes from a clean source, such as a solar panel or a wind turbine, they make no pollution.

FUTURE**HOVER**BIKE

Everyone hates sitting in traffic jams. With more cars on the roads and fewer places to put them, jams will happen much more often in future—unless we start taking to the air. In the future, people may swap motorcycles and cars for hoverbikes, powered by mini jet engines, that leave the city streets struggling far below.

Hover bird

Birds are brilliantly designed flying machines. They use wind and thermals (rising pockets of warm air) to help them stay airborne. Hummingbirds have an extra trick: they can hover on the spot by flapping their wings around 50 times a second. They can also fly in any direction by changing the angle, or pitch, of their wings as they flap, just like helicopter blades.

Handlebars control computer that keeps bike flying safely at all times

Front fan keeps the bike stable as it flies

Stereo system

Air intake

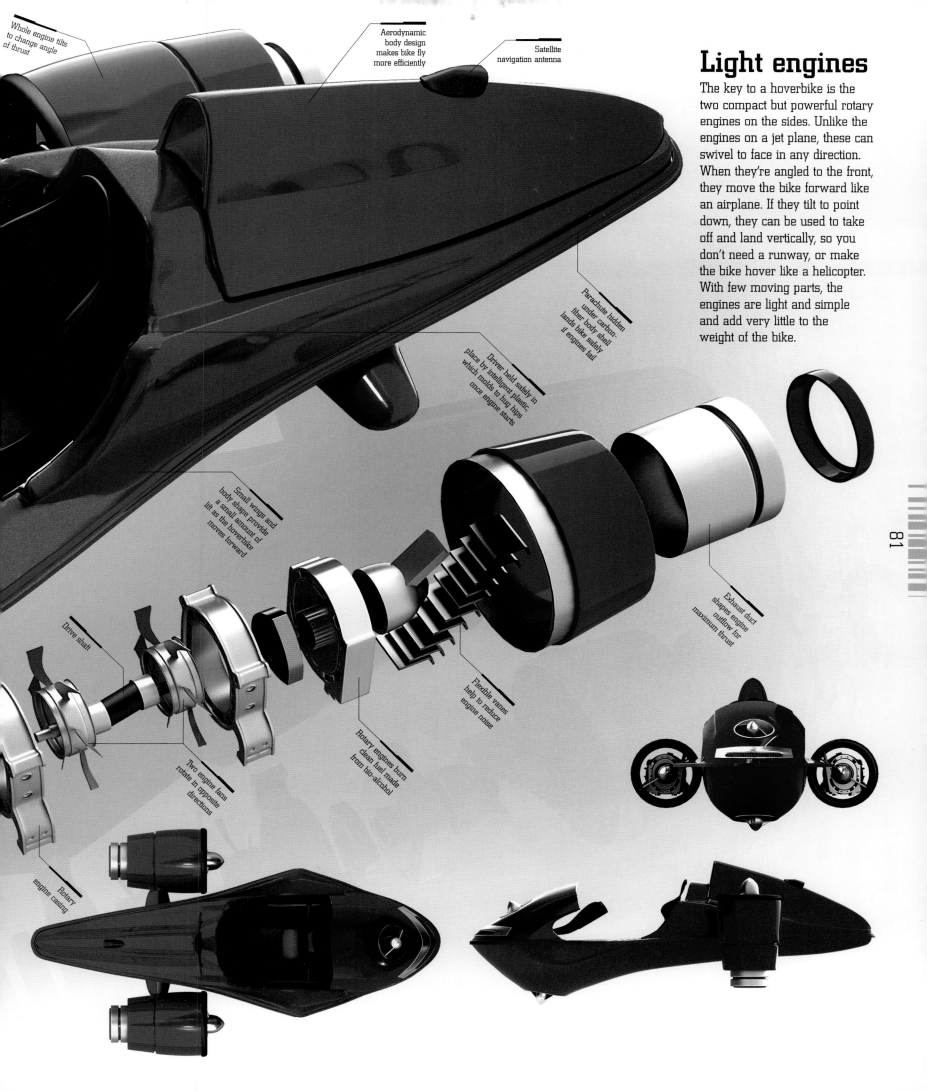

Whole engine tilts to change angle of thrust

Aerodynamic body design makes bike fly more efficiently

Satellite navigation antenna

Light engines

The key to a hoverbike is the two compact but powerful rotary engines on the sides. Unlike the engines on a jet plane, these can swivel to face in any direction. When they're angled to the front, they move the bike forward like an airplane. If they tilt to point down, they can be used to take off and land vertically, so you don't need a runway, or make the bike hover like a helicopter. With few moving parts, the engines are light and simple and add very little to the weight of the bike.

Parachute hidden under carbon-fiber body shell lands bike safely if engines fail

Driver held safely in place by intelligent plastic, which molds to hug hips once engine starts

Small wings and body shape provide a small amount of lift as the hoverbike moves forward

Exhaust duct shapes engine outflow for maximum thrust

Drive shaft

Flexible vanes help to reduce engine noise

Two engine fans rotate in opposite directions

Rotary engines burn clean fuel made from bio-alcohol

Rotary engine casing

Solar panels catch the Sun's rays and turn them into electricity. If we covered just 1 percent of the Sahara Desert with panels like these, we could generate enough electricity to power the entire world.

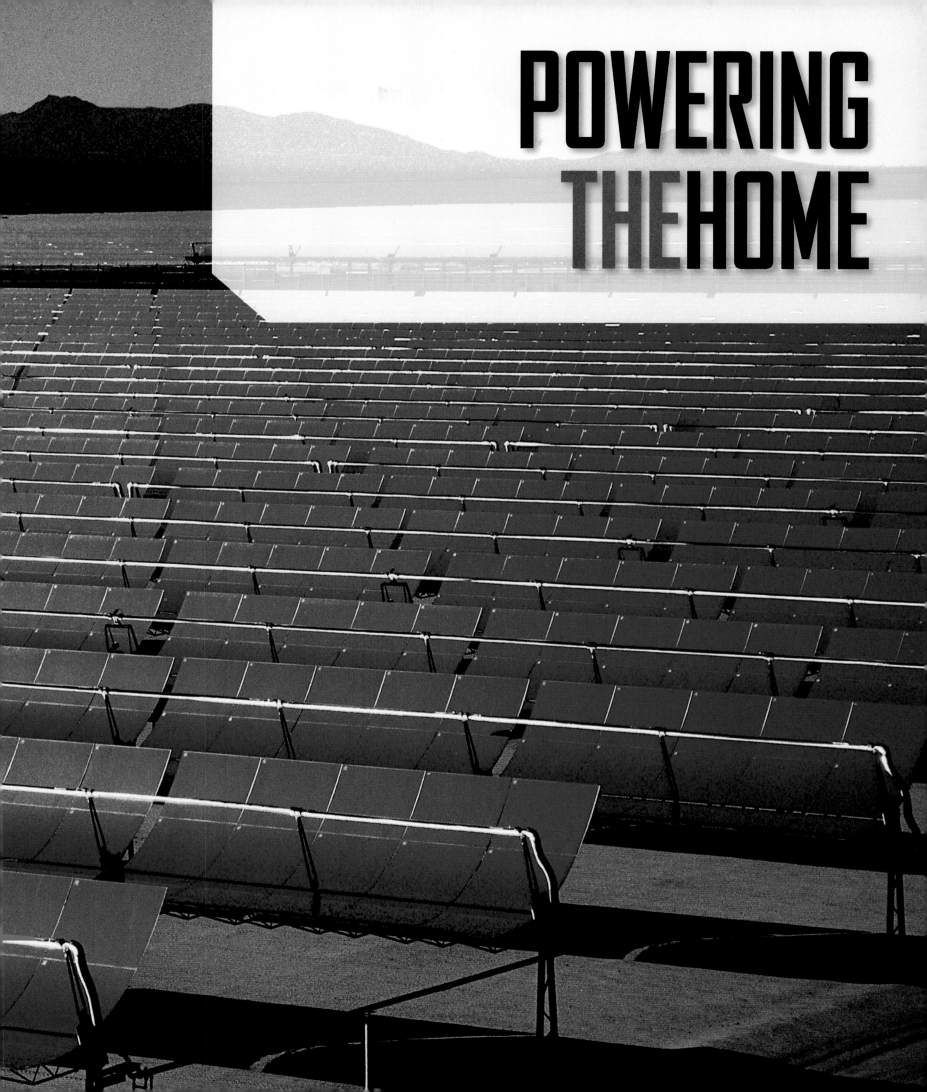

POWERING
THEHOME

Look down on Earth from a spaceship at night and you'll see small pinpricks of light where cities are burning with life. Zoom in on one of those cities and you'll find thousands or even millions of homes. If you could lift the roof off just one home, you would find that it is packed with ingenious gadgets and extraordinary appliances. Inside each gadget, hard-won scientific discoveries are being put to work to make our lives easier. Have you ever stopped to wonder how something as simple as an espresso machine can flush every last drop of flavor from a coffee bean? Or how a microwave oven cooks your dinner without ever getting hot itself? There's only really one way to find out, and that's to take a look inside.

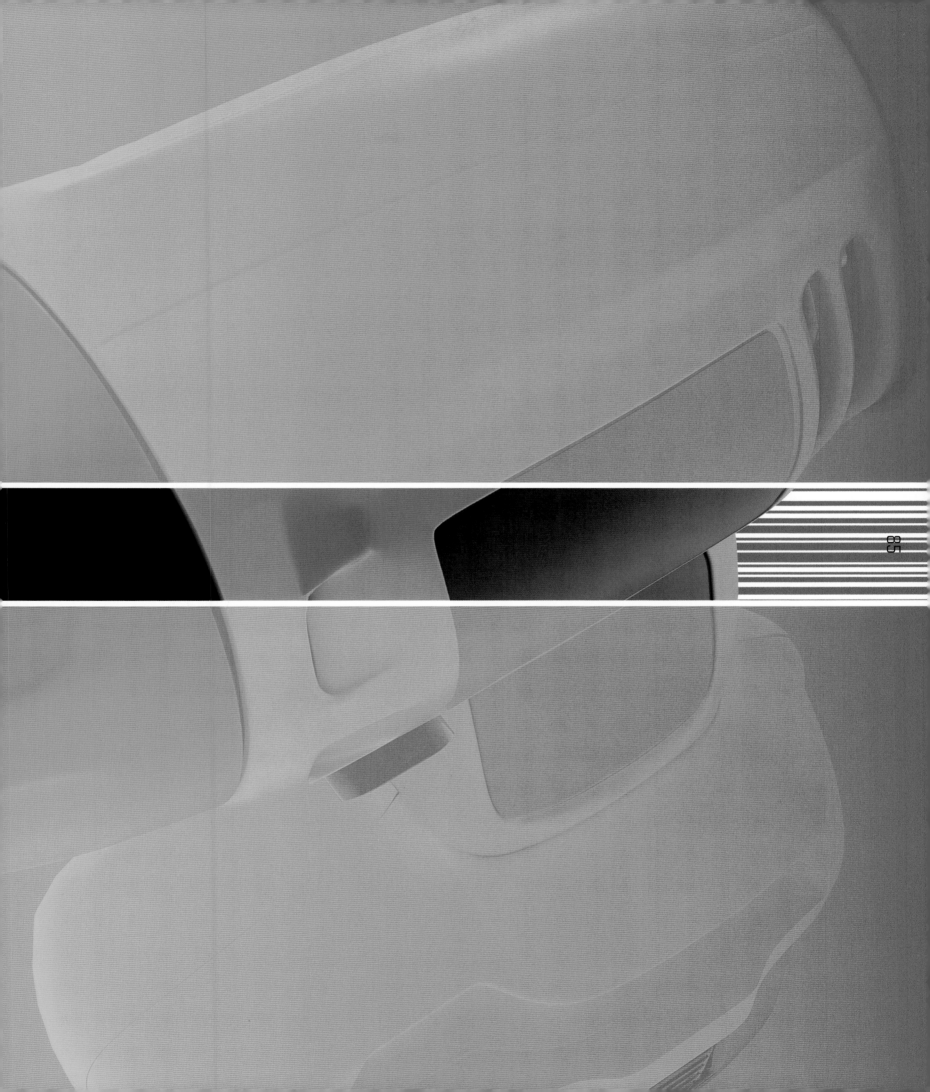

Wind farms

A big coal-fired or nuclear power plant makes about 2,000 megawatts (a megawatt is a million watts) of electricity—enough to power a million toasters all at the same time! You need about 1,000 wind turbines to make this much power, which is why turbines tend to be placed together in large groups called wind farms.

VESTAS WIND TURBINE

Our landscapes are flowering with elegant towers that produce energy from nothing but the wind. Just as well, because the oil and gas we rely on now may well be gone within decades. Coal, though plentiful, is too dirty to burn, and nuclear power produces dangerous waste. But soon we'll catch enough of the wind whistling around our planet to supply 10–20 percent of our energy. Slowly spinning in the breeze, each wind turbine generates enough electricity to supply 1,000 homes, creates no pollution, and helps us tackle global warming.

Tall tower

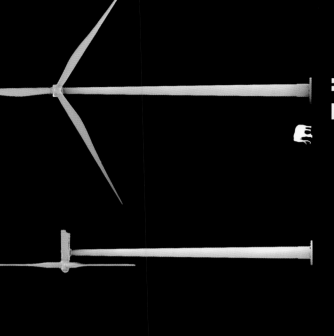

Wind moves faster high up than at ground level. Doubling the height of a wind turbine increases the energy it can produce by more than a third.

FAST FACTS

Tower height	262 ft–344 ft (80 m–105 m)
Rotor diameter	Up to 295 ft (90 m)
Maximum wind speed	55 mph (90 kph)
Blade material	Fiberglass and carbon fiber
Turbine weight	120 tons (110 metric tons)
Tower weight	190 tons (175 metric tons) 265 ft (80 m) height 300 tons (275 metric tons) 345 ft (105 m) height
Power output	Up to 3 megawatts

CD ROM

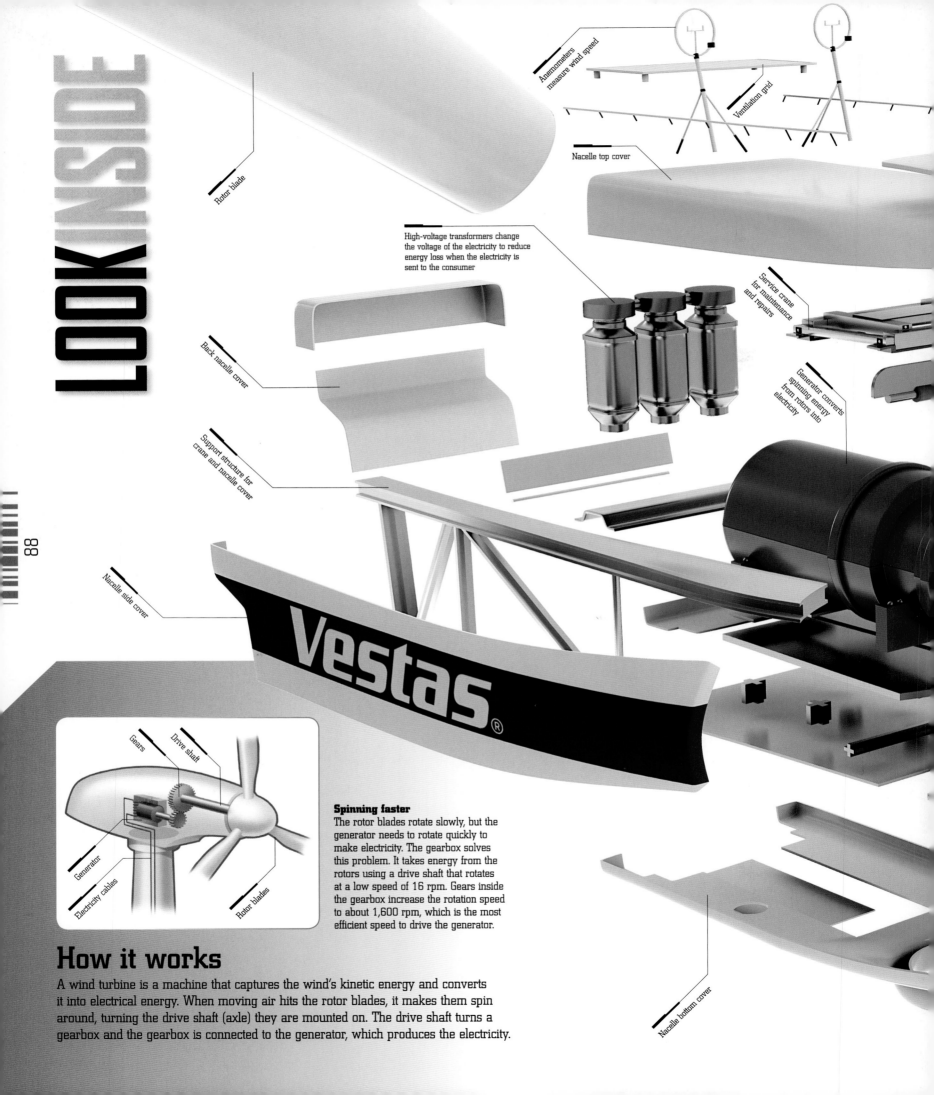

LOOK INSIDE

Anemometers measure wind speed

Ventilation grid

Nacelle top cover

Rotor blade

High-voltage transformers change the voltage of the electricity to reduce energy loss when the electricity is sent to the consumer

Service crane for maintenance and repairs

Back nacelle cover

Generator converts spinning energy from rotors into electricity

Support structure for crane and nacelle cover

Nacelle side cover

Vestas®

Nacelle bottom cover

Gears
Drive shaft

Generator
Electricity cables
Rotor blades

Spinning faster
The rotor blades rotate slowly, but the generator needs to rotate quickly to make electricity. The gearbox solves this problem. It takes energy from the rotors using a drive shaft that rotates at a low speed of 16 rpm. Gears inside the gearbox increase the rotation speed to about 1,600 rpm, which is the most efficient speed to drive the generator.

How it works

A wind turbine is a machine that captures the wind's kinetic energy and converts it into electrical energy. When moving air hits the rotor blades, it makes them spin around, turning the drive shaft (axle) they are mounted on. The drive shaft turns a gearbox and the gearbox is connected to the generator, which produces the electricity.

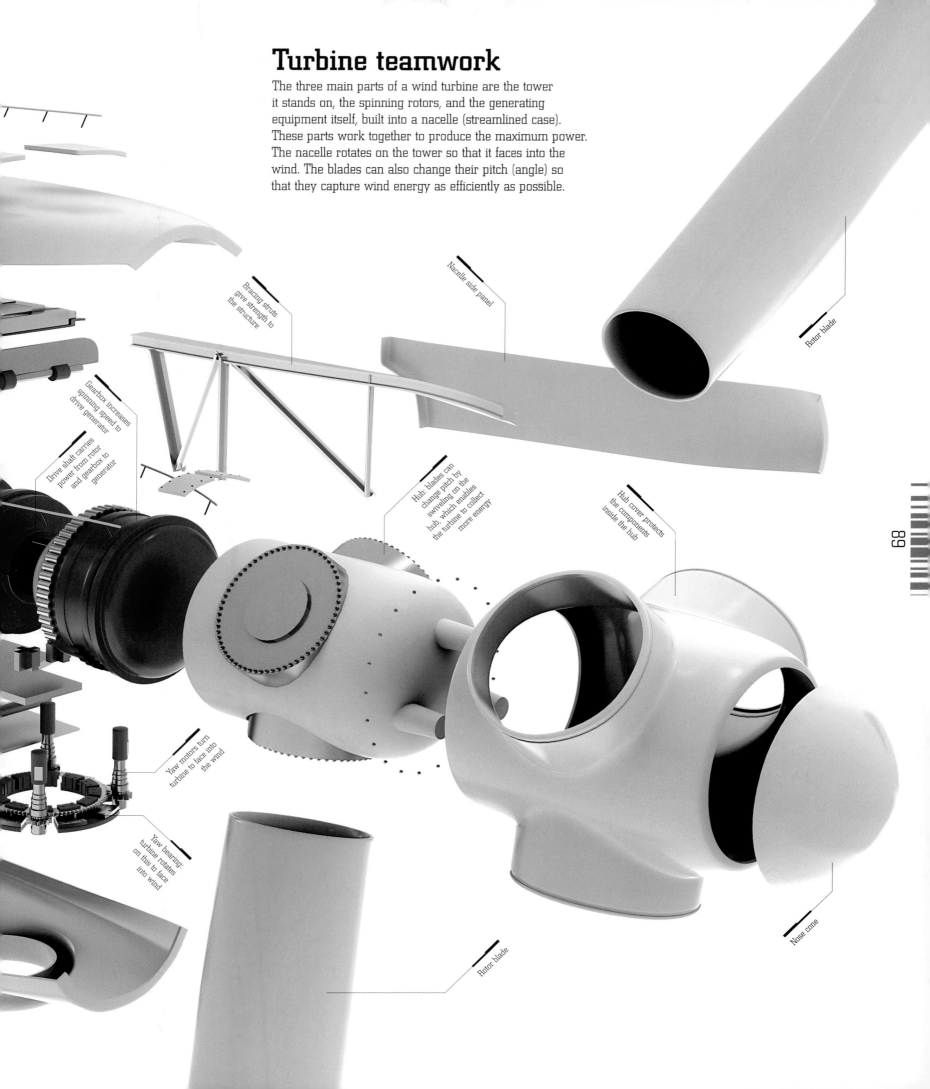

Turbine teamwork

The three main parts of a wind turbine are the tower it stands on, the spinning rotors, and the generating equipment itself, built into a nacelle (streamlined case). These parts work together to produce the maximum power. The nacelle rotates on the tower so that it faces into the wind. The blades can also change their pitch (angle) so that they capture wind energy as efficiently as possible.

Bracing struts give strength to the structure

Nacelle side panel

Rotor blade

Gearbox increases spinning speed to drive generator

Drive shaft carries power from rotor and gearbox to generator

Hub: blades can change pitch by swiveling on the hub, which enables the turbine to collect more energy

Hub cover protects the components inside the hub

Yaw motors turn turbine to face into the wind

Yaw bearing: turbine rotates on this to face into wind

Rotor blade

Nose cone

What is wind?

The power we think of as wind energy actually comes from the Sun. Wind is made when the Sun heats different places by different amounts. Hot air rises over warmer places and cool air rushes in underneath. Differences in temperature and air pressure between different places cause winds to blow over huge distances. People can harness the power of the wind to fill sails and push yachts along (left).

Lost at sea

This satellite image shows winds over the surface of the Pacific Ocean. The dark red areas, in the stormy south, have gale force eight winds with speeds reaching 45 mph (72 kph).

Offshore wind

It takes about 1,000 wind turbines to make as much electricity as one large coal or nuclear power plant. Countries with a coastline, such as Denmark, have built offshore wind farms to take advantage of the windy conditions at sea.

WIND POWER

Wind power is the world's fastest growing source of renewable energy. More than 10 times as much power is made with wind turbines today than a decade ago. In Europe, wind provides electricity for around 40 million people; in the US, about two million get their power this way. Some people think wind could one day provide much of the world's energy, but currently just 1 percent of electricity is made this way.

Wind dangers

Some people think wind turbines should be banned because their spinning blades can kill birds, but very few studies have been done. German conservationists have estimated that 20 times as many birds and bats are killed each year by traffic and high-voltage power lines than by wind turbines. Ornithologists (people who study birds) believe that wind farms should be situated away from important bird habitats and migration routes.

Micro power

Small wind turbines can make enough electricity for a single building. This turbine (above) is on the roof of an environmental center in the UK. It makes enough power for lights, computers, and a small workshop. By saving electricity, the turbine will pay back the cost of installing it in about 12 years.

Wind in the sails

Wind power is nothing new. Historians think windmills were invented in Persia (now Iran) about 1,400 years ago. It then took another 500 years for the idea to spread to Europe. In the past, windmills were primarily used for grinding grain into flour. These windmills (above) stand on the windy plateau of La Mancha in central Spain.

Windbreaks

Wind power can sometimes be a nuisance, particularly for farmers. In China's Gobi Desert (right), fierce winds blow sand into towering dunes that can suddenly wipe out fields and homes. In an attempt to stop this, farmers grow windbreaks of tall trees, both to hold back the sand and to stop the gales from devastating their crops.

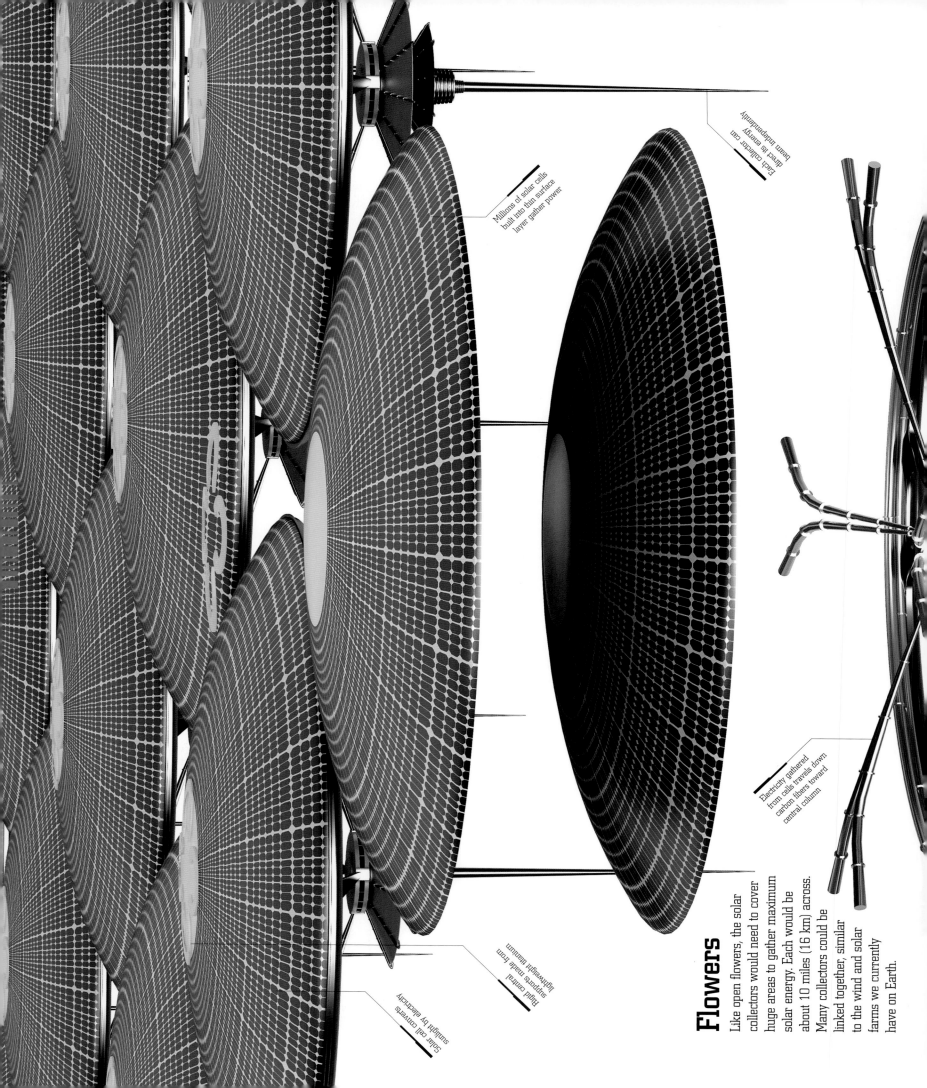

Each collector can
direct its energy
beam independently

Millions of solar cells
built into thin surface
layer gather power

Electricity gathered
from cells travels down
carbon fibers toward
central column

Rigid central
supports made from
lightweight titanium

Solar cell converts
sunlight by electricity

Flowers

Like open flowers, the solar
collectors would need to cover
huge areas to gather maximum
solar energy. Each would be
about 10 miles (16 km) across.
Many collectors could be
linked together, similar
to the wind and solar
farms we currently
have on Earth.

FUTURE POWER

With Earth's fuel supplies running low, we may soon need to look to the sky for power. Most of our energy already comes from the Sun, one way or another, but we could harvest this power more efficiently by building solar-electric power plants in space. Once the electricity had been generated, giant masers (microwave lasers) would beam it down to central collectors on Earth, from where it would flow to our homes as normal.

Going up

To build space power plants, we'd need to transport equipment into orbit about 22,000 miles (36,000 km) above Earth's surface. Scientists have already suggested a possible solution: an elevator into space. The motorized lifting equipment would crawl up and down a strong cable, shuttling back and forth between Earth and space.

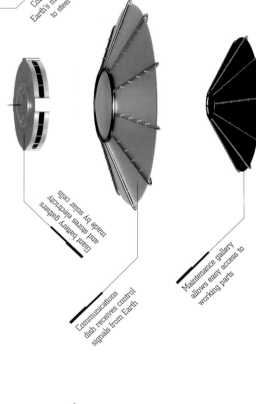

Coils react against Earth's magnetic field to steer collector

Giant battery gathers and stores electricity made by solar cells

Communications dish receives control signals from Earth

Maintenance gallery allows easy access to working parts

Inflatable outer structure allows station to be easily constructed and moved around

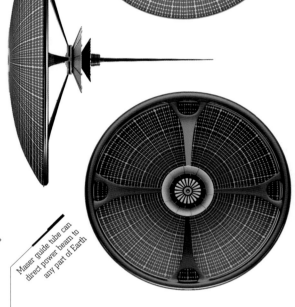

Capacitor stores electricity ready for conversion to microwaves

Maser (microwave laser) turns electricity into microwaves

Maser guide tube can direct power beam to any part of Earth

The race is on. Can you wash 36 plates, 12 cups and saucers, 12 glasses, and 60 pieces of cutlery in just 29 minutes? This dishwasher can. It works intelligently, using light-beams to measure how many dishes are inside. Then it saves energy by using only as much water and detergent as it needs.

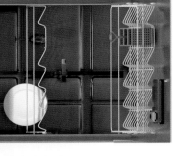

Stainless

Inside, a dishwasher is made of stainless steel: an alloy in which steel is combined with chromium to make it rustproof and stain-resistant. It can withstand years of hot water and powerful detergents.

FAST FACTS

Dimensions	32 in x 24 in x 22 in (81 cm x 60 cm x 55 cm)
Capacity	12 place settings
Water consumption	3 gallons (12 liters)
Annual water consumption	Approx. 63 gallons (240 liters)
Quick wash	29 minutes

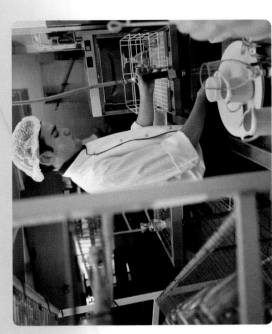

Industrial strength

Some hotels and restaurants still employ people to wash dishes by hand, but most use industrial dishwashers. Many are like bigger versions of home machines, but the biggest models use conveyor belts to wash up to 5,000 plates per hour!

LOOK INSIDE

Top case

Weight

Holding brackets secure tub inside machine

Insulation stops heat from escaping and makes machine more efficient

Back panel and heat exchanger

Side plate

Hose

Tub: rustproof, water-tight, stainless steel inner case

Sump removes water from tub

Exhaust duct helps dry dishes by removing hot, moist air after wash

Float mechanism controls amount of water in tub

High-temperature bottom rack for dishes

Drain hose

Filter catches food scraps and other debris

Water softener helps prevent limescale buildup

Seals

Base plate and drain

Water cycle

The heart of a dishwasher is a water-tight box called the tub. The pump at its base keeps the hot water circulating. It sucks water up from the bottom of the tub and squirts it out through spinning spray arms onto the dirty dishes.

Chemical helper

The detergent you use is just as important as the mechanical parts of your dishwasher. Its soapy chemicals cling to food remains and help to break them into small pieces. During the rinse cycle, the detergent and scraps of food stick to the water and get flushed away, leaving the plates clean.

Cutlery basket

Control module case

Electronic circuit controls wash programs

Digital temperature indicator

40

Handle and control panel

Program control buttons

Connector plug links to circuit

On/off button

Low-temperature top rack for glassware

Rollers allow racks to slide in and out

Shelf brackets work with rollers

Spray arm micro filter

Upper rotating spray arm squirts water jets onto top rack

Detergent box seal

Detergent dispenser box opens automatically when machine starts

Lower spray arm squirts water onto bottom rack

Electric pump motor

Inner door

Outer door

Pump housing

Seals

Motorized pump squirts water around inner tub

Rubber gasket seals door and stops water from escaping

Insulating plate

KEEP IT CLEAN

The average person will eat 82,125 meals in their lifetime—which means an awful lot of dirty dishes. If you spend just 20 minutes a day doing dishes, that's a year of your life spent slaving over the kitchen sink. It's hardly surprising that many of us choose to use dishwashers. They use hotter water and stronger detergents, so they kill more germs than washing by hand—and they will dry the dishes, too. Used properly, dishwashers can also be better for the environment.

Energy saver

You might think a dishwasher wastes water and electricity, but it uses up to four times less water than hand washing and can save energy, too.

Hot stuff

Modern dishwashers work at temperatures of 140–150°F (60–65°C), about 35°F (20°C) hotter than hand washing. These machines remove almost 400 times more bacteria from dirty plates than hand washing.

Early dishwashers

The dishwasher was invented in 1886 by Josephine Cochrane (1839–1913), an American socialite. She was fed up with her servants chipping the china when they washed it by hand. In her machine, dishes were piled into baskets and squirted with water jets to clean it. This Thor machine from 1947 (left) could also wash clothes.

Dirty dishes

This photograph (below) was taken with an electron microscope. It shows the bacteria lurking on a kitchen scrubbing pad magnified about 10,000 times. After just one day's use, a typical sponge contains more than a billion bacteria!

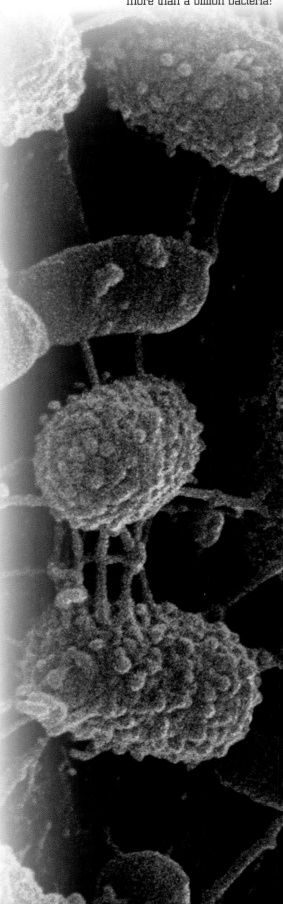

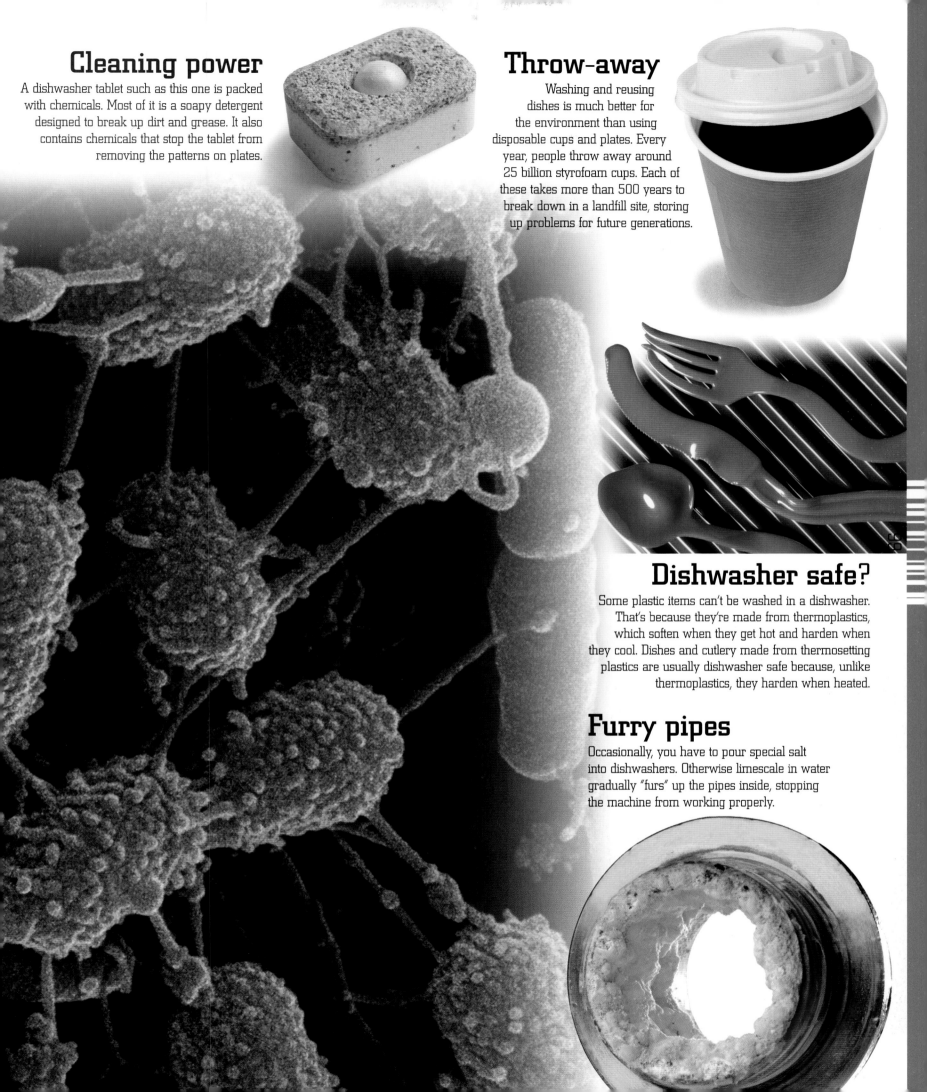

Cleaning power

A dishwasher tablet such as this one is packed with chemicals. Most of it is a soapy detergent designed to break up dirt and grease. It also contains chemicals that stop the tablet from removing the patterns on plates.

Throw-away

Washing and reusing dishes is much better for the environment than using disposable cups and plates. Every year, people throw away around 25 billion styrofoam cups. Each of these takes more than 500 years to break down in a landfill site, storing up problems for future generations.

Dishwasher safe?

Some plastic items can't be washed in a dishwasher. That's because they're made from thermoplastics, which soften when they get hot and harden when they cool. Dishes and cutlery made from thermosetting plastics are usually dishwasher safe because, unlike thermoplastics, they harden when heated.

Furry pipes

Occasionally, you have to pour special salt into dishwashers. Otherwise limescale in water gradually "furs" up the pipes inside, stopping the machine from working properly.

WASHING MACHINE

In many parts of the world, fresh water is so scarce that some people believe wars will be fought over it in future. Yet many of us still use up to 105 gallons (400 liters) worth each day. With many water-saving features, this intelligent washing machine could help to reduce this amount. During a rinse, it uses invisible infrared beams to measure how much soap is left inside, and uses no more water to flush the soap away than absolutely necessary.

In a spin

Early machines left clothes sopping wet—modern ones spin at incredibly high speeds to remove most of the water. This machine has a top speed of 1,400 rpm (revolutions per minute), which is equivalent to about 80 mph (130 kph)!

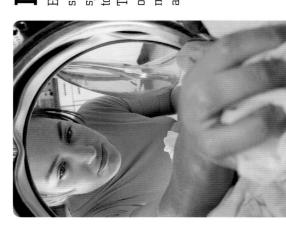

FAST FACTS

Dimensions	33 in x 23 in x 23 in (84 cm x 60 cm x 59 cm)
Load capacity	15 lb (7 kg)
Final spin speed	1,400 rpm
Water consumption	13 gallons (49 liters)
Number of programs	15

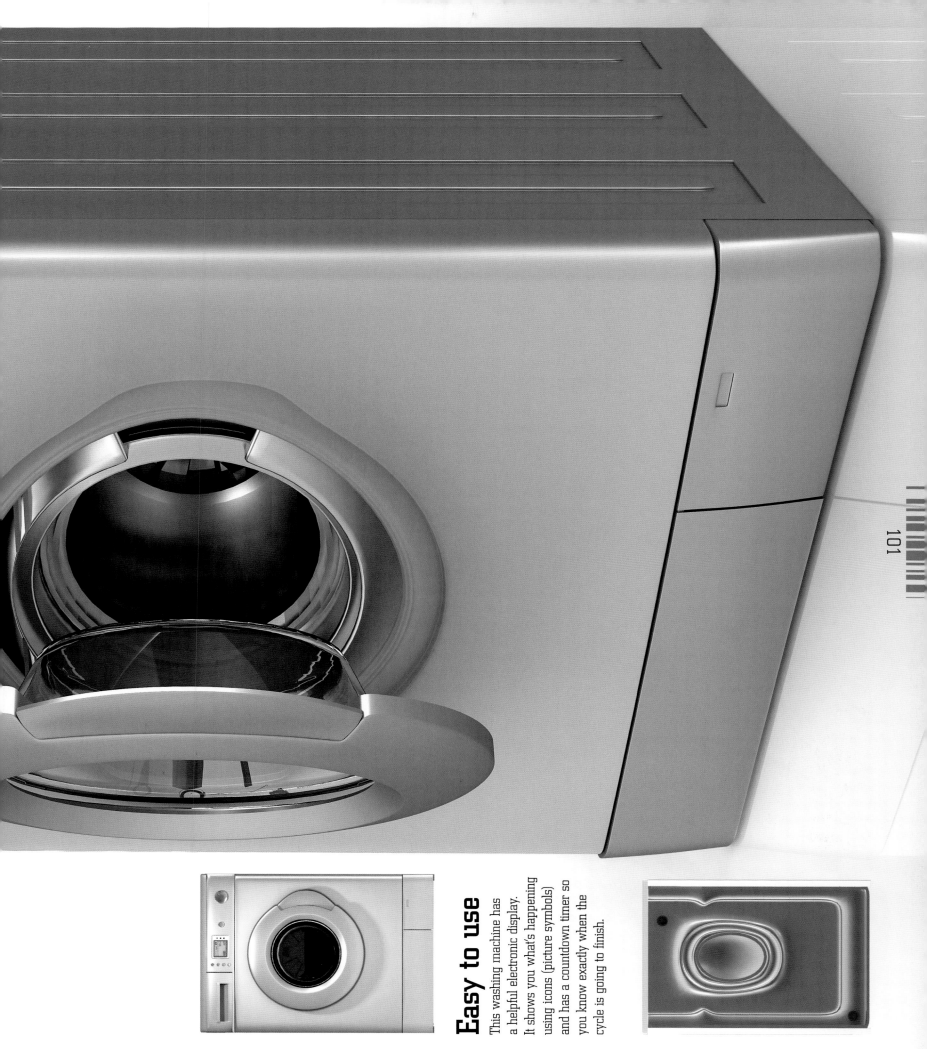

Easy to use

This washing machine has a helpful electronic display. It shows you what's happening using icons (picture symbols) and has a countdown timer so you know exactly when the cycle is going to finish.

101

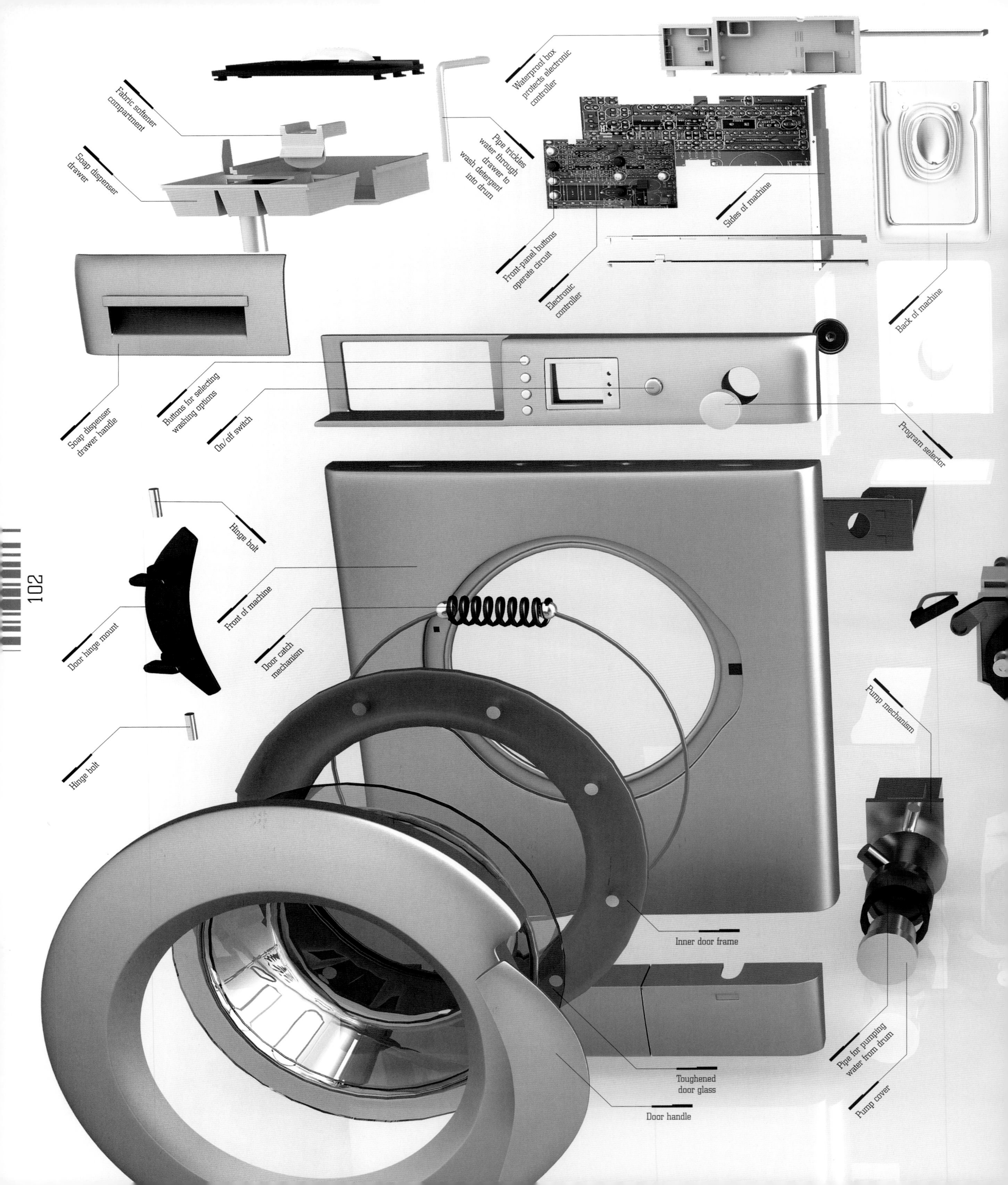

Fabric softener compartment

Soap dispenser drawer

Waterproof box protects electronic controller

Pipe trickles water through drawer to wash detergent into drum

Sides of machine

Front-panel buttons operate circuit

Electronic controller

Back of machine

Soap dispenser drawer handle

Buttons for selecting washing options

On/off switch

Program selector

Hinge bolt

Door hinge mount

Front of machine

Door catch mechanism

Hinge bolt

Pump mechanism

Inner door frame

Toughened door glass

Door handle

Pipe for pumping water from drum

Pump cover

LOOKINSIDE

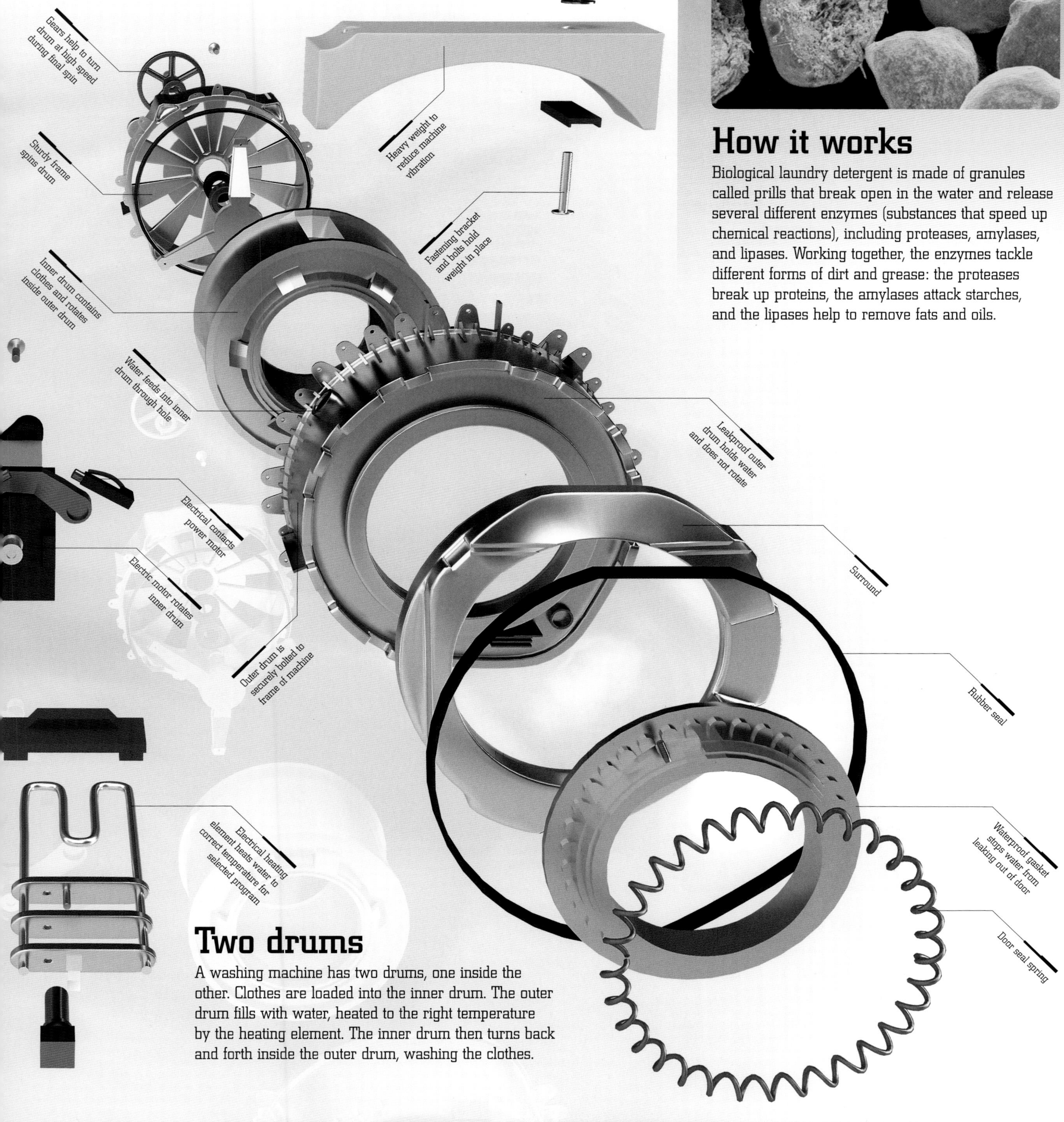

Gears help to turn drum at high speed during final spin

Sturdy frame spins drum

Inner drum contains clothes and rotates inside outer drum

Water feeds into inner drum through hole

Electrical contacts power motor

Electric motor rotates inner drum

Heavy weight to reduce machine vibration

Fastening bracket and bolts hold weight in place

Outer drum is securely bolted to frame of machine

Electrical heating element heats water to correct temperature for selected program

Leakproof outer drum holds water and does not rotate

Surround

Rubber seal

Waterproof gasket stops water from leaking out of door

Door seal spring

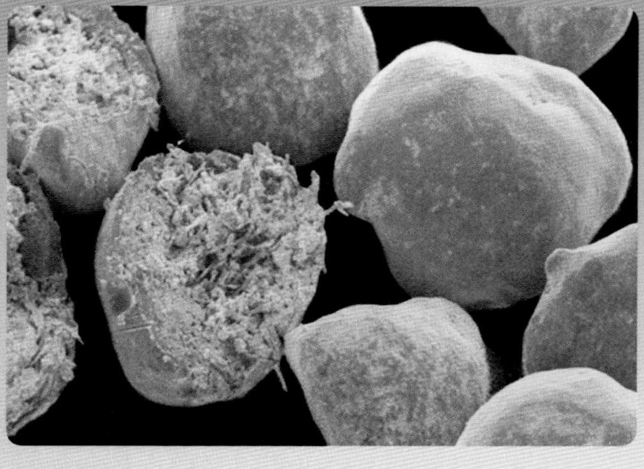

How it works

Biological laundry detergent is made of granules called prills that break open in the water and release several different enzymes (substances that speed up chemical reactions), including proteases, amylases, and lipases. Working together, the enzymes tackle different forms of dirt and grease: the proteases break up proteins, the amylases attack starches, and the lipases help to remove fats and oils.

Two drums

A washing machine has two drums, one inside the other. Clothes are loaded into the inner drum. The outer drum fills with water, heated to the right temperature by the heating element. The inner drum then turns back and forth inside the outer drum, washing the clothes.

A CLEANWORLD

Washing clothes can be a real chore—it's a problem that inventors have been trying to solve for more than 200 years. The first breakthrough, in 1797, was the invention of the scrubbing board: a ribbed piece of wood on which clothes were laid flat and brushed clean with soapy water. Technology has come a long way since then. The latest washing machines are microchip-controlled and eco-friendly: they wash at lower temperatures, but get your clothes cleaner and drier than ever.

Antique machine

By the 1920s, electric washing machines like the one pictured above had become popular. You placed your clothes in a metal drum, which swirled them through soapy water using a spinning paddle. Then you squeezed the clothes dry by feeding them through the "mangle" rollers on top.

Detergents

Powerful detergents get clothes clean—but they contain a chemical cocktail that harms the environment when they are flushed down the drain. Phosphates in detergents (which soften water) work like fertilizers when they reach our rivers and seas, causing huge growths of algae (water plants) that can suffocate fish. Perfumes in detergents and optical brighteners (which make our clothes gleam in sunlight) can also be toxic to fish and sea creatures. Some chemical companies now make eco-friendly detergents that do not contain these harmful ingredients.

Washing without...

We take clean water and electricity for granted—but billions of people across the world still have neither. In India, people wash their clothes in the Yamuna River (below), near the Taj Mahal, where pollution levels are 3,000 times higher than those considered safe.

Testing, testing

Water conducts electricity, so electric washing machines have to be carefully tested to make sure none of the electrics get wet. Each finished machine is sprayed with water from the outside to make sure it is leak-proof.

Toploader

Washing machines vary around the world. In Europe, people prefer front-loading machines that tumble clothes inside a rotating drum. In the United States and Asia, toploaders like this (above) are more common. Clothes are loaded from above, the drum stays still, and a big paddle wheel swishes the clothes around.

Laundromat

People who live in cities can choose to take their clothes to a laundromat. They can use the coin-operated machines themselves, or an attendant can wash their clothes for them. Laundromats are cheaper for occasional washing, but work out to be more expensive in the long term.

Waste not...

Most washing machines are sent to landfills when they wear out, but they can easily be recycled. Half a typical machine is made of valuable steel, and the rest contains useful materials such as aluminum, copper, and a mixture of plastics.

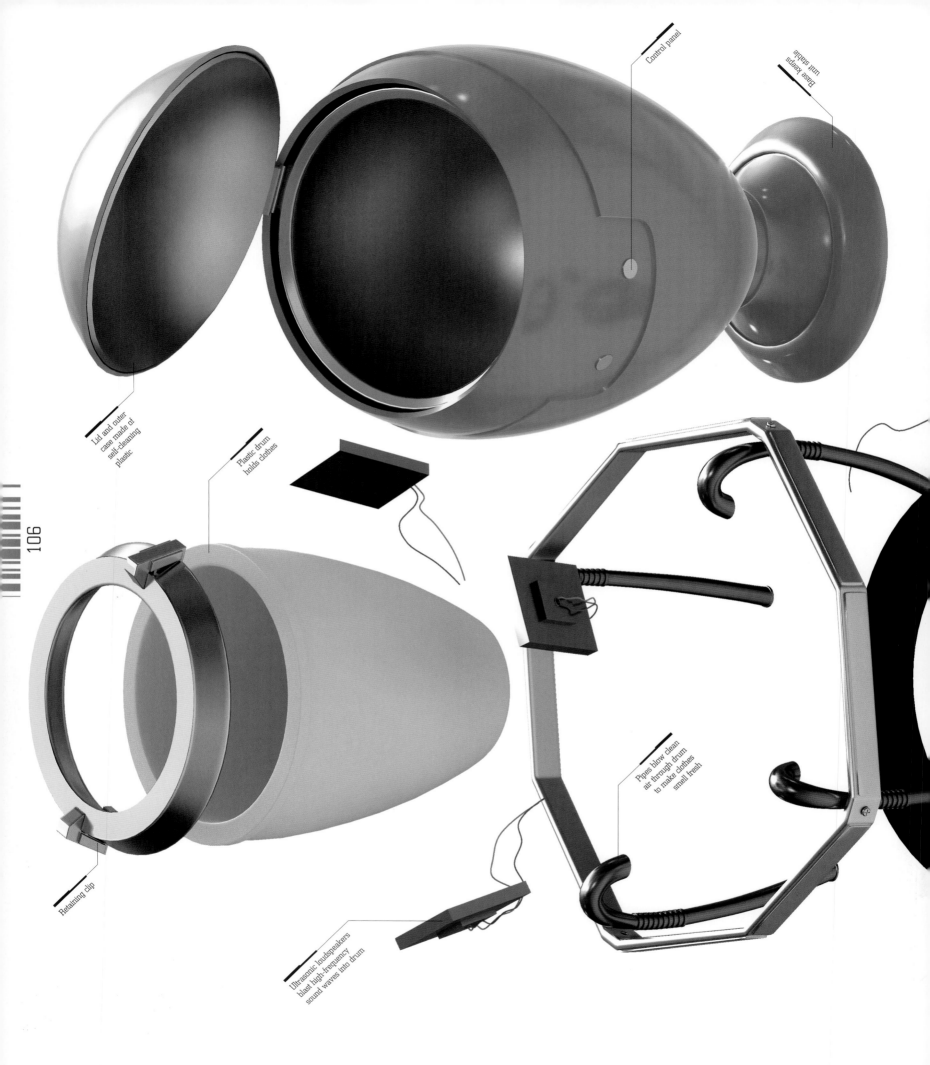

Control panel

Base keeps
unit stable

Lid and outer
case made of
self-cleaning
plastic

Plastic drum
holds clothes

106

Retaining clip

Pipes blow clean
air through drum
to make clothes
smell fresh

Ultrasonic loudspeakers
blast high-frequency
sound waves into drum

FUTURE SONIC WASHER

Everyone likes clean clothes, but washing and drying is a chore. In the future, washing machines could work a different way, using ultrasound and static electricity instead of soap and water. It'll take under a minute to turn dirty jeans back into clean ones—and because your clothes won't get wet, you'll be able to wear them right away.

Sound asleep

Ultrasound (high-frequency sound) is best known as a way of monitoring unborn babies. High-frequency sound is beamed into the mother's womb from a probe on her abdomen. A computer uses the sound waves reflected back to build up 3-D images like this.

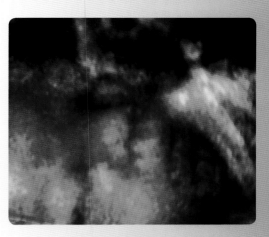

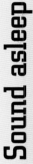

Electrostatic attractors use static electricity to pull loose dirt away

Ultraviolet light beams upward into clothes to kill germs

Ring holds inner drum in place

Dry clean

This future washer fires ultrasound waves into your clothes to shake the dirt loose, while electrostatic attractors outside the drum pull the loose dirt away. Gears spin the attractors around the drum to dislodge the dirt, which then collects in a trap at the bottom of the machine.

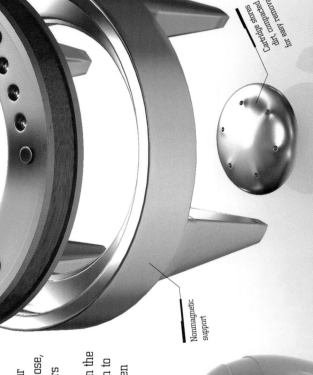

Filter collects dirt

Motorized carriage spins attractors around drum to release dirt

Nonmagnetic support

Cartridge stores compacted dirt, removed for easy removal

MICRO**WAVE**

A box that can cook food with a quick blast of energy waves seems like something out of science fiction—but you've probably got one standing in a corner of your kitchen right now. Every time you hear a microwave oven buzzing, it's pumping powerful radio waves into your dinner at the speed of light. A microwave can cook food around six times faster than a conventional oven.

Accidental invention

American engineer Percy Spencer (1894–1970) was experimenting with a radar (navigation) set one day. When stray waves of energy from his radar melted the candy bar in his pocket, Spencer realized he had found a new way of heating food.

Fast or slow

Microwaves cook liquid foods, such as soups, much faster than solid foods. That's because the entire liquid absorbs microwaves very quickly. But when you cook a large piece of solid food, the microwaves heat only the outer edge. The center of the food cooks more slowly as the heat flows inward. This takes much longer, so it is important to leave microwaved foods to stand after you take them out of the oven.

FAST FACTS

Typical dimensions	10.2 in x 19.5 in x 12.4 in (26 cm x 49.5 cm x 31.5 cm)
Power	800 watts
Materials	Wipe-clean, stainless-steel interior
Number of programs	3 cooking and 3 reheating

How it works

Microwaves are generated by a device called a magnetron and channeled into the cooking cavity. Inside the cavity, they bounce repeatedly off the metal walls and enter the food. When food absorbs microwaves, the water molecules it contains vibrate, and this causes a rise in temperature that cooks the food.

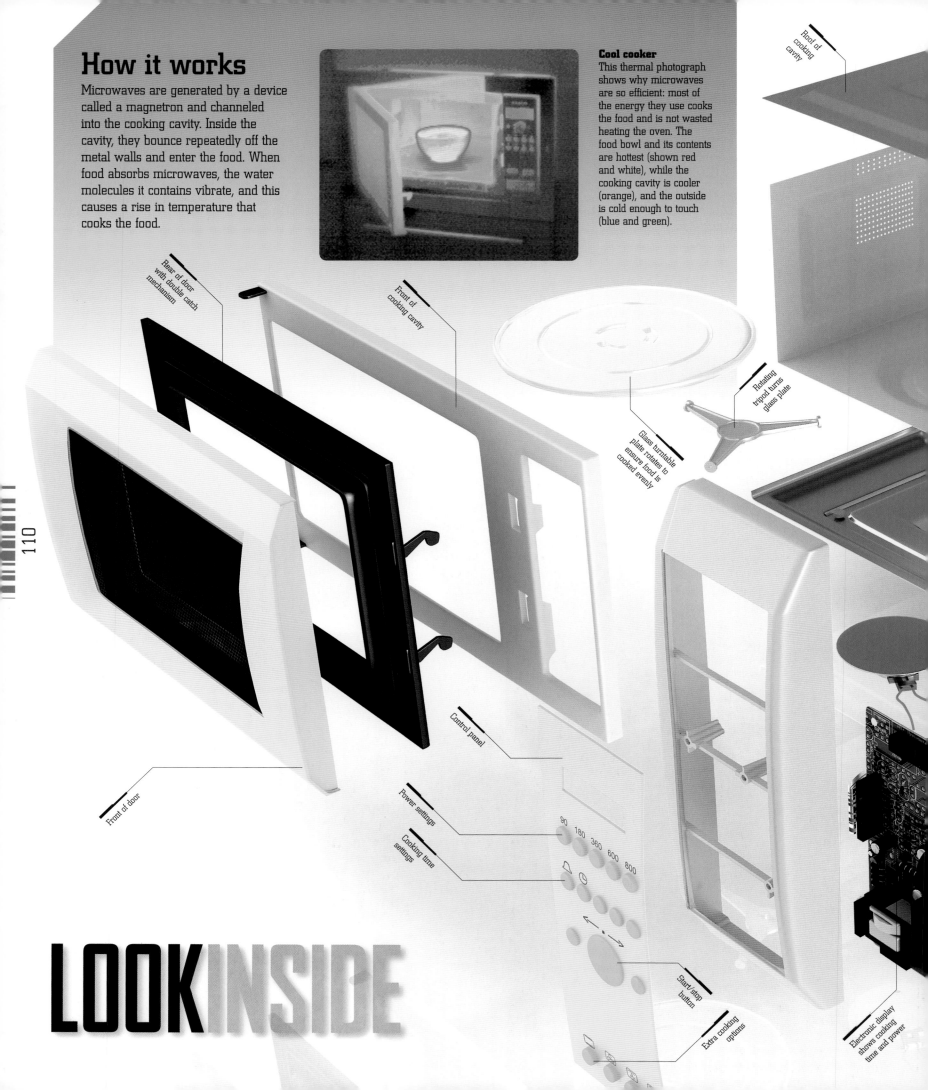

Cool cooker
This thermal photograph shows why microwaves are so efficient: most of the energy they use cooks the food and is not wasted heating the oven. The food bowl and its contents are hottest (shown red and white), while the cooking cavity is cooler (orange), and the outside is cold enough to touch (blue and green).

Roof of cooking cavity

Rear of door with double catch mechanism

Front of cooking cavity

Rotating tripod turns glass plate

Glass turntable plate rotates to ensure food is cooked evenly

Front of door

Control panel

Power settings

Cooking time settings

90 180 360 600 800

Start/stop button

Extra cooking options

Electronic display shows cooking time and power

LOOK**INSIDE**

Wipe-clean metal
outer case

Radiation-proof back
panel has ventilation
holes to let steam
escape

Cooking cavity
has perforations to
let steam (but not
microwaves) escape

Power
connector
and fuse

Transformer
produces high voltage
to power magnetron

Bottom cover

Magnetron
(microwave
generator)

111

Magnetron
cooling fins

Magnetron
casing

High-voltage
capacitor works
with transformer
to power
magnetron

Electric motor
powers cooling fan

Electric turntable
drive motor

Cooling fan

Fan housing

Magnetron
control circuit

Lamp holder and
power supply

Mounting bracket

Lamp lights up
cooking cavity

Door catch has
electronic sensors
to switch off oven if
door is opened

Electronic circuit
controls oven

Safe inside

Microwaves can be harmful to people, so a microwave
oven has to be properly sealed to stop them from
escaping. Inside the easy-to-clean case, there is a metal
box called the cooking cavity. Holes in the cavity allow
steam to escape, but microwaves cannot get through
them. The door also has a gauze metal lining to keep
microwaves inside.

ENERGY WAVES

We all think we know what the world looks like—it's right in front of us—but there's a whole other world that we can't see. All we can see is the light reflected off objects, but light is only one kind of electromagnetic energy buzzing around us. If our eyes could detect other kinds of energy, too, we might see radio and TV programs whizzing past our heads, phone calls soaring through the sky, and microwaves zapping around inside our ovens. We can't see these forms of energy, but we know they're there—and we can use them in all kinds of interesting ways.

Fast phones

The dishes on telephone towers like this (left) send and receive phone calls to and from similar towers in other cities using microwave beams. The towers have to be within each other's line of sight, which is why they're so tall.

Missile spotting

These strange-looking "golf balls" (right) were built in the 1960s to house missile detectors at Fylingdales in Yorkshire, England. Working with similar bases in Greenland and Alaska, the detectors used microwave beams to scan the sky. The golf balls were 84 ft (26 m) across and could spot a missile from almost 3,000 miles (5,000 km) away. They were dismantled in the early 1990s.

Big Bang

This picture of the sky was taken by a satellite called COBE (Cosmic Background Explorer), which can "see" microwaves. Different colors show areas of different temperatures (pink is hottest and blue coldest). Scientists have used this temperature map to help them understand how the universe was formed about 14 billion years ago in a giant explosion called the Big Bang.

Electromagnetic spectrum

Light, X-rays, radio waves, and microwaves are all kinds of electromagnetic energy. All travel at the speed of light as undulating waves of electricity and magnetism, but the waves they contain are of different lengths and carry different amounts of energy. Gamma rays are shortest and radio waves longest.

Gamma rays
Short, high-energy waves made by radioactivity

X-rays
Penetrating waves that are useful in medicine

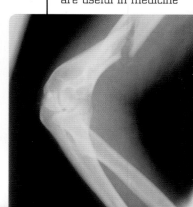

Microwave science

Scientists can study many things with microwaves. This satellite image shows how much water vapor (gas) there is in Earth's atmosphere. Areas with most water vapor are dark blue; areas with less are light blue. This kind of research helps scientists to understand Earth's water cycle.

Tornado chasing

Trucks like this (below) help weather forecasters predict when tornadoes will strike. The Doppler radar dish on the back fires a microwave beam into a storm. The reflected beam can be used to calculate the storm's speed and direction.

Curing cancer

Cancer is caused when runaway cells grow in people's bodies to make tumors. One way to kill tumors is to blast them with high-energy radiation, such as X-rays and microwaves.

Visible light

Ultraviolet rays
Present in sunlight

Infrared rays
Given off by hot objects

Microwaves
Short radio waves that can be used to cook food

Radio waves
Long waves that carry TV and radio signals

FAST FACTS

Capacity	Makes up to 6 cups
Time to make coffee	5–8 minutes
Materials	Stainless steel and plastic
Weight	10 lb (4.5 kg)
Cost	Approx. $80

Espresso yourself

In a coffee bar, espresso (a shot of hot, concentrated coffee) is the starting point for all coffee drinks. You can serve it as it is, add it to steamed milk (a latte), mix it with hot water (an Americano), or serve it with foamed milk and chocolate (a cappuccino).

Instant coffee may be convenient, but when it comes to flavor, there is no substitute for a velvety-rich espresso. An espresso machine extracts the maximum flavor by blasting high-pressure hot water through the coffee grains. A coffee maker like this uses water at 15 times the pressure of the air around us—roughly the same pressure a diver feels at 450 ft (150 m) under the sea!

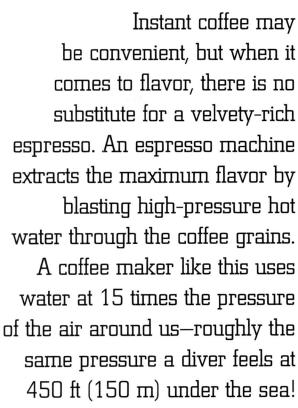

ESPRESSO MACHINE

Home coffee shop

Coffee makers such as this one have two separate halves for making different drinks. On one side, strong espresso drips into the pitcher below, while on the other side, a hotplate heats milk that can be frothed up for a cappuccino or a latte.

LOOKINSIDE

Two in one

The most important part of an espresso maker is the water heater and pressurizer unit on the left. Hot milk is prepared separately with the frother attachment on the right.

How it works

There are many different types of coffee maker. Most of them extract the flavor from ground coffee (coffee beans crushed into a fine powder) by soaking it in near-boiling water for several minutes. An espresso machine makes coffee faster and stronger than other methods by forcing hot, high-pressure water through the ground coffee.

1 Water tank
2 Electric element heats water
3 Pressurizer increases water pressure
4 Hot, high-pressure water forced through coffee

Perfect espresso

The water is heated to just below boiling point (about 195°F or 90°C), and is then pressurized and forced through the coffee.

Plastic top

Pressure cap

Frother on/off button

Electronic circuit board

Milk frother motor and blade

Heating element heats water in tank

Strength selector

Pressurizer unit

Washable metal filter

Filter holder

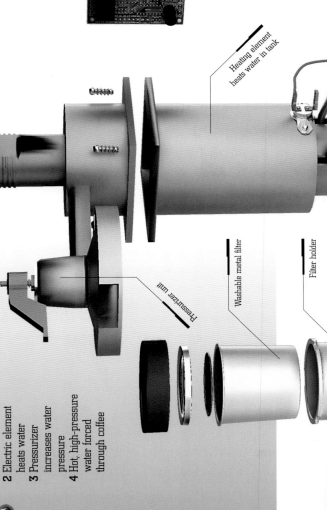

Milk frother cover

Milk frother hot plate cover

Milk frother hot plate

Milk frother hot plate on/off switch and indicator light

Air vents to cool machine

Milk frother hot plate

Water tank

Underside of casing

Glass coffee pitcher

Drip tray metal plate

Drip tray

Base plate

Plastic trim

Coffee maker on/off switch and indicator light

DRINK UP

People drink two billion cups of coffee every single day, making it the world's favorite hot drink. Coffee has been popular for more than a thousand years. According to legend, it was discovered around 850 CE when an Ethiopian goatherd named Kaldi noticed that his animals danced around after nibbling coffee beans. When Kaldi tried one himself, he felt much more alert. Coffee beans were soon being turned into stimulating drinks that gradually spread from Africa and the Middle East to Europe and America.

Cash crop

Coffee is one of the world's top 10 most important agricultural crops: the seven million tons of coffee produced each year is enough to fill a line of trucks 800 miles (1,300 km) long. Around 50 countries (including Brazil, Colombia, and Indonesia) grow coffee that they export to the rest of the world.

Making coffee

Coffee is made from two main plant species named *Coffea arabica* and *Coffea canephora* (also called *Coffea robusta*). Arabica beans come mostly from Latin America, the Caribbean, and Indonesia, and make a stronger and more aromatic coffee than robusta beans, which come from Africa.

In an instant

Instant coffee powder (seen here under an electron microscope) is made by taking a very strong liquid coffee and removing its water. That can be done either by spray drying (using hot air) or freeze drying (cooling quickly). The grains formed this way are light and hollow and can be turned back into coffee by adding hot water.

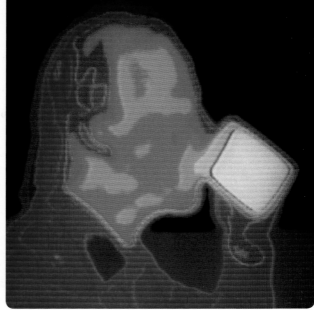

Feel the heat

This thermal photograph of a coffee drinker shows the hottest areas in white and red, and the cooler ones in blue and green. Hot drinks provide warmth to our bodies and can sometimes help to aid digestion.

Old school

Bedouins (Arab nomads) make coffee the traditional way. They roast the beans over an open fire to concentrate their flavor. The roasted beans are cooled, ground, and mixed with spices to make a delicious brew called *qahwah* or *gahwa*.

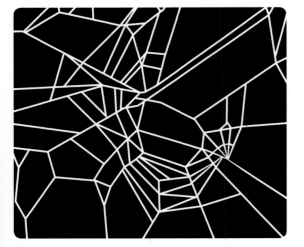

Hyperactive

Caffeine (the stimulating chemical in coffee) makes you more alert and active, but too much can make you restless and erratic. Scientists tested this by giving coffee to a spider. It became hyperactive and could build only this very chaotic web.

Coffee shopping

Coffee shops look similar the world over, but not all use espresso machines. In Turkey, coffee is more likely to be made by boiling ground coffee in a small metal pot. Filter coffee is popular in Vietnam. In Europe, many coffee shops serve cafetières (French presses), which use a metal gauze and plunger to remove coffee grounds.

Servants or slaves?

Before electric appliances were popular, wealthy people relied on servants, who were often little more than slaves. When appliances were first introduced, it was the servants who used them. Now most people have dispensed with servants and use appliances to do the chores themselves.

Women's liberation

The burden of housework used to fall on women, so advertisers sold appliances by making women feel guilty that their homes were not clean enough. As appliances became more affordable, housework became more automated. It's partly due to electric appliances that many more women now have challenging careers outside the home.

Culture clash

In 1959, two world leaders had a famous debate about electric homes. American Vice President Richard Nixon (1913–1994) argued with Nikita Khrushchev (1894–1971), leader of the Soviet Union (nations led by Russia), about which country's appliances were best. Nixon said that capitalism (the American system) gave people better homes and lives, while Khrushchev insisted communism (the Russian system) was just as good.

ELECTRIC FRIENDS

The electric power that zaps and buzzes through our homes is a relatively modern invention. Electric washing machines, vacuum cleaners, toasters, and televisions have been popular for only a few decades. They didn't exist at all before US inventor Thomas Edison (1847–1931) opened the world's first power plants in the 1880s. More than a century later, household appliances are the friends we can't live without. We take electricity for granted and notice it only in a power cut—when it disappears.

Material world

People in developing countries are less likely to own household appliances. In India, 600 million people (half the population) are not connected to the electricity grid. Indian people who have electricity consume only about 7 percent as much as people in Western countries.

Has it helped?

People spend as much time on housework today as they did decades ago. The main reason is that we have higher standards now and appliances let us do more: we own and wash more clothes, get our homes cleaner, and cook more sophisticated meals. Although men help more, women still do the majority of household chores.

FACTOIDS

• The world will use 76 percent more electricity in 2020 than it did in 1997. Industrialized countries will use 40 percent more, but developing countries will use 164 percent more. • In industrialized countries, there are more than three times as many TV sets in use now than in 1980.

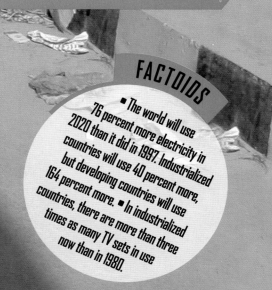

CORDLESS DRILL

Squeeze the trigger of a cordless drill and you've got a good deal of power at your fingertips. It takes real effort to force a hole through brick, wood, or steel—materials that simply don't like giving way. Fortunately, this drill has a hefty electric motor and battery pack to make light of the work. Another of its secrets is the spinning drill bit, tipped with supertough tungsten carbide. It is three times stronger than steel, lasts at least 10 times longer, and cuts like a diamond.

Drill science

Drilling won't work just by applying brute force. That force needs to be properly directed and concentrated in just the right areas. The drill bit is smaller than the chuck that grips it. As the chuck rotates, the surface of the drill bit moves a shorter distance, but with greater force. The bit is also smaller than the body of the drill. As you push from behind, it's like pressing on the flat head of a thumbtack: the force you apply to the drill case is concentrated into a smaller area on the drill bit, so that it pushes into the surface.

FAST FACTS

Speed	Up to 750 rpm
Drill depth	Can drill 1 in (25 mm) of wood or a half inch (10 mm) of steel
Power settings	5
Cost	Approx. $50

Power pack

Cordless drills are easier and safer to use than drills
with long electric cables that you could trip over. The
black power pack on the base of this drill contains
rechargeable batteries. They give around three hours
of power before they need to be charged again.

Torque torque

At the heart of a cordless drill is an electric motor, which gets its power from the battery pack underneath. The motor drives the drill bit through the transmission gears in the middle. The transmission reduces the speed provided by the motor so the drill bit turns more slowly but with extra torque (turning force), and this makes drilling easier. Five different torque settings give five levels of power for drilling different materials.

Phillips head screwdriver bit

Chuck holds drill and screwdriver bits tightly

Selection of drill bits

Twist grip for tightening chuck

Twist grip adjusts level of torque

Connection between battery pack and base of drill

Batteries inside battery pack

Outer case of battery pack

LOOKINSIDE

How it works

An electric motor is a machine that uses electricity and magnetism to produce movement. If you pass electricity through a wire that is sitting between the poles of a magnet, the wire will jump up or down very briefly. If you bend the wire into a loop and connect it to a circuit, you can make it spin continuously. In an electric motor, thousands of loops of wire are bunched tightly together. Large curved magnets turn the motor in a drill with a great deal of force.

Wire loop

Electric current flows through wire loop

Magnet

Wire loop spins inside magnetic field

Battery

Motor axle rotates at high speed

Coil inside motor

Curved magnets wrapped around coil

Electric motor

Vents in plastic case let air in to cool electric motor

Toughened polycarbonate (plastic) case designed to survive knocks

Selection of screwdriver bits

Transmission gears provide five different power settings for different materials

Back panel

Electric motor casing

Finger-operated trigger

Switch turns motor on when trigger is pressed

Electric cables take power from battery to motor

Copper contact feeds electric current to motor

Pecking order

Woodpeckers are nature's best-known drillers. Their tough, sharp beaks can hammer into trees at 100 beats per minute in search of ants and other insects to eat. The birds blink before each peck to prevent wood chips from damaging their eyes. Shock-absorbing structures in their heads prevent damage to their brains from the impact.

Early drills

People were drilling holes long before there was electricity. This prehistoric wooden drill has a bow string at the top. As you slide the bow back and forth, the string rotates the drill in the centre, grinding the bit into the material you want to drill.

Construction work

This pneumatic (air-powered) drill (right) uses compressed (squeezed) air to punch a metal bit into the road at high speed. A typical drill bangs up and down 25 times per second.

Bad tooth day

Dentists can save your teeth by drilling out the rotten parts and replacing them with a hard substitute such as porcelain. The dentist's drill shown in this false-colored photo (right) is coated with diamond fragments (shown in light orange) and spins at more than 100,000 times per minute.

DRILLING DOWN

People have been drilling holes since the Stone Age, but there's nothing prehistoric about modern drills. Big holes or small, there's a machine that can do the job for you. When railroad engineers decided to link the UK and France with the 31-mile (50-km) Channel Tunnel, it took 11 huge spinning drills seven years to finish the task. At the opposite end of the scale, scientists have recently found a way of drilling holes several times thinner than a human hair using tiny electrical sparks.

Drilling for oil

Oil rigs are very sophisticated drills. Instead of a short metal bit, they use a "string" of hollow metal pipes that can stretch 5 miles (8 km) or more underground. The latest drills, known as "snakes," can be steered along curving paths to extract much more oil than conventional drills.

Going underground

This tunnel boring machine (TBM), or "mole," drills railroads and roads. Its rotating cutter is about 30 ft (9 m) across and deposits rock onto rail trucks following behind. Machines like this can drill just over half a mile (1 km) of tunnel per month.

Laser drills

Laser drills like this one are used to make precision parts for aircraft. They can drill microscopic holes about the size of a human hair.

Screaming as they go, these people are
experiencing the terrifying delights of the Nemesis
Inferno corkscrew ride at Thorpe Park, UK.
In the final loop, riders experience forces
4.5 times stronger than gravity.

ENTERTAINMENT ANDLEISURE

A grand piano looks like a bizarre piece of wooden furniture—until someone lifts the lid and starts playing it. Even then, you'd never guess that the notes you're listening to are being made by an intricate machine, first designed in the 18th century, that has more than 12,000 separate parts. Other gadgets that entertain us have their secrets, too. Many people love the challenge of computer games, especially ones that are fast and realistic. What makes today's game consoles so much better than yesterday's are incredibly powerful microchips that work like supercomputers. Technology makes play time more interesting and fun—and you'll find out why if you look inside it.

PLAYST

FREEPLAY RADIO

Radio brings the world closer: spin slowly through the dial and you'll hear voices and songs that have crossed continents to reach your home. If you live in a country where electricity is hard to come by, radio may have been out of reach—until now. This Freeplay radio is powered by winding a handle, so it can work anywhere on Earth. One minute of winding gives an hour of play. It even has a built-in flashlight!

See through

Manufacturers usually go to great lengths to hide an appliance's working parts neatly inside it, but Freeplay has built this radio into a clear plastic case. You can see its powerful electricity generator spinning as you crank the handle. You can also see the electronic parts that turn incoming radio signals into sounds.

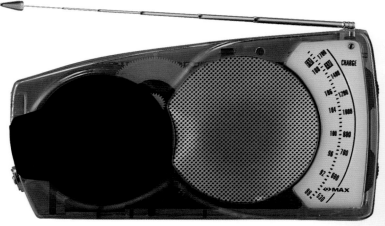

FAST FACTS

Power source	Windup generator, solar power, or outlet
Torch	Uses long-lasting LED (light-emitting diode)
Battery life	One full charge gives 25 hours of play. Battery lasts more than 5,000 hours
Cost	Approx. $50

FM 1700
108 AM CHARGE
1400
106 1200
104 1000
100 800
96 700
92 600
MAX
88 530

Clockwork universe

Before electric power became popular, many
machines were driven by clockwork. This was a way
of storing power in a machine by winding a handle.
The handle tightened a stiff metal spring which, as it
slowly unwound, turned gears that drove the machine.
This orrery (model of the planets) is clockwork-driven.

LOOKINSIDE

Wire connections
link generator to
circuit board

Body and
antenna holder

Main radio
circuit board

Volume control

Thumb controls

Radio tuning dial

Side plate with
holes for tuning
and volume dials

FM
AM

TUNING

VOLUME

DC-6V

Windup
generator magnets

Medium-wave
(AM/MW) antenna

DC input socket for
running radio from
external power

Windup
generator coils

Long-lasting
LED flashlight

Heavy flywheel helps
generator produce
power more smoothly

Rechargeable
batteries store windup
and solar power

Making power

Most radios are entirely electronic. This means that they have
no visibly moving parts. The Freeplay has lots of moving parts
in the mechanical generator that makes its power. When you crank
the handle at the front, you turn gear wheels inside that spin the
generator at speed. The generator works like a bicycle dynamo,
using magnets to make electricity. This electricity charges batteries,
which release their energy slowly as you listen to the radio.

How it works

Radio is a way of sending sounds, music, and other information between two places without using any wires. At a radio station, people's voices are captured using microphones and turned into electrical signals. These signals are encoded in radio waves and then beamed through the air, in all directions, using a powerful transmitter antenna. The radio set you have at home is a receiving device that captures the radio waves, decodes the signals they contain, and turns them back into sounds you can hear. A radio set looks complex, but the way it works can be broken down into a series of simple stages.

From signal to sound
Five of the electronic parts connected to a radio's circuit board are especially important. The antenna (1) captures incoming radio waves. The capacitor (2) tunes the radio by selecting a single frequency of radio wave. The diode (3) helps turn the radio waves back into sound. The transistor (4) boosts the sound so that it is powerful enough to drive a loudspeaker (5), which makes the sounds you can hear.

❶

❷

❸

❹

❺

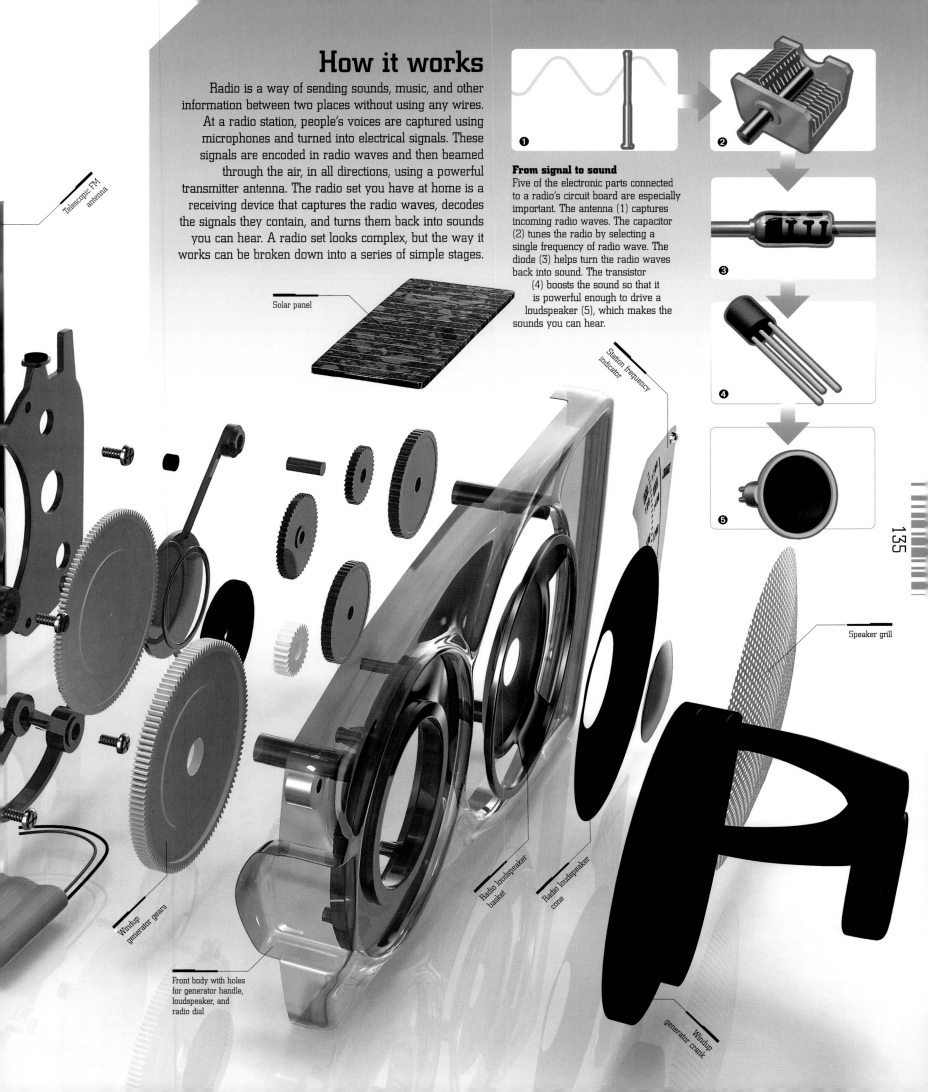

Telescopic FM antenna

Solar panel

Station frequency indicator

Speaker grill

Windup generator gears

Front body with holes for generator handle, loudspeaker, and radio dial

Radio loudspeaker basket

Radio loudspeaker cone

Windup generator crank

Solar television

TV pictures are beamed by radio waves, so you can pick them up anywhere. But you still need electricity to power the set. These villagers in Niger, West Africa, are watching a battery-powered TV run from solar panels.

Solar panels

Solar panels, such as this one (above) in a remote part of Bolivia, convert the Sun's energy directly into electricity. A panel this size makes about 100 watts—enough to power a light bulb. The electricity can be used immediately or stored in batteries for later.

PEOPLEPOWER

More than a century since the first power plants were built, a quarter of the world's people still have no electricity. Until recently, there were two problems in bringing power to developing countries—one was constructing the power plants themselves, which cost as much as $4 billion and take years to build. The other problem was transmitting power to remote places, which means building expensive overhead power lines or underground cables. Poor countries have often seen electricity as a luxury that must come after clean water and basic health care. That's now changing, thanks to technologies like solar power and rechargeable batteries, which allow people to make and store electricity whenever and wherever they need it.

Cell phone

Landlines (ordinary wired telephone lines) are uncommon in most developing countries. In Africa, fewer than one person in a hundred has a phone of this kind. Cell phones are much more common than landlines because they need no expensive wiring to a local exchange. Their batteries can be charged with small solar cells.

Solar water pump

More than 1.1 billion people (one-sixth of the world's population) still lack access to clean water. Solar-powered pumps such as this one in Namibia (below) could reduce that number. The solar panels drive an electric motor that sucks water up from under the ground. Some pumps also use the ultraviolet part of sunlight to disinfect the water they collect.

Solar cooking

People in some developing countries get up to 80 percent of their energy by burning wood. It's usually the job of women and children to spend several hours a day walking to collect the fuel. An alternative is a solar "stove" like this one (below). The huge dish-shaped mirror gathers the Sun's hot rays and reflects them onto the cooking pot in the middle.

Solar lanterns

Solar lights can help people work or study at night in places with no electricity. During daytime, solar panels capture sunlight and store its power in batteries that power the light at night.

Windup laptop

With no electricity and few telephones or books, many children in developing countries struggle to get an education. This new, low-cost laptop could help. It's powered by a windup handle and has a wireless (Wi-Fi) link to the internet.

KEF MUON SPEAKERS

Loudspeakers that sound fantastic usually come in ugly black boxes. These KEF Muons, which are among the world's most expensive speakers, are something else entirely. With curvy aluminum cases swimming in reflections, they look good enough to stand in an art gallery. Each unit contains nine separate speakers (seven in the front and two in the back) and can make as much noise as a jet airplane taking off. Launched in a limited edition, only 100 pairs of Muons will ever be produced.

CD ROM

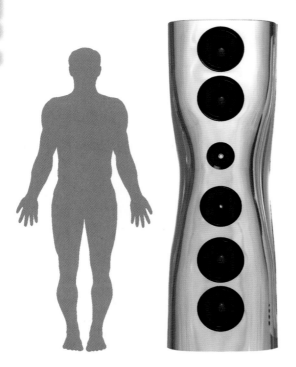

Sound sculptures

The prototype (test version) of the Muon speakers was sculpted by a computerized lathe (cutting machine) from an adult-sized block of solid aluminum. The final versions are made by a process called superforming, where giant sheets of aluminum are heated to high temperatures, bent using air pressure, and then trimmed to size.

Art of noise

The striking Muon speakers were developed by renowned British industrial designer Ross Lovegrove. Inspired by the twisting shapes he finds in nature, Lovegrove transforms humdrum products into works of art. His creations are exhibited in such places as New York's Museum of Modern Art.

FAST FACTS

Dimensions	79 in x 24 in x 16 in (200 cm x 60 cm x 38 cm)
Weight	250 lb (115 kg)
Material	Case made of quarter-inch-thick (6 mm) superformed aluminum
Cost	$140,000 per pair
Output	118 dB

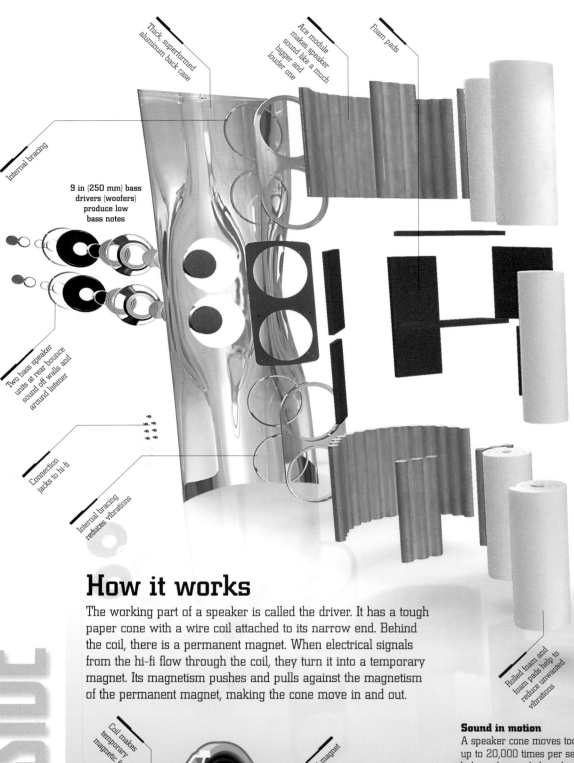

Thick, superformed aluminum back case

Ace module makes speaker sound like a much bigger and louder one

Foam pads

Internal bracing

9 in (250 mm) bass drivers (woofers) produce low bass notes

Two bass speaker units at rear bounce sound off walls and around listener

Connection jacks to hi-fi

Internal bracing reduces vibrations

Rolled foam and foam pads help to reduce unwanted vibrations

Thick, superformed aluminum front case

LOOK INSIDE

How it works

The working part of a speaker is called the driver. It has a tough paper cone with a wire coil attached to its narrow end. Behind the coil, there is a permanent magnet. When electrical signals from the hi-fi flow through the coil, they turn it into a temporary magnet. Its magnetism pushes and pulls against the magnetism of the permanent magnet, making the cone move in and out.

Coil makes temporary magnetic field

Permanent magnet

Cone is fixed at edges but central part can move

Moving cone produces sound

Wires carrying signals from hi-fi

Sound in motion

A speaker cone moves too fast to see—up to 20,000 times per second. If you balanced some light polystyrene balls on the cone, you would be able to see them jumping up and down as the cone moves in and out.

Energy converter

The driver's job is to turn electrical energy into sound energy using magnetism. As electrical signals feed into the driver, the cone pushes the air in front of it back and forth, pumping waves of sound toward our ears.

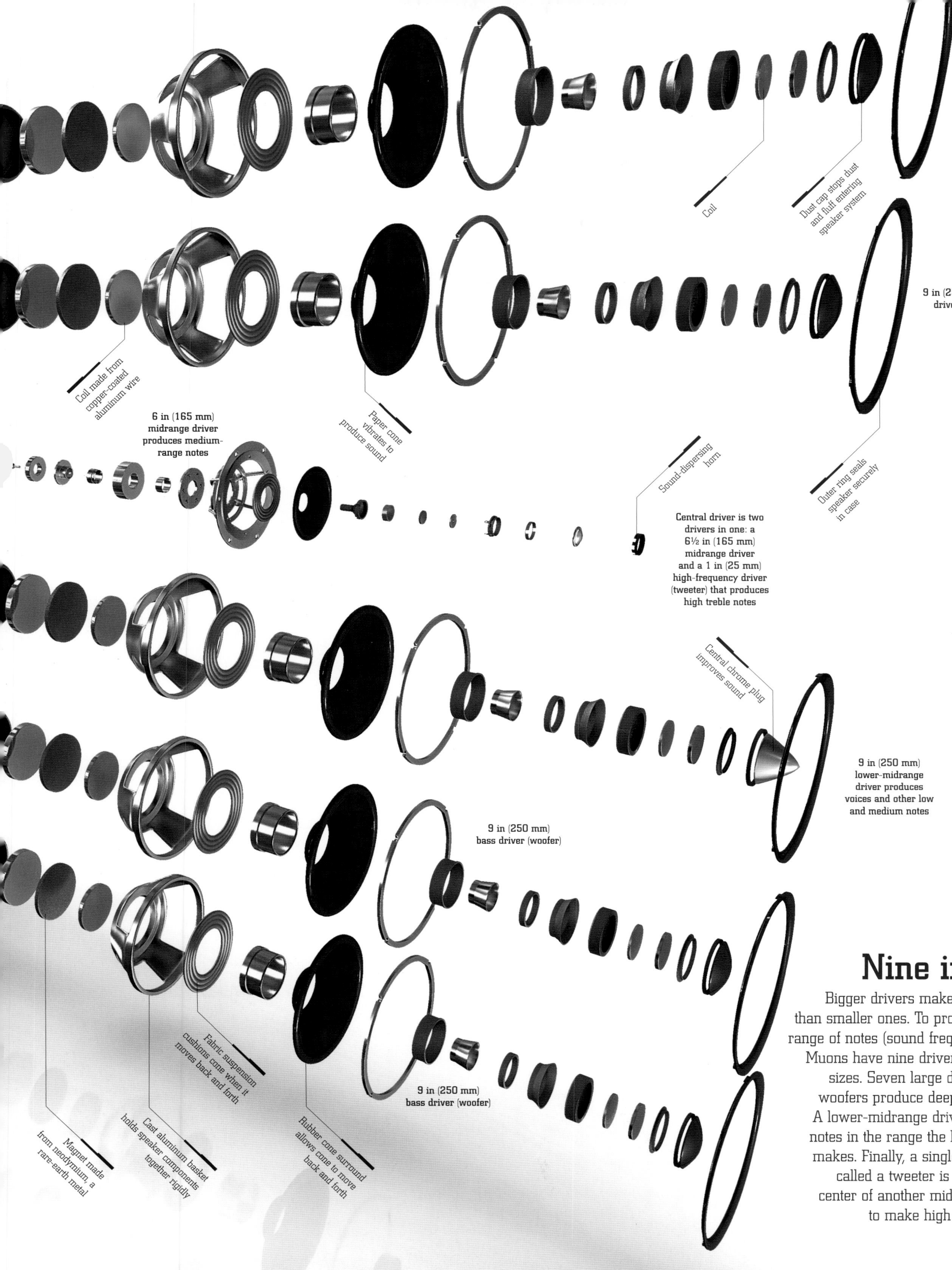

9 in (250 mm) bass driver (woofer)

Coil

Dust cap stops dust and fluff entering speaker system

9 in (250 mm) bass driver (woofer)

Coil made from copper-coated aluminum wire

6 in (165 mm) midrange driver produces medium-range notes

Paper cone vibrates to produce sound

Sound-dispersing horn

Central driver is two drivers in one: a 6½ in (165 mm) midrange driver and a 1 in (25 mm) high-frequency driver (tweeter) that produces high treble notes

Outer ring seals speaker securely in case

Central chrome plug improves sound

9 in (250 mm) lower-midrange driver produces voices and other low and medium notes

9 in (250 mm) bass driver (woofer)

Magnet made from neodymium a rare-earth metal

Cast aluminum basket holds speaker components together rigidly

Fabric suspension cushions cone when it moves back and forth

Rubber cone surround allows cone to move back and forth

9 in (250 mm) bass driver (woofer)

Nine in one

Bigger drivers make lower notes than smaller ones. To produce the full range of notes (sound frequencies), the Muons have nine drivers of varying sizes. Seven large drivers called woofers produce deep bass notes. A lower-midrange driver produces notes in the range the human voice makes. Finally, a single, tiny driver called a tweeter is built into the center of another midrange driver to make high treble notes.

SOUND WORLD

Birds chirping, friends laughing, sirens blaring, drums beating—our world is swimming with sounds that carry information. Animals interpret sounds to warn them of approaching dangers, but not all creatures hear things the same way. Snakes, for example, can hear through the muscles in their bellies, while crickets' "ears" are just below their knees! Human ears are sophisticated organs that allow us to hear sounds in stereo. They work like loudspeakers in reverse. Incoming sounds move our eardrums back and forth to make electrical signals, which our brains decode to give us the experience of hearing. Since the 19th century, we've developed sound equipment outside our bodies using science. With amazing loudspeakers and sound-recording machines, we can now make sounds and listen to them whenever and wherever we like.

Soundscape

Using a system with four or more loudspeakers, you can create a three-dimensional "sound landscape." Your brain is fooled into thinking you're outside in the real world, instead of sitting still in your living room. This effect, known as surround sound, is used to add realism and excitement to many adventure films.

Big noise

Rock bands have to make enough noise to fill stadiums packed with thousands of people. Their microphones and instruments feed sounds into electrical amplifiers, which boost the noise many times. These amplified signals then drive huge loudspeakers that recreate the original sounds many times louder.

Milestones

Phonograph cylinders

Although the great American inventor Thomas Edison (1847–1931) had hearing problems, he pioneered the idea of recording sounds so people could listen to things any time they wanted to. His mechanical phonograph, invented in 1877, recorded sounds onto a cylinder covered

Gramophone

Gramophones replaced the phonograph cylinder in the 1910s. They played music by running a needle through a spiral-shaped groove in a circular plastic disk. The sounds were made louder by feeding them into a huge, trumpet-shaped horn.

Sound of silence

These noise-canceling headphones (above) use a microphone and electronics to silence outside noises. The headphones play a reversed version of the noise into the pilot's ears, canceling out unwanted sounds almost entirely.

Recording studios

Musicians can make complex music tracks by recording different instruments separately and then "mixing" the recordings together. In the studio, engineers use computerized desks to alter the sounds when they are played back through speakers or headphones.

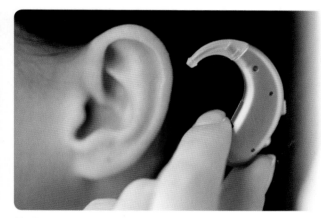

Micro-speakers

A hearing aid has a microphone on the outside that picks up the sounds a deaf person cannot normally hear. The sounds are amplified and passed to a tiny loudspeaker, which plays them back much louder inside the person's ear canal.

Record players
Compact record players first appeared in the 1950s. Like gramophones, they used a needle to play back sound from flat plastic records. Instead of horns, they used small electric loudspeakers to amplify the sound.

Walkman
Sony invented the Walkman music player in 1979. People could now take their music anywhere. The walkman played back sound stored on magnetic tape through headphones.

MP3 player
The first MP3 player was made in 1998. MP3 players can store hundreds or thousands of music tracks in compressed (electronically squeezed) computer files. The tracks can be listened to using speakers or tiny earbud headphones.

BREITLING**WATCH**

Time machine

The case of a Breitling is meticulously made. It's stamped from a single sheet of superstrong steel alloy or titanium by weights totaling 480 tons (435 metric tons). It is then bathed and cleaned nine times and polished 15 times. The case alone consists of 59 separate parts.

Tick tock, tick tock—most watches speak the same language. If Breitling watches could talk, you sense they'd have more to say. Their movement (inner mechanism) contains more than 140 high-precision pieces. Even the simplest parts, the hands, are diamond-polished and machined by computer to an accuracy of less than one-thirtieth of a hair's breadth. It takes 41 painstaking processes to give a watch like this its "voice."

Crystal clear

The "glass" on a Breitling watch is actually a scratch-resistant sapphire crystal. Microscopically fine powder is grown into stalactite-shaped crystals that are sliced like salami, then ground and polished into shape. The slices are then coated on both sides to cut out 99 percent of the glare from reflected light.

FAST FACTS

Materials	Steel case and bracelet
Diameter	1¾ in (44 mm)
Weight	4 oz (120 g)
Water resistant	1,000 ft (300 m)
Cost	$5,000–$45,000

TAKING TIME

Thanks to long-distance travel and communication technologies such as the telegraph, telephone, and internet, people have found themselves telling time in increasingly sophisticated ways. In ancient times, it was fine to measure hours vaguely with the creeping shadow of a sundial or a trickle of sand grains. In the modern world, we count seconds with quartz watches and nanoseconds using the superaccurate pulses of atomic clocks. Time moves no faster, but we're more aware of it passing than ever before.

Atomic clock

In an old-fashioned clock, the pendulum swings roughly once a second. In an atomic clock, atoms of the chemical element caesium "swing" back and forth more than 9 billion times each second. The best atomic clocks lose only one second in 20 million years!

Milestones of sound

Sundial
Thousands of years ago, people saw the heavens as one big clock and told time by watching the Sun, Moon, and stars. Ancient monuments such as Stonehenge may have been built as giant Sun clocks. This ornate sundial is typical of the "watches" sailors used to tell time in the 17th century.

Sand clock
Before accurate clocks appeared, hourglasses like this were used to measure short periods of time. Each glass drains sand in exactly 15 minutes, so the whole clock can keep time accurately for an hour. It was made in Italy from finely carved ebony and ivory.

Shipping time

To measure longitude (your east-west position) accurately, you need to know the time. This meant that navigating the seas was a risky business until Englishman John Harrison (1693–1776) developed the chronometer, a clock that could keep time on rough seas. Watches like the Breitling, which many pilots wear to help them navigate, are the modern-day equivalent.

Railroad time

Originally, every place in the world kept its own time. In England, for instance, Bristol was 10 minutes behind London. When long-distance railroads and telegraphs started linking cities in the 19th century, people had to agree on a shared time system and synchronize their watches.

Airport time

Thanks to jet airplanes, we can fly around the world so fast that we arrive before we started! This "time travel" is possible because everyone in the world tells time using an agreed system of "zones" centered on Greenwich in London.

Internet time

Time zones make no difference on the internet—all that matters is whether you're online. Internet time divides the day into 1,000 units called ".beats" and is the same wherever you are. When it's 5 p.m. in Tokyo, 8 a.m. in London, and 3 a.m. in New York, the Internet time is @375 .beats in all three cities.

Pendulum clock
A pendulum (swinging weight) of a certain length takes exactly the same time to move back and forth. Dutch physicist Christiaan Huygens (1629–1695) built the first pendulum clock in December 1656.

Spring-driven watch
Once people had learned to make miniature metal gears and springs, clocks shrunk into watches small enough to carry. This spring-driven watch dates from the 18th century.

Quartz electronic clock
Instead of telling time with a moving pendulum or gears, this watch counts the vibrations of a tiny quartz crystal when electricity passes through it.

ENTERTAINMENT SYSTEM

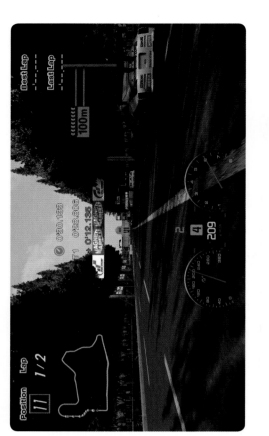

Serious games call for a serious games machine. Where an ordinary personal computer has a single microchip as its "brain," Sony's PlayStation 3 uses a more advanced chip called a cell broadband engine, split into nine parts, that can work much faster. It has roughly the same power as a supercomputer (massively powerful scientific computer) from the mid-1990s.

Lifelike

To produce realistic graphics, games programs need to contain a huge amount of information. To deal with all this data, the PlayStation uses a type of high-capacity DVD drive called Blu-ray. A Blu-ray disc can store 10 times more information than a normal DVD, which means game graphics can be much more detailed.

FAST FACTS

Memory	Hard drive: 20GB–80GB
Microprocessor	3.2GHz cell processor
Performance	218 GFLOPS
Disc media	CD, DVD, and Blu-ray
Connections	USB, Wi-Fi, and Bluetooth

PLAYSTATION 3

Power tower

The PlayStation 3 has a built-in Wi-Fi (wireless Internet) connection that lets you play games with up to 40 other people at a time, anywhere in the world. You can also download extra games, chat to your friends, and automatically update your system.

Circuit board controls
Blu-ray player

Ribbon cables
connect small
circuit boards
to motherboard

Front case with slots
for memory cards

Blu-ray disc player
can also play CDs
and DVDs

Motor spindle
rotates Blu-ray disc
at high speed

Inner case

Top case

PLAYSTATION 3

154

Card reader for
memory sticks
and cards

Wi-Fi and Bluetooth
circuit board

Power supply
unit cover

Transformer

Capacitors smooth
power supply to
delicate electronic
parts

16V

5.0V

5.0V

Front case

LOOKINSIDE

Hot stuff

Microprocessors (the "brains" inside computers) get
hot because massive amounts of electrical activity take
place in a tiny space inside them. The PlayStation gets
hotter than less powerful computers and needs a huge
internal cooling system. The giant cooling fan at the
back is several times bigger than the ones in laptop
computers, and the huge copper cooling pipes also
help to channel heat away.

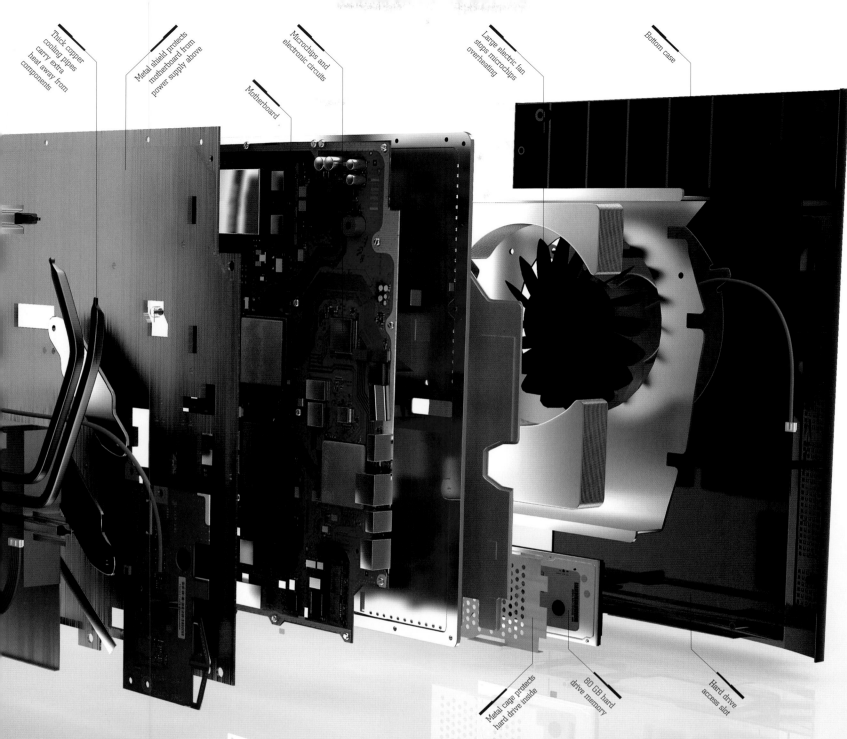

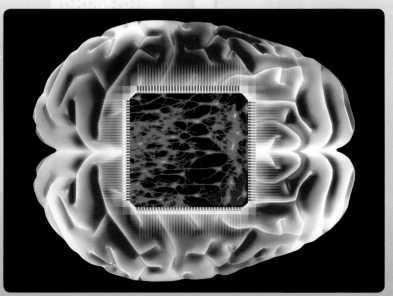

Thick copper cooling pipes carry extra heat away from components

Metal shield protects motherboard from power supply above

Motherboard

Microchips and electronic circuits

Large electric fan stops microchips overheating

Bottom case

Metal cage protects hard drive inside

80 GB hard drive memory

Hard drive access slot

How it works

The most important part of the PlayStation is a powerful microprocessor chip, which consists of nine separate processors built into a single computer chip. Eight of these processors help the PlayStation to process information at blistering, supercomputer speeds. The ninth acts as a supervisor, controlling and overseeing the work of the other eight.

Brain power
An ordinary computer has to finish one job completely before it can start another. This is called serial processing and it's sometimes very slow. The eight processors in the PlayStation can work on several different jobs at once so they finish much faster. This is called parallel processing and it's how our brains work.

GAME ON

Playing computer games may be fun, but it's also a serious business—a leading entertainment industry worth billions to the world economy. Computer games used to be things you could play only by yourself. Now, thanks to the internet, millions of us go online each day to play with people we've never met on the other side of the world. As more and more people discover the internet, and games move from consoles to handheld devices such as cell phones, computer games will become even more popular.

Go anywhere

Unlike a hefty PlayStation, this handheld Nintendo DS is light enough to take anywhere. It has a bright display, touchscreen input, and wireless internet access. The battery lasts 19 hours—long enough to survive the most boring journey!

Cyber cafés

Cyber cafés are very popular in Asian countries, especially with young people who want to play games or access the internet. In democratic countries such as South Korea and Japan, people can use the internet freely, but in nations like China, Vietnam, and Burma, governments monitor access and block any websites they disapprove of.

Bad for you?

Some people argue that video games may cause problems, such as bad eyesight, if you play them too much. However, research has found that strategy games can improve children's thinking and reasoning, while online games boost social skills (dealing with other people).

Milestones

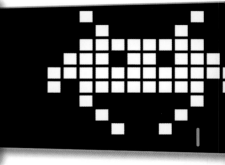

One-armed bandit (1880s)
Before computer games were invented, there were mechanical slot machines. You pulled a metal lever on the side to try to line up colored wheels and win a prize called the jackpot. Also known as one-armed bandits, machines like this are still popular in arcades today.

Pong (1970s)
Pong (computerized ping-pong) became the first widely popular computer game in 1972. Originally a coin-operated arcade game, it was later sold as a console that plugged into a home TV.

Serious play

Hardware (equipment) and software (programs) developed for playing games can be used to help the disabled and people with other special needs. Playing games can also help people recover strength and coordination after accidents and illnesses.

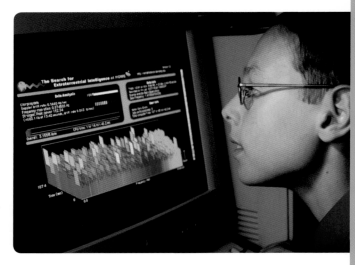

Aliens online

Is there life out in space? A project called SETI@home (Search for Extra-Terrestrial Intelligence at home) aims to find out. It uses spare time and processing power on people's home computers to search telescope data for alien signals.

Supercomputer

Computer games consoles are as powerful today as supercomputers used to be in the mid-1990s. You might have the power of this Cray supercomputer (above) in your home!

Space Invaders (1980s)

By the early 1980s, computers were fast, affordable, and had color screens. *Space Invaders* was a popular 1980s game in which you had to fight off an attack from flying aliens. It was one of the first computer games to have sound effects.

Myst (1990s)

In the 1990s, games with stunning artwork came on compact discs. In one best-seller, *Myst*, the player had to solve mysteries on a fantasy island.

Virtual reality

Virtual reality (VR) uses headsets and other interactive devices such as gloves to immerse you fully in a computer-generated world. Although the technology is still in development, future games may use VR to create a more realistic experience than ever before.

Body double

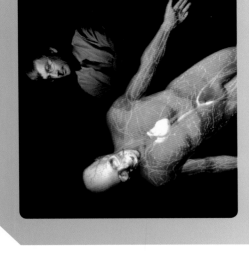

Holograms have many important practical uses. Doctors at the University of Calgary, Canada, are building detailed holographic models of the body to help them study diseases. They can even "walk around" inside computer reconstructions of cells, body tissues, and entire organs.

Graphics processing circuit board and memory chips

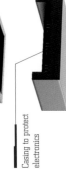

Casing to protect electronics

Projection screen shows image made by crisscrossing laser beams

Dome protects holoscreen

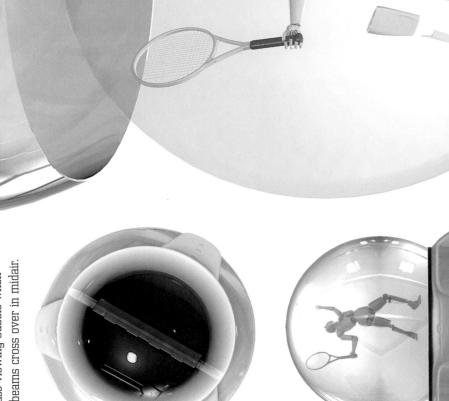

Holograms

Holograms, like the security pictures you may have seen on credit cards, are 3-D images that seem to be frozen inside plastic or glass. They are made by scanning laser beams over objects. Unlike a normal photograph, which is just a pattern of light and dark, a hologram stores all the details of the laser light waves reflected from objects. Realistic, 3-D images of those objects can be re-created by shining light onto the hologram. In this 3-D television, holograms are created moment by moment inside the glass viewing bubble when laser beams cross over in midair.

FUTURE HOLOGRAPHIC TV

It's said that if you gaze into a crystal ball, you can see the future. You can certainly see the future in this ball—it's a TV that uses holography (based on crossing laser beams) to create captivating moving images in 3-D.

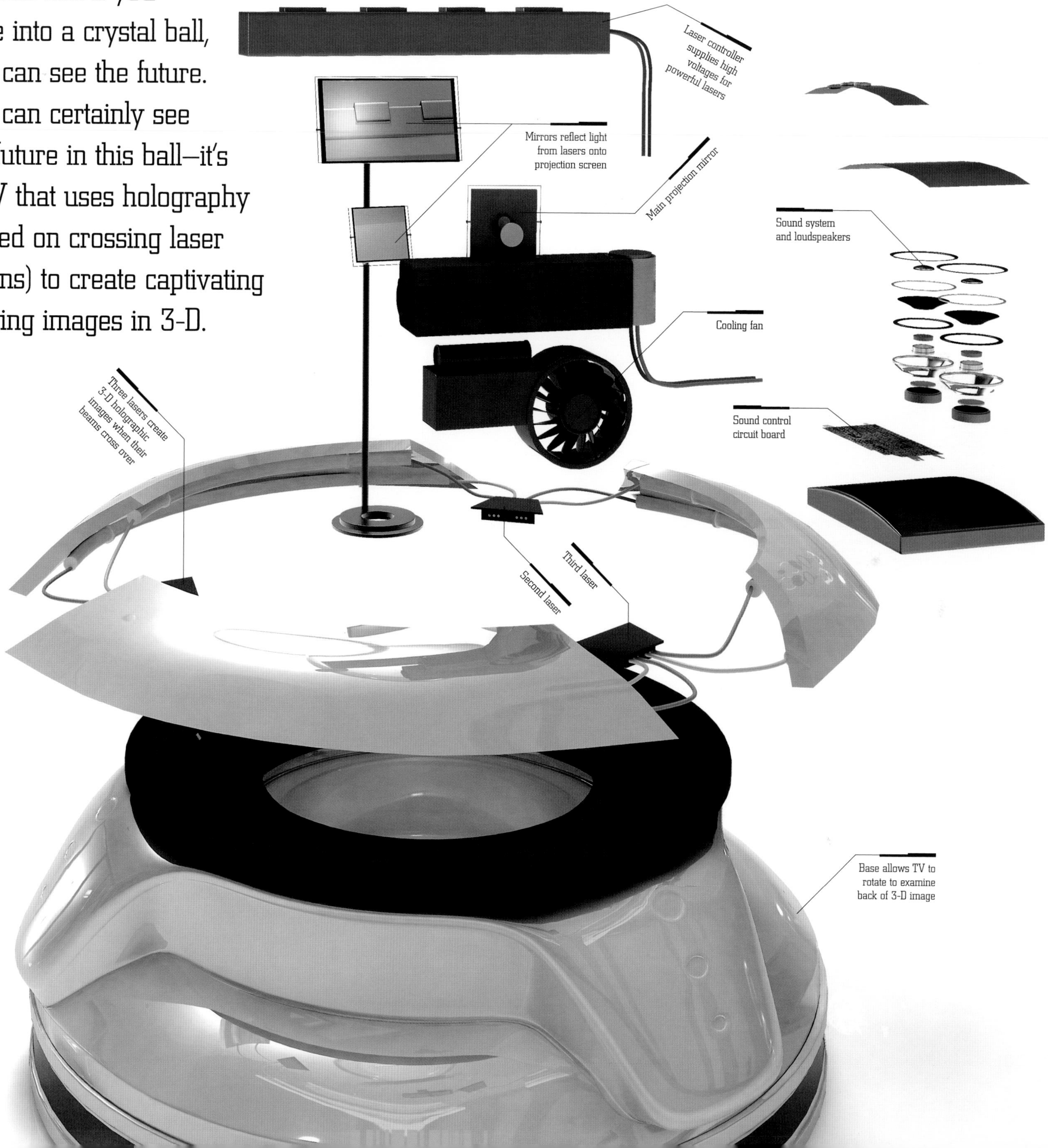

Sound system and loudspeakers

Cooling fan

Sound control circuit board

Laser controller supplies high voltages for powerful lasers

Main projection mirror

Mirrors reflect light from lasers onto projection screen

Third laser

Second laser

Base allows TV to rotate to examine back of 3-D image

Three lasers create 3-D holographic images when their beams cross over

FACTOIDS

• Workers in Europe enjoy the longest vacations: up to 42 days leave per year. In the United States, the average is only 13 days off per year. ■ More than 90 percent of working adults believe time away from work makes them more productive when they return.

Pleasure center

Experiments with animals are very controversial, but they can sometimes help us learn more about ourselves. In 1954, American scientists Peter Milner and James Olds tried an experiment where they allowed rats to give tiny electric shocks to their own brains by pressing a switch. Instead of hating the shocks, the rats loved them, and pressed the switches more than 2,000 times an hour. This is because the shocks triggered the rats' brains to release a pleasure-giving chemical called dopamine. Our brains release similar feel-good chemicals. This may explain why we like to do things we enjoy again and again.

Creative play

Everyone can be creative—it just means doing things in original, surprising, and fun new ways. This sculpture is a good example of all three. It was made out of pencils by South-African-born artist Jennifer Maestre.

People enjoy their work when they do it in creative ways, making it feel more like play. That could mean something as simple as decorating your desk, or you may invent a new way to do your job that is unique to you. For example, scientists have found that chefs find their job more rewarding when they spend time arranging food attractively on the plate.

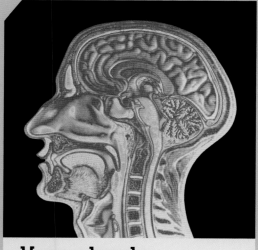

Happy heads

Images such as this one are produced by scanners to show which parts of people's brains are active when they are happy, angry, or sad. Scientists have found that these emotions are complex and can be produced by many different combinations of brain activity.

PLAY TIME

Watch a soccer player shooting for goal, a dancer spinning across the stage, or a pianist pounding the keys, and you'll see people at the very peak of their powers. When we do things we love, even work feels like play. But why do we need to play and why is it so much fun? Children play to discover how the world works. Adults play, too—and scientists have been studying them to work out why they enjoy it so much.

Endorphins

When we push our bodies to their limits, our brains release natural painkillers called endorphins into our bloodstream, which make us feel better. Scientists believe that people may choose to do frightening activities such as parachute jumping and rock climbing to produce a release of pleasure-giving endorphins.

Learning to play

Stress at work can cause serious health problems, but people often find it hard to relax and sometimes need encouragement to take time off work. Postcards and posters such as this one give us some ideas about how we might enjoy our leisure time.

SPLITKEIN
Flexible Flyer

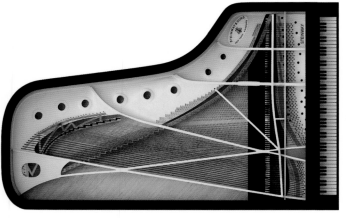

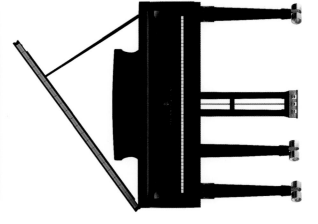

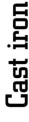

STEINWAY PIANO

Musicians are only as good as the instruments they play, so the finest pianists demand the finest pianos. A thousand tiny details make a Steinway grand piano the instrument of choice for 90 percent of the world's professionals. The case, for example, comes in a choice of 11 different wood finishes. They include everything from rich, golden satinwood, patterned like a bee's wing, to the deep, dark shine of ebony veneer (shown here). All the veneer is carved from a single tree to ensure the case polishes up to perfection. Such careful craftsmanship pays dividends—Steinway grand pianos have gained more in value over time than vintage cars, fine wines, and even gold! Lovingly built by hand, an instrument like this takes a year to make—and will last for a lifetime.

Cast iron

One essential part of a piano is a heavy cast iron plate (the part with holes in). The 200 or so strings pull inward with 45,373 lb (20,581 kg) of tension. This is a force equivalent to that of three elephants sitting on the case, and without the iron plate, the piano would implode.

In the bank

Steinway maintains a "bank" of 300 pianos across North America that pianists can borrow for performances. They simply choose one they like from the nearest dealer. Chinese pianist Lang Lang (1982–) is shown here testing a piano in the Steinway basement in New York City.

STEINWAY & SONS

FAST FACTS

Length	8ft 11¾ in (274 cm)
Width	5ft 1¼ in (156 cm)
Weight	990 lb (480 kg)
Cost	$75,000–$150,000

LOOK INSIDE

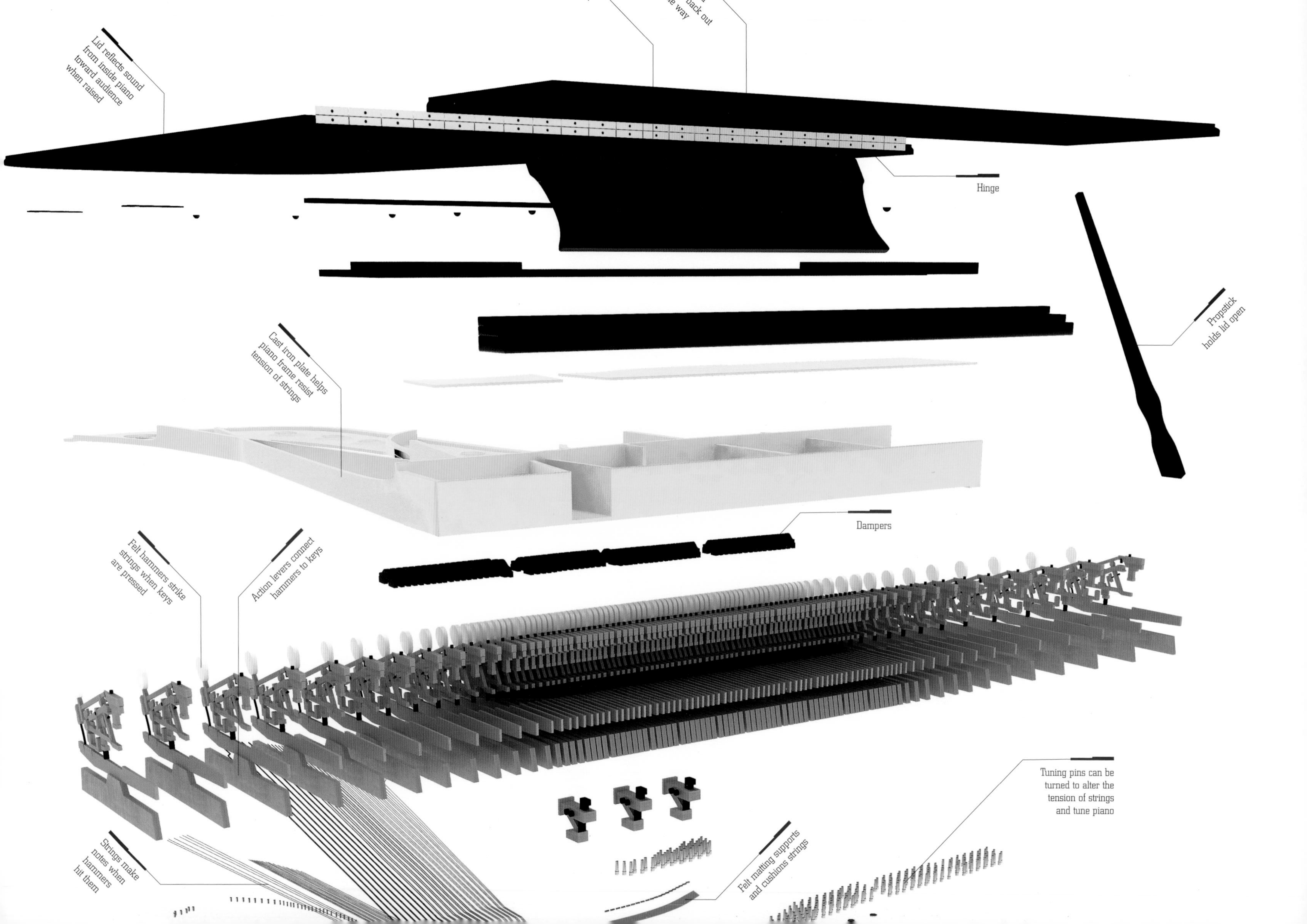

Propstick holds lid open

Hinge

Front of lid hinges back out of the way

Music rest

Lid reflects sound from inside piano toward audience when raised

Dampers

Cast iron plate helps piano frame resist tension of strings

Action levers connect hammers to keys

Felt hammers strike strings when keys are pressed

Strings make notes when hammers hit them

Tuning pins can be turned to alter the tension of strings and tune piano

Felt matting supports and cushions strings

Making notes

When you press a key, it pushes a lever. The middle of the lever flicks a hammer up, which vibrates the string and makes a note. The back of the lever pushes up a felt damper above the string. When the key is released, the damper falls back and stops the vibration to end the note.

Hammer

Key

Lever

Damper

How it works

A piano is a string instrument, because strings make the sounds you hear. But it's also a percussion instrument because the strings are hit by tiny hammers linked to the keys you press. Each key hits up to three strings when pressed, giving a richer sound.

Bridge holds strings above soundboard so they vibrate freely

White keys play notes A to G

Keyboard lid

Black keys play sharp and flat notes

Pedal lyre rods operate soft and sustain mechanisms when you press pedals

Right, sustain pedal makes all notes last longer by holding all the dampers up

Middle pedal makes pressed keys produce longer-lasting notes

Left, soft pedal

Lyre pillar supports pedals

Lyre block houses pedals

STEINWAY & SONS

165

Under the lid

There are more than 12,000 parts in a Steinway piano, most of them hidden from view. Some parts help to generate the musical sounds. Others change the quality of those sounds. When you press the pedals, these parts can make the sound quieter or keep a note going after you stop pressing the key. You might think that the lid is simply there to keep the dust out, but it, too, has an important job to do: reflecting sound toward the audience.

Soundboard, made of spruce wood amplifies the sounds the strings make

Castors make it easy to move piano, which weighs as much as seven men

Rear leg

Rear leg block

Sturdy wooden case covered in polished veneer

Laminated rim made from layers of hard maple wood, bent by hand

PIANOPLAY

Many great composers, including Mozart and Beethoven, were also great pianists. But pianos are not just used to play classical music: you can find them everywhere, from churches to schools and bars. One reason they're so popular is the sweeping scale of 88 keys—big enough for two hands to play two separate tunes, which is impossible on most instruments.

Pianola

Player pianos (or pianolas) were invented in the late 19th century for people who liked piano music but couldn't play. These intricate automated machines played themselves by reading patterns of holes punched in reels of paper.

Synthesizer

French musician Jean-Michel Jarre (1948–) (right) helped to popularize electronic music in the 1970s. The synthesizers he plays are electronic keyboards that can create any sound you can imagine and modify existing sounds in unusual ways. Electronic music dates back to the early 20th century, when inventors made the first electronic instruments from radio parts.

Milestones

Spinet

Keyboard instruments such as the spinet made music by plucking strings. Using a simple mechanism, pressing each key caused a different string to be plucked. Spinets had about half as many keys as a modern piano and date from the early 17th century.

Harpischord

Harpsichords are bigger and more sophisticated than spinets and also work by plucking strings. Although they make a wonderful sound, all their notes sound equally loud.

Bartolomeo Cristofori

Most people credit the invention of the modern piano to Bartolomeo Cristofori (1655–1731), an Italian who looked after harpsichords for Grand Prince Ferdinando of Florence. Cristofori's fortepianos had only 54 keys, but were complex, expensive, and slow to catch on. Only three survive today.

J. S. Bach

Piano music became popular after German composer Johann Sebastian Bach (1685–1750) wrote a series of 48 short pieces called *The Well-Tempered Clavier*. These tunes, known as preludes and fugues, illustrated the dazzling possibilities of what was then still a relatively new instrument.

John Cage

Musicians are still finding new ways to use pianos. In the 20th century, radical American composer John Cage (1912–1992) popularized the use of a "prepared piano." This involves changing the sound of a piano in striking ways by placing nuts, bolts, and other objects under the strings.

Fortepiano
Bartolomeo Cristofori developed the harpsichord into a more versatile instrument that could play both loud and soft notes, which he called a *gravicembalo col piano e forte* (harpsichord with soft and loud). Known as a fortepiano, it was smaller and quieter than a modern piano.

Upright piano
Before recorded music was invented, many bars employed pianists, who played upright pianos such as this. The mechanisms were built into compact, upright cases.

Modern electronic piano
Table-top keyboards such as this one make sounds using electronic circuits and small speakers. With almost no moving parts, they are much less expensive than pianos.

GIBSON ELECTRIC GUITAR

Six-string sound

Traditional acoustic guitars have hollow wooden bodies and make more or less the same sound however they are played. The notes they make last only as long as the guitar vibrates when you pluck the string. Electric guitars are very different. Their six steel strings can make a huge range of sounds, from thumping bass notes and staccato rhythms to high-pitched screams like a human voice. The notes can last as long as the guitar player wants because their sounds are produced electrically.

CD ROM

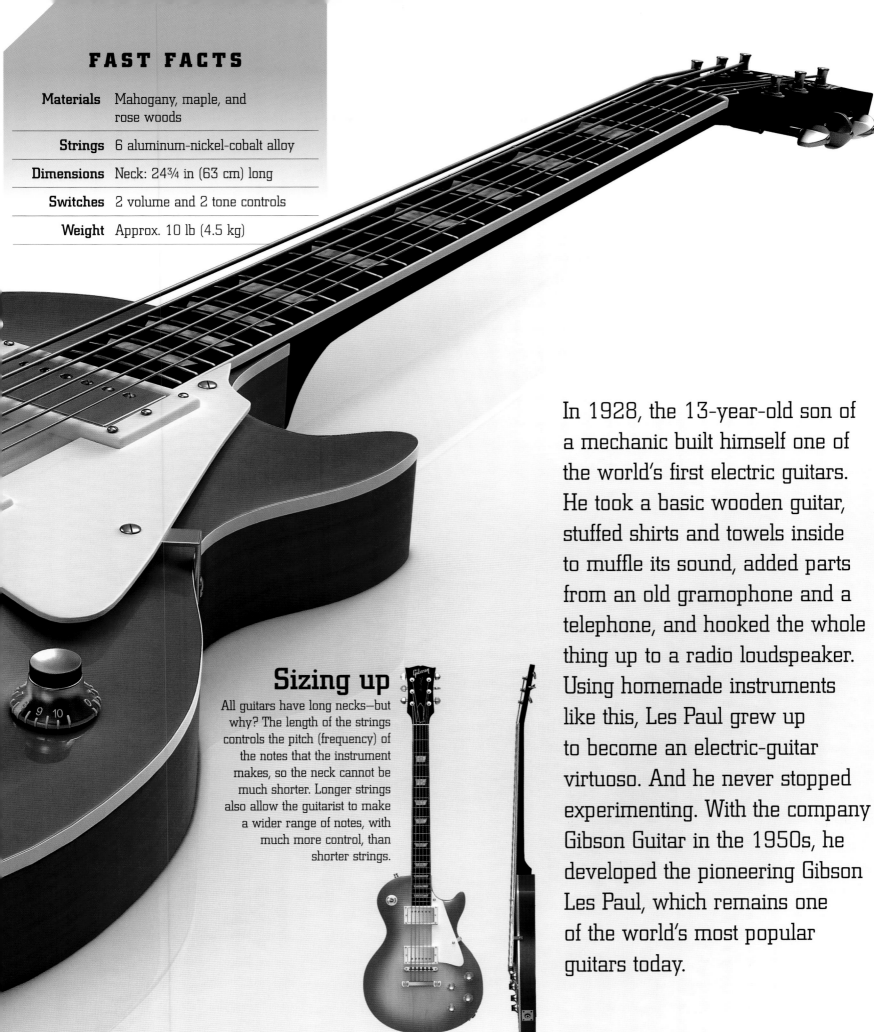

FAST FACTS

Materials	Mahogany, maple, and rose woods
Strings	6 aluminum-nickel-cobalt alloy
Dimensions	Neck: 24¾ in (63 cm) long
Switches	2 volume and 2 tone controls
Weight	Approx. 10 lb (4.5 kg)

Sizing up

All guitars have long necks—but why? The length of the strings controls the pitch (frequency) of the notes that the instrument makes, so the neck cannot be much shorter. Longer strings also allow the guitarist to make a wider range of notes, with much more control, than shorter strings.

In 1928, the 13-year-old son of a mechanic built himself one of the world's first electric guitars. He took a basic wooden guitar, stuffed shirts and towels inside to muffle its sound, added parts from an old gramophone and a telephone, and hooked the whole thing up to a radio loudspeaker. Using homemade instruments like this, Les Paul grew up to become an electric-guitar virtuoso. And he never stopped experimenting. With the company Gibson Guitar in the 1950s, he developed the pioneering Gibson Les Paul, which remains one of the world's most popular guitars today.

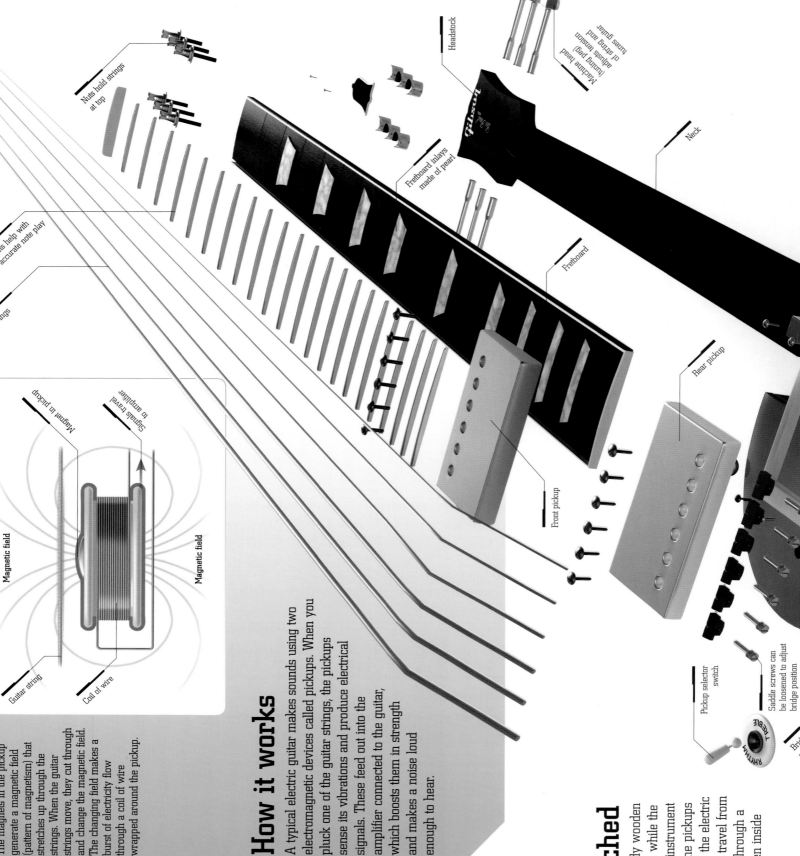

LOOK INSIDE

Strings attached

An electric guitar has a sturdy wooden neck to keep the strings taut, while the large body is shaped so the instrument is easy to cradle and play. The pickups underneath the strings make the electric sound signals. These signals travel from the pickups to the amplifier through a simple electrical circuit hidden inside the guitar's body.

How it works

A typical electric guitar makes sounds using two electromagnetic devices called pickups. When you pluck one of the guitar strings, the pickups sense its vibrations and produce electrical signals. These feed out into the amplifier connected to the guitar, which boosts them in strength and makes a noise loud enough to hear.

Pickup power

The magnets in the pickup generate a magnetic field (pattern of magnetism) that stretches up through the strings. When the guitar strings move, they cut through and change the magnetic field. The changing field makes a burst of electricity flow through a coil of wire wrapped around the pickup.

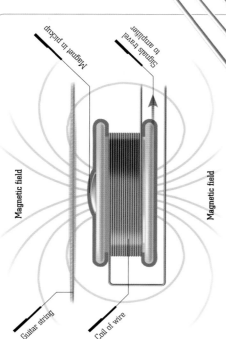

Magnet in pickup

Signals travel to amplifier

Magnetic field

Magnetic field

Guitar string

Coil of wire

Labels

Machine head (tuning peg) adjusts tension of string and tunes guitar

Headstock

Neck

Fretboard inlays made of pearl

Fretboard

Nuts hold strings at top

Frets help with accurate note play

Strings

Rear pickup

Front pickup

Pickup selector switch

Saddle screws can be loosened to adjust bridge position

Bridge supports strings so they vibrate freely

RHYTHM TREBLE

Gibson

Pickguard

Tone control for
rear pickup

Output socket
connects guitar
to amplifier

Volume control for
rear pickup

Inner wiring
and electronics

Pickup mount

Bridge mount

Tailpiece fastens
strings to case

Volume control for
front pickup

Front case

Tone control for
front pickup

Strap connector

THE WORLD'S FAVORITE

People have been making music since prehistoric times, using musical instruments made from the things around them. Horns made from conch shells have been used for millennia and, in the 1990s, historians discovered a flute made from a hollowed-out bear bone that was 45,000 years old. Stone-Age people were ingenious, but they had nothing to rival the electric guitar—a music machine powerful enough to shake a stadium. Loud and angry or soft and sweet, guitars can be used to play all kinds of music, from rock and soul to jazz and folk. And a guitar is small enough to carry around. No wonder it's the world's favorite instrument.

Les Paul

Now in his nineties, Les Paul remains one of the world's best-loved guitarists. With painful arthritis in his hands, he can no longer play chords the way he used to. Even so, he still won two Grammy awards in 2006 for his latest album—aged 91!

Ancient ancestors

Electric guitars were invented in the 20th century, based on six-string acoustic guitars developed a century or so before. These, in turn, evolved from string instruments such as the mandolin and lute (right). Popular in Renaissance Europe, the lute can be traced back to ancient Egyptian times.

Classic sound

Many people learn to play acoustic (classical) guitars like these (above) before moving on to electric guitars. Acoustic guitars are quieter than electric ones, but they are cheaper and easier to carry around since they don't require an electric amplifier.

Guitar heroes

Electric guitars make music—but they also make a statement. Rowdy and rebellious, guitar-driven rock has been the soundtrack to young people's lives since the 1950s. No two players sound exactly the same. The best electric guitarists, such as Keith Richards, shown here with his band The Rolling Stones, have instantly recognizable styles.

Spanish guitar
Acoustic guitars such as this are also known as Spanish or classical guitars. They have wooden bodies and six strings made from nylon or metal.

Guitar synthesizer
This unusual Roland G-707 (below) dates from the 1980s. It was played like a guitar but had a similar sound to a synthesizer.

12-string Rickenbacker
Twelve-string guitars produce a much richer tone than six-string ones. Guitars like this one (left) were popularized by The Beatles.

Otwin 4/6
This unusual instrument (right) is two guitars in one. The top part is a four-string bass, while the bottom part is a six-string rhythm guitar.

Making a guitar

Most electric guitars are molded from solid plastic, but prestigious makes like the Gibson and acoustic guitars are still built by hand (left). The wooden sides of an acoustic guitar are bent into curves by rolling them over a hot pipe.

Variety

Electric guitars come in every shape and size. Guitars that play the melody (main tune) of a song typically have six or 12 strings, while bass guitars have four strings and play low, deep notes. Some make a mixture of electric and acoustic sounds.

LEGO ROBOT

Can you build a robot that walks like a human? It's one of the hardest problems that robot scientists have to grapple with. You can try it, too, with a construction kit called LEGO Mindstorms. It comes with a programmable computer brain and 519 plastic body parts. That's still not quite as sophisticated as the human body, with its 206 bones and 700 muscles, but it's a step in the right direction.

Touch sensitive

This factory-style robot arm can tell the difference between a red ball and a blue one. When its claw closes over a ball, a light sensor measures the color. If the ball is red, the robot keeps its claw closed and carries the ball away. If the ball is blue, the robot opens its claw and drops the ball.

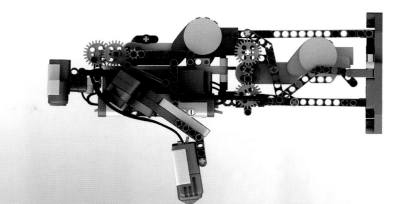

Stepping out

This LEGO robot walks like a human but works like a machine. For muscles, it has servo motors: electric motors that can move very smoothly and with great precision. Instead of a brain, it has a powerful computer in its chest called an NXT. You can connect this to an outside computer to program the robot with its instructions.

FAST FACTS

Sensors Touch, sound, light, and ultrasonic

Processor NXT computer can connect to 3 motors and 4 sensors

Power 6 AA batteries

Computer Connects to a PC with USB link or wireless Bluetooth link

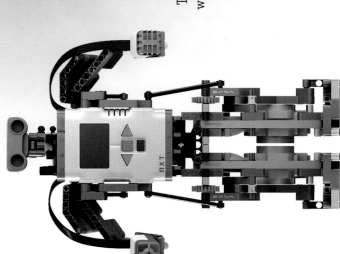

Block party

You can put six basic LEGO blocks together in 915 million different ways, so imagine how many different robots you can make with just the pieces shown here! LEGO Mindstorms was developed in 1998, and became LEGO NXT in 2006.

Gear wheel transmits force from servo motor

Angled blocks form shoulders

Straight blocks form upper arms

Axle allows parts to rotate

Pin to fix different parts together

Cog to move legs

Touch sensor on end of robot's arm

Servo motors control arms and legs

Display screen

How it works

Robots work in roughly the same way as computers because they have computers as their "brains." To kick a ball, a robot has to follow three stages called input, processing, and output. Humans do things in a similar way, but for us, the stages are called perception, cognition, and action.

Input (perception)
First, the robot has to see the approaching object as a ball. Color, shape, and movement help the robot to tell the difference between the ball and other nearby objects.

Processing (cognition)
Now the ball has been recognized, the robot has to decide what to do with it. It does this by following a series of instructions in its computer program.

Output (action)
The program tells the robot to move its foot forward so that it makes contact with the ball. The robot's servo motors allow it to kick the ball accurately.

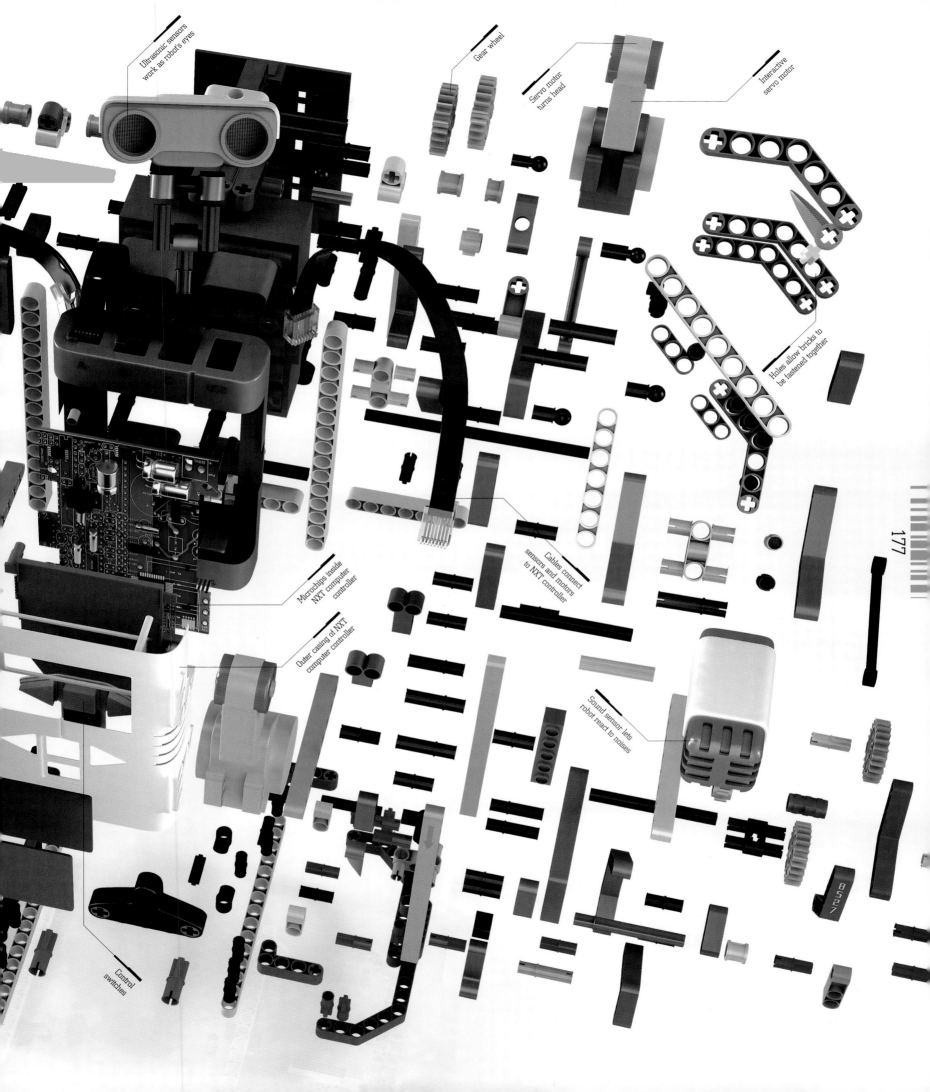

Ultrasonic sensors
work as robot's eyes

Gear wheel

Servo motor
turns head

Interactive
servo motor

Holes allow bricks to
be fastened together

Microchips inside
NXT computer
controller

Cables connect
sensors and motors
to NXT controller

Outer casing of NXT
computer controller

Sound sensor lets
robot react to noises

177

Control
switches

ROBOCULTURE

Robots seem like visitors from the future, but they're just as much a part of the past. The ancient Greeks had automata (steam-powered automatic machines) more than 2,000 years ago. Since the word "robot" was coined in 1938, scary metal monsters have appeared in many books and films. Even now, when most people think of robots, they imagine clanking contraptions taking over the world. The reality is different: robots are more likely to help us weld cars, run factories, and care for the sick. They're very much our friends, not our foes.

Magic Mike

Toy robots like this Magic Mike became hugely popular in the 1950s and 1960s, when robots started to appear in science-fiction films and TV series. Mike talks, makes space sounds, trundles along, flashes his eyes, and opens and closes his hands.

Metropolis

A German film called *Metropolis*, made in 1926, was one of the first to feature robots. Set in a bleak futuristic city in 2026, it features a robot that encourages workers in an underground city to stage a revolution.

Transformers

Transformers, a film made by Steven Spielberg in 2007, features robots that can disguise themselves as cars, trucks, and other real-world machines. Like many robot characters, the ones in *Transformers* have humanlike emotions and machinelike powers.

Driving force

Robots have been helping people make cars since 1961, when the first robot was used at a General Motors factory in New Jersey. Factory robots don't need bodies: they can manage with a single, computer-controlled arm.

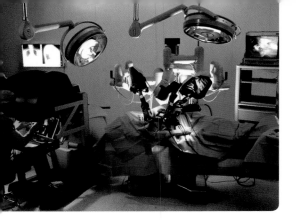

Robot surgery

Difficult medical operations call for the world's best surgeons, but what if they're in another country from the patients who need their help? Robot surgery may be the answer. The surgeon sits at a console, like a video game, controlling a robot that might be on the other side of the world. As the surgeon steers the controls, the robot carries out its instructions with utmost precision.

ASIMO

This Japanese robot is so lifelike, you might think there was a person hiding inside. About the size of a 10-year-old, ASIMO walks, runs, climbs stairs, waves, and dances with incredibly realistic movements. It's powered by a rechargeable battery that gives it an hour of life between charges.

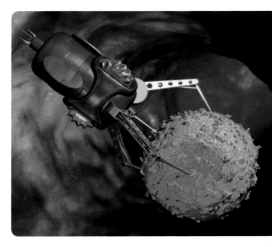

Nanorobots

Some scientists think robots will eventually be small enough to inject into our bodies. Known as nanorobots (or nanobots), they could hunt down viruses or cure illnesses that are too complex for doctors to treat from outside.

FUTURE ROBOT

If you're aiming for a gold medal, you need the world's best coach. In the future, when sportsmen and women are reaching the limits of what humans can do, robots like this could help them go further. It's a fully computerized sports coach that trains with you, videos what you do, and analyzes your performance.

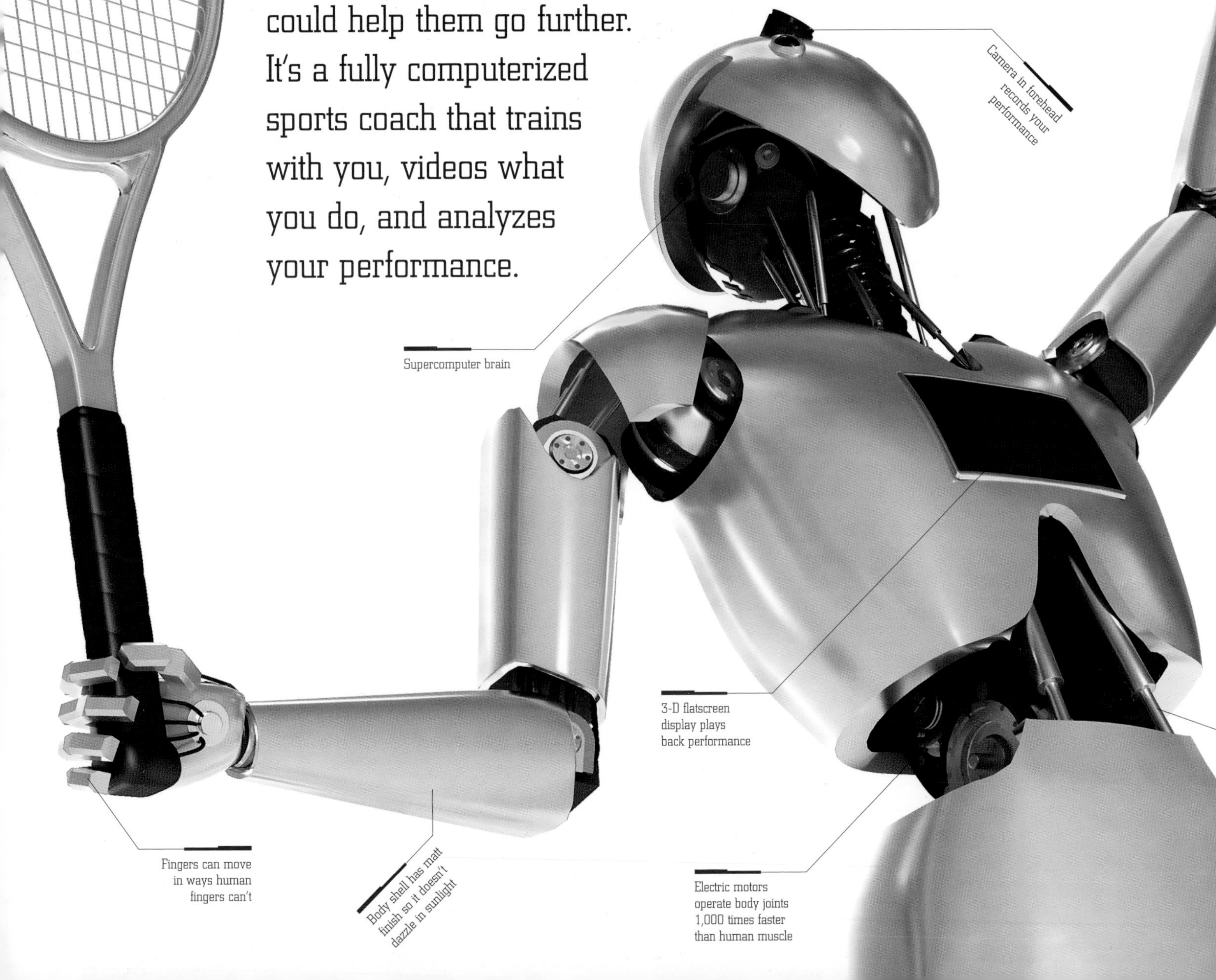

Hands are strong enough to crush steel

Camera in forehead records your performance

Supercomputer brain

3-D flatscreen display plays back performance

Robot "abdominal" muscles

Electric motors operate body joints 1,000 times faster than human muscle

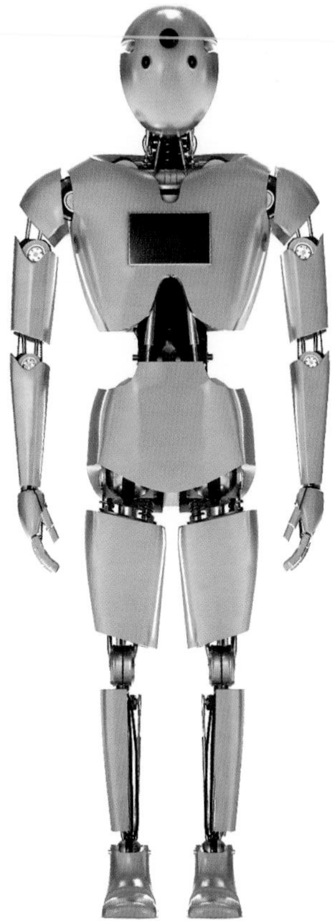

Body shell has matt finish so it doesn't dazzle in sunlight

Fingers can move in ways human fingers can't

Perfect partner

Robo-coach helps you practice any sport, from archery to swimming. Standing more than 7 ft (2.1 m) tall, it's 10 times stronger than most humans and can play nonstop sports for 36 hours, until its batteries run flat. The video camera records your performance, and you can watch the playback later on the TV in the chest. Robo-coach even gives you a massage when you're tired!

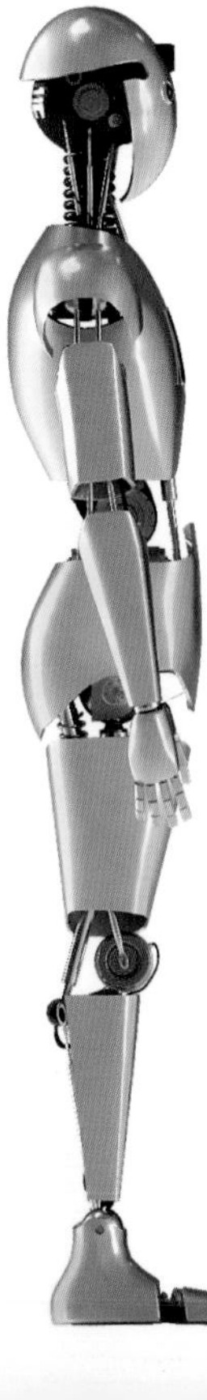

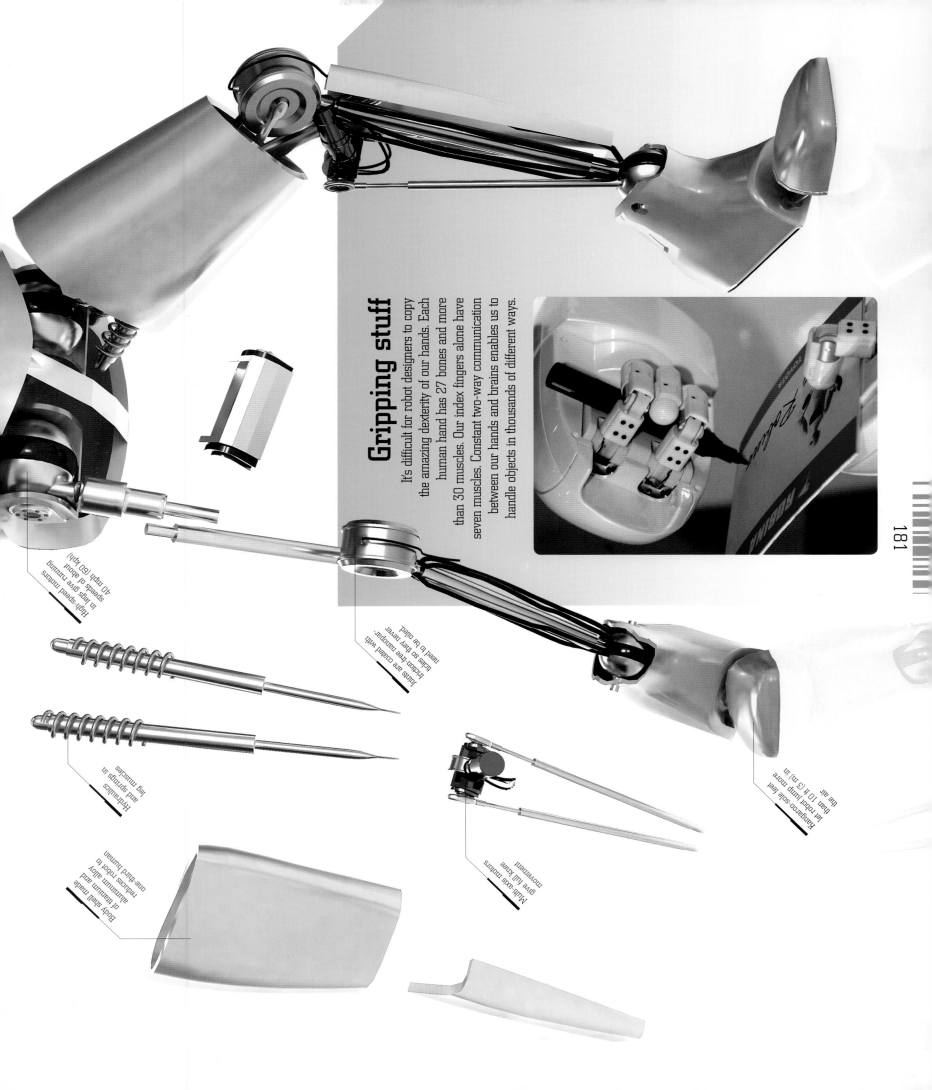

Gripping stuff

It's difficult for robot designers to copy the amazing dexterity of our hands. Each human hand has 27 bones and more than 30 muscles. Our index fingers alone have seven muscles. Constant two-way communication between our hands and brains enables us to handle objects in thousands of different ways.

High-speed motors in legs give running speeds of about 40 mph (60 kph).

Joints are coated with friction-free nanoparticles so they never need to be oiled.

Kangaroo-sole feet let robot jump more than 10 ft (3 m) in the air.

Hydraulics and springs in leg muscles

Multi-axis motors give full knee movement

Body shell made of titanium and aluminum alloy reduces robot to one-third human weight.

LONDON EYE

CD ROM

Spinning slowly on the South Bank of the Thames River, the London Eye has a diameter more than 150 times that of a bicycle wheel. Up to 800 people at a time can fly in the London Eye's 32 sleek glass capsules. From the top, they are treated to fantastic views right across London.

Balancing act

When you sit on a bicycle, your weight pushes down on the frame. The frame in turn balances on the wheels, supported by the spokes. The London Eye is more like a bike resting upside down on its saddle. The wheel and capsules, which together weigh more than 300 elephants, are supported by the spokes and hub, which hang from a frame resting on the ground.

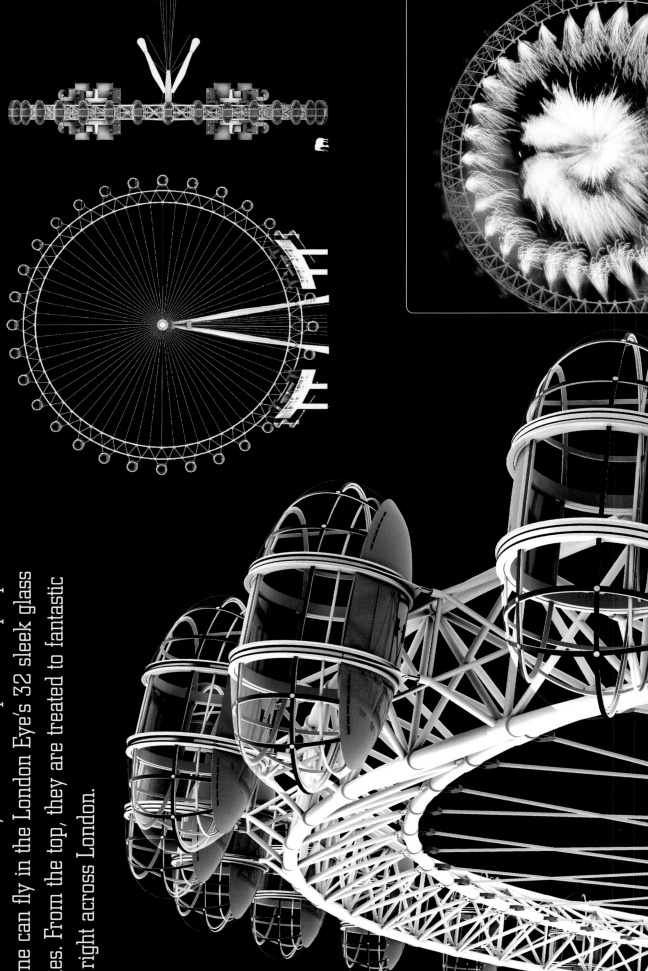

Millennium Wheel

Built to celebrate the Millennium, the London Eye was officially opened on December 31, 1999, with a spectacular firework display. A line of 2,000 precisely synchronized fireworks fired up from floating barges in sequence, making it appear as if a sheet of flames was moving up the river. This was followed by a giant display that the organizers hoped would be visible from space.

FAST FACTS

Height to top	443 ft (135 m)
Capsule weight	11 tons each
Total weight	2,300 tons
Rotation speed	0.6 mph (0.9 kph)
Time to rotate	Approx. 30 minutes

Steel frame

184

Building the Eye

Parts of the London Eye were built in six European countries before being shipped to London. They were put together a bit like flatpack furniture, using a floating crane, on a temporary "island" on the Thames River. The engineers then made the bold decision to lift the finished structure into place in a single day.

Testing, testing
Before the London Eye could be lifted, the crane's strength had to be tested. The wheel was firmly bolted to the river island and the crane pulled upward with immense force to prove that none of the cables would break.

Panels made from laminated glass

Space capsule

The London Eye is much more glamorous than an old-fashioned Ferris wheel. Each of the spacious glass capsules is fully enclosed and climate-controlled, with a mechanism underneath that keeps it perfectly level. The working parts are all under the floor, so you get an uninterrupted 360° view stretching up to 25 miles (40 km) in each direction.

Two sets of batteries for emergencies

Capsule drive motor

Self-levelling stability system

LOOKINSIDE

185

RIDE TIME

There's nothing we like more than being scared out of our wits. Many people will pay to be flung through the air or spun around at top speed. Rides work in many different ways. We see the world from high up so it looks strange and surprising. We feel weird sensations as our bodies twist and turn. We can get all the thrills of doing something dangerous on rides designed to keep us safe.

Ferris wheel

The first Ferris wheel had an iron frame and wooden cars, and was half the size of the London Eye wheel that now stands by the Thames River. It was built in Chicago in 1893 by American bridge-builder George Ferris (1859–1896). It cost $400,000 (about $10 million today).

Icy roller coaster

On the first roller coasters, built in 15th-century Russia, you clambered up about 100 rickety stairs and whizzed back down on a sled made of ice and straw at around 50 mph (80 kph).

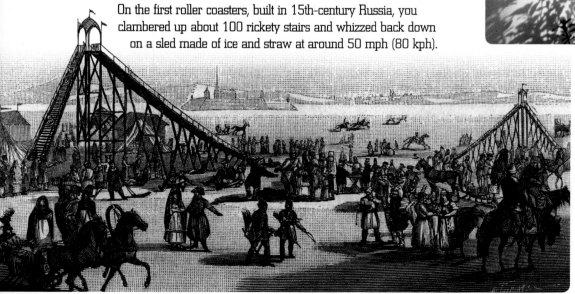

Modern rides

This roller coaster (right) is one of many that were built in the US in the first half of the 20th century by John A. Miller (1874–1941), the pioneer of modern roller coasters. His cars had safety brakes to stop them from rolling backward and extra wheels under the track to stop them from coming off on tight bends.

Wooden roller coaster

Wooden coasters, such as the Roar in California, United States, (left), deliberately shake and rattle to provide a truly terrifying ride. It takes just two minutes to get from one end to the other, but in that time you race down over half a mile (1 km) of twisty track at 50 mph (80 kph), while feeling 3.5 times the force of gravity.

Metal rollers

Roller coasters made from superstrong steel can have more steeply twisting track and overhead corkscrew turns than wooden ones. Powered by the force of gravity, the cars can reach speeds of more than 100 mph (160 kph).

Zorbing

Zorbing is like a roller coaster without the track. Instead of sitting in a car, you're strapped inside a gigantic bouncy ball and pushed down a hill. You tumble head over heels till you reach the bottom.

Kingda Ka

The world's highest and fastest ride is Kingda Ka in New Jersey. The cars can reach a staggering 128 mph (200 kph) after plunging down a vertical track three times taller than the Statue of Liberty.

Spinning stars

Roller coasters and Ferris wheels are only two of many kinds of ride. Star Flyers (above) spin 24 people at a time from a huge central tower more than 300 ft (90 m) off the ground.

187

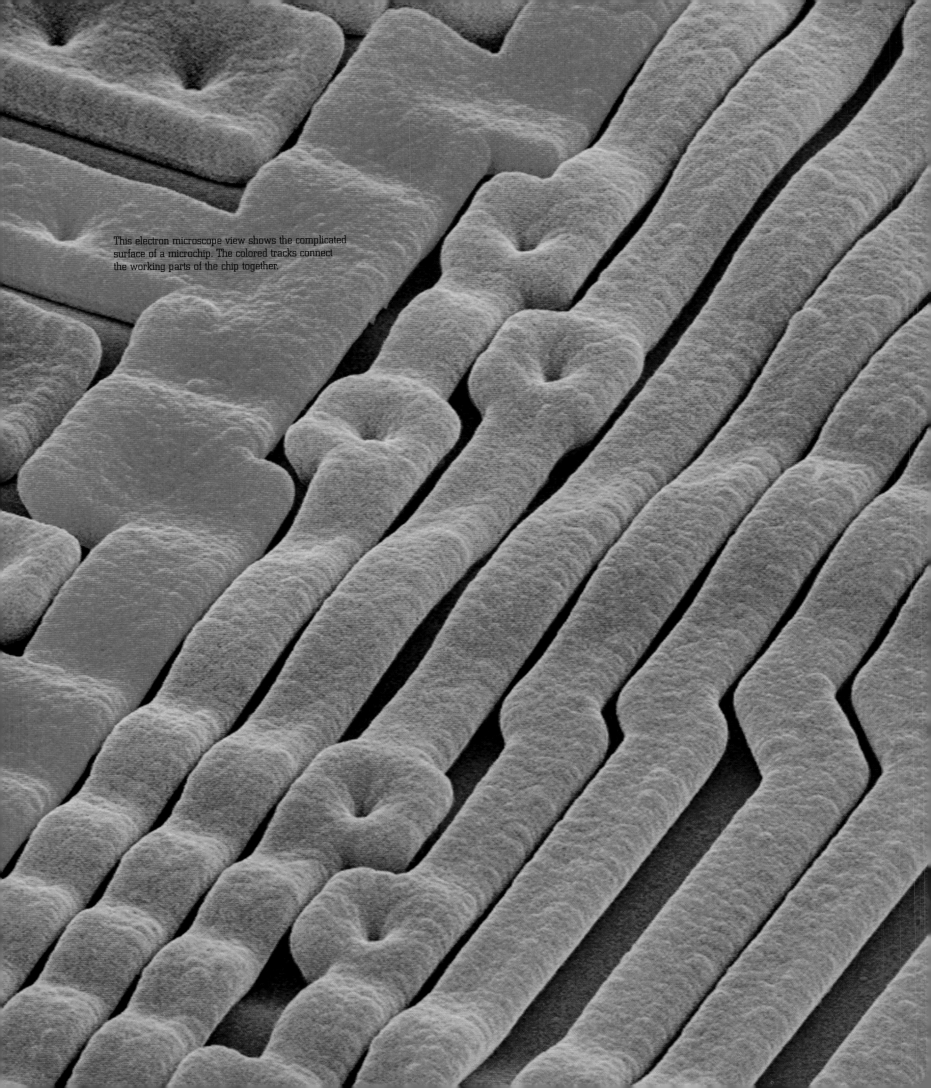

This electron microscope view shows the complicated surface of a microchip. The colored tracks connect the working parts of the chip together.

DIGITAL TECHNOLOGY

There are no cogs, levers, engines, or wheels in electronic gadgets—and to the naked eye, it looks like there is nothing going on inside them. But if our eyes could zoom in on the atomic world, we'd find that the insides of laptops and cell phones are humming like the busiest of factories. We can't see what an atom looks like because it's about a million times thinner than a human hair. Whizzing around these are electrons whose movement creates electricity. Every email you send, every phone call you make, and every digital photo you take sets circuits buzzing, making billions of these unimaginably tiny particles march around like soldiers on parade. You can't see it happening—but it's all there on the inside.

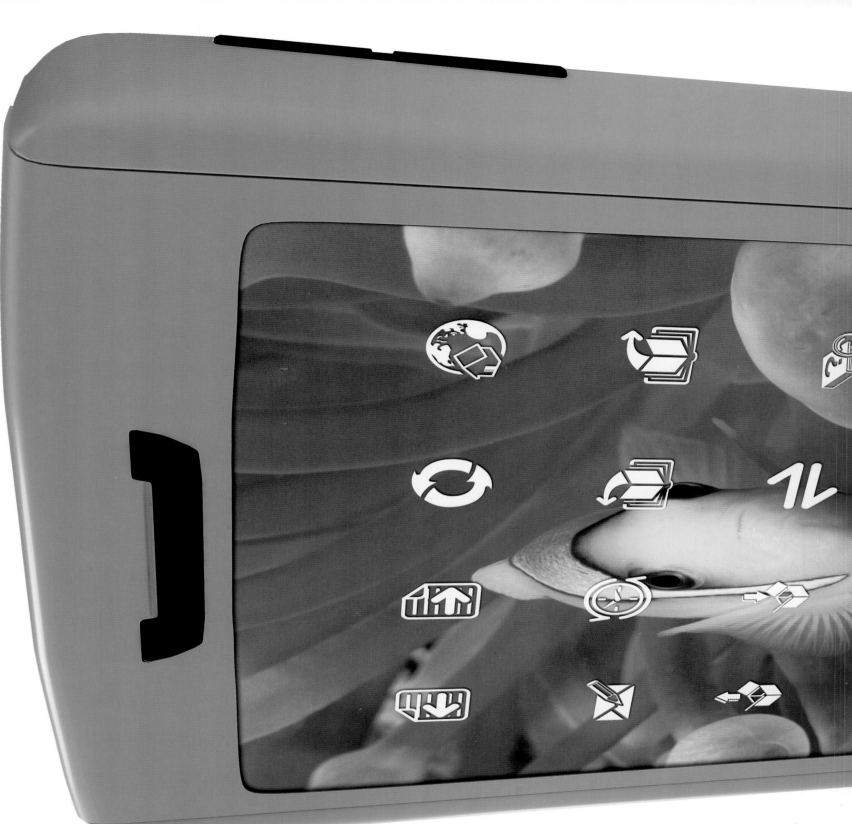

Think thin

Phones are packed with more and more features, but they seem to get thinner and lighter every year. In 1983, a cell phone was as big as a brick and weighed 28 oz (800 g). Made from strong but lightweight plastic, a modern touchscreen phone is six times lighter and slips easily into your pocket.

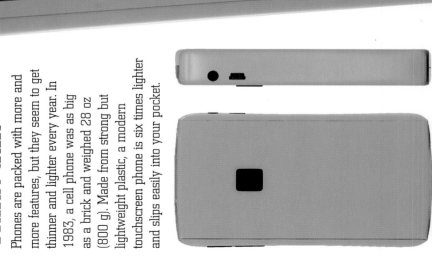

CELL PHONE

CD ROM

Touching is natural. Instinctively, we reach for the things we want—it's one of the first things babies learn to do. Lots of people are now reaching for cool gadgets like this cell phone.

Instead of a fiddly keyboard, it has a sleek, touch-sensitive screen dancing with colorful pictures and text. Touch the screen and it changes instantly from a phone to an internet browser, camera, news reader, or music player.

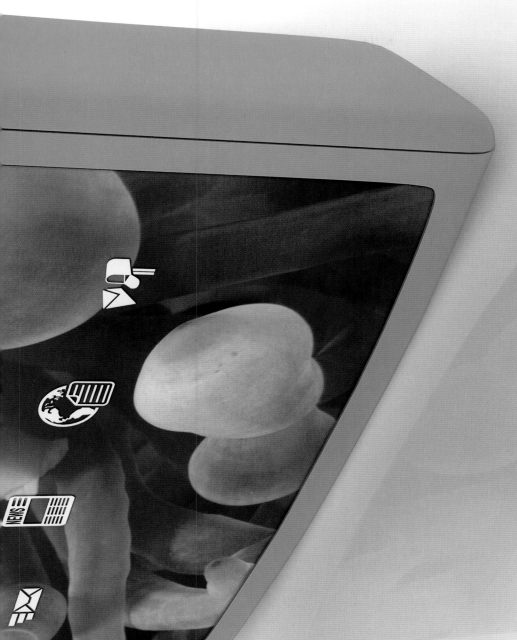

FAST FACTS

Dimensions	4½ in x 2½ in x ½ in (115 mm x 61 mm x 12 mm)
Weight	4½ oz (130 g)
Display	3½ in (9 cm) color multitouch
Camera	3 megapixels
Battery	Lithium-ion with 8 hours of talk time

Pocket computer

The gadgets we carry may be mobile, but they're no longer just phones. With touchscreen technology, a cell phone becomes as powerful and flexible as a portable computer. It can link to the internet through the radio-wave connection that normally carries your calls, so you can send emails, browse websites, or download music and videos.

Layers upon layers

The touchscreen of a cell phone is made up of lots of different layers. At the base, the LCD creates images and words by lighting up patterns of pixels (tiny colored squares). The touch-sensitive transparent layer sits above it. The various other layers include shims (spacing and filling layers) to protect the LCD and touchscreen from knocks, scratches, moisture, and dirt.

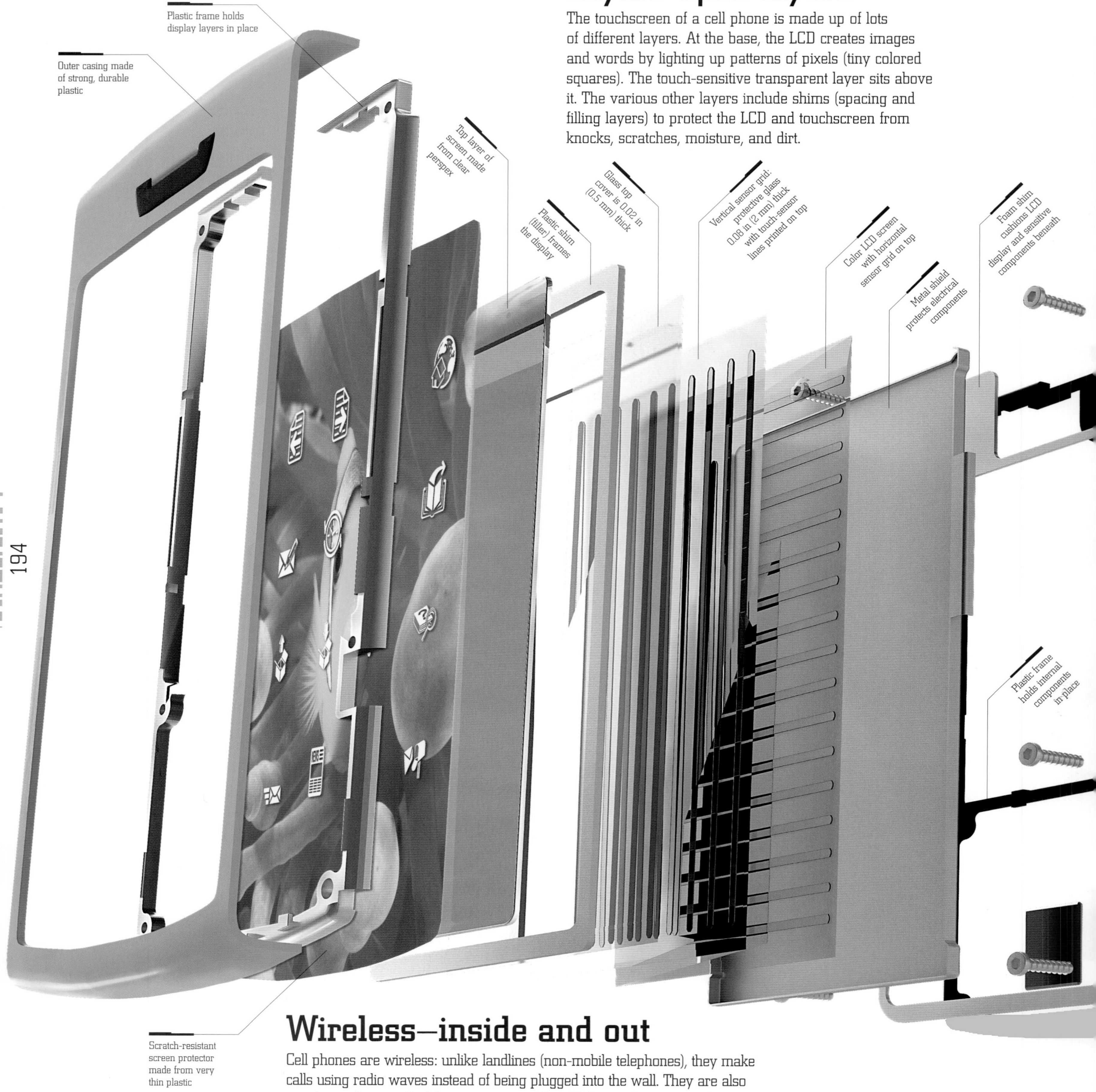

Plastic frame holds display layers in place

Outer casing made of strong, durable plastic

Top layer of screen made from clear perspex

Plastic shim (filler) frames the display

Glass top cover is 0.02 in (0.5 mm) thick

Vertical sensor grid: protective glass 0.08 in (2 mm) thick with touch-sensor lines printed on top

Color LCD screen with horizontal sensor grid on top

Metal shield protects electrical components

Foam shim cushions LCD display and sensitive components beneath

Plastic frame holds internal components in place

Scratch-resistant screen protector made from very thin plastic

Wireless—inside and out

Cell phones are wireless: unlike landlines (non-mobile telephones), they make calls using radio waves instead of being plugged into the wall. They are also mostly wireless inside. Many parts are soldered (electrically connected) to a circuit board (a piece of plastic covered in metal connections). Other components, such as the LCD screen, plug directly into the circuit board or have very short wires.

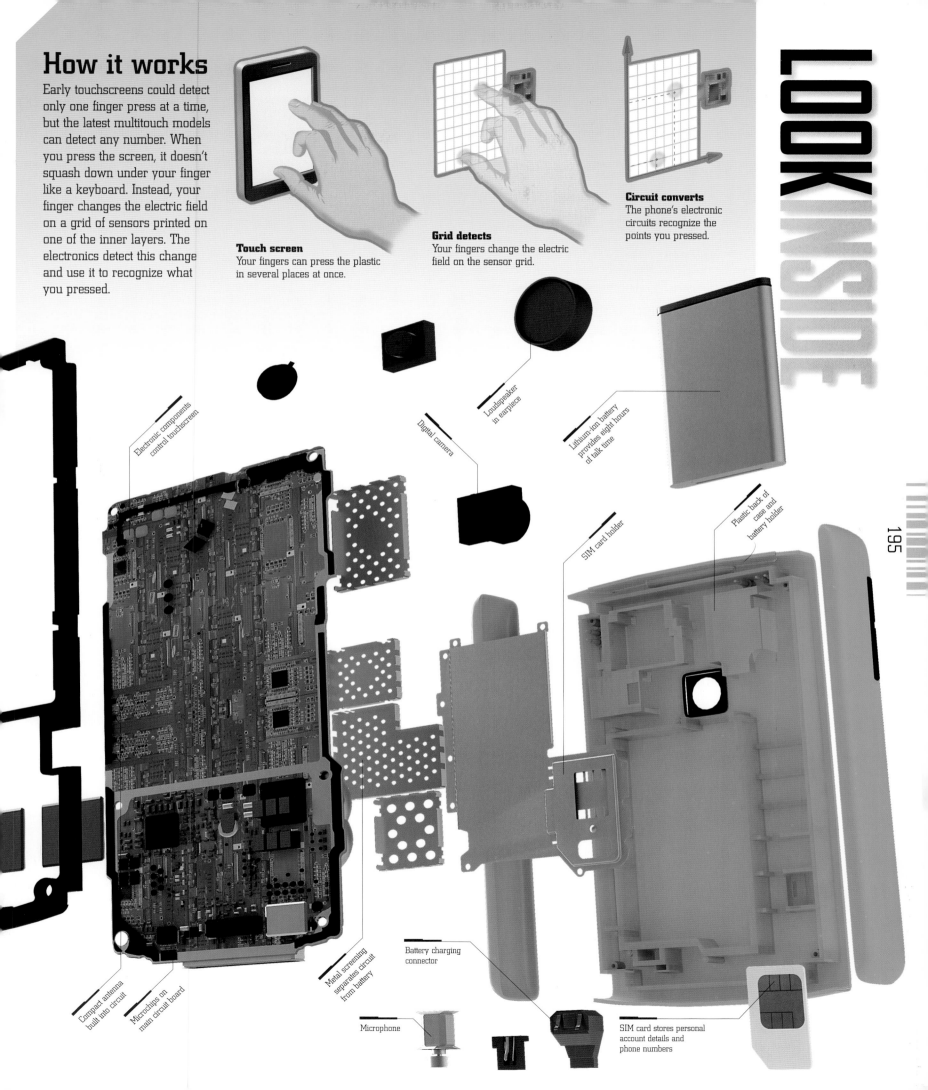

How it works

Early touchscreens could detect only one finger press at a time, but the latest multitouch models can detect any number. When you press the screen, it doesn't squash down under your finger like a keyboard. Instead, your finger changes the electric field on a grid of sensors printed on one of the inner layers. The electronics detect this change and use it to recognize what you pressed.

Touch screen
Your fingers can press the plastic in several places at once.

Grid detects
Your fingers change the electric field on the sensor grid.

Circuit converts
The phone's electronic circuits recognize the points you pressed.

Electronic components control touchscreen

Loudspeaker in earpiece

Digital camera

Lithium-ion battery provides eight hours of talk time

SIM card holder

Plastic back of case and battery holder

Compact antenna built into circuit

Microchips on main circuit board

Metal screening separates circuit from battery

Battery charging connector

Microphone

SIM card stores personal account details and phone numbers

IN TOUCH

There are more than six billion people in the world, and more than three billion cell phones. Every minute, 1,000 more people buy a phone for the first time and join in with the most versatile medium of communication ever invented. The growth in cell phones has been spectacular. It took 20 years for the first billion people to get connected, but the most recent billion have bought their phones in the last two years alone. In some parts of the world, including Europe, many people own more than one phone—and there are more cell phones in these places than people!

Early cell phones

This is what cell phones looked like in 1985. The handset (similar to an ordinary telephone handset) was connected to a heavy but portable case filled mostly with batteries. The antenna on the back could be extended for better reception in rural areas.

Mast in disguise

Phone masts relay calls between cell phones and the phone networks they use. To work properly, masts have to be mounted on hilltops or tall buildings. Many people find ordinary metal masts (which look like giant TV antennas) unattractive. This one has been disguised with fake plastic branches to look like a tree.

Waste of phones

Most people replace their cell phone every 18 months or so, but only 4 percent of phones are properly recycled. Many end up in landfills. Their plastic cases take up to 500 years to break down, while their batteries and electronic components can release toxic metals such as cadmium, mercury, and lead into the environment.

World favorite

Phone keyboards tend to have symbols on the function buttons instead of letters or words, so people in every country can understand them. The most popular mobile phone system, GSM, is used in more than 200 countries.

Health risk?

Scientists have not proved that cell phones are safe—or unsafe. Some have found that phone users have more risk of brain tumors, while others say there's no effect at all. These images show how people's brain activity changes when they use phones.

Big in Japan

Cell phones are more than just portable phones—they also work as cameras and music players. In Japan, people use a system called i-mode to send emails, play games, and browse the web. Some phones even work as wallets, paying for your shopping when you swipe them over the checkout (right).

Distractions

Drivers are four times more likely to have an accident if they use a cell phone, so driving with a phone is now illegal or restricted in at least 30 countries. Some research has shown that talking to a passenger is just as distracting, however.

FUTURE FLEXIPHONE

Bone phone

Handheld phones could become obsolete if we find a way of beaming sound signals directly into a person's head. One possibility is to give people tooth implants containing microchip radio receivers and vibration devices. The chips would vibrate in response to incoming phone calls, passing the sound to your inner ear through your jawbone. Nobody would even know you were on the phone!

Magnets hold phone strap closed when it wraps around your wrist

Case can flex and twist in any direction

Electronic components on ultrathin circuit board

The 19th century gave us the telephone. The 20th century brought us the cell phone. In the 21st century, phones will develop into flexiphones—personal communicators that are flexible in more ways than one. Today, people carry cell phones and music players, paper diaries and address books. In the future, our phones will help us do just about anything we want, from sending emails and ordering shopping online to having live video chats with friends anywhere in the world.

Ultrathin and lightweight plastic battery charged by solar cells

Lightweight

All the phone's electronic components, including the screen, are printed onto thin layers of flexible plastic. Power comes from ultrathin solar cells in the outer case, so only a small battery is needed. With a more compact screen and battery, the phone weighs as little as a pencil. Magnets in the case strap it onto your wrist like a watch.

Display layers as thin as cellophane can produce pin-sharp video pictures

Solar cells built into plastic case charge battery

Multiple flexible layers are built up to give phone its unique properties

SIM card stores phone numbers and account details

DIGITAL PEN

The old saying "The pen is mightier than the sword" highlights the power of well-chosen words. Combine a pen with a computer, and you have something even more impressive. A digital pen doesn't simply write on paper: its built-in camera automatically detects the marks you make, so the words you write can be beamed to your computer and edited as easily as if you'd typed them in.

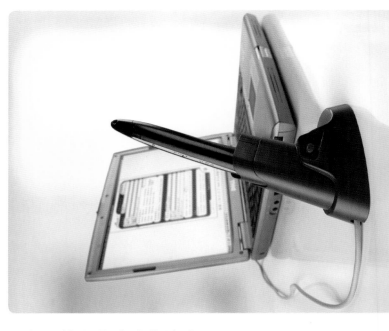

Well connected

A digital pen is electrically powered. Every so often, you have to put it back in its docking station to recharge the battery inside. The docking station also links to a computer with a USB cable. When the pen is docked, all the things you've written with it are uploaded automatically to your computer.

Hard copy

When computers first became popular, people spoke of a "paperless society" with all communication in electronic form. Two-thirds of people now use email at work, but there's 50 percent more paper in our offices than there was in the 1960s. It seems that people still prefer the convenience of a hard copy that they can write their comments on.

FAST FACTS

Memory	100 8½ x 11 in pages of text
Weight	32 oz (908 g) in box
Dimensions	½ in x 1 in x ¾ in (157 mm x 24 mm x 21 mm)
Operating time	Up to 3 hours
Standby time	Up to 20 hours
Data transfer	Wireless Bluetooth or USB connection to computer

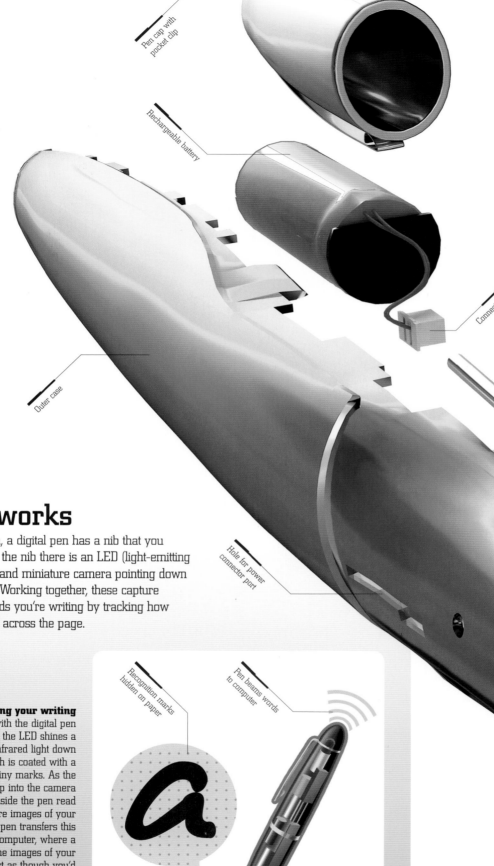

Pen cap with pocket clip

Rechargeable battery

Top screw mounting

Top clip

Refill holder

Outer case

Connector links battery to circuit board

Flexible circuit connector

Hole for power connector port

Recognition marks hidden on paper

Pen beams words to computer

Wires carry electrical power and signals

Connection to docking stand

How it works

Like a normal pen, a digital pen has a nib that you write with. Next to the nib there is an LED (light-emitting diode) transmitter and miniature camera pointing down toward the paper. Working together, these capture images of the words you're writing by tracking how you move the pen across the page.

Reading your writing

When you write with the digital pen on special paper, the LED shines a beam of invisible infrared light down onto the paper, which is coated with a grid of extremely tiny marks. As the light reflects back up into the camera lens, microchips inside the pen read the marks and store images of your handwriting. The pen transfers this information to your computer, where a program converts the images of your writing into text, just as though you'd typed it with the keyboard.

abcde

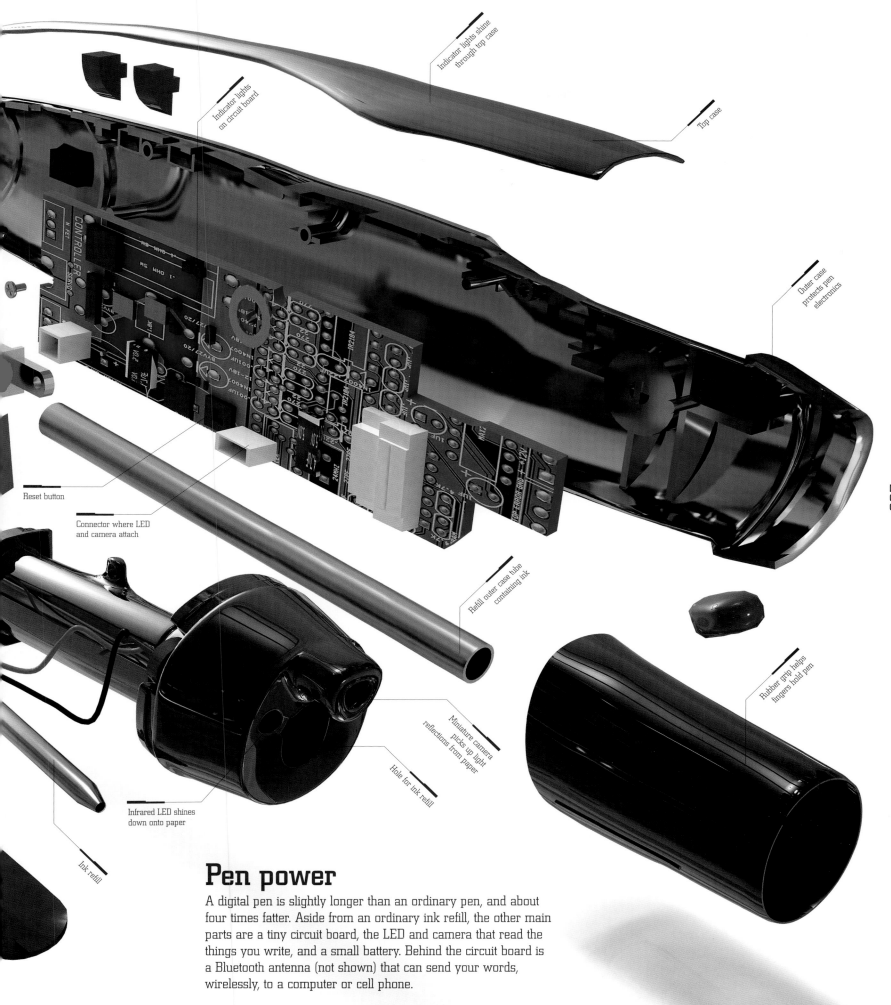

Indicator lights shine through top case

Top case

Indicator lights on circuit board

Outer case protects pen electronics

CONTROLLER

Reset button

Connector where LED and camera attach

Refill outer case tube containing ink

Rubber grip helps fingers hold pen

Miniature camera picks up light reflections from paper

Hole for ink refill

Infrared LED shines down onto paper

Ink refill

Pen power

A digital pen is slightly longer than an ordinary pen, and about four times fatter. Aside from an ordinary ink refill, the other main parts are a tiny circuit board, the LED and camera that read the things you write, and a small battery. Behind the circuit board is a Bluetooth antenna (not shown) that can send your words, wirelessly, to a computer or cell phone.

SAVINGDATA

Humans have invented some ingenious ways to store information, which means that we can draw on the knowledge of the generations that came before us. Even after we have died, others can build on our achievements, and this is how civilization has advanced. Ancient inventions such as paper and writing marked the beginning of the age of recorded history. In our age, very recent inventions such as computers and the World Wide Web will carry the history we make today far into the future.

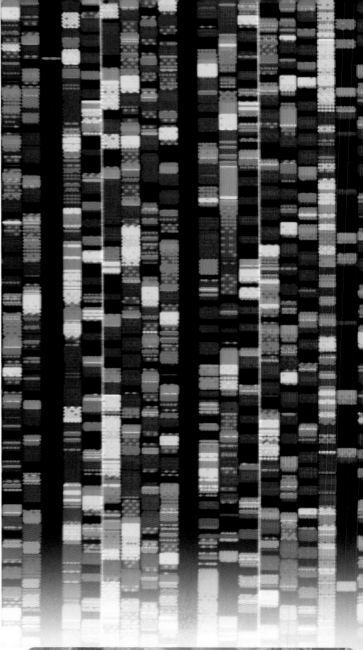

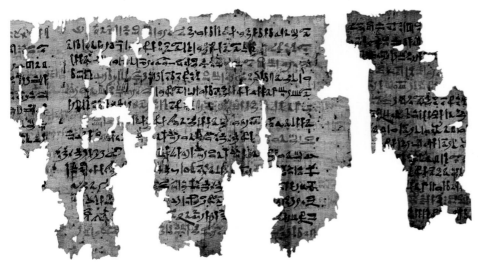

Papyrus

Paper was invented about 5,000 years ago by the ancient Egyptians, who made it from the stem of a plant called papyrus. The 3,700-year-old Edwin Smith Papyrus, above, is the world's oldest medical book. It describes how the body works and lists some medical cures that are still used today.

Cuneiform

Writing materials are useless without an agreed to system to record your ideas. The first ever written language, called cuneiform, involved making line marks in clay with a piece of wood called a stylus. Cuneiform was invented in Mesopotamia (now part of Iraq) about 5,500 years ago.

Information is power

If knowledge is power, the owners of libraries are very powerful indeed. Here, the accumulated knowledge of whole civilizations is stored. Ornate libraries such as this one in the Strahov Monastery, Prague, Czech Republic, celebrate the power of books and words.

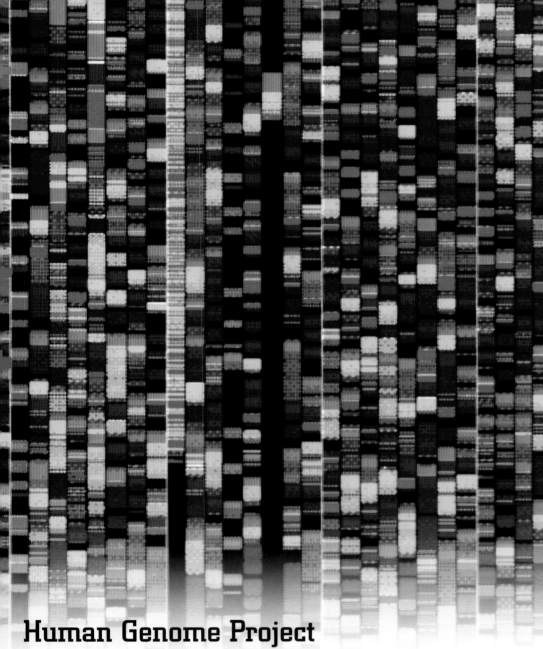

Digital libraries

The British Library shares some of its rare and valuable books on a website called Turning the Pages. You read digital books by dragging the pages with your mouse. These detailed plant pictures are from *A Curious Herbal* by Elizabeth Blackwell, dating from 1737.

Human Genome Project

Thanks to computers, information is easier to store and share than ever before. The Human Genome Project is a huge computer database of genetic information (shown here as colored bands) that scientists can access using the internet to develop cures for illnesses such as cancer.

Recognizing writing

People can read computer printouts, but most computers can't yet read human writing. This mail sorting machine (above) uses a laser to read postal codes written on envelopes. It prints the codes on the paper as a pattern of fluorescent dots that other sorting machines can read.

Easy access

Blind people find it hard to access information in books, but computers can help. Instead of using screens, screen readers speak words aloud. Some blind people use Braille displays like this one (left). It converts documents into raised dots that blind people read with their fingers.

Semantic Web

Tim Berners-Lee (right, 1955–) invented the World Wide Web so that scientists could share their work. His next project, the Semantic Web, will let machines share information too. In the Semantic Web, all Web content will be written in a language that computers can understand as well as in human languages such as English.

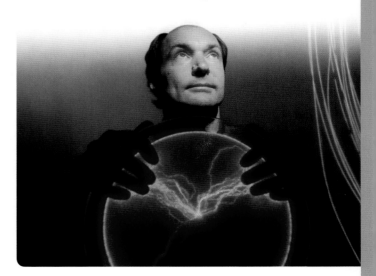

CAMCORDER

CD ROM

If you watch a film lasting two hours, more than 170,000 photographs dance briefly before your eyes. Your brain doesn't see them as separate images but blends them into a continuous moving picture. Until recently, making movies was something only professional filmmakers could do. But modern electronics have made cameras smaller, simpler, and more affordable, and anyone can now make a film with a camcorder. Pictures are stored on tape or in digital memory, so if you don't like your film, you can record over it.

FAST FACTS

Dimensions	4¾ in x 3½ in x 2½ in (118 mm x 92 mm x 64 mm)
LCD screen size	2¾ in (7 cm)
Optical zoom	34 times
Weight	12 oz (350 g)
Recording system	MiniDV tape

Instant playback

Until video was invented, movie cameras worked like old-fashioned film cameras: the pictures you recorded had to be slowly and laboriously developed. With a modern camcorder, you can instantly play back what you have filmed. Pictures are stored in digital form, so you can easily upload them onto websites and share them with your friends.

Handheld film crew

Hollywood films have expensive budgets, giant sets, and dozens of people in the film crew. If you're filming with a camcorder, you have everything you need in the palm of your hand. Weighing only a fifth as much as professional video cameras, camcorders are light and portable enough to film almost anywhere.

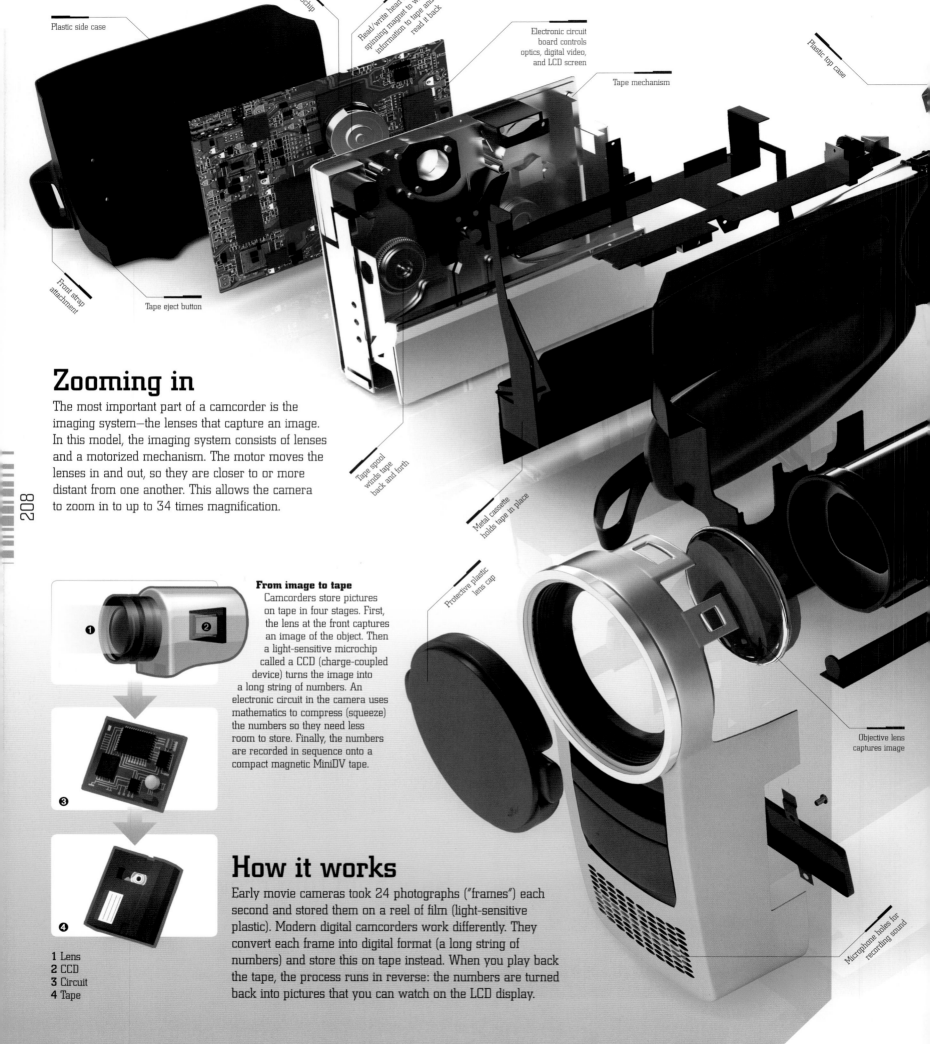

Plastic side case

Microchip

Read/write head uses a spinning magnet to write information to tape and read it back

Electronic circuit board controls optics, digital video, and LCD screen

Tape mechanism

Plastic top case

Front strap attachment

Tape eject button

Tape spool winds tape back and forth

Metal cassette holds tape in place

Protective plastic lens cap

Objective lens captures image

Microphone holes for recording sound

Zooming in

The most important part of a camcorder is the imaging system—the lenses that capture an image. In this model, the imaging system consists of lenses and a motorized mechanism. The motor moves the lenses in and out, so they are closer to or more distant from one another. This allows the camera to zoom in to up to 34 times magnification.

From image to tape

Camcorders store pictures on tape in four stages. First, the lens at the front captures an image of the object. Then a light-sensitive microchip called a CCD (charge-coupled device) turns the image into a long string of numbers. An electronic circuit in the camera uses mathematics to compress (squeeze) the numbers so they need less room to store. Finally, the numbers are recorded in sequence onto a compact magnetic MiniDV tape.

❶

❷

❸

❹

1 Lens
2 CCD
3 Circuit
4 Tape

How it works

Early movie cameras took 24 photographs ("frames") each second and stored them on a reel of film (light-sensitive plastic). Modern digital camcorders work differently. They convert each frame into digital format (a long string of numbers) and store this on tape instead. When you play back the tape, the process runs in reverse: the numbers are turned back into pictures that you can watch on the LCD display.

Viewfinder lets you see what you're filming

Rechargeable battery pack

CCD captures image

Circuit board

Button-cell battery

Tape control buttons

Connecting tracks on circuit board link electronic parts together

LCD display

Motorized mechanism for moving zoom lenses

Loudspeaker in side of case plays back recorded sound

Zoom lenses

Hinge allows LCD display to fold in and out

Microphone

Fold-out plastic LCD display surround

Push-button controls for playback

Slots house playback buttons

LOOK INSIDE

ON SCREEN

When a huge steam locomotive came charging toward a crowd in Paris, France, in 1896, people screamed, panicked, and dived out of the way to save themselves. In fact, the train was just an enormous filmed image projected onto a screen, but it seemed frighteningly real at the time. The people who watched it were the audience in the world's first movie theater, and they had never seen a film before. More than a century later, films haven't lost the power to move us, but some things have changed. We're more likely to watch a film at home on the television than in an auditorium with other people, and we've learned to use the technology of capturing moving pictures in other interesting ways.

Electronic news-gathering

It can take several years to make a feature film, but sometimes we need pictures more quickly. TV news cameras instantly capture pictures with digital video. Then they transmit them immediately back to a studio, anywhere in the world, using satellite trucks like this one.

Big screen

In many western countries, movie theaters reached the peak of their popularity in the 1940s. Audiences have fallen by more than 90 percent since then, largely because of television and home video. That's not the case in India, which has the world's biggest film business. Indian filmmakers produce more than 1,000 films a year, shown in more than 13,000 movie theaters. Most Indian people still prefer to watch films in theaters and only 8 percent of films in India are watched on videos at home.

Milestones

Zoetrope (1860s)
This zoetrope shows the scientific idea behind films, called persistence of vision. This is when you see a series of pictures so fast that your brain merges them together. If you peer through a slit on the spinning zoetrope, you don't see lots of still pictures—you see a single moving image. The Zoetrope was invented by Austrian scientist Simon Stampfer (1792–1864).

Cinématographe (1895)
The French brothers Auguste and Louis Lumière invented the first practical film camera and projector in 1895. The following year, they opened the world's first movie theater in the Grand Café in Paris.

Scientific study

Filmmaking technology lets us study the world at a safe distance. This vulcanologist (volcano scientist) is filming the lava flowing down Mount Etna, the largest active volcano in Europe. Films have important scientific value because they can be stored and compared over time.

Big Brother

Most of us appear in films every day without knowing it because security cameras like these watch our every move. Cameras have helped to solve some high-profile crimes, but it is uncertain whether they reduce crime more generally.

Piracy

Video and DVD recorders make it easier than ever for people to make illegal copies. According to the film industry, piracy costs the major film studios about $24 billion a year in lost earnings. Most happens in China, Russia, and Thailand.

Video cassettes (1970s)
Video recorders were invented in the 1950s, but were too expensive for most people. They became popular in the 1970s when Sony released this affordable machine called the Betamax, which could record from a video camera or direct from a home television.

DVD players (1990s)
Video recorders were unreliable, and their tapes often broke or wore out. Many people have now switched to DVD recorders, which are more reliable and easier to use.

Internet video (2000s)
In the future, even things like DVDs may become obsolete. Already, people use webcams to record videos and send them directly over the internet. Soon, we may download all our films instead of buying them from stores.

CAMERA

Moments vanish in the blink of an eye, but you can capture them forever with a camera like this. The pictures digital cameras take are like mosaics of tiny squares called pixels. The Canon EOS-5D takes pictures made up of an impressive 13 megapixels (one megapixel is a million pixels). Our eyes have 10 times more light-detecting cells in their retinas, but no way of storing the images they see or showing them to others.

CD ROM

Under control

Until microchips became popular in the 1980s, cameras were heavy and entirely mechanical. Virtually everything on the Canon is electronically controlled by buttons on the top, back, and sides. That makes it lighter, more reliable, and easier to use.

FAST FACTS

Weight	28 oz (810 g) without lens
Materials	Case made from polycarbonate (plastic) and magnesium alloy
Image quality	4,368 x 2,912 pixels
Shutter speed	1/8,000s to 30s
Monitor	2½ in (6.4 cm) LCD screen
Cost	$2,500 (with lens)

Zooming in

Unlike a compact camera, you can change the lens on a professional camera to get different effects. The Canon can use lenses from 14 mm (wide-angle lenses for taking close-ups of nearby objects) to 800 mm (telephoto lenses that zoom in on distant objects like a telescope).

TAKING PICTURES

Photographs freeze a moment in time forever. By taking a photo, we can show other people things that are far away in both distance and time. For some people, photography is a serious, creative art form; for others, it's a convenient way to remember happy events. But photographs have more serious uses, too. There are limits to what our eyes can see and our brains can remember. Photographs help us overcome our limits and record the world in ways that can be crucial to our daily lives.

Nature close-ups

Stunning photography brings nature to life. Words would struggle to capture the intricate details on the face of this fly, and no artist could make it sit still long enough to sketch the myriad colors of its eyes. Macro (close-up) photographs like this reveal minute features we could never see with the naked eye.

Milestones

Camera Obscura
Around 2,500 years ago, the Chinese discovered that images could be projected through a small hole onto a surface in a darkened room. Europeans called this "camera obscura" (Latin for dark chamber). This is where the word camera comes from.

First photographs
Englishman William Henry Fox Talbot (1800–1877) helped to invent modern photography. His method involved using silver chemicals to make pictures from "negatives" (reversed versions) of what his cameras saw.

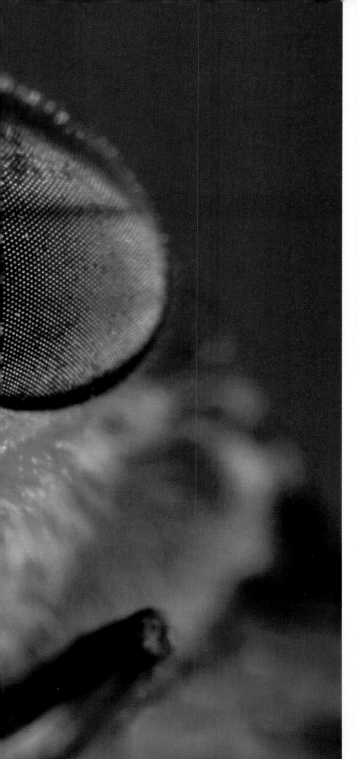

Solving crime

Photographic evidence can help the police bring criminals to justice. This forensic scientist is using a camera mounted on a tripod to photograph a footprint left at a crime scene. The flashlight in his left hand shows up the print more clearly when it's captured on film. Photographs have to be taken with great precision because they may be needed as evidence in court.

Journalism

Photographs record history as it happens. The moments just before President John F. Kennedy was assassinated in his car in November 1963 have been captured forever in photographs such as this.

Scientific research

Scientists find photographs extremely useful. Our eyes can't see what happens when atoms smash apart into smaller particles, but this photograph shows us. It was taken using a piece of apparatus called a bubble chamber. As fragments from smashed atoms move through the chamber, they leave tracks behind, a bit like the vapor trails airplanes make in the sky. Photos like this reveal the deep secrets of matter.

Film cameras
Photography was messy and time-consuming until American George Eastman (1854–1932) developed convenient plastic film. With cameras like the Brownie, his Kodak company turned photography into a popular hobby in the 1890s.

Instant cameras
Many people like to see photos as soon as they are taken. In 1947 American inventor Edwin Land (1909–1991) developed the Polaroid camera, which made instant pictures on chemically treated paper.

Photo sharing
Anyone can make instant photographs using a camera phone like this. Because the photos are made as digital files, you can email them to your family and friends or instantly upload them onto the web.

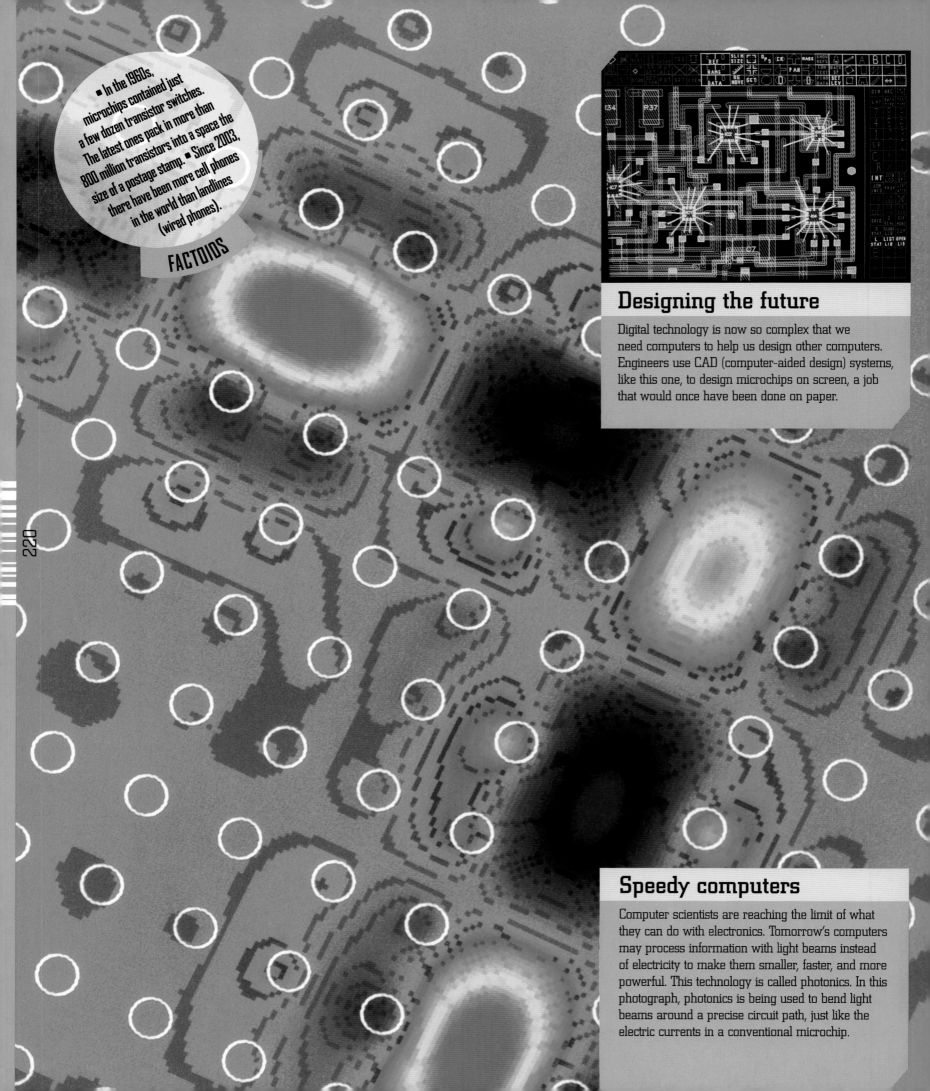

● In the 1960s, microchips contained just a few dozen transistor switches. The latest ones pack in more than 800 million transistors into a space the size of a postage stamp. ● Since 2003, there have been more cell phones in the world than landlines (wired phones).

FACTOIDS

Designing the future

Digital technology is now so complex that we need computers to help us design other computers. Engineers use CAD (computer-aided design) systems, like this one, to design microchips on screen, a job that would once have been done on paper.

Speedy computers

Computer scientists are reaching the limit of what they can do with electronics. Tomorrow's computers may process information with light beams instead of electricity to make them smaller, faster, and more powerful. This technology is called photonics. In this photograph, photonics is being used to bend light beams around a precise circuit path, just like the electric currents in a conventional microchip.

Convergence

It is easy to share digital information between different gadgets. That's why cell phones can play videos, and music players can store photographs. Soon we may not need separate phones, music players, cameras, and computers—one device will do everything. This idea is called convergence: it means our gadgets are gradually merging together.

LIVING BY NUMBERS

Gone tomorrow?

Museums have scraps of written information several thousand years old, but no one has the first email or cell phone call, even though they are just a few decades old. Information stored on web pages can seem to vanish as quickly as it appears. Organizations such as the Internet Archive maintain online libraries of web pages to ensure that they are not lost.

Sometimes it seems like the whole world is turning into numbers. Digital photographs, music tracks, Web pages, and TV programs are at their heart long strings of zeros and ones. That's because electronic gadgets ultimately store and process all these things in number form. It's much easier to handle information this way but it's risky, too, because digital information is less private, and easier to steal.

Space race

One of the best things about digital technology is that you can pack vast amounts of information into tiny volumes of space. You could fit 10,000 copies of the complete works of Shakespeare onto a single DVD, so all the books shown here would fit on just a few discs.

Prying eyes

When people shop online, the websites they visit use encryption (mathematical scrambling) to keep their personal details secure. Information sent in light beams down fiber-optic cables can now be protected using quantum encryption machines. If a criminal tries to unscramble the information locked in a light beam, the beam changes subtly, and it becomes obvious that someone has tried to break in.

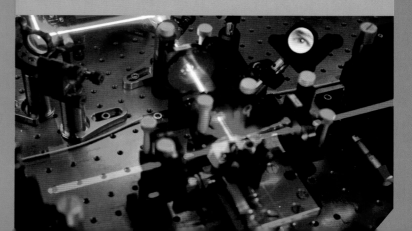

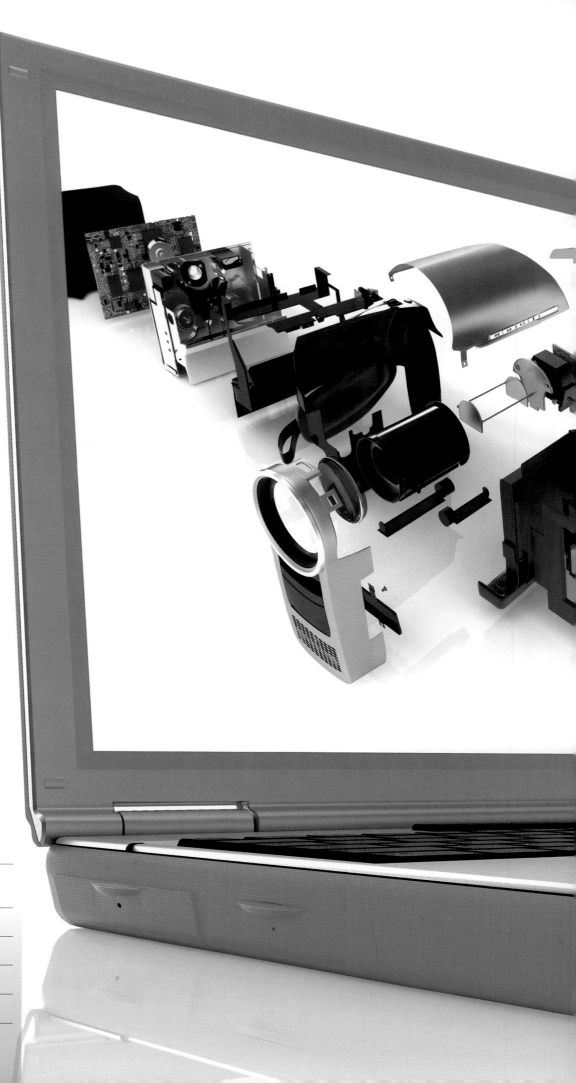

Flat pack

A laptop computer has smaller and thinner components inside than a desktop. The case is usually made of a sturdy plastic such as polycarbonate. More expensive models use strong, light metals such as titanium.

FAST FACTS

Screen	15 in (38 cm) widescreen
Memory	2GB RAM and 250GB hard drive
Processor	Dual core
Battery life	4 hours
Network	Wi-Fi wireless Internet
Weight	4½ lb (2 kg)

LAPTOP COMPUTER

In 1949, an issue of the hobby magazine *Popular Mechanics* daringly suggested: "Computers in the future may weigh no more than 1.5 tons." Back then, the idea of a laptop computer would have seemed utterly absurd. But thanks to incredible advances in miniaturized electronics, modern laptops are about 1,000 times lighter than *Popular Mechanics* predicted (weighing in at only 2–4 lb, or 1–2 kg), and compact enough to carry almost anywhere.

Class of '77

Hardly any offices or schools had computers until the mid-1980s. A few lucky ones had chunky computers such as this 1977 Commodore PET. It had a tiny keyboard and screen, and a cassette tape recorder instead of a hard drive.

LOOK INSIDE

How it works

A computer is an "information processing" machine: you feed it data (such as words or images), it works on the data, and then it displays the results. Feeding in data is input, changing data is processing, and showing the results is output. Input comes mostly from the keyboard, mouse, memory, or disk drives, processing happens in the microchips, and output is usually displayed on an LCD screen.

Tablet screens

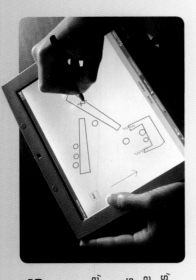

Liquid crystal display (LCD) screens became popular in the 1990s. Some are touch-sensitive, and can be used as flat drawing tablets. Screens like this work as both input and output at the same time, recognizing your penstrokes, and displaying them, too.

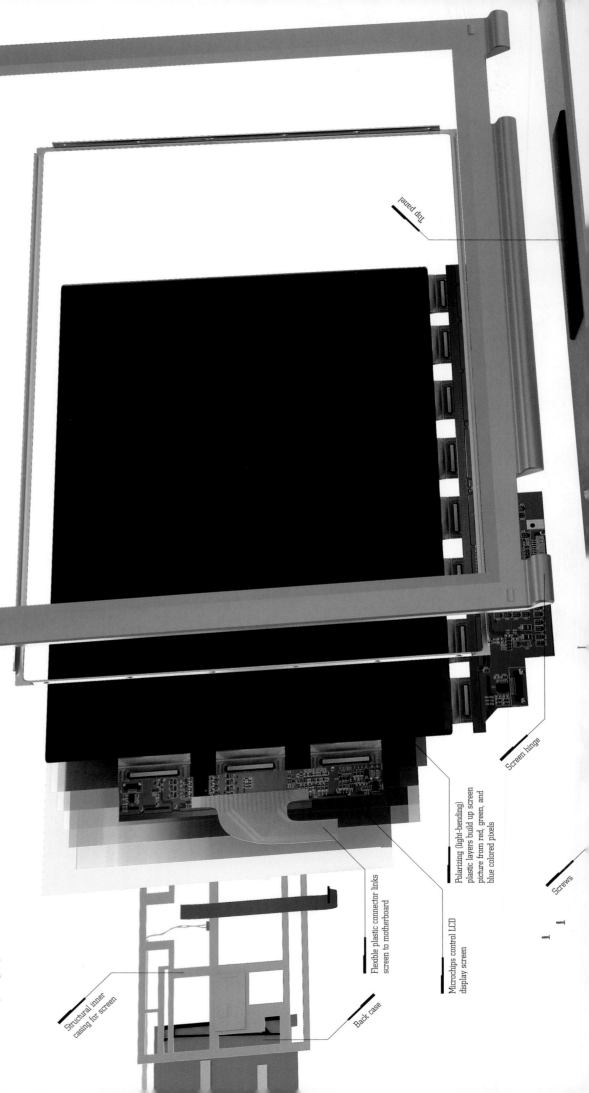

Top panel

Plastic screen surround seals screen into case

Screen hinge

Screws

Polarizing (light-bending) plastic layers build up screen picture from red, green, and blue colored pixels

Microchips control LCD display screen

Flexible plastic connector links screen to motherboard

Structural inner casing for screen

Back case

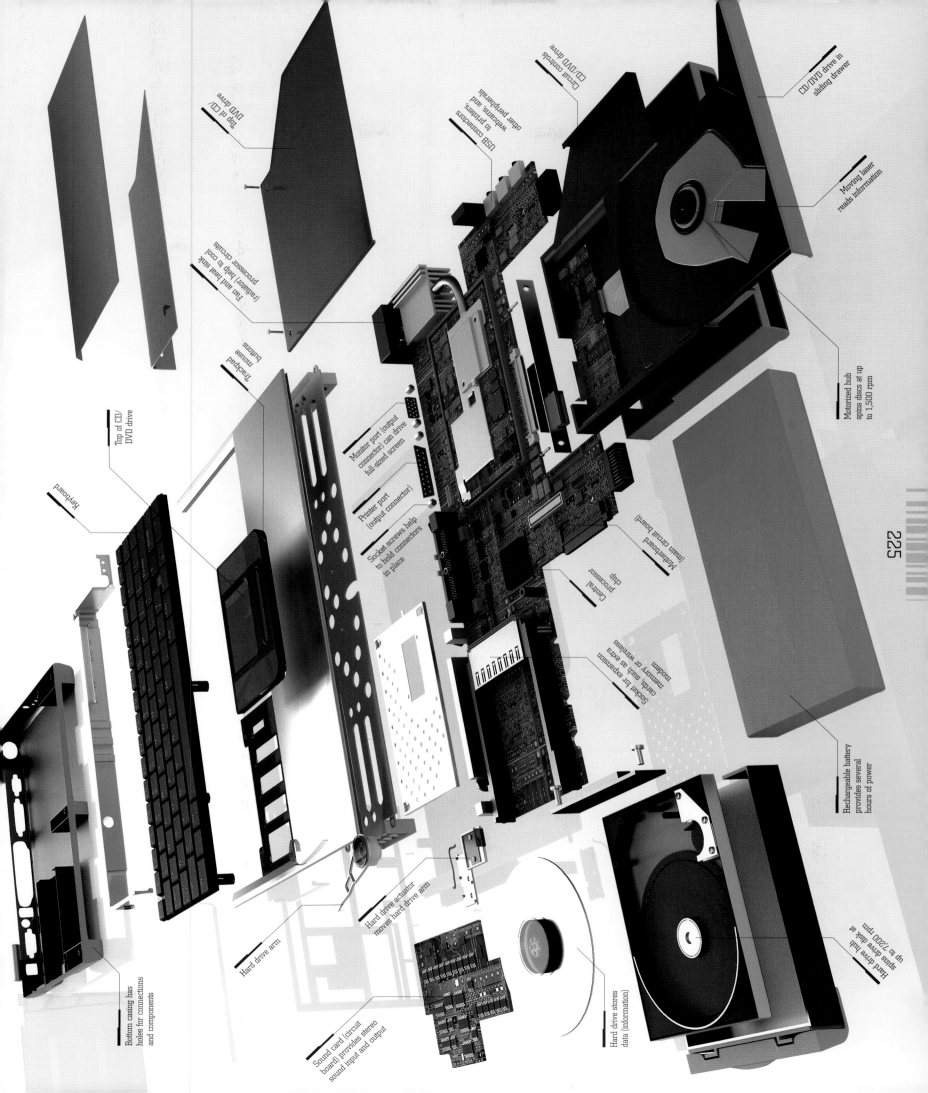

Top of CD/
DVD drive

DVD drive

Top of CD/
DVD drive

Keyboard

Trackpad
mouse
buttons

Bottom casing has
holes for connections
and components

Fan and heat sink
(radiator) help to cool
processor circuits

USB connectors
to printers,
webcams, and
other peripherals

Circuit controls
CD/DVD drive

CD/DVD drive in
sliding drawer

Moving laser
reads information

Motorized hub
spins discs at up
to 1,500 rpm

Monitor port (output
connector) can drive
full-sized screen

Printer port
(output connector)

Socket screws help
to hold connectors
in place

Motherboard
(main circuit board)

Central
processor
chip

Socket for expansion
cards, such as extra
memory or wireless
modem

Rechargeable battery
provides several
hours of power

Hard drive actuator
moves hard drive arm

Hard drive arm

Sound card (circuit
board) provides stereo
sound input and output

Hard drive stores
data (information)

Hard drive hub
spins drive disk at
up to 7,200 rpm

225

MICROCHIPS

In 1943, Thomas Watson, founder of the IBM computer company, guessed that there would be a market for "about five computers." How wrong he was. It's now estimated that there are two billion computers in the world. No one knows exactly, because many modern computers are actually microprocessors (tiny computer chips) built into mobile phones, music players, and other gadgets. Watson's prediction was wrong because he never imagined computers would develop as they have. In the 1940s, a state-of-the-art computer cost about $10 million. Today, a microprocessor works a million times faster and costs 25,000 times less.

Portable power

Laptops became practical when the parts inside computers could be made smaller and lighter. One big difficulty was making powerful batteries that were small enough to carry. Fortunately, modern batteries are much smaller than this voltaic pile, the world's first ever battery, invented in 1800 by Italian physicist Alessandro Volta (1745–1827).

Always online

People originally found computers useful because they could process information quickly. Now it's just as important that computers can access and share information over the internet. With wireless networking, you can go online almost anywhere—even up a mountain!

Remote computing

You can find computers in some unexpected places. Wrist computers give scuba divers precise information about their dives, including how long they can stay safely under water and how quickly they can resurface.

Milestones

Abacus
The abacus, a frame with beads that slide along wires, was the world's first "portable computer." Invented in its most primitive form more than 4,500 years ago, it is still used in many countries today.

Babbage engines
In the 19th century, English mathematician Charles Babbage (1791–1871) tried to build complex calculators using thousands of moving parts. He ran out of money and the machines were never completed.

Little wonder

This millipede is holding a microprocessor: a complete computer, built onto a single tiny chip of silicon, that you might find working away inside a laptop computer or MP3 music player. A modern microprocessor contains 400–800 million tiny switches called transistors. That may sound powerful, but by contrast, the human brain contains about 100 billion switching cells (neurons).

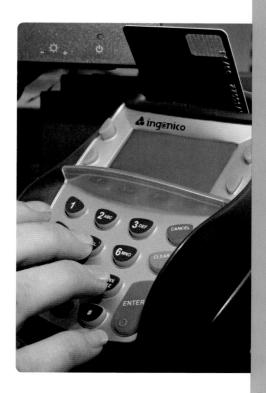
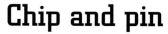

Chip and pin

Most credit cards now have built-in computers. A "chip and pin" card has a microchip in one corner that stores your security number. When you pay for something, you have to enter the same number on a keypad to prove you really own the card.

Laptop for all

These laptops cost only $100, so schools in developing countries can afford them, and are ruggedly built to survive in hot and humid places. Their screens are designed to be visible in direct sunlight, because many children in these countries have classes outdoors.

Superpowered

In May 1997, an IBM supercomputer called Deep Blue beat Russian chess champion Garry Kasparov (1963–). The newest microprocessors used in PCs (personal computers) and laptops are already several times faster than those found in Deep Blue.

IBM mainframe
IBM dominated the computer industry in the 20th century. Its revolutionary System/360 was announced in 1964 and came with 150 different peripherals (add-on devices). It was very popular with businesses because it could easily be expanded into a more powerful machine as their needs changed.

Osborne 1
Launched in 1981, the Osborne 1 was the world's first real portable computer. It had a tiny 5 in (12.5 cm) screen and weighed 26 lb (12 kg)—six times as much as a modern laptop.

BlackBerry
These popular handhelds are like cell phones crossed with computers. You can use them to send emails or messages, make phone calls, or browse the Web.

FUTURE SMART GLASSES

Our eyes are our windows on the world, but sometimes the world isn't the only thing you want to see. If you're walking in a strange place, you need to see a map. If you're expecting an urgent email, you might want to see a computer screen. In the future, smart glasses will help us with things like this. They'll also be able to zoom in and out like binoculars and even help us see at night.

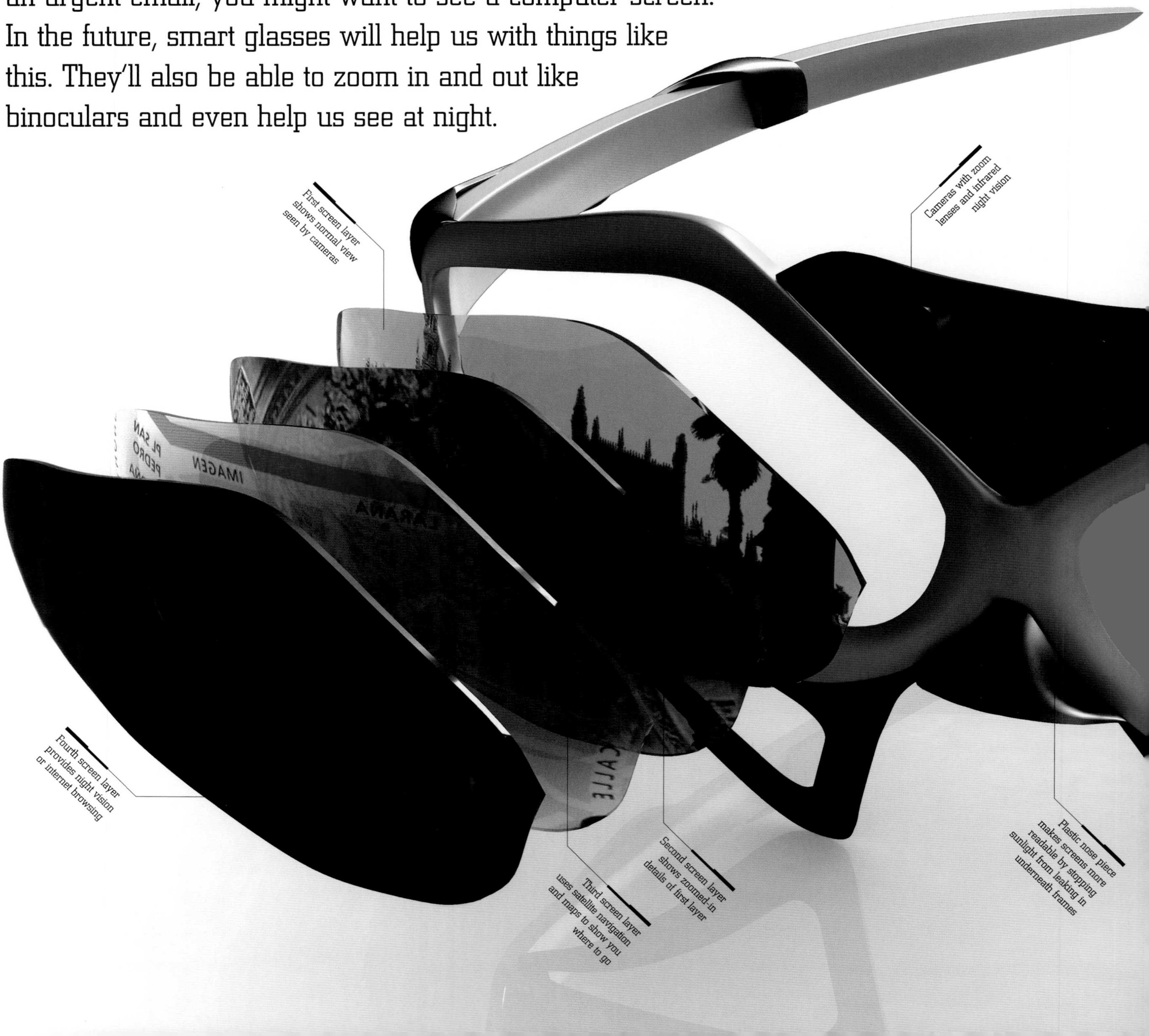

First screen layer shows normal view seen by cameras

Cameras with zoom lenses and infrared night vision

Fourth screen layer provides night vision or internet browsing

Third screen layer uses satellite navigation and maps to show you where to go

Second screen layer shows zoomed-in details of first layer

Plastic nose piece makes screens more readable by stopping sunlight from leaking in underneath frames

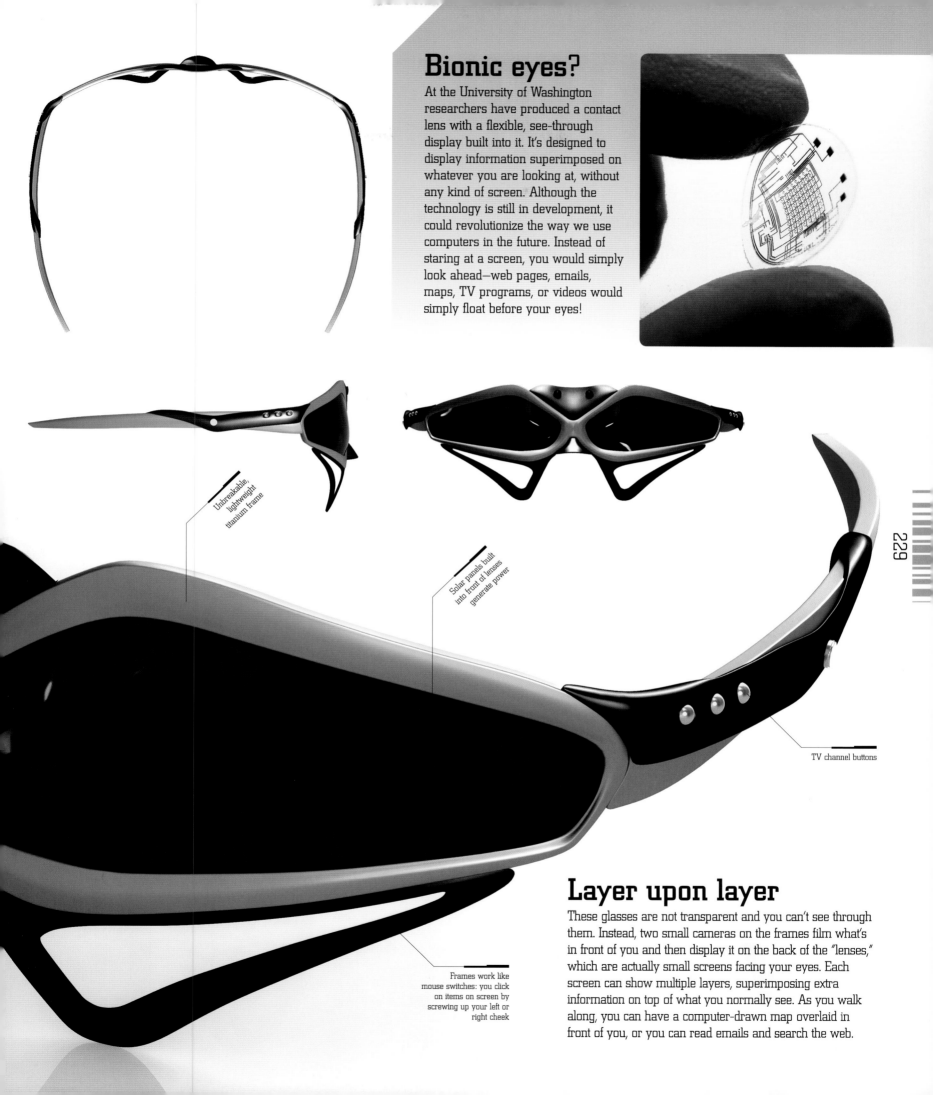

Bionic eyes?

At the University of Washington researchers have produced a contact lens with a flexible, see-through display built into it. It's designed to display information superimposed on whatever you are looking at, without any kind of screen. Although the technology is still in development, it could revolutionize the way we use computers in the future. Instead of staring at a screen, you would simply look ahead—web pages, emails, maps, TV programs, or videos would simply float before your eyes!

Unbreakable, lightweight titanium frame

Solar panels built into front of lenses generate power

TV channel buttons

Frames work like mouse switches: you click on items on screen by screwing up your left or right cheek

Layer upon layer

These glasses are not transparent and you can't see through them. Instead, two small cameras on the frames film what's in front of you and then display it on the back of the "lenses," which are actually small screens facing your eyes. Each screen can show multiple layers, superimposing extra information on top of what you normally see. As you walk along, you can have a computer-drawn map overlaid in front of you, or you can read emails and search the web.

COMPUTER MOUSE

You might think you get little exercise sitting at a desk, but if you push your computer mouse just 10 times a minute, your hand will move something like 50 miles (80 km) a year. If you click the buttons a few times a minute as well, that's about a million clicks each year on top. All this can punish the muscles in your wrist and forearm, so mice have to be well designed to reduce the risk of injury and long-term damage.

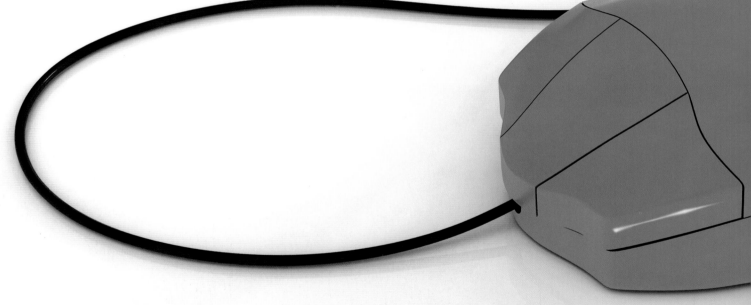

FAST FACTS

Weight	3½ oz (100 g)
Connection	USB/wireless
Dimensions	4¼ in x 2½ in x 1½ in (110 mm x 60 mm x 35 mm)

Cordless mice

Some computer mice still send signals to computers through cables, but newer ones tend to be cordless (wireless) and use invisible radio waves instead. Older computers can be converted to use newer, cordless mice with plug-in radio-transmitter sticks like the one shown here (far right).

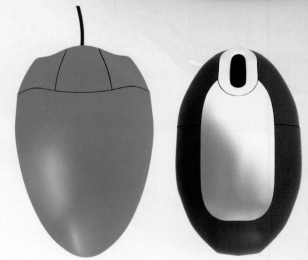

Shining down

Optical mice recognize where they are by reflecting a light off your desk. You don't need a mouse pad, and slightly rough surfaces are better than very smooth, polished ones. This is because the grooves and bumps work like tiny landmarks, helping the mouse to work out where it is.

LOOK INSIDE

Mechanical mouse

A mechanical mouse has a large rubber ball inside. As you move the mouse, the ball moves as well, turning two plastic wheels. The wheels have little spokes around their edges that interrupt a pair of light beams as they turn. The electronic circuit works out where you are moving the mouse to by counting the number of times the light beams are broken.

USB stick enables computer to receive radio-wave signals from mouse

Top case made of light, rigid ABS plastic

USB cable attaches to computer

Top case made of light, rigid ABS plastic

Optical detectors measure movements by shining infrared light through holes in tracking wheels

Small switches detect mouse button clicks

Processor chip

Processor chip with built-in light detector underneath

Scroll wheel for reading pages quickly

Scroll wheel holder

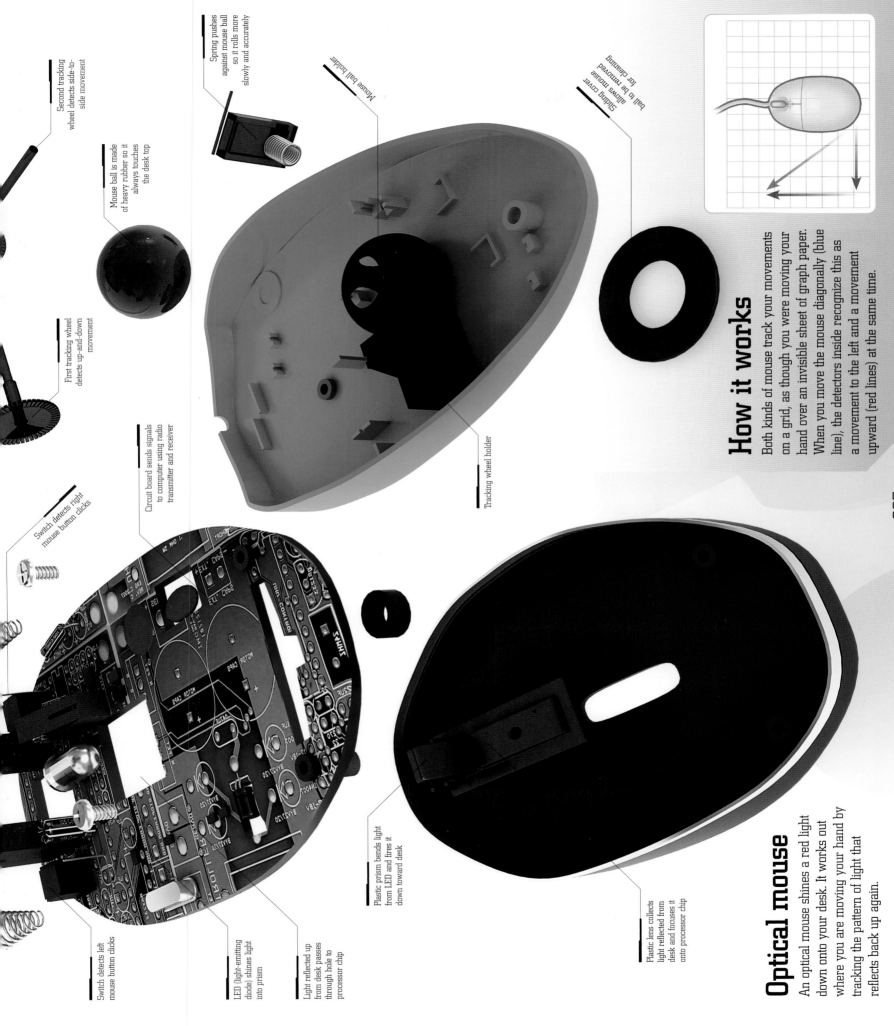

Second tracking wheel detects side-to-side movement

Spring pushes against mouse ball so it rolls more slowly and accurately

Mouse ball holder

Sliding cover allows mouse ball to be removed for cleaning

Mouse ball is made of heavy rubber so it always touches the desk top

First tracking wheel detects up-and-down movement

How it works

Both kinds of mouse track your movements on a grid, as though you were moving your hand over an invisible sheet of graph paper. When you move the mouse diagonally (blue line), the detectors inside recognize this as a movement to the left and a movement upward (red lines) at the same time.

Circuit board sends signals to computer using radio transmitter and receiver

Tracking wheel holder

Switch detects right mouse button clicks

233

Switch detects left mouse button clicks

LED (light-emitting diode) shines light into prism

Light reflected up from desk passes through hole to processor chip

Plastic prism bends light from LED and fires it down toward desk

Plastic lens collects light reflected from desk and focuses it onto processor chip

Optical mouse

An optical mouse shines a red light down onto your desk. It works out where you are moving your hand by tracking the pattern of light that reflects back up again.

VIRTUAL WORLD

Computers put the world at our fingertips. Thanks to the invention of the internet, many things we used to do in the "real world"—such as shopping, visiting a library, and making friends—we now do in the virtual world, online. Fifty years ago, the only people who used computers were mathematicians and scientists. Today, people have computers on their desks, in their homes, and even in their pockets. Tiny electronics have made computers much smaller and, crucially, devices like the mouse have made them easier to use. In the 21st century, we cannot imagine life without computers. As we reach for the mouse and become absorbed by the screen, our computers become extensions of our own minds and bodies.

234

ENIAC

Modern computers look friendly, but they used to be like this (above). Built in 1946, the enormous ENIAC (Electronic Numerical Integrator and Calculator) was 80 ft (24 m) long, weighed 33 tons (30 metric tons), and contained over 100,000 electronic parts. It was so unreliable, it never went more than five days without breaking down.

The first mouse

Modern mice are made of plastic, but the first one was built out of wood. It was invented in 1963–1964 by American computer scientist Douglas Engelbart (1925–), who called it an "X-Y position indicator." Someone thought the curly cable looked like a mouse's tail, and the name "mouse" has been used ever since.

Second life

Millions of people use their computers to live out their fantasies. On the popular *Second Life* website (right), you can create a graphical version of yourself called an avatar and move it around an imaginary world. Real-world laws don't apply: you can create anything you can imagine—you can even fly!

The Apple Lisa

Launched in 1983, the Lisa was the first mass-produced computer with a mouse and picture-based screen. It was a flop, because it cost $9,995—several times more than its rivals. But it led to the hugely popular Apple Macintosh, launched a year later.

Ergonomic mouse

Using a mouse or keyboard for too long can cause a painful condition called repetitive strain injury (RSI). This mouse has a ball on the side to minimize wrist movements and reduce the risk of RSI. Designing products people can use more easily is called ergonomics.

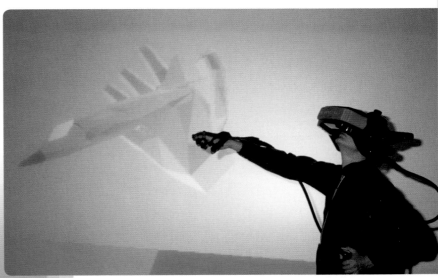

Virtual reality

Virtual reality takes the mouse a step further. You wear a wraparound headset and sensor gloves. As you move, the computer detects what you do and changes the picture you see, so you feel yourself floating through its imaginary world.

Humans obsolete?

From forecasting climate change to curing disease, computers are our partners in solving humanity's biggest problems. In the future, computers will become even more "intelligent" and helpful. There will never be a time when we don't need computers—but could there come a time when computers don't need us?

Precision printing

If you enjoy painting, you'll know you need a fine brush to do detailed work. Imagine the precision of using a paintbrush with a single hair and you'll have some idea of how detailed an inkjet printer can make its pictures. Canon's PIXMA can print 4,800 dots across and 1,200 dots down in an area slightly bigger than a postage stamp. Our eyes can't see dots that small, so pictures printed with this resolution (amount of detail) look as clear as photographs.

FAST FACTS

Dimensions	17¼ in x 5¾ in x 11¾ in (43.7 cm x 14.7 cm x 30 cm)
Number of ink nozzles	1,600
Speed	25 pages per minute (ppm) for black and white or 10.8 ppm for colour
Ink	Separate tanks for black, cyan, magenta, and yellow
Cost	$60

INKJET PRINTER

Printing is one of the most important technologies of all time, but machines that can print on paper are quite a recent invention. Before the 15th century everything had to be copied out by hand, mostly by educated monks and nuns who took two to three hours to write a single page. Compare that to today's inkjet printers, which can run off a page in just 2.4 seconds—about 3,000 times faster!

Personal print store

High-quality printing takes longer because more ink needs to be sprayed on the page. The printer also has to move the paper more slowly so that it has time to dry. The type of paper makes a big difference. Ordinary office paper soaks up ink like tissue. Photo-quality paper is coated with plastics or clays that stop the ink from soaking in and spreading, which makes the printing more precise.

How it works

Inside the printer, the print head glides repeatedly from side to side, squirting ink onto a sheet of paper that moves from the hopper at the back to the tray at the front. By combining different amounts of four separate inks (black plus the three colors cyan, magenta, and yellow), the printer can make any color. The print head's 1,600 nozzles allow it to print at near-photographic quality.

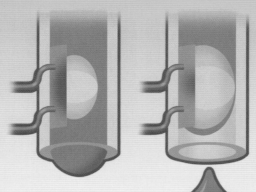

Ink drops
As the bubble grows, it squirts an ink drop out onto the paper. More ink is sucked in from the tank on top.

Heating up
Electricity flows through a heating element on the side of the ink reservoir.

Bubble forms
The heat vaporizes some of the ink and makes a bubble form in the reservoir.

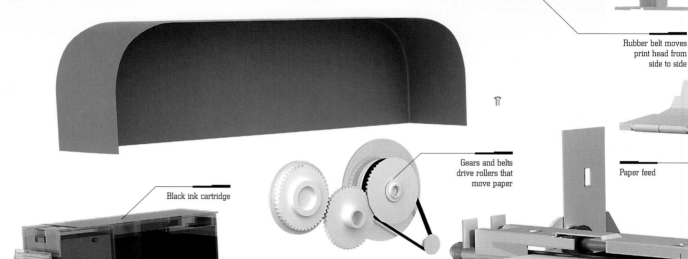

Rubber belt moves print head from side to side

Gears and belts drive rollers that move paper

Paper feed

Black ink cartridge

Cyan, magenta, and yellow ink cartridges

Rollers and spiked wheels pull paper forward through printer

Print head squirts ink from cartridges down onto page

Plastic base

Front folds out to make a tray for newly printed sheets

Left side case

Servo motor moves gears, belts, and paper rollers

LOOK INSIDE

LTR   B5

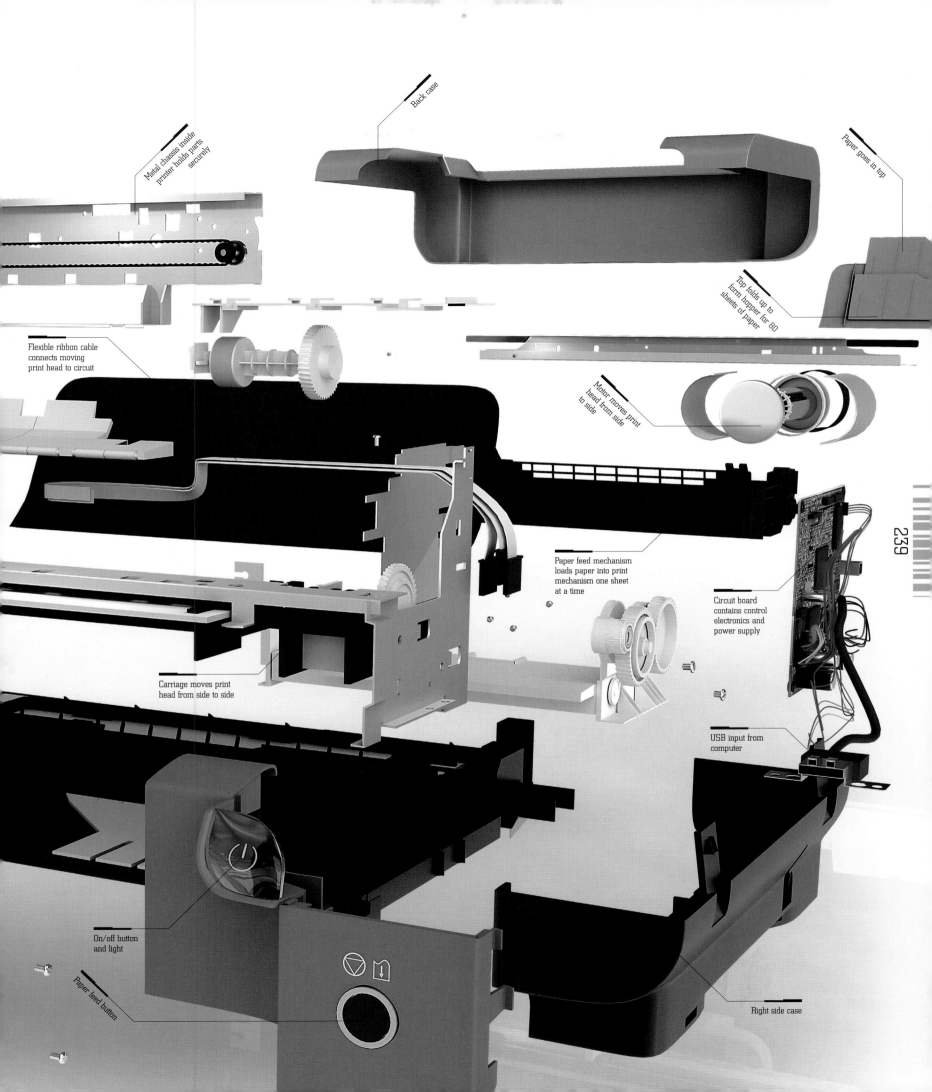

Metal chassis inside printer holds parts securely

Back case

Paper goes in top

Flexible ribbon cable connects moving print head to circuit

Top folds up to form hopper for 80 sheets of paper

Motor moves print head from side to side

239

Paper feed mechanism loads paper into print mechanism one sheet at a time

Circuit board contains control electronics and power supply

Carriage moves print head from side to side

USB input from computer

On/off button and light

Paper feed button

Right side case

Paper maker

Paper was developed in 105 CE by Ts'ai Lun, who worked for the Emperor of China. Made from hemp fiber, it was smoother and easier to write on than previous writing materials such as papyrus. From China, paper technology spread to Korea, Japan, and the rest of the world.

Type cast

Gutenberg didn't invent printing, but he greatly improved it. He developed thick, sticky ink, a new printing table based on a wine press, and metal type (blocks with raised letters on them that could be rearranged to print any page).

PRINTEDPAGES

The printed book you're reading now would have seemed like something from another world 550 years ago, when a German named Johannes Gutenberg (c. 1400–1468) invented the modern printing process. Few books existed, hardly anyone could read, and there was no easy way to spread ideas. Printing changed all this. It became possible to copy books in huge numbers, which allowed civilization to advance more rapidly. Much of the information we share these days is in electronic form, in emails or on web pages. But we still talk about "type" and "printing"—ideas that survive from Gutenberg's time.

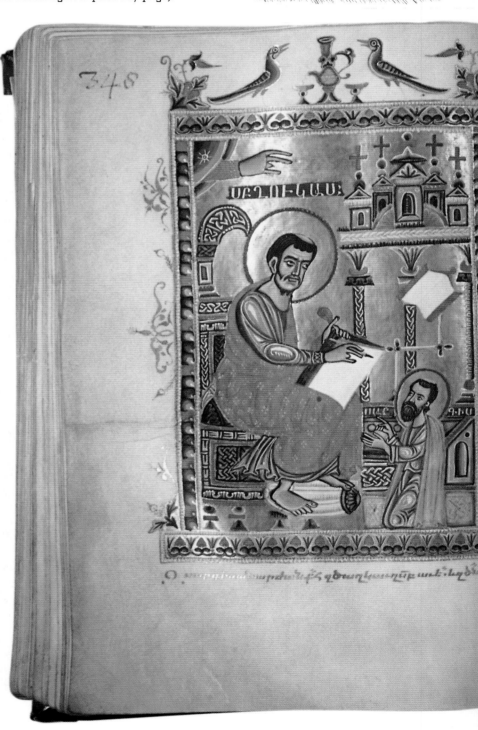

Illuminated manuscripts

This is what books looked liked before Gutenberg developed the printing press. Each page is a work of art, laboriously handpainted and lettered with gold. Books like this were called illuminated manuscripts. This one is part of a collection of 200,000 priceless volumes kept at the monastery of San Lazzaro degli Armeni in Venice, Italy.

Making news

Newspapers were invented in ancient Rome. Since the Romans had no printers, news was written on sheets that were then pinned up on walls. Printed newspapers first appeared in the 17th century. Modern newspapers and magazines are printed with rotary presses (high-speed spinning drums), such as this one (left), controlled by computers.

Carlson's copier

Chester Carlson (1906–1968) was determined to make his fortune from a great invention. But when he first showed big companies his idea for an "electrophotography" machine, none of them showed any interest. Later renamed the xerography machine (photocopier), it became the most important printing invention since the Gutenberg press.

Printing without paper?

Many of us now read books and newspapers online, but the words and pictures are still typically arranged like a printed page. Our eyes find it easy to scan and digest information laid out in this convenient way.

FUTURE 3-D PRINTER

Wouldn't it be good if you could make a copy of any object? Future printers will be able to make 3-D copies by building up billions of atoms. Three atomic blasters will fire the atoms, making a perfect copy in less than five minutes. Instead of expensive ink, the machine will use nothing but tap water—it will simply extract hydrogen and oxygen atoms from the water and transform them into any other atoms it needs.

3-D today

3-D printers already exist. The one shown here (below) makes 3-D models from detailed designs drawn on a computer. The machine builds models from the bottom up by printing one thin layer of powder or resin on top of another—a little like building a house up from layers of bricks. The whole process takes about four hours.

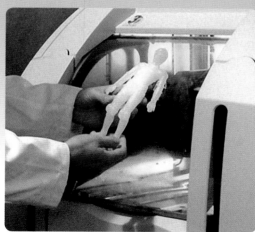

Vacuum compartment is sealed during copying to keep air and dirt from contaminating the process

Third atom blaster

Water tank and atom creation unit

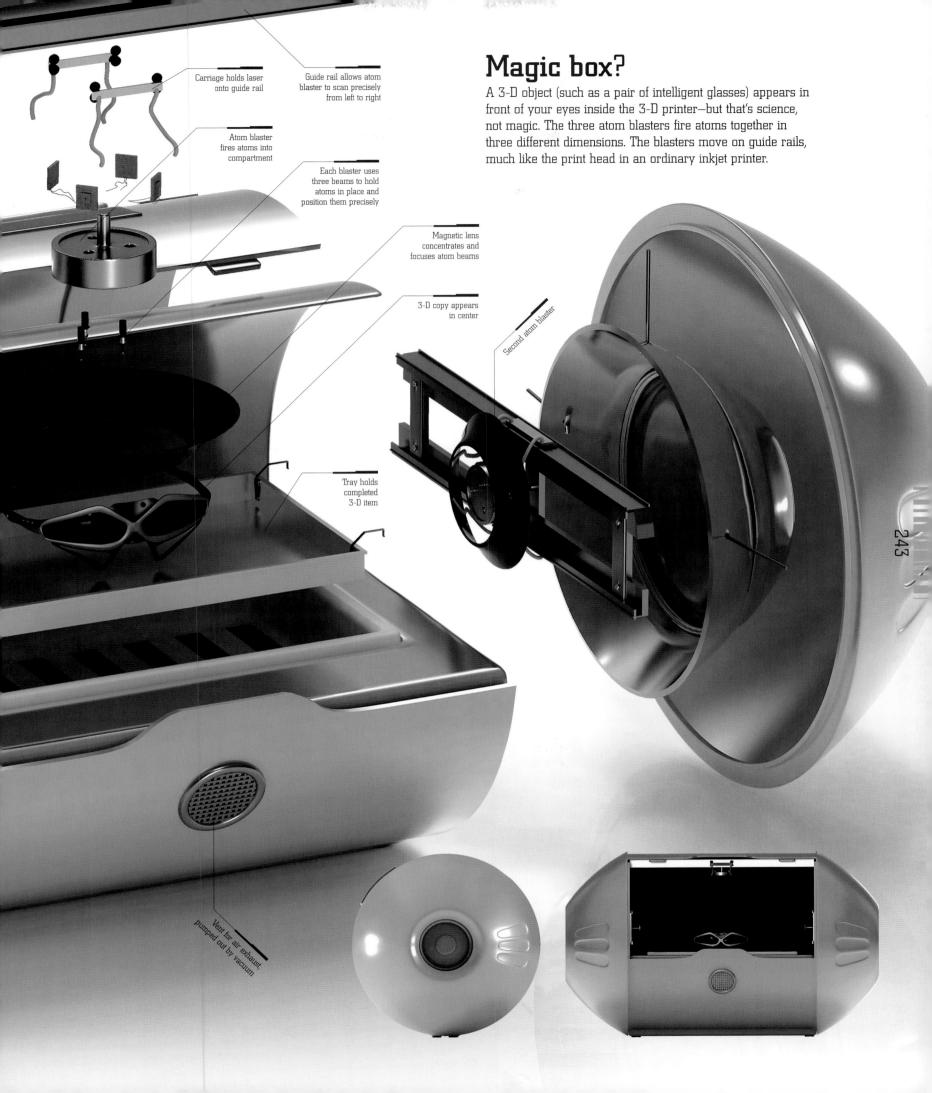

Magic box?

A 3-D object (such as a pair of intelligent glasses) appears in front of your eyes inside the 3-D printer—but that's science, not magic. The three atom blasters fire atoms together in three different dimensions. The blasters move on guide rails, much like the print head in an ordinary inkjet printer.

Carriage holds laser onto guide rail

Guide rail allows atom blaster to scan precisely from left to right

Atom blaster fires atoms into compartment

Each blaster uses three beams to hold atoms in place and position them precisely

Magnetic lens concentrates and focuses atom beams

3-D copy appears in center

Second atom blaster

Tray holds completed 3-D item

Vent for air exhaust pumped out by vacuum

243

GLOSSARY

A

AC
Alternating current. A type of electric current that reverses direction every so often in a circuit.

acoustic
A type of guitar that makes sound from a hollow wooden body, without electric amplification.

additive
A chemical added to a material to change its properties.

aerodynamic
The curved or angled shape something has to make it move more smoothly through the air.

aerofoil
The shape of an airplane wing, with a curved upper surface and a straight lower surface. An aerofoil is designed to produce an upward force called lift as air flows over it.

air intake
An opening in a vehicle that allows oxygen to enter the engine to help burn fuel.

air pressure
The force that acts on things in the world around us, caused by invisible air molecules crashing into them.

air resistance
The force that slows down a moving vehicle caused by air flowing around it.

alloy
A metal mixed with smaller amounts of other metals (or sometimes nonmetals) to make it stronger, harder, or improve it in some other way.

aluminum
A strong and lightweight metal widely used to make airplane and spacecraft parts.

amplifier
A device that increases size or strength. The amplifier in an electric guitar makes sound louder. A transistor amplifier in a radio makes weak incoming radio signals stronger.

analog
A way of representing an amount of something without using numbers—for example, with a pointer on a dial. An analog watch has hands, while an analog speedometer shows a car's speed with a moving pointer. See also digital.

appliance
A piece of electrical equipment used to perform jobs around the home, such as a washing machine, iron, or drill.

atom
The smallest amount of a chemical element that can exist.

avatar
A cartoonlike character that people use to represent themselves in computer games and internet chat rooms.

axle
The strong rod on a moving vehicle around which the wheels turn.

B

bacteria
A single-celled microorganism. Some bacteria can be harmful because they carry disease; others can be helpful, such as those that aid digestion in our bodies.

battery
A portable power supply that generates electricity when chemical reactions happen inside it.

binary
A code for representing information using only the numbers zero and one. Binary code is used in computers and other forms of electronic equipment.

Bluetooth
A way of linking together electronic equipment over short distances without using wires. Many cell phones use Bluetooth to connect to wireless headsets and personal computers.

bogie
A small truck carrying a set of wheels underneath a train or plane.

bulkhead
A strong partition separating one internal part of a vehicle (such as a ship or rocket) from another.

C

capacitor
A component in a circuit that stores electrical charge.

carbon dioxide
An invisible gas produced when things made of carbon burn in the oxygen that air contains. When carbon dioxide collects in the atmosphere, it contributes to the problems of global warming and climate change.

catalytic converter
A device that fits inside a car's exhaust and uses chemical reactions to turn pollution into harmless gases.

CCD
Charge-coupled device. A rectangular grid of light detectors used to generate a digital picture in a digital camera.

CD
Compact disc. A thin plastic disc, coated with reflective metal, used to store music or other information in digital form.

ceramic
A nonmetallic solid material, typically made from clay or porcelain. Ceramics can withstand high temperatures so they are widely used in situations where other materials might melt.

circuit
The closed path around which electricity flows.

circuit board
A flat piece of plastic covered with metal tracks that connect electrical components into a circuit.

climate change
The gradual transformation of Earth's weather that is being caused by global warming.

combustion
The chemical reaction in which a fuel burns with oxygen, usually from the air, to release energy. Carbon dioxide, water, and pollution gases are made as by-products.

component
A small electronic part on a circuit board. Diodes, transistors, and capacitors are examples of electronic components.

composite
A material made by combining two or more others to produce an entirely new material with better properties.

computer
An electronic device that stores and processes information by following a series of instructions called a program.

crank
The handle on a machine such as a generator.

current
The flow of electricity through a material. Compare AC (alternating current) and DC (direct current).

cylinder
A strong metal can in a car engine where fuel is burned to produce energy. Power is produced when pistons move up and down inside the car's cylinders.

D data
The information that computers (and other types of digital technology) store, process, and share.

DC
Direct current. A type of electric current that always moves in the same direction around a circuit.

derailleur
A part of a bicycle gear that keeps the chain taut as it moves between sprockets (gear wheels) of different sizes.

detergent
A soaplike substance that makes washing more effective. A detergent breaks up and removes dirt and grease with the help of water.

diesel engine
A type of internal combustion engine that makes power by compressing fuel much more than an ordinary gasoline engine.

digital
A way of representing information using only numbers. A digital watch represents the time using only a series of numbers. See also analog.

diode
A component in a circuit that allows electricity to flow in one direction only. A diode is also called a rectifier.

disk brake
A brake that stops a vehicle by pressing rubber pads against a disk of metal positioned just inside the main wheel and tire.

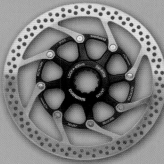

download
The process of copying files from the internet onto your own computer.

drag
The force of air resistance that slows down moving objects.

DVD
Digital video/versatile disc. A thin plastic disc, coated with reflective metal, used to store information in digital form. A DVD is similar to a CD but can store around seven times more information.

E efficiency
The amount of energy that a machine uses effectively. If a machine is 60 percent efficient, it uses 60 percent of the energy supplied to do useful work and wastes the other 40 percent.

electrical
A process that uses electricity to produce energy.

electricity
A flow of energy caused by electrons moving in a circuit.

electromagnetism
A combination of electricity and magnetism. An electric motor is electromagnetic because it uses both electricity and magnetism to make something move.

electron
A tiny particle inside an atom that carries a small negative electrical charge.

electronic
A type of appliance in which large electric currents are controlled precisely by smaller, more precise ones.

electron microscope
A type of microscope that makes much more detailed images than a conventional one by using beams of electrons instead of beams of light.

element
A chemical substance that cannot be broken down into anything simpler using only chemical reactions.

emission
A gas produced during a chemical reaction. Carbon dioxide emissions made by engines are one cause of global warming.

encryption
A way of making information secure by scrambling it using a mathematical process. For example, websites use encryption to protect people's credit card information when they shop online.

245

energy
A source of power or an ability to do something (such as climb stairs or move an object). In science, when something has energy it can work against a force.

engine
A machine that produces energy by burning fuel, such as a rocket or internal combustion engine.

exhaust
A pipe used to remove waste gases from an engine.

F **fiber optics**
A way of sending digital information down flexible glass or plastic pipes (known as fiber-optic cables) using precisely controlled beams of light.

force
A pushing or pulling action that alters the way an object moves or changes its shape.

four-wheel drive
A type of vehicle in which the engine powers all four wheels.

friction
The rubbing force between two objects that are in contact.

fuel
A carbon-rich substance, such as oil or coal, that releases energy when it burns in oxygen from the air.

fuel cell
A device similar to a battery that produces electrical energy from a chemical reaction, usually involving the gases hydrogen and oxygen. Unlike a battery, a fuel cell is supplied by a tank and keeps running as long as it has fuel.

fuselage
The main body of an airplane, not including the wings, containing the passenger seats and cargo hold.

G **gasket**
A seal that stops water from escaping from a joint between two parts inside a machine.

gear
A pair of wheels with teeth that mesh together. Gears can be used to change the power, speed, or direction of movement inside a machine.

generator
A machine that uses magnets and tightly wrapped coils of metal to turn movement into electricity. The generator in a wind turbine converts the movement of the turbine's rotor blades into electric power. See also motor.

global warming
The gradual increase in Earth's surface temperature caused by (among other things) a buildup of the gas carbon dioxide in the atmosphere. Global warming is causing Earth's climate to change.

gravity
The pulling force (force of attraction) between any two objects (masses) in the universe. On Earth, we experience gravity as a strong pulling force toward the center of the planet.

H **hard drive**
A magnetic disk, rotating at high speed, that stores data inside a computer even when the power is switched off.

hardware
The various electrical, electronic, and mechanical components that make up a computer system. See also software.

hub
The strong, central part of a wheel.

hydraulic
A mechanical system of fluid-filled pipes in a machine such as a digger or crane. Hydraulics help to increase the pushing, pulling, or lifting force a machine can exert. See also pneumatic.

hydrogen
A gas made from simple atoms that is lighter than air and can be used as a fuel.

I **immersive**
A type of virtual reality computer system in which all the things people can see, hear, and touch are created by a computer. In immersive virtual reality, people feel they are entirely within a computer-generated world.

infrared
A type of electromagnetic radiation produced by hot objects. Infrared radiation is similar to light, but the waves that carry it are longer.

input
The process of getting information into a computer. Typing things into a computer using a keyboard is a form of input.

internal combustion engine
A machine that produces heat energy by burning fuel with oxygen inside closed metal containers called cylinders.

internet
A global network of computers that are informally connected by telephone and other telecommunications links.

K

Kevlar
A very strong fabric made from tightly woven carbon fibers. Kevlar is used to make bulletproof vests and other protective materials.

kinetic energy
The energy something has because it is moving.

L

landline
An ordinary telephone line, connected directly to the main phone network. Unlike a cell phone, a landline cannot roam from place to place.

laser
A powerful and precise beam of light in which the waves all travel in step.

LCD
Liquid crystal display. A display on a piece of electronic equipment in which the numbers and other characters are produced by passing electric currents through crystals.

loudspeaker
A device that turns electricity into sound using a magnet and coil of wire to push a paper cone back and forth.

M

machine
A device usually powered by electricity or fuel that uses wheels, levers, gears, and other moving parts to do a job.

mechanical
A process carried out by a machine with moving parts.

memory
An electronic device that can store information.

microchip
An informal name for a microprocessor.

microprocessor
A computer built into a tiny piece of silicon about the size of a fingernail.

microwave
A type of electromagnetic radiation produced by a device called a magnetron and used in microwave ovens, radar, and telecommunications. Microwaves are similar to light, but invisible, and the waves that carry them are much longer.

mineral
A useful, nonliving solid substance mined from the ground. Coal, sand, and gold are examples of minerals.

molecule
The smallest amount of a chemical compound that can exist. A molecule consists of two or more atoms joined together.

motherboard
The main electronic circuit board in a computer or electronic device.

motor
A machine that uses magnets and tightly wrapped coils of metal to turn electricity into movement. See also generator.

MP3
Moving Picture Experts Group (MPEG) Audio Layer 3. A type of computer file that stores music in a very compressed (squeezed) form. This makes it easy to store the file in a smaller space or send it more quickly over the internet.

N

nacelle
The housing (outer case) of a machine, such as a jet engine or wind turbine, that contains the main components.

nanotechnology
A technology through which people are attempting to create useful new materials by manipulating individual atoms and molecules.

NASA
National Aeronautics and Space Administration. An American government agency that conducts space research and runs missions into space (such as the Apollo Moon landings and the Space Shuttle missions).

O

optical
A device that carries or detects light, such as a camera or camcorder lens.

P

parallel processing
A way of designing a computer so it solves a problem more quickly by working on more than one piece of it at once.

piston
A tight-fitting metal plunger that moves up and down inside the cylinder in an engine to convert heat energy into movement (mechanical energy).

pixel
A small colored square that makes up part of the picture in a digital camera image or a computer or television screen. A typical digital photograph is made up of millions of pixels.

plastic
A material usually made from petroleum-based chemicals that is flexible when first created and easy to mold into different shapes.

pneumatic
A machine powered by compressed air flowing through pipes, such as a pneumatic road drill. See also hydraulic.

polarized
A type of light that has been passed through a filter so its waves move in only one direction.

pollution
A waste substance that is harmful to people or the environment.

polycarbonate
A tough, durable, and virtually shatterproof form of plastic.

port
The left side of a ship or airplane.

pressure
The force acting on a certain area of an object's surface. If the same force acts over half the area, it produces twice as much pressure.

processor
The central "brain" inside a computer where most information processing happens. The processor is usually built onto a single microchip.

pump

A mechanical device that moves a liquid or gas from one place to another. A pump typically has a piston that moves back and forth (as in a bicycle pump) or a rotating mechanism called an impeller (as in a dishwasher).

R radar

A device that uses beams of invisible microwaves to detect approaching ships, airplanes, or other objects. Radar stands for radio detection and ranging.

radiation

A type of energy given off by a physical process. Hot objects give off invisible waves of heat, which consist of infrared radiation.

radiator

A device that gives off heat to the air around it when a hot liquid or gas flows through it. The radiators in homes give off heat when hot water flows through them. The radiator in a car cools the engine by giving off waste heat.

radio

A way of sending sound or other information between two places using beams of radio waves instead of wires.

receiver

An electrical device that picks up radio waves sent through the air by a transmitter.

rechargeable

A type of battery that can be recharged with energy hundreds of times by connecting it to an electrical power supply. An ordinary disposable battery cannot normally be recharged.

renewable energy

A type of energy, such as wind or solar power, that is made without burning fossil fuels such as coal, gas, or oil.

retina

The light-sensitive surface inside the human eyeball.

rotor

A moving blade, shaped like an aerofoil, used in an aircraft, wind turbine, or similar device.

S satellite

An object, such as a spacecraft, that moves in orbit around a planet. The Moon is a natural satellite of Earth.

sensor

A mechanical, electrical, or electronic device on a machine designed to respond to a change in the environment around it.

servo motor

An electric motor that can be rotated in small steps so it moves something (like a robot arm) with high precision. A servo motor is also known as a stepper motor.

shim

A thin layer of material that separates different parts.

shock absorber

A hydraulic component on a vehicle's suspension that uses a fluid-filled piston to absorb energy and smooth out bumps in the road.

software

The programs stored in a computer that control how it operates. See also hardware.

solar power

A type of energy made from the Sun's light or heat. Solar power can be used to heat something or to make electricity.

spoiler

A curved wing at the front or back of a car designed to deflect airflow and improve the car's handling or performance.

sprocket

A gear wheel.

starboard

The right side of a ship or airplane.

streamlining

A way of designing vehicles so that air moves over them more easily. By reducing drag, streamlining helps to increase speed and reduce fuel consumption.

supercomputer

An extremely powerful computer typically used to solve difficult scientific problems such as weather forecasting.

suspension

The mechanical system underneath a car that uses hydraulics and springs to cushion passengers from bumps in the road.

T Teflon

An extremely slippery material used as a protective material in spacesuits and as a coating in nonstick frying pans.

thermogram

A photograph showing patterns of heat given off

by objects. A conventional photograph shows the light that objects reflect, whereas a thermogram shows the infrared energy they give off.

transformer
An electrical device that increases or decreases the voltage of an electrical supply.

transistor
A small component that can work as an amplifier (current booster) or switch in an electronic circuit.

transmitter
An electrical device that produces radio waves and beams them through the air. See also receiver.

turbine
A machine similar to a windmill that spins around in a moving gas or liquid, capturing some of its energy. A wind turbine captures the energy from the moving airstream we call wind.

turbocharger
A device attached to the exhaust of a car or airplane that boosts the power created by the engine.

type
Pieces of metal or plastic used to print letters, numbers, or other characters in a printing press.

U **ultrasonic**
A sound with a frequency (pitch) too high for humans to hear.

ultraviolet
A type of invisible electromagnetic radiation similar to light, but the waves that carry it are shorter and carry more energy. Sunlight contains harmful ultraviolet light that we block out with suncreams and sunglasses.

upload
The process of copying files from your computer to the internet.

USB
Universal serial bus. A standardized connection on a computer that can be used to attach and power printers, webcams, disk drives, and other devices (known as peripherals).

V **velocity**
The speed at which an object moves in a particular direction.

video
A way of permanently recording pictures filmed with a camera onto a tape or disc.

virtual reality
A computer-generated model of a real or imaginary world inside which a person can move around.

voltage
The amount of electrical force produced by something like a battery.

W **watt**
The amount of energy that something uses or produces in one second.

wave
A back-and-forth or up-and-down movement that carries energy from one place to another.

webcam
A small digital camera, usually connected to a computer with a USB lead, that sends pictures live (in real time) over the Internet.

Wi-Fi
Wireless Fidelity. A way of connecting computer systems together without wires over medium ranges (typically up to 300 ft or about 100 m).

wireless
A way of sending information or connecting electronic devices by using radio waves instead of cables.

INDEX

A

abacus 226
acid rain 79
acoustic guitar 168, 172, 173
advanced passenger train (APT) 30
aerodynamics 73
aerofoils 17, 42, 49
aerospace:
    research 58–59
    space plane 52–53
air ambulance 45
Airbus:
    A380 14, 46–49
    Beluga Super Transporter 51
aircraft 30, 31, 39, 46–51
    Airbus A380 14, 46–49
    space plane 52–53
air pollution 74, 78–79
airports 51
air travel 50–51, 151
amplifier 142, 170
animals 142, 160
antenna 135, 196
Apple Lisa computer 235
Ariane 5 rocket 14, 60–65, 67
Asia 156
ASIMO robot 179
assembly line 21
Atlantic Ocean 31, 50, 51
atmosphere 113
atomic blaster 242–243
atomic clock 150
atoms 191, 219, 242–243
autogyro 45
automata 178
automatic watch 148
avatar 234

B

Babbage, Charles 226
Bach, Johann Sebastian 167
backhoe loader 14, 32–35

bacteria 98
Bagger 288 excavator 37
batteries 134, 136, 156, 196
    rechargeable 123, 136, 137, 200
    voltaic pile 226
Bedouins 119
Benz, Karl 20
Berners-Lee, Tim 205
Big Bang 112
bikes 68–73, 182
    hover bike 80–81
    motorcycle 74–77
    mountain bike 68–71
biological detergent 103
birds 80, 91, 126
BlackBerry 227
blind people 205
Bluetooth 203
Blu-ray 152
Boeing 747 "jumbo jet" 51
bogies, train, 29
Bolivia 136
books 204, 221, 240
Braille 205
brain 155, 161, 197, 227
brakes, disk 68, 71
Braun, Werner von 67
Breitling watch 144–149, 151
British Library 205
bronchitis 78, 79
bubble chamber 219
bucket excavator 37
Bugatti Veyron car 21
Bullet train 31

C

CAD (computer-aided design) 220
caffeine 119
Cage, John 167
camcorder 206–209
camera 202, 218–219
    cell phone 219
    digital 212–217
    instant 219

    security 211
    smart glasses 229
    webcam 211
camera obscura 218
cancer 113, 205
Canon:
    EOS-5D digital camera 212–217
    PIXMA inkjet printer 236–239
capacitor 135
carbon dioxide gas 20, 31, 38
carbon composites 69, 73
cargo planes 49, 51
Carlson, Chester 241
carriages, tilting 24, 26–28
cars 20–21, 30, 39, 74
    intelligent 22–23
    rally 14, 16–19
catalytic converter 74
caterpillar tracks 33
CCD (charge-coupled device) 208, 216
cell phone 137, 192–197, 220
    camera 219
    games 156
cell processor 152, 155
cesium 150
Channel Tunnel 126
chariot 20
chemicals 104
chess computer 227
child labor 36
China 21, 66, 72, 156, 240
Chinook helicopter 45
chip and pin cards 227
chronometer 151
Cierva, Juan de la 44
cinema 210
    see also films
circuit board 194
cities 38, 72, 78, 85
clocks 150–151
clockwork 133
coal 37, 78, 87
COBE (Cosmic Background Explorer) 112
Cochrane, Josephine 98
coffee 118–119
coffee makers 114–117

ACKNOWLEDGMENTS

The publisher would like to thank the following:

Chris Bernstein for indexing; Kieran Macdonald for proofreading; Johnny Pau and Rebecca Wright for additional design; Claire Bowers and Rose Horridge in the DK Picture Library; Rachael Hender, Jason Harding, Rob Quantrell, and Stanislav Shcherbakov at Nikid Design Ltd; Chris Heal, FBHI; Nicola Woodcock.

The publisher would also like to thank the following manufacturers for their kind cooperation and help in producing the computer-generated artworks of their products:

Pendolino Train – Alstom Transport
Ariane 5 – ESA/CNES/ARIANESPACE
ENV Fuel Cell Bike – Seymourpowell/Intelligent Energy
Vestas Wind Turbine – Vestas
Freeplay Radio – Freeplay Energy PLC
KEF Muon speakers – KEF and Uni-Q are registered trademarks. Uni-Q is protected under GB patent 2 236929, U.S. patent No. 5,548,657 and other worldwide patents. ACE technology is protected under GB patent 2146871. U.S. patent No.4657108 and other worldwide patents.
Breitling Watch – Breitling
Steinway Piano – courtesy of Steinway & Sons
Gibson Electric Guitar – Gibson Guitar, part of the Gibson Guitar Corporation which is Trademarked - www.gibson.com
Lego Robot – MINDSTORMS is a trademark of the LEGO Group
London Eye – conceived and designed by Marks Barfield Architects. Operated by the London Eye Company Limited, a Merlin Entertainments Group Company.
Canon Camera and Canon Inkjet Printer – Canon UK Ltd. For more information please visit www.canon.co.uk

The publisher would like to thank the following for their kind permission to reproduce their photographs:

(Key: a-above; b-below/bottom; c-center; f-far; l-left; r-right; t-top)

The Advertising Archives: 142br, 156bc, 210br; **Alamy Images:** Alvey & Towers Picture Library 25br; BCA&D Photo Illustration 99cr; Blackout Concepts 44cl; Bobo 99tl; Martin Bond 168tl; Richard Broadwell 90ftl; David Burton 105bl; Buzz Pictures 68b; ClassicStock 31tl; David Hoffman Photo Library 210t; Danita Delimont 118bl; Ianni Dimitrov 196-197c; Chad Ehlers 31tr; Andrew Fox 112tl; geldi 237r; Sean Gladwell 156br; Peter Huggins 79bl; ImageState 241tl; Jupiter Images/ BananaStock 95r; Vincent Lowe 33br; Mary Evans Picture Library 240tr; Eric Nathan 156bl; David Osborn 51br; Photofusion Picture Library 157tl; John Robertson 196b; Howard Sayer 128-129; Alex Segre 156cl; Shout 38bl; Skyscan Photolibrary 112-113c; Charles Stirling 119cr; Stockbyte 99tl; John Sturrock 221cl; The Print Collector 157cr; The Stock Asylum, LLC 173bl; David Wall 31cr, 186c; Zak Waters 136tl; **Anoto:** 200t; **Auger-Loizeau:** 198t; **Anthony Bernier:** 23; **British Library:** 204t, 205t; **Camera Press:** Keystone 186t; © **CERN Geneva:** 219cb; **Corbis:** 30t, 187tl; Piyal Adhikary 21crb; Bettmann 45bl, 120cl, 219ca; Stefano Bianchetti 186bl; Iñigo Bujedo Aguirre 151cl; Construction

Photography 127cr; Jerry Cooke 234tl; Andreu Dalmau 44-45c; Arko Datta 120-121c; DK Limited 241tr; Najlah Feanny 227br; Owen Franken 105cr; Stephen Frink 226cl; Chinch Gryniewicz 104b; Tim Hawkins 45t; Amet Jean Pierre 73br; Bembaron Jeremy 166-167c; Lake County Museum 187bl; Jonny Le Fortune 197t; Lester Lefkowitz 37bc; Jo Lillini 16b; Araldo de Luca 150br; Stephanie Maze 36bl; Tom & Dee Ann McCarthy 38br; Moodboard 226cr; NASA 8; Hashimoto Noboru 31b; Alain Nogues 67cr; David Pollack 161br; David Reed 21bl; Reuters 179tc; Bob Rowan 226br; Zack Seckler 105t; The Art Archive 226tl; Sunny S. Unal 197b; John Van Hasselt 166br; Martin B. Withers 137tr; Jim Zuckerman 38tr; **DK Images:** Rowan Greenwood 50cl; NASA 246b; National Motor Museum, Beaulieu 20bc; Robert Opie Collection, The Museum of Advertising and Packaging, Gloucester, England 218br; **Eyevine Ltd:** 241br; Floris Leeuwenberg 235; New York Times/Redux/ 163t, 210-211c; Redux 161tr; **2004 Funtime Group:** 187cl; **Getty Images:** 3D Systems Corp 242bl; 21tl, 36br, 73t, 120tl, 127t, 211br; AFP 21tr, 51cl, 59bl, 173t, 187br, 235br; Altrendo images 59br, 105br; Alejandro Balaguer 44t; Peter Cade 100l; Cousteau Society 59t; Adrian Dennis 182tr; Michael Dunning 12-13; Tim Flach 108bl; Bruce Forster 143tl; Marco Garcia 72cr; Garry Gay 160; Catrina Genovese 205br; Gavin Hellier 30-31c; Hulton Archive 67fbr, 98bl, 151cr; Koichi Kamoshida 181r; Brian Kenney 126tl; Dennis McColeman 66fbl; Roberto Mettifogo 161bl; Hans Neleman 112br; Patagonik Works 207tr; Andrew Paterson 231t; Mark Ralston 156-157c; Chris M. Rogers 187cr; Mario Tama 227cb; The Bridgeman Art Library 151t, 204bl; Time & Life Pictures 50br, 51bl, 72br; David Tipling 80bl; Roger Viollet 104l; **Reaksmy Gloriana:** 227ca; **Impact Photos:** Yann Arthus-Bertrand 90bl; **KEF Audio:** 142t; **The Kobal Collection:** 178-179bc; **Lebrecht Music and Arts Photo Library:** 166bc, 167cr, 167tl, 167tr; **Jennifer Maestre:** 161tl; **Mary Evans Picture Library:** 20bl, 36c, 50bc, 66bc, 66bl, 166tl, 218bl; **Maxppp:** 72t; **Milepost:** 30l; **Myst:** 157bc; **NASA:** 53br, 55r, 67br, 93t; Dryden Flight Research Center Photo Collection 50t; **NHPA/Photoshot:** Stephen Dalton 218-219c; **PA Photos:** 45cl, 120bl, 172t, 234b, 235t; **Panos Pictures:** Mark Henley 104-105c; Abbie Trayler-Smith 137tl; **Reuters:** Kimberley White 221tl; **Rex Features:** 20tr, 20-21c, 37t, 45cr, 47br, 72l, 73bl, 73cl, 119br, 121b, 137br, 143br, 143cr, 205bl, 218bc, 219br; Everett Collection 178cr; Eye Ubiquitous 211bl; Richard Jones 211cl; Alisdair Macdonald 39; David Pearson 156t; Chris Ratcliffe 193b; Sunset 86b; Sutton-Hibbert 197cb; Ray Tang 185tl; Times Newspapers 185tr; E. M. Welch 227tr; **Science & Society Picture Library:** 72bl, 78bc, 150bc, 151bl, 196t, 210bc, 210bl, 219bl, 226bc, 227bl, 235tr; **Science Photo Library:** 37br, 44bc, 58b; Steve Allen 38tl; Andrew Lambert Photography 79br, 140br; Julian Baum 112bl; Jeremy Bishop 211tr; Martin Bond 91cr; Andrew Brookes 150-151c; Tony Buxton 67t; Conor Caffrey 78c; Martyn F. Chillmaid 99br; Thomas Deerinck 78t; Martin Dohrn 113cl; Carlos Dominguez 98tr; Michael Donne 240tl; David Ducros 60b; P. Dumas 197ca; Ray Ellis 127b; Pascal Goetgheluck 78-79c; Roger Harris 179tr; James Holmes 205cr; J. Joannopoulos / Mit 220-221; Cavallini James 79t; Jacques Jangoux 37bl; Ted Kinsman 98c, 113bl; C.s. Langlois 143tr; Living Art Enterprises, Llc 107t; Jerry Mason 221tr; Andrew Mcclenaghan

79cr; Tony Mcconnell 110t; Peter Menzel 179tl; Cordelia Molloy 211cr; NASA 57r, 90fcla, 112c, 113t, 119bl; Susumu Nishinaga 118br; David Nunuk 113br; Sam Ogden 224tl; Pbaeza, Publiophoto Diffusion 118-119c; David Parker 178b, 204-205c; Alfred Pasieka 155br, 161c; Detlev Van Ravensswaay 66c; Jim Reed 113cr; David Scharf 98-99c; Heini Schneebeli 137cr; Simon Fraser / Welwyn Electronics 220t; Pasquale Sorrentino 76t; Volker Steger 126-127, 221br, 226-227c; George Steinmetz 58-59c, 91br; Bjorn Svensson 78bl; Andrew Syred 103tr, 188-189; Sheila Terry 44bl; Jim Varney 219t; **Second Life** is a trademark of Linden Research, Inc. Certain materials have been reproduced with the permission of Linden Research, Inc. Copyright © 2001–2007 Linden Research, Inc. All rights reserved: 234-235c; **Sony Computer Entertainment:** 152tl; **Still Pictures:** 44cr; Mark Edwards 136tr, 136-137c; Danna Patricia 91tl; **StockFood.com:** 114l; **SuperStock:** Corbis 82-83, Swatch AG: 151b; **University of Calgary / Dr Christoph Sensen:** 158t; University of Washington: 229tr; **US Department of Defense:** 40l, 45br; USGS: EROS 67c, 67ca, **Yamaha:** © 2007 Yamaha Corporation 167br

Jacket images: *Front: DK Images:* 2008 The LEGO Group/ MINDSTORMS is a trademark of the LEGO Group

All other images © Dorling Kindersley
For further information see: www.dkimages.com

Japonisme

Cultural Crossings between Japan and the West

Lionel Lambourne

Φ

Phaidon Press Limited,
Regent's Wharf,
All Saints Street,
London N1 9PA

Phaidon Press Inc.,
180 Varick Street,
New York, NY 10014

www.phaidon.com

First published 2005
© 2005 Phaidon Press Limited

ISBN 0 7148 4105 6

A CIP catalogue record for this book is
available from the British Library

Design: Phil Cleaver and James Cartledge
of etal-design
Printed in Hong Kong

Endpaper: **Vincent van Gogh, Branches
of Almond Tree in Bloom. Saint-Rémy**
(detail), 1880. Oil on canvas, 73·5 x 92 cm
(29 x 36¼ in). Rijksmuseum, Amsterdam

Frontispiece: **Edmund Evans, after Walter
Crane, Aladdin; or The Wonderful Lamp,**
from the 'Shilling Series', 1875
(detail of 137)

Previous page: **Robert Blum, L'Ameya:
The Sweet Stall,** 1892 (detail of 159)

Adriaan Reland,
Map of Japan (detail),
1715,
reissued in *Atlas Minor,*
Reiner and Joshua
Ottens, *c.*1740

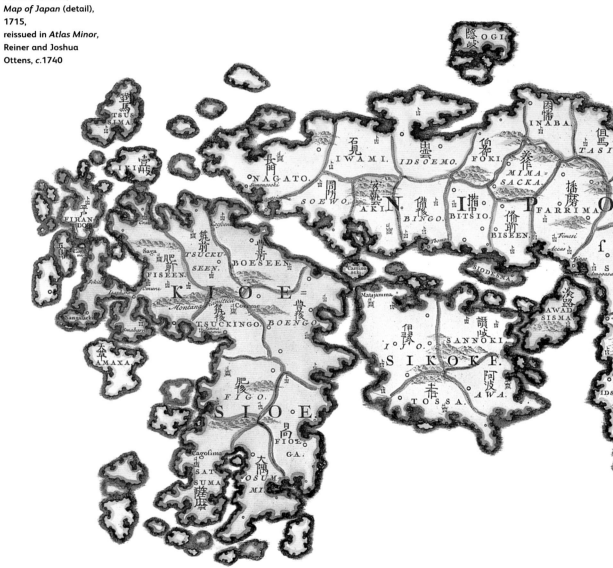

Contents

Introduction

Japonisme is not just a style; it does not lend itself to being used as a concept in place of a style, and it cannot be pinned down to a specific period.
Siegfried Wichmann, 1981

The European taste for things Japanese was at its height in the 1880s. However, the story of Japonisme begins much earlier as indicated by the comments of the influential French writer Charles Baudelaire in 1861:

Quite a while ago I received a packet of Japoneries. *I've split them up among my friends.*

The word 'Japonisme' was coined in 1872 by the French author and collector, Philippe Burty, 'to designate a new field of study of artistic, historic and ethnographic borrowings from the arts of Japan'. To eyes sated with Neoclassicism and the Gothic revival, then in full spate, Japanese art was far more than just a refreshing visual novelty. It is, however, misleading to use the word 'Japonisme' as it infers that it was solely a French phenomenon. While in France it gained its widest acceptance by intellectuals, artists and writers, and became a fashionable craze, it also flourished outside of France in the Netherlands, Great Britain, America, Germany (as *Japanismus*) and many other countries. Indeed, Japanese works of art became potent catalysts for new designs in many disciplines, particularly affecting the ceramic industry, furniture making and textile design.

1
Katsukawa Shunsho,
*Girls Airing Out Books
and Scrolls by Drying
Them on a Line*,
Edo period, 18th century.
Painting on silk,
157·1 x 82·6 cm
(61³⁄₄ x 32¹⁄₂ in).
Freer Gallery of Art,
Smithsonian Institution,
Washington, DC

The catalyst for the phenomenon of Japonisme was the opening up of Japan to international trade in 1858. For over 200 years previously – from 1639 to 1858 – the great maritime nations of Europe (Portugal, Spain, the Netherlands and Great Britain) had been unable to breach the defences of the enclosed world of Japan, which embraced a policy known as *sakoku* – 'the secluded country'. However, the isolation was never total. From behind this barrier there emerged an extraordinarily exotic mixture of goods ranging from the amazing imagery of Japanese prints and screens to delicate porcelain, powerful pottery and the ornate elaboration of wares. Moreover, in recent years we have come to realize more and more that Japan's relations with the outside world were the result of a gradual, complex process. The fall of an imaginary 'bamboo curtain' in 1858 has analogies with the breakdown of the Iron Curtain and the fall of the Berlin Wall in our own time. In each case curiosity concerning events in the outside world provided the motivation that eventually led to the fall of restrictions and prohibitions. The West's love affair with Japan had been slowly growing for two centuries before it finally blossomed after 1858.

Within a few years of 1858, European technology and American brashness transformed the troubled waters of internal Japanese political manoeuvring.

As early as 1867, the young Meiji emperor (r.1867–1912), although only fifteen years of age, had clear ideas concerning the future direction of Japan. The new era, described as 'the Enlightened Government of Brilliant Rule', was firmly established in April 1868 at an imperial palace in Kyoto, when the emperor signed Article 5 of the Imperial Oath stating, 'Knowledge shall be sought for throughout the world, so that the foundations of the empire may be strengthened', or, loosely translated, 'If you can't beat them, join them, and then perhaps you can beat them later.'

The successful cultivation of this policy would bring Japan into the modern world, although, of course, at a cost. While Japan strove energetically to modernize the country, the process of rapid industrialization took its relentless course. Many people were eager to see the old Japan before it became completely changed by modernization. Foreign visitors and artists were enticed to Japan in quite large numbers from the late 1860s. These early tourists were often initially inspired to make the trip after enjoying the charms of Japanese works in major international industrial and trade exhibitions. These shows created huge interest in the Western world throughout the second half of the nineteenth century.

At these exhibitions and via specialized dealers many Europeans made their first acquisitions of Japanese prints, an experience that for them could possess almost the thrill of a first love affair. In feeling such hedonistic emotions they mirrored the reactions of Edmond and Jules de Goncourt, who in their novel *Manette Salomon* (1867) devoted the whole of one chapter to the fantasies of the hero as he peruses an album of Japanese woodcuts.

The arousal of such emotions owes much to the visions conjured up in the world described by the artists who made *ukiyo-e* prints – 'pictures of the floating world'. This school of popular graphic art recorded the life, fashions and entertainments of the Japanese urban population in the seventeenth, eighteenth and early nineteenth centuries. During this period Japan was virtually isolated under the repressive and censorious regime of the Tokugawa shoguns (1603–1867). Thus *ukiyo-e* paintings, prints and books depicted a society unknown to the rest of the world. It was, according to Edmond de Goncourt in his monograph *Hokusai* (1896), 'life in flux, seen strictly as it presents itself to the eyes of the artist'.

This society was first described in 1665 in the *Tales of the Floating World*, by the Kyoto author Asai Ryoi. A memorable passage reads:

Living only for the moment, turning our full attention to the pleasures of the moon, the snow, the cherry blossoms and the maple, singing songs, drinking wine, and diverting ourselves just in floating, caring not a whit for the poverty staring us in the face, refusing to be disheartened, like a gourd floating along with the river current: this is what we call ukiyo-e.

The hedonistic implications of this ephemeral and stylish floating world are mirrored in an attractive work by Katsukawa Shunsho (1726–92), *Girls airing out books and scrolls by drying them on a line* (1). The scene depicted is not a print but a painting on silk. It shows a house in which a vigorous cleaning-up is in progress. The summer rains have ceased and the women of the household dry out books and scrolls while a little boy hands the volumes to a girl drying them on a line. On the verandah two women spread out the volumes, and one becomes involved in reading.

This charming painting, with its homely yet stylized and exotic glimpse of a mysterious world, presents a paradigm of the qualities that proved irresistible to Westerners on their first encounter with Japanese art and artefacts. It can also serve as an allegory for the many books on the fascinating subject of Japanese art, and remind us to try, in our own way, to start out on a historical survey of a rich subject.

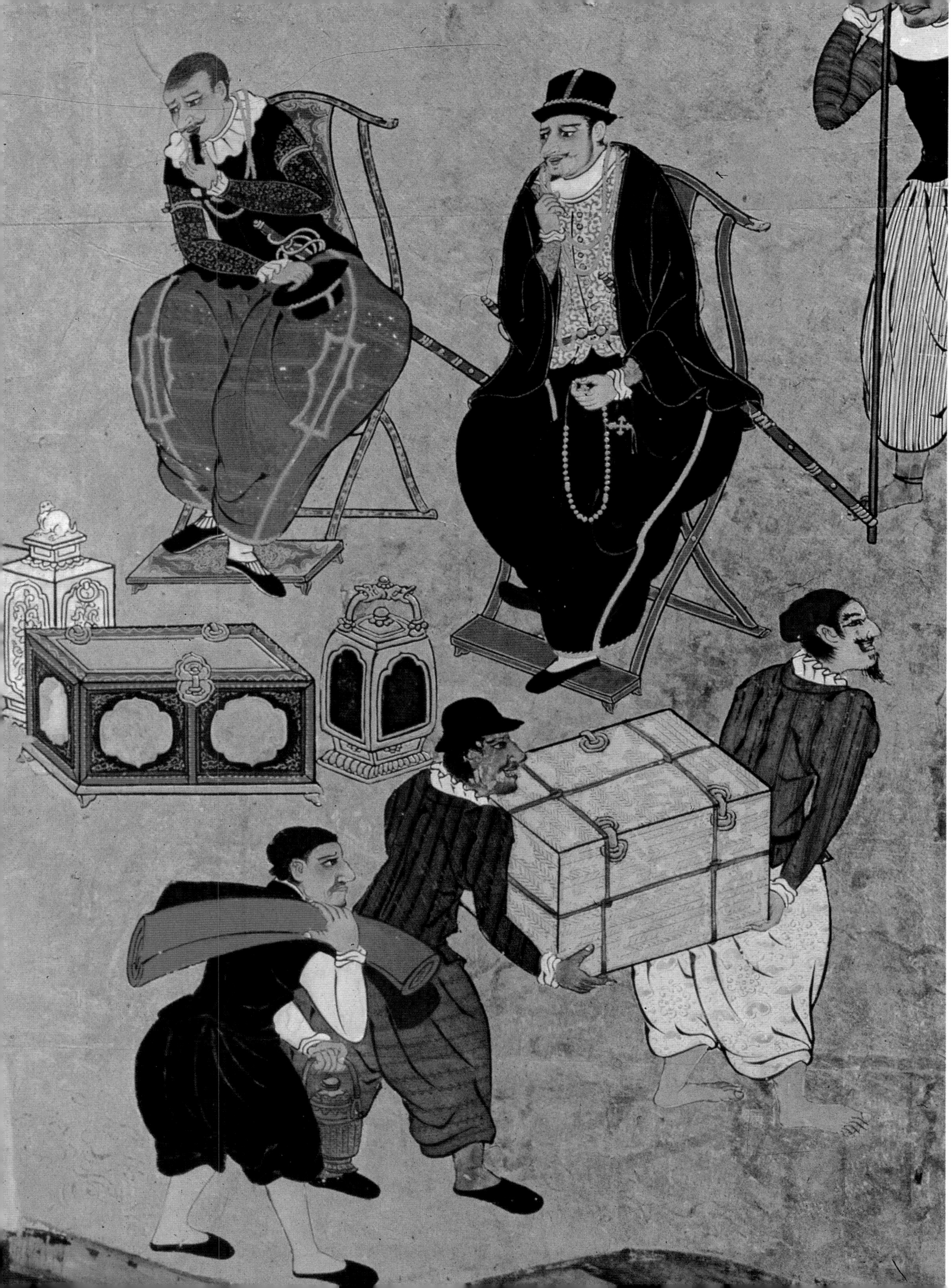

It is in general the unexplored that attracts us …

Lady Murasaki, The Tale of Genji, turn of the eleventh century

Here, remember, the people really eat lotuses, they form a common article of diet …
Lafcadio Hearn, 1891

The history of Japan really begins with the accession of the first 'human' emperor, Jimmu Tenno, in about 660 BC, from whom all the emperors of Japan descended. Until the year 710 AD the imperial family had no fixed long-term abode and with each new emperor the capital of the country also changed. In 710, however, a 'permanent' capital was established at Nara, some 40 miles (64 km) from Kyoto, which, though it lasted for less than a century as a capital, saw the creation of some of the most exquisite buildings in Japan. Nara became a veritable Buddhist crossroads, steeped in the religious and artistic influences of the differing forms of the Buddhist faith from India, China and Korea.

To escape from this deeply religious environment and the influence of the monks, the worldly Emperor Kammu (r.781–806) decided to build a new capital, and the court was moved again at the beginning of the Heian period (794–1185) to a new location in Kyoto, otherwise known as Heian-kyo, the 'Capital of Peace'.

This proved an auspicious title, for the Heian era and the ensuing centuries would enjoy years of relative peace, the population having little contact with the outside world, and turning to their own artistic pursuits. For landscape painters the beetling mountain tops and precipices of Chinese art gave way to native *yamato-e* ('pure Japanese painting') landscapes depicting the gentle, rolling hills of Yamato (the heart of Japan containing both Nara and Kyoto). Narrative picture scrolls with calligraphy of exquisite formality illustrated some of the masterpieces of Japanese literature, notably the *monogatari*, prose tales with poetic interludes. These tales abound with tragic, dewy-eyed lovers, selfless servants, gossipy diaries and passionate love letters, all of which are combined in the thoroughly readable *Genji Monogatari* (*The Tale of Genji*). Written by a court lady, Murasaki Shikabu, it is claimed to be the world's first novel, and is full of delightfully observed incidents of family life which would for centuries inspire Japanese artists and print-makers.

The elegant formality of the Heian court saw the dwindling of Japan's contacts with the rest of Asia. Internally, however, the proliferation of many Buddhist sects, notably Zen Buddhism, had a strong influence on art, not only on landscape scrolls, but on the art of the sword-smith, whose blades became legendary, synonymous with honesty and valour, good faith and the suppression of evil.

Such blades were put to both symbolic and practical use during the long period of conflict between the Taira and Minamoto clans and the establishment of a separate capital at Kamakura, where in 1185 after a great sea battle the Minamoto clan gained the ascendancy and began the dual system of emperor and shogun which lasted for several centuries. One shogunate was established in Muromachi, a suburb of Kyoto, leading to the period from 1339 to 1573 being known as the Muromachi era. It was not a happy time, for clan fought against clan, and bandits took advantage of the decay of noble families to seize temporary possession of land and treasures.

It is against this stormy background of warring factions that we must place the arrival in 1543 of a ship from Macao, the Portuguese trading port in China. The ship was driven ashore off the coast of Kyushu in the southeast of Japan. The Portuguese sailors were well treated, and soon afterwards other ships from Macao began to call at Kyushu, some going on as far as Honshu or Kyoto. Trading flourished, the Japanese delighting particularly in the smooth-bore musket, an instrument of destruction which they soon learnt to make for themselves, decorating them superbly and elevating the gunsmith's craft, like the sword-smith's, to an art form.

These firearms hastened the rise of Oda Nobunaga (1534–82), a warlord who aspired to unify the country and seized power in 1568 from the imperial court in Kyoto. The power of the musket had arrived at just the right moment for this ambitious man and by using this new and lethal weapon, he was able to bring nearly half of Japan's sixty-six provinces under his control. Although Nobunaga was murdered before the complete pacification of the country took place, his successor, Toyotomi Hideoyoshi (1536–98), almost managed to achieve this elusive goal. Nicknamed 'the Japanese Napoleon', Hideoyoshi was physically almost a dwarf, but had immense charisma. Acutely conscious of his low birth, he hoped by his valour to achieve aristocratic distinction on the battle-field, but two unsuccessful campaigns against China and Korea, in 1592 and 1597, led to dire defeats.

Nobunaga and Hideoyoshi were renowned patrons of the arts. Hideoyoshi loved public spectacle, and on one occasion he held a huge open-air tea ceremony to which everyone in the country, from peasant to lord, was invited. The festivities went on for ten days. One of Hideoyoshi's palaces, Momoyama-jo, or Momoyama castle, was decorated with profuse carvings of flowers, mythical monsters, visionary screens glowing with bright colours and gold leaf, curving eaves and heavy roof tiles. This style consequently gave its name to a period in Japanese history: the Momoyama period (1573–1614).

2
School of Kanu,
Portuguese merchants,
detail from a *namban*
screen depicting the
arrival of the Portuguese
in Japan,
*c.*1600–10.
Paint and gold leaf on
wood,
height: 170 cm (67 in).
Museu Nacional de
Soares dos Reis, Oporto

The spread of Christianity also played a large part in the relationships between Japan and European powers. It began with the arrival of several Catholic missionaries from Portugal who are often credited with introducing chiaroscuro prints to Japan, which showed the Western use of light and shade as opposed to the flat unshaded areas of colour used by the Japanese. The most notable of these priests was St Francis Xavier, who came to Kagoshima in 1549 and began to preach with the full permission of the Lord of Satsuma. Xavier stayed for two years and founded a highly successful mission before leaving to find martyrdom in China. Unease grew, however, at the rapid expansion of Christianity (150,000 converts by 1582), a process marred by the dissent between the Jesuit, Franciscan and Dominican missions in converting the Japanese to the new faith. The Japanese were amazed at the unedifying spectacle of Europeans quarrelling over rival brands of a fanatical and merciless creed, which, it was felt, might subvert the social structure of Japanese life. In 1597 there was an outburst of persecution, which led to the martyrdom of twenty-six Christians at Nagasaki, and an edict of 1614 that expelled all missionaries.

The Spaniards were expelled in 1624, and the Portuguese in 1639, which finally ended foreign trade with Japan and severely curtailed all Japanese contact with the outside world.

Before Hideoyoshi died, he came to an arrangement with a rising young member of the Tokugawa family, Tokugawa Ieyasu (1542–1616), who in 1585 established a rigorous military system by posting samurai warriors as police and tax collectors in every district, and beginning a dual system of rule by emperor and shogun military dictators. In 1590, Ieyasu, acting upon Hideoyoshi's advice, settled upon Edo, present-day Tokyo, as his military headquarters, which became the greatest city in Japan. It was Ieyasu who established the lasting dynasty of the Tokugawa shoguns who ruled the country until the restoration of the Meiji emperor in 1868.

On 12 April 1600, the Dutch ship, *Liefde* (*Charity*), from Rotterdam limped into the Japanese port of Bungo in distress. Its pilot, William Adams from Gillingham, Kent, was the first Englishman to enter Japan. As a boy Adams learnt the arts of shipbuilding and navigation, and served against Spain in the rout of the Spanish Armada. Later, with the Dutch fleet he voyaged to the Arctic and Pacific, acting as both buccaneer and pilot, plundering the coasts of Chile and Peru before crossing the Pacific to trade in Indonesia.

Unfortunately, in the Straits of Magellan, the fleet broke up in bad weather and only the *Liefde* reached Japan.

Ieyasu liked Adams and persuaded him to stay in Japan and teach mathematics, navigation, maritime lore and other subjects, while supervising the building of two ships in the European style. Adams, clearly a man of great charisma and individual talents, became a direct retainer of the shogun and a 'naturalized Japanner' who married a Japanese woman by whom he had two children. A bold swash-buckler, Adams loved to dress up as a samurai wearing the two swords of his rank, which upset the Jesuits, jealous of Ieyasu's favour. They denounced Adams as a pirate; but he displayed greater forbearance to them when Ieyasu began to clamp down on the corruption of Japanese officials by European traders, and to issue anti-Christian edicts. Adams became a diplomatic go-between when Dutch and English traders arrived in 1609 and 1613 respectively. Known to the Japanese as Miura Anjin, he lived in Edo in a street named Anjin-cho (Pilot Street), which stood until the great earthquake of 1923. He is still a cult figure today, the hero of novels, films and television to the extent that an area of Tokyo, Anjin-cho, is named after him.

The Dutch trading voyages to the East, which started around 1600, were preceded by almost a century of Portuguese and Spanish expansion to the east and west. In Nagasaki and Kobe the busy activities of both Portuguese and Dutch traders (the Dutch East India Company, or VOC [Verenigde Oostindische Compagnie], was established in 1602) were vividly depicted in the *namban byobu*. These were a type of screen created by Japanese pupils of Portuguese Jesuit teachers to satisfy the deep interest of Japanese society in the strange visitors from abroad, the *namban-jin*, literally meaning 'southern barbarians'. Neither Oriental nor European, the style was a result of the intermingling of the two cultures (see pp.8–9). Typical screens show the arrival of Portuguese ships into the harbour, and the reception of their crews, many of whom are wearing the extraordinary breeches then in fashion, which look as though they have been inflated like balloons (2). Others show the procession of the arriving captain and his retinue greeted by Jesuits in long cassocks. No attempt is made at accurate perspective, but there are myriad anecdotal situations painted in red, green, blue and white on gold paper.

3
World Map Screen,
second half of the
18th century.
Folding screen,
163·8 x 362·8 cm
(64½ x 142¾ in).
Kobe City Museum of
Namban Art

4
*The Deshima Trading
Post Before 1699* from
A Montanus, *Memorable
Embassies*, 1699

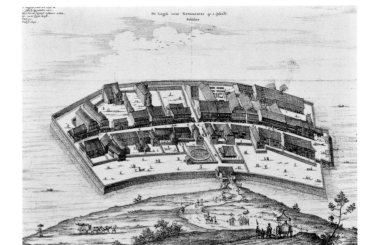

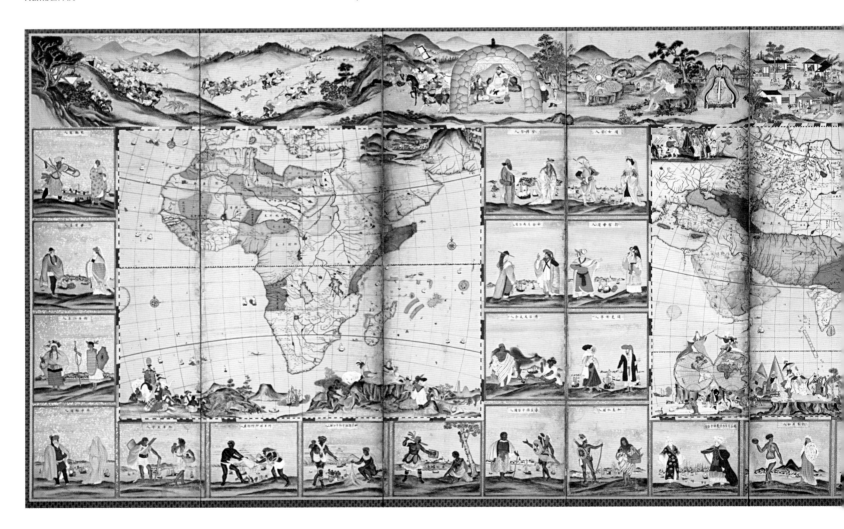

5
Nagasaki School,
The Dutch Factory on the Island of Deshima
detail from a scroll painting, Edo period, 18th century.
Paint on paper, height: 26·7 cm (10½ in).
British Museum, London

The subjects of other similar screens reflect the attempts by the Jesuits to teach Western geography, notably the *World Map Screen* (1593; 3) and its pair *Four Major Cities of the World* (Lisbon, Seville, Rome and Constantinople). Around the edges of the *World Map Screen* are figures dressed in the fashion of their countries and mounted knights, painted by Japanese students in 1593. These screens possess a naive yet powerful fascination, representing the starting point in the artistic exchange between Europe and Japan.

The exact extent of Japan's isolation after 1639 remains an academic minefield. Throughout the shogunate a small population of Calvinist Dutch traders (with no spiritual designs on the population) were allowed to remain on an artificial island in the bay at Nagasaki. Although he had banished the Jesuits and persecuted the indigenous Christian community, Tokugawa Iemetsu, the shogun who ruled from 1622 to 1651, continued to consider trade desirable. He ordered the flattening of one of the hills in the bay of Nagasaki so that its rocks could be used to construct the artificial island of Deshima, a name derived from the Japanese words *deru* (go out), and *shima* (island). The shape of the island is said to have been settled by a shogun who, when asked what shape the new artificial island, roughly the size of a modern athletics track, should be, threw down his fan and pointed to it without a word (4).

Today it is hard not to draw an ironic analogy between Deshima and Osaka's international airport, which, just over three centuries later, has offshore runways also constructed by the demolition of a mountain. But unlike the vast runways of Osaka, which is designed to attract foreigners by the thousands, the fan-shaped Deshima 'shop window' to the West was relatively tiny – 65-m (71-yds) deep and 175-m (191-yds) wide on the side facing the city, and 215-m (235-yds) wide on the side facing the sea. It was surrounded by a basalt wall.

The pioneering European arrivals in Japan shared one aim – to establish trading posts which could act as stages in bringing various luxury goods back to the West; goods ranging from rolls of silk from China to spices and peppers from the Spice islands and Arita porcelain from Japan. All such goods were kept in compounds comprising living quarters and warehouses, collectively called a 'factory', a term which simply meant a place where factors, or representatives of a merchant company, could live and trade. Where trade flourished, so did hospitality, as we see in one of a series of scenes of Dutch life in the factory on Deshima (5).

The claustrophobic boredom of living on Deshima in such straitened circumstances was alleviated once a year by an annual visit of a delegation to the shogun in Edo. This was the highlight of the year, the only occasion to gain a tantalizing glimpse of the outside world. Otherwise, social contacts with the Japanese were restricted to the prostitutes who were allowed to visit the Dutch on the island, which for 200 years was to play the role not only of a window on the West, but also that of a 'cat-flap' through which some goods could enter or leave, although subject to strict controls. During the more liberal shogunate of Yoshimune (r.1716–45), prohibitions were relaxed, allowing the importation of foreign books (except those relating to Christianity). Slowly and laboriously a Dutch-Japanese dictionary was compiled and translations into Japanese were made of books on anatomy, medicine and astronomy. Eventually Japan became a small but vital link in the trade network of the Dutch in Asia, who sailed under the familiar initials VOC, which for many years was the largest commercial enterprise in the world. In order to maintain good trading relations, the Dutch were expected to present gifts to the shogun every year during their visits to the Japanese court

6
Shiba Kokan,
The Pewterer's Shop,
late Edo period,
18th century.
Painting on silk,
63·9 x 129·1 cm
(25 x 50⅞ in).
Kobe City Museum
of Namban Art

7
Shiba Kokan,
The Archery Gallery,
c.1771–4.
Colour woodblock,
25·2 x 19 cm
(10 x 7½ in)

They handed over sumptuous and original gifts, including books, maps and scientific instruments. The Dutch were also obliged to communicate new information, and news of the outside world.

From its headquarters in Batavia (now Indonesia), the Dutch annually sent a fleet of ships to Japan, laden to the gunnels with the exciting secrets of the West, craved for by the intellectual Japanese. So great was the dominance of *rangaku*, or Dutch learning, that it became a term for all Western studies. Among the cargoes were a number of Dutch treatises on landscape painting, and individual prints which were eagerly studied by several Japanese artists, notably Shiba Kokan (1747–1818), who had the most far-ranging interests and made a unique contribution to Japan's contacts with the West. He is credited with producing the first etching made in Japan, a technique learnt from a manual brought to Nagasaki by Dutch traders. He also painted copies on silk, based on a series of etchings showing Dutch crafts and trades (6). In 1799 Kokan published a book, *On Western Painting*, in which he wrote:

Western painting captures the very soul of creation. Japanese and Chinese paintings are like toys and are not of much practical good. Western painters use light and shade to express contrasting effects – smoothness and roughness, distance and proximity, depth and shallowness.

Although attracted by the surface gloss of Dutch and other Western painting, Kokan was even more fascinated by the Western use of perspective, and introduced the novelty of vanishing-point perspective in one of his own prints using *ukiyo-e* techniques learnt from his famous master, Suzuki Harunobu (1725–70). One of Kokan's most interesting prints is *The Archery Gallery* (c.1771–4; 7), which shows a woman giving an arrow to a male archer at a shooting booth, with the caption, 'Ten Arrows for Two Mon'. The illusion of depth is created by the lines focusing on the distant target on the far wall, and is augmented by a landscape glimpsed through the windows of the booth.

On one long-desired journey to Nagasaki, Kokan travelled armed with magnifying glasses, copperplates for etchings, and a camera obscura which he had made based upon a European prototype. Assisted by these 'visual aids', his lectures on world geography and foreign inventions were popular with both peasants and prostitutes. In his entertaining journal he described how much in demand his pictures of Edo were to an audience forbidden to travel.

8
Okumura Masanobu,
*A Scene from the Play
Dojoji at the Nakamura-
za Theatre* (detail),
mid-18th century.
Colour woodblock,
full page: 29·3 x 43·2 cm
(11½ x 17 in)

The fame of Kokan's discoveries preceded him, as he described amusingly:

*September 4 … To my embarrass-
ment, at least twelve or thirteen
women waited on me at the brothel
… The women were completely
dumbfounded when I showed them
my pictures* Ryogoku Bridge *and*
Enjoying the Evening Cool by the
River *through the camera obscura
that I brought with me … and from
then on we chatted freely. When I
left the brothel, the women begged
me to return the next day to talk to
them again.*

Kokan eventually became interested
in Western-style oil painting. Faced
with such images Japanese artists
began to understand the artistic
capital to be made by elaborating
a new visual language.

The great importance of Kokan's prints
lies in the fact that they influenced
early masters of new print-making
schools, such as Okumura Masanobu
(1686–1764). He was the proprietor
of a publishing house that made many
experiments and may have originated
the tall vertical pillar prints (*hashira-e*).
He also enthusiastically adopted the
exotic European convention of the
vanishing point, and modified it by
Japanese practice to produce *uki-e*
(perspective prints). His prints vividly
capture the gossip and noise of a first
night at a *kabuki* theatre (8). In this
scene the heroine is entering left on
the raised walkway (*hana-michi*) or
'flower way'.

15

9
**Bow factory dish with a
Kakiemon pattern,
*c.*1752–8.**
Soft paste porcelain,
diameter: 17·2 cm
(6¾ in).
Victoria and Albert
Museum, London

Throughout the closure of Japan, European monarchs continued to vie with each other in forming collections of luxury goods such as Japanese lacquer ware and porcelain. Japanese porcelain manufacture began early in the seventeenth century following the discovery of kaolin clay at Arita, not far from Nagasaki. Some pieces were especially made for the export trade, depicting Dutch merchant ships and brocaded 'Japan' patterns.

One of the most important collectors of porcelain was Augustus II, Elector of Saxony and King of Poland (1670–1733), known as 'the Strong' perhaps because of his large family of over 350 children. He avidly collected Chinese and Japanese porcelain, often paying enormous sums for single specimens. He justified his passion in a letter to a friend:

Are you not aware that the same is true for oranges as for porcelain, that once one has the sickness for one or the other, one can never get enough of the things and wishes to have more and more.

At Dresden, Augustus created one of his most cherished, yet never fully realized projects to celebrate this passion for porcelain, the 'Japanese Pavilion', across the river Elbe from the main palace complex.

The collection was arranged in categories, with Chinese and Japanese porcelain on the ground floor, and Meissen on the first floor. In the panelled rooms furnished with mirrors and chandeliers, the porcelain was shown in cabinets and skilfully arranged on plinths on the walls in formal patterns according to their style and decoration. Today these dazzling displays can still be seen in the Zwinger, the restored Baroque palace. Legends abound about the porcelain collection, a typical story relating to the huge baluster 'Dragoon' vases decorated with Chinese cobalt blue glazes, which were supposedly acquired by Augustus from Frederick William I of Prussia (r.1713–40) in exchange for 600 cavalry soldiers. Other rooms contain some of the finest Japanese Imari porcelain outside Japan, including monumental covered jars and vases. With other less grandiose collectors throughout Europe, Augustus established the immense popularity of export Japanese Kakiemon porcelain, named after the Kakiemon family who worked in Arita from the seventeenth century onwards. Their wares were painted with a restricted palette of turquoise green, light blue, yellow and iron-red, with such themes as the 'Quail', 'Hob-in-the-Well', and 'the Three Friends' (pine, prunus and bamboo). These motifs were depicted in a characteristically asymmetric manner, leaving much of the surface plain and showing the milky-white porcelain to advantage.

10
Japanese black lacquer
cabinet on a William and
Mary giltwood stand,
17th century.
Lacquer and giltwood,
height: 98·5 cm
(38¼ in).
Private collection

The Japanese Kakiemon style of decoration on export wares was copied by many European factories as diverse as Meissen, Chantilly, Chelsea and Bow, often so carefully that the imitations can barely be distinguished (9).

This insatiable European demand for Japanese porcelain was rivalled by a fierce enthusiasm for the lacquer work which poured out through Deshima. One great collector of lacquer ware was the Empress Marie Theresa of Austria (r.1740–80), who bequeathed a collection to her daughter, Marie Antoinette (r.1774–93). When it arrived in France, Marie Antoinette had individual pieces graded as being objects of the highest calibre, a process which led to their preservation during the overthrow of the *ancien régime* in the French Revolution.

At first, in the seventeenth century, screens, cabinets or panels of lacquer were imported, cut up and adapted to form hybrid mirror frames, cabinets, tables and chests. Just as *ormolu* was used to marry Oriental porcelain with European Rococo settings, so Japanese lacquered panels were mounted on elaborate Baroque stands, which formed compositions that still last today in palaces and grand houses all over Europe (10).

There was, however, an easier and cheaper way to meet the demand for lacquered furniture, which was to produce imitation lacquer. The art of 'japanning' quickly became a fashion and a social accomplishment for a young lady. We know this from a letter of 1689 from Sir Ralph Verney, in which he agrees to pay 'a guinay entrance and 40 shillings more' to buy materials for his daughter Molly to be taught japanning at school. To cater for this demand John Stalker and George Parker published in 1688 a useful volume entitled *A Treatise of Japanning and Varnishing*. In a famous passage they proclaimed:

Let not the Europeans any longer flatter themselves with the empty notions of having surpassed all the world beside in stately Palaces, costly Temples and sumptuous Fabricks: Ancient and Modern Rome must now give place. The glory of one country, Japan alone, has exceeded in beauty and magnificence all the pride of the Vatican at this time and the Pantheon heretofore.

The book contains recipes for the preparation of lacquer and instructions on techniques. Standards were, of course, variable and while some pieces of japanning were acceptable, vast quantities of inferior amateur work were also produced.

Rivalling the compulsive demand in Europe for the fine and decorative arts of Japan was a thirst to possess specimens and paintings of exotic and unknown flowers, for there was huge European curiosity concerning Japan's flora and fauna. For over a century a number of eager naturalists were employed on short-term contracts by the VOC. They covered their real aims by working as physicians in Deshima and, providing they did not get too involved in internal affairs, they could peer at the flora of Japan through the limited view afforded by specimens brought in via Deshima.

Despite stringent security, smuggling was rife. It was indeed encouraged by the fact that the Dutchman, Isaac Titsingh, who held the post of official overseer (1779–84), was exempt from body searches. He had a special garment made which looked like a diver's suit, and was stuffed full of contraband. Supported by two wild-looking youths, Titsingh staggered out to meet the bowing Japanese. To facilitate other more serious espionage activities he acquired a fluent knowledge of Japanese.

After his return from three tours of duty in Deshima, Titsingh wrote and lectured extensively in England and Europe, keeping an interest in Japan alive for the outside world. He is known to have brought back antiquities and prints, and it was possibly through him that the eighteenth-century botanist, Sir Joseph Banks, acquired his 1788 copy of *Ehon Mushi Erabi* (*Picture-book of Selected Insects*; 11) by Kitagawa Utamaro (1753–1806), which became one of the first Japanese works of art to enter the British Museum collections after Banks' library was left to the museum.

At that time this exquisite example of woodblock printing was regarded solely as a botanical source book. Indeed, plants are far more evident in it than the insects promised by the title. Utamaro also produced entrancing 'Shell' and 'Bird' books. The Swedish botanist and collector, Carl Peter Thunberg, visited Nagasaki en route to Deshima in 1775. He returned with works by the early masters, Harunobu and Isoda Koryusai (*fl*.1765–80s), the most fashionable *ukiyo-e* artists of the day, which can now be seen in the Ethnographical Museum in Stockholm.

The greatest early botanist and collector, however, was Dr Philipp Franz von Siebold (1796–1866), a German working for the VOC, who brought back a comprehensive group of Japanese cultural artefacts and plants. He was perhaps the most important visitor to Japan before it opened its doors to the outside world.

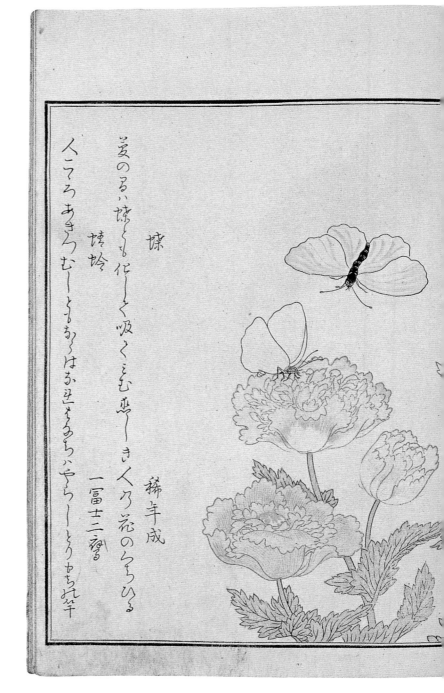

11
Kitagawa Utamaro,
Dragonfly, Butterflies
and Poppies, from the
Ehon Mushi Erabi
(*Picture-book of Selected*
Insects),
1788.
Colour woodblock,
each page: 27·1 x 18·5 cm
(10³₄ x 7¹₄ in)

Siebold arrived at Nagasaki on 23 August 1823, to take up his post as surgeon-physician at Deshima. His initial reception was very similar to that which was given twenty years later to Captain Van Assendelft de Coningh, who visited Nagasaki in 1845 and 1851 and had a nasty brush with the Japanese authorities, later recalling how:

I was filled with fear after I had managed to escape from the clutches of the inspectors and entered Deshima through the two solemn gateways where the guards were sitting on mats like silent mummies. The high walls, which enclosed the island, gave me the feeling that we were criminals who had been imprisoned in some sort of institution.

On Siebold's arrival at Deshima he found eleven houses which were at the disposal of Dutch officials, and a number of buildings which were used as warehouses, kitchens, a sick-bay, a cow byre and pigsty. Siebold moved into the doctor's quarters and fitted it out with such Western luxuries as a piano, which he played frequently. We gain a vivid idea of his daily life in the Dutch quarter from an album dating from 1847 showing a jolly lunch party (12) and a group making use of a telescope to look round the harbour.

Despite these excitements it was hard work adjusting to the 'time capsule' inhabited by the long-term resident Dutchmen in Deshima, of whom Siebold wrote:

Initially, we did not have a pleasant impression of the formal court behaviour these men adopted towards each other and to the Japanese officials, nor of the old-fashioned clothing which they wore … which consisted of quilted velvet coats and black cloaks, hats with feathers, steel swords and Spanish canes with gold handles … the prevailing atmosphere … felt as though we were taking part in a seventeenth-century ceremony.

This description sounds almost as though Siebold's colleagues had walked out of a *namban* screen (see 2).

As a doctor Siebold particularly excelled at eye operations such as cataracts, which if successful can produce such amazing results, and which earned him the soubriquet 'Miracle Doctor'. He actually started a school of medicine in Nagasaki for students who were not allowed to visit Deshima. The local fame and admiration that this aroused inevitably caused friction with the Dutchmen in the settlement, who also criticized Siebold's lifestyle when romance entered his life in the form of his 'marriage' to a beautiful and devoted Japanese girl.

In retrospect, the emotional vicissitudes of her life with Siebold form virtually a precursor of the Madame Butterfly story (see Chapter 9). During the winter of 1823–4, the 27-year-old doctor made house calls to sick patients in Nagasaki and met the 16-year-old Kusumoto Otaki, whom he affectionately called by the diminutive name, Sonogi. This may have been her courtesan name for, according to some authorities, she was one of the prostitutes who were allowed to visit the island to satisfy male needs.

Siebold confided in a letter to an uncle:

I have given in to that old Dutch habit and have temporarily become quite attached to a sweet sixteen-year-old Japanese girl, whom I would not willingly exchange for a European one.

Some sources maintain that Sonogi loved Siebold so much that she allowed a red courtesan stamp to be placed in her passport to enable her to visit Deshima, as at that time it was forbidden for a foreigner to marry a Japanese woman. On 10 May 1827 a daughter was born, whom they named Oine.

Following his official duties, Siebold set off on a trip to Edo to pay homage to the shogun and to report on events, a journey that took place only once every four years. The round trip measured approximately 1,750 miles (2,815 km), and was the only opportunity to see more of Japan.

Siebold set out on 15 February 1826 accompanied by the store-house manager J F Van Overmeer Fisscher. Both men were eager to bring back to Europe works which would convey the realities of daily life in the exotic land, and were particularly excited by Japanese woodcuts. Siebold wrote:

panoramas of the large cities and of the famous temple grounds are usual, as well as views of beautiful places and remarkable mountains. Such woodcuts, printed in black or with colours, often produce very naturalistic pictures and they are for sale everywhere.

In another reference to prints he says:

views of landscapes, temples and other buildings, the garments and depictions of notable men and women in the form of coloured woodcut prints are widely spread in Japan, and in Osaka and Edo these prints are worked out very beautifully.

Siebold's companion, Fisscher, was full of admiration for the way in which the Japanese use pigments to:

produce such marvellous colours as are not to be found in Europe … and give reason to believe that the Japanese would make very great progress once they studied the European painting school.

12
Kawahara Keiga,
Life in the Dutch Quarters of Deshima (detail),
c.1847.
Painted scroll,
22·5 x 35·3 cm
(8⅞ x 13⅞ in).
Nagasaki City Museum

13
Katsushika Hokusai
*Peasants Surprised by
a Sudden Rainstorm,*
*c.*1826.
Watercolour and ink,
27·1 x 40 cm
(10³₄ x 15³₄ in).
National Museum of
Ethnology, Leiden

The journey took two months, for the rules on the itinerary were very strict (although frequently violated by Siebold, who treated many sick people on the way for skin and eye diseases and syphilis). Once in Edo, Siebold became a great attraction for many intellectual individuals eager for knowledge of the outside world. An encounter with Takahashi Sakuzaemon, the court astronomer and supervisor of the Imperial Library, led to an imprudent exchange of maps which was eventually to be Siebold's downfall. If discovered, it made him vulnerable to the accusation of espionage at a time when Russia was threatening Japan's northern borders. Supplying maps to foreigners was punishable by death.

The journey back to Nagasaki passed smoothly, enlivened by such excitements as the illicit act of measuring the height of Mount Fuji with a sextant, and less controversially by visits to a *kabuki* performance in Osaka. Siebold left a vivid description of the theatre:

The gallery, which in Europe opens on a corridor, is left open to let in light, since plays are performed during the day in Japan, not at night, with artificial lighting. Two high, bridge-like passages leading from the back of the theatre to the stage, allow actors to enter, exit and act in the midst of the audience.

Many first-class artists performed ... their luxurious costumes were enough to make us forget the poor appearance of the theatre itself ... instead of having movable flats, they change scenery very quickly with a revolving stage.

Back in Deshima (reached on 20 June 1826), Siebold was happy for a year cataloguing and enlarging his vast botanical, zoological and ethnographic collections, which had increased dramatically on his court journey. But on 18 September 1828, a typhoon caused the ship *Cornelius Houtman* with eighty-nine crates containing Siebold's collection to run aground on the coast.

Among the cargo were forbidden maps, which when discovered led to the arrest of Siebold, Sakuzaemon, fifty interpreters and forty Japanese who had come in contact with Siebold on his journeys to and from Edo. Sakuzaemon was beaten, and died in prison before sentence of death was passed in March 1829.

After his arrest, Siebold was rigorously interrogated for over a year by the authorities at Deshima, and on 22 October 1829 he was banished from Japan for life. Siebold regarded the sentence as extremely severe for it meant that he could never return to see his wife and two-year-old daughter again.

He had two miniatures painted of them, which he placed in lacquer boxes together with locks of their hair, and left Japan on 30 December 1829, asking his two best students to share the responsibilities of bringing up his daughter.

As his ship, the same *Cornelius Houtman*, left the next morning a small boat emerged through the mists with his wife, daughter and two students on board to say their final farewells, a moment surely of operatic intensity. Remarkably, Oine and her father would remain in contact through his years of exile from Japan, and he supplied her with Western medicines while Siebold's students gave her Western medical training. She achieved fame by becoming the first woman doctor in Japan and by running a gynaecology clinic in Nagasaki.

Siebold was lucky to escape with his life, and also lucky to return to Holland with over 2,000 illustrated books and prints. Among the more notable artists whose works he brought back were Katsushika Hokusai (1760–1849), Ando Hiroshige (1797–1858), Utagawa Kunisada (1786–1864) and earlier artists such as Utamaro, Suzuki Haranobu, Torii Kiyonaga (1752–1815), together with examples of the rare prints of Sharaku Toshusai (*fl.*1794–5). Siebold was to use copperplate engravings after Hokusai's illustrations in his book, *Nippon* (1832–58).

One work with which Siebold returned is of particular interest, Hokusai's watercolour sketch in the Western style painted in ink and colours on Dutch paper entitled *Peasants Surprised by a Sudden Rainstorm* (*c.*1826; 13), from a series depicting Japanese customs and festivities. It was ordered by Jan Cock Blomhoff, one of Siebold's colleagues at Deshima, and may have been selected and purchased by Siebold from Hokusai himself. The subject of falling rain and snow or high winds fascinated Hokusai, who returned to the theme again and again.

During the next thirty years Siebold's fortunes waxed and waned. On a visit to the health resort of Bad Kissingen in 1840 in his native Germany he met the Baroness Von Garden, twenty-five years his junior. Five years later they were married, and were to have five children, the two oldest sons inheriting his love of Japan. Although appointed adviser on Japanese affairs to the Bavarian court, Siebold was no courtier and was eventually dismissed, only to be re-employed in 1858. The same year he heard, to his delight, that his banishment from Japan had been withdrawn. On 4 August 1859 Siebold returned to Japan with his eldest son, Alexander.

They were met by his Japanese daughter, Oine, now 32, with a daughter of her own. Sonogi had remarried twice in the interim, rather to Siebold's surprise, but we do not know what Sonogi thought of Siebold's marriage and family. One cannot help but consider how the story presents further operatic opportunities, such as memorable solos, duets, trios and quartets. The final solo, however, would surely belong to Siebold's Japanese daughter, whom he met for the last time in Nagasaki on his second and final enforced return to Europe at the end of April 1862. He died in Munich in October 1866.

Denied contact with the outside world, alert Japanese eyes were eager to see more of the exotic figures from the West. This led to the production of the so-called Nagasaki prints, inexpensive souvenirs of foreign ships, visitors and their amazing animals. Like the animals, the Japanese felt that they too were imprisoned, and they stirred uneasily under the dictatorial rule of the shoguns. Russian, British and American ships risked putting in to Japanese ports hoping to do some trading and break the monopoly of the Dutch and Chinese. Some crews were massacred. Others were ordered to leave at once.

After protests the Japanese agreed that ships in distress might put in for water and fuel to their ports. But in 1839, when Congress in Washington sent Commodore Biddle to try to negotiate a trade agreement, the request was contemptuously refused. American pride had been wounded, and even worse, commercial interests were threatened. Enterprising Americans wanted a foothold in Japan, so that they might become the principal traders both there and in China.

A race for a trade treaty with Japan began between America and Russia, just as a century later the two countries would vie with each other to be the first to place a man on the moon. In October 1852 the Russian Admiral Putyatin sailed with four ships for Japan, but he arrived at Nagasaki in August 1853, a few weeks too late, for another fleet of four American ships had reached Japan in July. They were the famous 'black' ships, two steamers and two sailing boats, with nearly 600 men under the command of Commodore Matthew Perry, US Navy. His predecessor, Biddle, had been forbidden to deal firmly with the Japanese but Perry had a free hand. The following year, in February 1854, he returned with seven ships and 2,000 men, and the shogunate realized that no defences would keep out the Americans for long. The first treaties were extremely limited in effect for only Nagasaki, Hakodate and Shimoda were opened to foreign shipping.

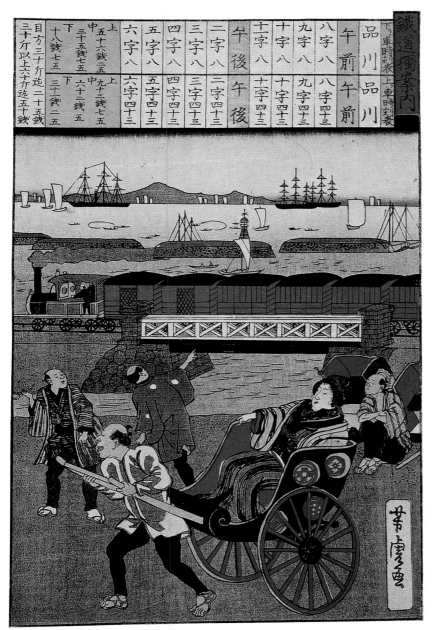

But the commercial process of opening Japan had begun and was not confined to the United States of America; before the end of the 1850s a series of treaties was signed with Great Britain, France, Russia and The Netherlands.

On the second American mission visit to Japan in the *Macedonian* in 1854, Dr Francis Hawks, who kept the official journal, recorded the intense interest in a miniature train given to Japan to introduce the power of steam. It was designed to run on an 46-cm (18-in) gauge track on a 107-m (117-yds) circular railway line at a speed of 20 miles (32 km) an hour.

It was a spectacle not a little ludicrous to behold a dignified mandarin [sic] whirling around a circular road at the rate of twenty miles per hour with his loose robes flying in the wind. As he clung with a desperate hold to the edge of the roof, grinning with intense interest and his huddled up body shaking convulsively with a kind of laughing timidity while the car spun rapidly round the circle, you might have supposed that the movement somehow was dependent rather upon the enormous exertion of the uneasy mandarin than upon the power of the little puffing locomotive which was easily performing its work.

Less than thirty years later, in 1872, a real railway would make its way between Tokyo and Yokohama, and above it would soar the wires of the first telegraph lines (14).

The age of steam would also make its mark in the guise of the company founded in 1840 which would become the Peninsular and Oriental Steam Navigation Company, always known as P & O. For the first three decades of its history passengers and goods had to be transported on camels by land across the narrow isthmus which separated Suez from the Nile. But the opening of the Suez canal in 1869 (celebrated in Cairo with the first production of Verdi's opera *Aida* against a background of the pyramids) gave the opportunity for P & O to use the latest steam ships to destinations in the Pacific and the Far East. Very soon educated Europeans began to visit Japan in surprising numbers.

The first British citizens had arrived in 1859, and while some settled in Nagasaki and Hakodate, most stayed at Yokohama, notably Sir Rutherford Alcock, the first British Minister to Japan. He returned to England in time to organize the Japanese stand at the International Exhibition of 1862, which contained many artefacts that he had collected. His book, *The Capital of the Tycoon* (1863), describes his years in Japan and is still very readable.

15
Utagawa Yoshitora,
American Drinking
and Carousing,
1861.
Colour woodblock,
35·4 x 24 cm
(14 x 9³⁄₈ in)

A vivid record of these exciting days, with the ups and downs of daily life of the foreign community, and the rapid adoption of Western ways by the indigenous population, is provided by Nagasaki and Yokohama prints. The first Nagasaki prints had been made at the turn of the century and depicted quaint Chinese and lecherous Dutchmen in a semi-foreign style, but printed according to traditional *ukiyo-e* methods (15). The Yokohama prints (16) are at their most amusing in the naive depictions of 'foreign' capitals, hilarious popular images of London or Rome, which were sold as cheap souvenirs (17). These engaging works were highly successful when depicting foreign ships on the open sea. Although entertaining, they differ greatly from the earlier masterpieces of the *ukiyo-e* school, which when they reached Europe would have a striking effect on the artists and designers of the day.

Utagawa Sadahide,
A Sunday in Yokohama,
1861–2.
Colour woodblock,
36·4 x 74·2 cm
(14¹₄ x 29¹₈ in)

International exhibitions and world fairs began with the Great Exhibition in the Crystal Palace, London, 1851. Japan was not represented at this first world fair, for there were still a few years to go before the end of seclusion. Once Japan started to be involved with them, however, they became one of the most enthusiastic participants in an endless round of international exhibitions. The London exhibition of 1862 had a Japanese section chosen by the first British Minister in Japan, but it was not until 1867 in Paris that Japan officially participated, and although the shogun government was on the brink of collapse, Japan found much sympathetic support in France. During the more enlightened years of the Meiji era (1868–1912) the empire changed rapidly and enjoyed what has been described as Japan's Victorian age. With the support of the progressive new Meiji emperor, lavish displays were mounted at major and minor exhibition venues in France, thus providing an ideal opportunity for Japanese manufacturers to market their export lines. This competitive stimulus led many European manufacturers to produce reciprocal samples of goods destined for sale in Japan. These 'Japanese' displays also created enduring popular images, visual clichés of Japan that persisted throughout the West well into the twentieth century

Utagawa Yoshitora,
Port of London triptych,
1862.
Colour woodblock,
each section:
36·5 x 73·9 cm
(14³⁄₈ x 29 in).
Kobe City Museum of
Namban Art

Chapter two:
Japan and the Painters

18
Kitagawa Utamaro,
*Lovers in an Upstairs
Room* from *The Poem
of the Pillow*,
1788.
Colour woodblock,
25·5 x 36·9 cm
(10 x 14¹₂ in)

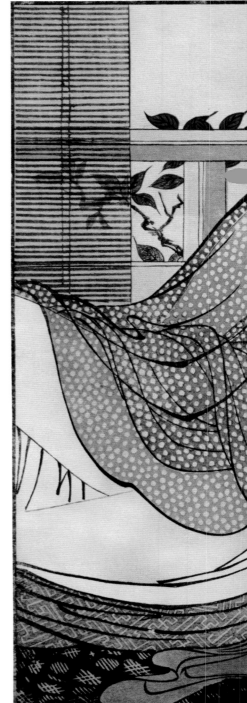

It is strange, this revolution brought by Japanese art in the taste of a people who, in matters of art, are the slaves of Greek symmetry and who, suddenly, are becoming impassioned over a plate on which the flower is not set dead in the middle, over a fabric in which harmony is not achieved by a gradation of tints but by a knowledge-able juxtaposition of raw colours.
Edmond de Goncourt, 1877

Japanese prints … penny plain and tuppence coloured – illustrations of Yeddo … excellent no doubt as decorative furnishings but absurd as pictures.
Joseph Péladan, 1884

The influence of Japan upon European art and literature of the nineteenth century was various. From the 1860s to the 1890s the themes of Japonisme provided an exciting new direction for artists such as James Abbott McNeill Whistler (1834–1903), Édouard Manet (1832–83) and Claude Monet (1840–1926), and authors such as the de Goncourt brothers, Guy de Maupassant and Pierre Loti. For thirty years few artists or writers could afford to ignore the obsession with 'things Japanese'. As early as 1867 the de Goncourt brothers published a novel, *Manette Salomon*, in which a chapter is devoted to the hero's Oriental daydreams as he studies albums of Japanese woodcuts, finding:

pages like ivory palettes laden with the colours of the Orient … sparkling with purple, ultramarine and emerald greens. And from these albums of Japanese drawings, there dawned for him a day in this magical country, a day without shadow, a day that was nothing but light.

This idyllic dream would later haunt many artists, notably Vincent van Gogh (1853–90) and Paul Gauguin (1848–1903), driving them to seek out Japanese themes, either in the form of woodcuts, or by visiting the south of France, a vision of bright sunlight, blue skies, intense starlight and bold colours.

The most important of all advocates for the Japoniste cause were the two brothers, Edmond and Jules de Goncourt. Within the pages of their intimate *Journal* (1851–70) lie the raw materials for a history of Japonisme, a subject they knew well as collectors, critics and novelists. Their most famous joint art-historical work was *French Eighteenth Century Painters* (1859–75), which reveals not only their passion for accuracy in research, but also their delight in extreme forms of art such as *singerie* (the decorative depiction of monkeys in human roles) and *chinoiserie* (decorative art inspired by the art of China).

Such enthusiasms prepared Edmond for his passionate interest in Japon-isme. Jules's early death, aged forty, ended their collaborative work, but Edmond continued to write the journal they had started in 1851. Its nine volumes chart with zest Parisian literary and artistic life, and often make reference to the progress of the cult of Japan, that was a powerful influence on the art of the Impressionists.

In an entry dated January 1862 the brothers express their views concerning the conflict between the two principles of beauty and truth ('*le beau versus le vrai*') which dominated French art throughout the second half of the nineteenth century. They came to be associated in the minds of the artistic establishment of the day with backing the Japanese side in the conflict between Japanese and Greek art, representing beauty and truth respectively. 'Art is not one,' they proclaimed:

or rather there is no single art. Japanese art is as great an art as Greek art. Greek art, frankly what is it? The realism of the beautiful. No fantasy, no dream. The absolute of line.

The de Goncourts shared more than their pens and paper, for their sexual lives were said to have been both erotic and economical – it was rumoured that they enjoyed the favours of the same mistress. Their delight in the Rococo sexual frisson possessed by the works of Jean-Antoine Watteau (1684–1721), François Boucher (1703–70) and Jean-Honoré Fragonard (1732–1806) found more explicit satisfaction in Japanese *shunga* or pillow books (18). As early as October 1863 Edmond described how:

The other day I bought some albums of Japanese obscenities. They delight me, amuse me, and charm my eyes. I look on them as being beyond obscenity, which is there, yet seems not to be there, and which I do not see, so completely does it disappear into fantasy.

The violence of the lines, the unexpectedness of the conjunctions, the arrangement of the accessories, the caprice in the poses and the objects, the picturesqueness, and, so to speak, the landscape of the genital parts. Looking at them, I think of Greek art, boredom in perfection, an art that will never free itself from the crime of being academic!

On 19 July 1864 Edmond made a note of the evening sky:

This evening the sun looks like a wafer of cherry-coloured sealing wax, glued onto the sky over a pearl-coloured sea. Only the Japanese have dared, in their colour albums, to give these strange effects of nature.

On 30 September 1864 he praised Japanese artists for their discernment:

Everything that they do is taken from observation. They represent what they see: the incredible effects of the sky, the stripes on a mushroom, the transparency of the jellyfish. Their art copies nature as does Gothic art. Basically there is no paradox in saying that a Japanese album and a painting by Watteau are drawn from an intimate study of nature. Nothing like this in the Greeks: their art, except for sculpture, is false and invented.

An artist who adopted a Japoniste agenda while also keeping a foot in the Hellenic camp was Whistler. His enthusiasm for collecting Japanese art began in the early 1860s when, as a gifted young American painter, he occupied a unique 'mid-channel' role in the artistic world of London and Paris, at a time of great change in the arts in both capital cities.

By the mid-1860s in England, Pre-Raphaelitism had begun to wane and a full-scale Neoclassical revival was underway. Yet for Whistler, like the de Goncourts, the word 'academic' was anathema. While admiring the lightly clad ladies painted by his friend Albert Moore (1841–93), Whistler himself used Japanese art to distance himself from the toga-clad Greeks and Romans of Lawrence Alma-Tadema (1836–1912) and the toiling Israelites goaded by Egyptians by Edward Poynter (1836–1919), which jostled for attention at the Royal Academy in London.

19
James Abbott McNeill Whistler,
*Symphony in White,
No. 2: The Little White Girl*,
1864.
Oil on canvas,
76·5 x 51·1 cm
(30¹⁄₈ x 20 in).
Tate Britain, London

20
James Abbott McNeill
Whistler,
*Caprice in Purple and
Gold, No. 2: The Golden
Screen*,
1864.
Oil on wood,
50·2 x 68·7 cm
(19³₄ x 27 in).
Freer Gallery of Art,
Smithsonian Institution,
Washington, DC

Placed against these pseudo-classical subjects Whistler's own paintings are strikingly original. His work would eventually display his profound sympathy for Japanese art, yet at first this expressed itself mainly in the fun of using unusual Japanese artefacts as studio props. In the most hauntingly beautiful of these works, *Symphony in White, No. 2: The Little White Girl* (19), Whistler used his beautiful Irish mistress, Jo Heffernan, as a model. Clad in a voluminous white dress, she leans on a white marble mantelpiece with a pier glass, while her right hand hangs by her side holding a colourful Japanese fan. She gazes at a blue and white jar, a red lacquer bowl and some colourful azaleas, all reflected in the mirror. Whistler would continue to explore the theme of a painting arranged around a single colour and devise unusual colour schemes for several of the apartments he occupied in London in the 1860s, all remarkable for their decor.

In all of them his Oriental porcelain collection played an important role. His mother, who came to live with him in the winter of 1863, wrote to a friend on 10 February 1864 describing her son's 'artistic abode … ornamented by a very rare collection of blue and white china'.

21
James Abbott McNeill Whistler,
Variations in Flesh Colour and Green: The Balcony,
*c.*1867–8.
Oil on wood,
61·4 x 48·8 cm
(24¹⁄₈ x 19¹⁄₄ in).
Freer Gallery of Art, Smithsonian Institution, Washington, DC

Whistler's motives for collecting were complex, including his delight in the search for exciting examples, and a personal enjoyment of the colour blue, used in Chinese and Japanese porcelain, subtle variations of which hue appear in so many of his paintings. He also delighted in depicting both his own treasured pieces and examples borrowed from the stock of the dealer, Murray Marks.

Whistler took pleasure in rivalling the freedom of the potter's brush, a theme developed in his *Purple and Rose: the Lange Leizen of the Six Marks* (1864), which shows the model as if intent on painting the tall figures on the vase. Whistler also collected prints which can be seen in another work, *Caprice in Purple and Gold, No. 2: The Golden Screen* (1864; 20). In it the model, Jo, clad not in a white dress but a kimono, looks at a pile of prints by Hiroshige from his landscape series *Famous Views in the Sixty-odd Provinces.* Jo's head is dramatically silhouetted against a magnificent *tosa* screen whose literary theme is taken from *The Tale of Genji.*

22

Torii Kiyonaga
The Fourth Month:
Gentleman Entertained
by Courtesans and
Geisha at a Teahouse
in Shihagawa **from the**
series *Twelve Months*
in the South,
*c.***1783.**
Colour woodblock,
36 x 51 cm
(14⅛ x 20 in)

To celebrate his return after his visit to Valparaíso, Chile, at the end of 1866, Whistler gave a memorable housewarming party at his new apartment in Chelsea, London, at 2 Lindsay Row. One guest, W M Rossetti, noted that Whistler 'has got-up the rooms with many delightful Japanisms, etc. Saw for the first time his pagoda cabinet', while Whistler's friend, Alan Cole, focused more critically on 'Jimmy's absurdities with pieces of Liberty silks on the floor' and 'flights of Japanese fans on the ceiling', a decorative innovation anticipating both Manet and Monet's use of the same conceit. These exotic artefacts were set off by the overall simple tonality of the rooms, in subtle and light hues unusual for the high Victorian era.

In possibly the most Japanese of all these early works, *Variations in Flesh Colour and Green: The Balcony* (*c.*1867–8; 21), Whistler posed his models on a Chelsea balcony before the distant factory chimneys of Battersea. The horizontal and verticals formed by the rolled bamboo blinds make this an extremely Japoniste composition. It is clearly related to two woodcuts by Torii Kiyonaga, from a five-sheet composition *Autumn Moon on the Sumida* and the same artist's *The Fourth Month: Gentleman Entertained by Courtesans and Geisha at a Teahouse in Shihagawa* from *Twelve Months in the South* of *c.*1783 (22), both of which Whistler owned.

Whistler's enthusiasm for collecting was infectious and he introduced the poet and painter, Dante Gabriel Rossetti (1828–82), to Madame Desoye's famous shop at 220 Rue de Rivoli in Paris, also known as *La Porte chinoise*. Opened in 1862, it had become the haunt of all those interested in Japanese art. There, as Edmond de Goncourt described (31 March 1875):

enthroned in her jewels like a Japanese idol, sits the fat Madame Desoye; almost a historic figure in our own time, for this shop has been the place, the school as it were, from which this great Japanese movement has evolved which today extends from painting to fashion.

On his first visit to the shop in November 1864, Rossetti bought four Japanese books. He was almost certainly on the hunt for an exotic costume accessory to use in his painting *The Bride* or *The Beloved*, but as he described in a letter:

found that all the costumes were being snapped up by a French artist, Tissot, who it seems is doing three Japanese pictures, which the mistress of the shop described to me as the three wonders of the world, evidently in her opinion quite throwing Whistler into the shade. She told me, with a great deal of laughing, about Whistler's consternation at my collection of china.

23
James Tissot
La Japonaise au bain,
1864.
Oil on canvas,
208 x 124 cm
(82 x 49 in).
Musée des Beaux-Arts,
Dijon

The shop became a legend. The critic and writer, Phillipe Burty, in his novel, *Grave Imprudence* (1880), has his hero Brissot (a mixture of Manet and Monet) take enormous pride in having bought the first album of flowers and birds printed in colours in Madame Desoye's shop after her arrival from Japan. Brissot also admires her 'collection of robes of *guecuhas* and *musmes* which filled her cupboards', using affectionate diminutives for geishas and their pupils, the *mousmés*. It would, however, be wrong to give the impression that Desoye's shop was unique. Ernest Chesneau, in recalling the early 1860s, wrote:

one kept oneself informed about new cargoes. Old Ivories, enamels, faience and porcelain, bronzes, lacquers, wood sculptures, sewn materials, embroidered satins, playthings, simply arrived at a merchant's shop and immediately left for artists' studios or writers' studies.

One of the paintings by James Tissot (1836–1902) described by Madame Desoye was probably *La Japonaise au bain* (1864; 23), perhaps the most sensuous of all his works, although painted from a Western model, and not as sexually explicit as a Japanese treatment of such a theme. Tissot also painted three versions of a picture of *Two Young Women Looking at Japanese Objects*. They were posed in Tissot's house on the Avenue de l'Impératrice, sumptuously furnished with Japanese objects, some of which were presented to Tissot by Prince Akitake.

24
James Tissot,
Portrait of Prince
Tokugawa Akitake,
1868.
Watercolour,
55 x 47 cm
(21⅝ x 18½ in).
Tokugawa Museum,
Mito

The prince was one of the pioneering Japanese visitors to Europe, who came to organize the Japanese display at the Exposition Universelle of 1867. After representing the Tokugawa government at the exhibition, the prince stayed on in Paris, taking drawing lessons from Tissot. A portrait of the prince wearing Japanese dress was painted in 1868 by Tissot with an affectionate dedication to the sitter inscribed on the back. When he returned to Japan, the prince had the watercolour portrait mounted in the Japanese manner in the form of a *kakemono*, a hanging scroll picture (24).

Tissot, like Whistler, was a key figure in bringing knowledge of Japonisme across the Channel to England, exhibiting with Whistler at the Grosvenor Gallery in 1877. In Paris Tissot also kept in touch with Edgar Degas (1834–1917), who, perhaps more than any other European artist, assimilated the lessons of Japanese dramatic composition, viewpoint and perspective, such as cutting off figures with the picture frame. His studies of nude women bathing (25), drying themselves, combing their hair or having their hair combed by someone else, were directly inspired by such prints from the *Manga* vol. 1, *A Noodle Vendor* and *Women at a Public Bath* (26).

25
Edgar Degas,
The Tub,
1886.
Pastel on paper,
60 x 83 cm
(23½ x 32½ in).
Musée d'Orsay, Paris

26
Katsushika Hokusai,
Women at Public Bath,
from the *Manga* vol. I,
c.1820.
Colour woodblock,
17·5 x 11·5 cm
(7 x 4½ in)

The *Manga* were a particularly popular Japanese source from which Europeans continually borrowed motifs. The fifteen volumes that comprise the set created intense interest and were rapidly passed from hand to hand, all over Europe. In France a copy first came into the hands of a printer of etchings, Auguste Delâtré (1822–1907). He showed it to both Whistler and the etcher, Félix Bracquemond (1833–1914), who acquired the books permanently, and introduced them to a wide range of practitioners in the 'fine' and 'decorative' arts.

Degas, after a classical training with an emphasis on purity of form, found welcome relief from Western idealization of 'the female form divine' in Hokusai's vibrant studies of life in the public baths. Such sketches were a bracing alternative to the conventional poses to be seen in the works of the French Salon painters.

Hokusai's vision was echoed in Degas's favoured themes of washerwomen at work in the hot sweaty atmosphere of steamy laundries, nude studies in the brothel, and especially the themes of ballerinas, whether at rehearsals, preparing for their appearances on stage or nursing sprains in the wings of the Opéra.

27
Edgar Degas,
Mary Cassatt at the Louvre: The Painting Gallery,
1879–80.
Etching, aquatint, drypoint and crayon électrique heightened with pastel on tan wove paper,
30·5 x 12·6 cm
(12 x 5 in).
The Art Institute of Chicago

A great admirer of Degas was the fiercely independent, Mary Cassatt (1844–1926), from Pennsylvania, who from the age of sixteen had studied art in Europe, exhibiting her first painting at the Paris Salon in 1868. She evolved her own special themes – women in boxes at the theatre, the intimate pleasures of maternity and the relationship between mother and baby – subjects she would treat with virtuoso success in every graphic medium. Degas admired her work, tersely perceiving it in 1877 to be 'by someone who thinks as I do', and advised her to exhibit exclusively with the new group of Impressionists, an invitation which, she wrote, 'I accepted with joy. I hated conventional art. I began to live.' She forged a close working relationship with Degas, who portrayed her in *Mary Cassatt at the Louvre: The Painting Gallery* (1879–80; 27), one of the painter's most consciously Japanese works, whose trimmed composition may derive from the tall, narrow *hashira-e* prints designed for hanging on pillars in Japanese houses.

In April 1890 Cassatt wrote to another great woman Impressionist, Berthe Morisot (1841–95), 'you must see the Japanese [prints] – come as soon as you can to the École des Beaux-Arts.' The exhibition had been arranged by Siegfried, also known as Samuel, Bing, the German-born French entrepreneur who was a key figure in influencing a wider understanding of Japanese art and who organized a number of exhibitions, notably the 1890 show which contained a vast display of 700 prints.

28
Mary Cassatt,
The Letter,
*c.*1890–1.
Coloured etching,
drypoint and aquatint,
34·5 x 22·8 cm
(13¹₂ x 9 in)

29
Kitagawa Utamaro,
*The Courtesan Hinazuru
at the Keizetsuru*, from
the series *Comparing the
Charms of Beautiful
Women*,
*c.*1794–5.
Colour woodcut

30
Mary Cassatt,
Young Woman Bathing,
1890–1.
Drypoint and aquatint,
36·8 x 26·3 cm
(14³⁄₈ x 10¹⁄₂ in)

There had been large exhibitions
of prints earlier but this was the first
historical retrospective, and, although
Cassatt was already familiar with
Japanese prints, the show had a
profound effect on her, leading her
to produce a series of ten aquatints,
which are among the finest of all
Japoniste works. Among them is
The Letter (1890–1; 28), in which
the sensual lips of the girl licking the
envelope, the curl of her fingers
and the distorted perspective of the
desk top, are surely direct tributes to
Kitagawa Utamaro (29), whom Cassatt
greatly admired.

Cassatt's *Young Woman Bathing*
(1890–1; 30) is one of her rare studies
of the female nude, and one of the
most successful marriages of Eastern
and Western styles. It was inspired
by her delight at the 1890 exhibition
in the prints of Nishikawa Sukenobu
(1671–1750), Toyokuni (1769–1825)
and most of all Utamaro. Degas was
immensely impressed when he saw
this print for the first time, remarking,
'this back, did you draw this?' Another
admirer of Cassatt's technical skills
was the Impressionist painter, Camille
Pissarro (1830–1903), who wrote to
his son Lucien praising Cassatt's
achievement in colour printing
in aquatint: 'the tone, even, subtle,
delicate … the result is admirable,
as beautiful as Japanese work, and
it's done with printer's ink!'

31
Mary Cassatt,
The Boating Party,
1893–4.
Oil on canvas,
90 x 117 cm
(35¹₂ x 46¹₄ in).
National Gallery of Art,
Washington, DC

Cassatt also continued to paint in oils, and *The Boating Party* (1893–4; 31), became the centrepiece of her first exhibition in the United States of America. Probably inspired by one of several annual summer visits to Antibes, it is seen by some as a variation of her favoured theme of mother and child by the insertion of the back view of a male figure, the rower. The oar and sail, cut off by the picture's frame and the man's black-clad back, form a composition reminiscent of Hiroshige's *The Benton Ford Across the Oi River* (1856) (see 61).

Vincent van Gogh first discovered Japanese prints in Nuenen, Holland, when reading Edmond de Goncourt's novel *Chérie* (1848), whose hero was the first to voice the famous phrase 'Japonaiserie forever'. Two years later in a letter to his brother Theo from Antwerp, he describes how the Japanese prints he has tacked upon his wall amuse him. This growing interest becomes even more intense in Paris, where in 1887 he organized two exhibitions of prints, one at the café, Le Tambourin, during his stormy relationship with its proprietor, Agostina Segatori, who was probably his mistress when he portrayed her sitting in her café in *Woman at Le Tambourin* (1887). Behind her some Japanese prints can be seen stuck on the walls.

Van Gogh also studied prints at the dealer Bing's premises, purchasing as many prints as he could afford and urging his friends to do the same. He also recommended that they read the de Goncourt novel, *Manette Salomon*, in which the hero, with whom Van Gogh felt a kinship of interests, leafs through a volume of Japanese prints. This experience in his imagination:

gave birth to a day in that enchanting land, a day without shadow, filled with light … a fantasy disturbed by the light of reality, by the wintry sun of Paris, and by the lamp brought into the studio.

Van Gogh's own personal image of Japan began to take palpable form in Paris in 1887 when he painted several careful copies in oils made from tracings and squared-up drawings. These *Japonaiseries* include his painstaking version of Hiroshige's *Sudden Shower over the Shin-Ohashi Bridge* (c.1857) from *One Hundred Views of Edo* (32, 33) painted with a thick, heavy impasto. Years later the great American architect and dealer of Japanese prints, Frank Lloyd Wright (1867–1959), said of this painting:

there's the one that Van Gogh has copied 'after Hiroshige' he called it – but I couldn't see that it was anything but just an oil painting of this print. I don't think he did a very good job of it either, the print was so far superior that it was too bad to look at what he did.

32
Utagawa Hiroshige,
*Sudden Shower over
the Shin-Ohashi Bridge*
from *One Hundred
Views of Edo,*
c.1857.
Colour woodcut,
23·7 x 36·2 cm
(9³⁄₈ x 14¹⁄₄ in)

33
Vincent van Gogh,
The Bridge in the Rain
(after Hiroshige),
1887.
Oil on canvas,
73 x 54 cm
(28³⁄₄ x 21¹⁄₄ in).
Van Gogh Museum,
Amsterdam

34
Vincent van Gogh,
Portrait of Père Tanguy,
1887–8.
Oil on canvas,
65 x 51 cm
(25¹₂ x 20 in).
Private collection

Around the borders of both this painting and *The Plum Tree Teahouse at Kameido* (*c.*1887), Vincent copied *kanji* characters which, once doctored by Van Gogh, became little more than gobbledygook, unlike the border of his large copy after the print *Oiran: The Courtesan* by Keisai Eisen (1790–1848). The print had been reproduced on the cover of the journal, *Paris Illustré*, in May 1886. In the borders around the central figure of the Oiran, Van Gogh added a pond with water lilies, reeds and bamboo, two toads and two cranes. Both frogs and cranes were, it should be remembered, slang terms for a prostitute. The 'frogs', actually toads in this print, are copies from Utagawa Yoshimaru's *New Prints of Worms and Insects* dating from 1883, a reminder of how quickly prints were making their way from Japan to Europe.

The most famous of all Van Gogh's works showing Japanese prints, his *Portrait of Père Tanguy* (34), the artist's colour man, was also painted at this time. Colour salesmen, like cobblers, are the subject of legend, for both perform tasks which give them plenty of time to philosophize upon the arts as well as life's ups and downs. Julien (Père) Tanguy started his career as a travelling paint salesman who often met up with Pissarro, Pierre-Auguste Renoir (1891–1919), Monet and other artists in the outer suburbs of Paris. A volunteer soldier for the Commune in 1870, he was captured by the Versailles army and condemned to death, but saved by Degas's friend, Henri Rouart.

After the war Tanguy set up shop in the Rue Clauzel and took a liking to Paul Cézanne (1839–1906), providing him with paints and canvases in return for paintings. Later Van Gogh and Tanguy, politically kindred spirits, also became friends, rather to the dismay of Tanguy's wife, seeing her husband yet again exchange perfectly saleable paints and canvases for unsaleable paintings. He and his shop became something of a legend for the Impressionists.

Van Gogh made three portraits of Tanguy, two oil paintings and one drawing. In all three Tanguy is depicted against a background totally covered with Japanese prints. These were probably from Van Gogh's own collection since Tanguy did not deal in them, but the two men may have shared a private joke of realizing, via the print, a dream visit to Japan composed of such familiar themes as Mount Fuji, geishas, 'morning glory' flowers and typical landscapes of all four seasons.

For Van Gogh Japan became a Utopian dream. In a letter to Gauguin, Vincent recalled the ecstatic feelings he had on his first discovery of the south of France. 'I always remember the emotions which the trip from Paris to Arles evoked. How I kept watching to see if I had already reached Japan! Childish, isn't it?' In the fields around Arles he experimented by using Japanese reed pens with results which, far from being merely Japanese pastiche, can be numbered amongst his most powerful drawings.

In a letter to his sister written shortly after his arrival at Arles in February 1888, Vincent described how his personal vision had changed, that he now saw things 'with an eye more Japanese', and that if she studied Japanese prints she would come to understand modern artists who used bright and pure colours. He added:

as for me here I have no need for Japanese art, for I always tell myself that here I am in Japan, and that consequently I have only to open my eyes and to take in what I have before me.

In late September 1887 Vincent wrote from Arles to his brother, Theo, extolling the benefits of studying Japanese art:

If we study Japanese art, we see a man who is undoubtedly wise, philosophic and intelligent, who spends his time how? In studying the distance between the earth and the moon? No. In studying the policy of Bismarck? No. He studies a single blade of grass … this blade of grass leads him to draw every plant and then the seasons, the wide aspects of the countryside, then animals, then the human figure. So he passes his life, and life is too short to do the whole.

Come now, isn't it almost an actual religion which these simple Japanese teach us, who live in nature as though they themselves were flowers?

In July 1888 Van Gogh read the first edition of Pierre Loti's novel *Madame Chrysanthème*, a cynical precursor of Puccini's *Madame Butterfly* (1904) with illustrations by Luigi Rossi (1853–1923) and Félicien de Myrbach-Rheinfeld (1853–1940) which Van Gogh would transform into his own personal visions of Japan:

Have you read Mme Chrysanthème? *It gave me the impression that the real Japanese have nothing on their walls, that description of the cloister or pagoda where there was nothing (the drawings and curiosities all being hidden in the drawers). That is how you must look at Japanese art, in a very bright room, quite bare and open to the country.*

Van Gogh's continued reading of Loti's novel led to him becoming intrigued by the Japanese word *mousmé* or *musume*, which Loti had defined as follows:

Mousmé is a word for a girl or a very young woman. It is one of the most appealing words in Japanese, for it contains suggestions of moue (the sweet, funny little moue they have), *and above all* frimousse (that impish little face of theirs).

Inspired by Rossi's illustration, Van Gogh made his own *Portrait of a Mousmé* (35, 36).

35
Luigi Rossi,
Madame Chrysanthème
from Pierre Loti's
Madame Chrysanthème,
1888

36
Vincent van Gogh,
Portrait of a Mousmé,
1888.
Ink on paper,
32·5 x 24·5 cm
(12¾ x 9⅝ in).
Pushkin Museum,
Moscow

Other illustrations in the novel of funeral processions led by Japanese priests, *bonze* or *bozu* (37), led Vincent to trim his hair, slant his eyes and paint a self-portrait as a *bonze* (38).

Van Gogh was not alone in finding an ideal Japan without actually visiting the 'empire of the rising sun', as Japan was described by the de Goncourt brothers in their novel, *Manette Salomon*. Writing from Norway on 1 March 1895, the painter Claude Monet declared:

I have here a delicious motif, little islands at water level covered by snow, and a mountain in the background. One would say Japan … I did a mountain which is seen everywhere and which makes me think of Fuji-yama.

Monet collected Japanese prints throughout his life (his collection can be seen at his home in Giverny; see Chapter 10). He believed passionately, as he wrote in 1878, that:

We needed the arrival of Japanese albums in our midst, before anyone dared to sit down on a river bank, and juxtapose on canvas a roof which was bright red, a wall which was white, a green poplar, a yellow road and blue water. Before the example given by the Japanese, this was impossible, the painter always lied … all one ever saw on a canvas were subdued colours, drowning in a half-tone.

37
Luigi Rossi,
Funeral Procession from
Pierre Loti's *Madame
Chrysanthème*, 1888

38
Vincent van Gogh,
*Self-Portrait Dedicated
to Paul Gauguin*,
1888.
Oil on canvas,
60·5 x 49·4 cm
(23³⁄₄ x 19¹⁄₂ in).
The Fogg Art Museum,
Harvard University,
Cambridge, MA

39
Katsushika Hokusai,
South Wind, Clear Dawn,
from *Thirty-Six Views of
Mount Fuji*,
c.1830–2.
Colour woodblock,
26 x 38·1 cm
(10¼ x 15 in)

It may well be that Hokusai's *Thirty-Six Views of Mount Fuji*, showing the great volcano in different weather conditions and at different times of day, inspired the sequence paintings such as those by Monet – of haystacks, poplars, the façade of Rouen Cathedral, Westminster Bridge and even the water lilies which occupied the last twenty-five years of his life.

This view is substantiated by the de Goncourt journal in which on 17 February 1892 Edmond noted:

As we were leafing through the big plates of Fujiyama by Hokusai, Manzi [Michel Manzi (1849–1915), Italian painter, publisher, and friend of Degas] said to me: 'Look, here are Monet's great yellow areas.' And he was right. People are not sufficiently aware of how much our contemporary landscape artists have borrowed from these pictures, especially Monet, whom I often encounter at Bing's in the little attic where Lévy is in charge of the Japanese prints.

This encounter took place only a year after Monet had first exhibited fifteen of his *Haystack* series of paintings, whose profound interrelationship with Hokusai's *Thirty-Six Views of Mount Fuji* can be seen particularly clearly between Hokusai's *South Wind, Clear Dawn* (*c*.1830–2), the so-called *Red Fuji* (a copy of which Monet owned; 39), and his own *Haystack, Sunset* (1891; 40).

This is one of twenty-three pictures of haystacks which Monet painted between 1891 and 1892 at different times of day and in different weather conditions. Monet could have seen the full Fuji series either in Bing's shop or at the famous exhibition of Japanese prints held in 1890 at the École des Beaux-Arts in Paris.

It is generally held that Paul Cézanne, of all his contemporaries, the Impressionists, is said to have had the least interest in Japanese art. However, his own long fascination with the depiction of the landscape of Provence led him to paint Mont Ste-Victoire more than sixty times from different viewpoints during two periods 1882–90 and 1901–6. Remarkably Hokusai did not begin his own endless variations on the theme of Fuji until he was seventy and pursued the subject until his death at ninety. All we shall ever know for certain is that both artists in their later years produced some of the most memorable works of their time, in homage to a specific mountain.

To conclude let us return to Van Gogh's explanation of what he conceived as being the essence of Japan, by turning to another of his letters:

I saw a magnificent and strange effect this evening. A very big boat loaded with coal on the Rhône, moored to the quay. Seen from above, it was all shining and still wet with rain; the water was yellowish white and the clouds pearl grey, the sky violet with an orange streak in the west: the town violet. On the boat some poor boatmen in dirty blue and white came and went carrying the cargo onto the shore. It was pure Hokusai.

Van Gogh might have added, that it was highly reminiscent of the effects of dawn so vividly described in the de Goncourt novel, *Manette Salomon,* which he, a keen reader of novels, had just enjoyed.

For thirty years the Japoniste option would spread from France across Europe and to America. The list of artists affected could be extended to include names as varied as Georges Seurat (1859–91), Paul Signac (1863–1935), Gustav Klimt (1862–1918) and Egon Schiele (1890–1918). The final years of the nineteenth century would see one of the most lasting of all the effects of the Japanese print in the graphic discipline of lithography and its use in the new art form of the coloured poster.

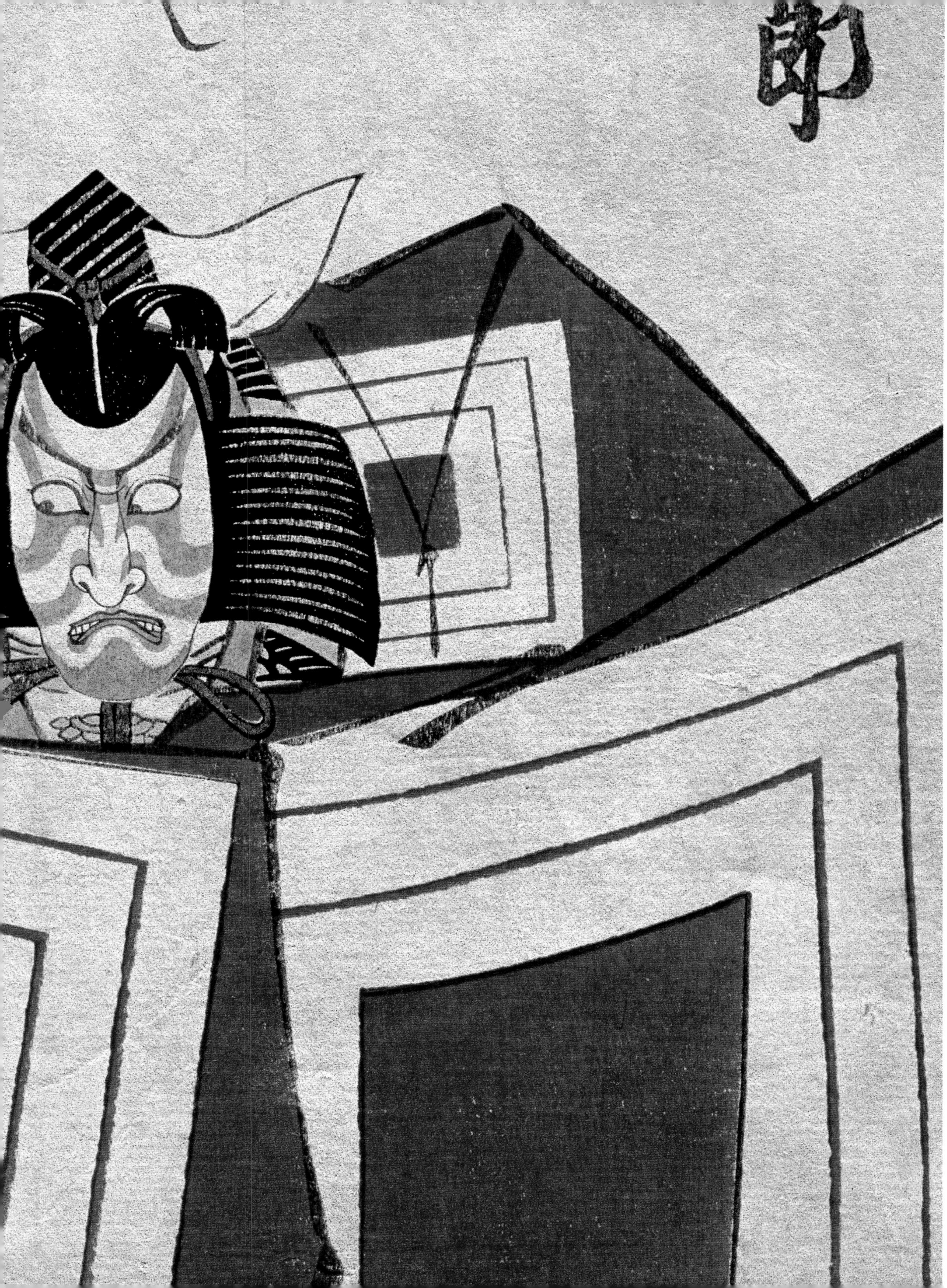

Chapter three: The Poster and the Japanese Print

CHAMPFLEURY – LES CHATS

DEUXIÈME ÉDITION avec 52 DESSINS

Un volume illustré, Prix 5 Francs
En Vente ici.

Previous page
Utagawa Toyokuni,
Ichikawa Danjuro VII
in the Shibaraku Role
of Kumai Taro
(detail of 44)

41
Édouard Manet,
The Cats' Rendezvous,
from the cover of *Les*
Chats by Champfleury,
1868.
Lithograph

42
Toshusai Sharaku,
The Actor, Sanogawa
Ichimatsu,
1794–5.
Colour woodblock,
38 x 25·7 cm
(15 x 10⅛)

Crazes and hobbies enough and
to spare
Our forebears have left us. Now,
say is it right
For leaders of taste a new cult
to declare
Postage stamps, book plates, blue
china and quite …
Dozens of things most aesthetic
and mystic
Pass for the moment away out of sight
Now is the cult of the poster artistic.
Anonymous, c.1890

Advertisement is an absolute necessity
of modern life … [yet] still there is a
general feeling that the artist who
puts his art into the poster is déclassé –
on the streets – and consequently
of light character.
Aubrey Beardsley, 1894

Today, as neon lights spell out their
imperative messages to the public in
the city centres of London, Paris and
Tokyo, or television commercials issue
their thirty-second categorical
demands, it is hard to understand fully
the dominance of the poster as an
advertising medium in the second
half of the nineteenth century.

The main thrust of commercial
advertising campaigns is now
televisual, for the poster's role is largely
confined to enlivening long waits for
motorists in traffic jams, or cheering up
waiting passengers on the platforms of
underground stations, with artwork
heavily reliant on photographic
imagery.

In the 1860s, before the technical
innovation of colour lithography began
to liberate poster art, the hoardings of
European cities were given over
completely to bill-stickers, who pasted
black-and-white typographical
advertisements one upon another,
creating a monotonous palimpsest of
print. This sorry state of affairs began
to change when it first became
possible for serious artists to pause
from their strict pursuit of 'high art',
and undertake a wider range of
graphic commissions, combining both
Japonisme and the new invention of
colour lithography to create the
'golden age of the poster'. The
poster's impact was greatest in France,
where it intriguingly paralleled the
Impressionist painters' delight in the
rainbow palette of Japanese prints.

There are striking similarities between
the two processes of lithography used
by Western artists and the complex
woodcut technique employed by the
Japanese print-makers. Both achieved
dramatic effects by the bold use of
colour and flat colour areas, thick
outlines and simplicity of design.

The Japanese woodcut was essentially
a team effort. The artist who drew the
original design passed it to an
assistant who pasted the drawing on
to a plank of cherrywood cut across
the grain, which was then taken to a
block-cutter who cut different blocks
for each individual pigment up to as
many as sixteen, far more than is usual
in Europe. The blocks were kept in strict
ratio to each other by *kento* marks,
which ensure the different hues are
exactly in relationship with one
another.

Lithography was discovered by the
German, Aloys Senefelder, in 1798, and
was at first named 'Poly Autography'
from the Greek, meaning literally
'many originals'. Unlike most graphic
disciplines it is not an intaglio process
achieved by cutting *into* a surface, but
a process whereby the picture is made
on top of a surface, using the principle
popularly known as 'water-off-a-
duck's-back' or the antipathy of grease
to water. A drawing with special greasy
chalks and ink is made on a prepared
slab of limestone. The stone is then
washed with nitric acid, wiped with
gum arabic and dampened. When
printing ink is rolled on, it adheres to
the greasy chalks but not to the wet
stone. A palette of different colours
can be achieved by using separate
stones and superimposing one colour
upon another to produce a third.

Manet's lithograph of *The Cats'*
Rendezvous (41), a feline glimpse of
the roofs of Paris, can claim the honour
of being one of the earliest posters, as
it was used to advertise his friend
Champfleury's book *Les Chats* of 1868.
Its weakness is that the coarse
lettering, almost certainly added by
the printer, is not integrated into the
design (the example of the Japanese
print had not yet been fully understood
by Western artists). Japanese prints
had circulated since the 1850s but it
was in the 1870s that they really
began to influence the new art form of
the poster. They could be studied by
poster artists in exhibitions, galleries
and special numbers on Japan in
magazines such as *Paris illustré*.

At the very heart of the *ukiyo-e* print
business was one of its most popular
subjects, *kabuki*, the most junior of the
three major forms of Japanese drama
stemming from the more spiritual *noh*
theatre and the puppet drama *bunraku*.
Kabuki is traditionally said to have
begun in the Tokugawa era in the
early seventeenth century with female
performers who included a number
of ladies of easy virtue. Over the years
their activities became so scandalous
that from 1629 female performers and
dancers were banned outright. From
early on, women's roles in *kabuki*
dramas were played by men known as
onnagata, who can be identified by the
small square of fabric fastened around
their brows to cover their shaven
foreheads, as in a portrait of Sanogawa
Ichimatsu (42) by Sharaku (*fl.*1794–5).

43
Attributed to the Torii
school,
Theatre signboard
depicting scenes from the
play *Nishikigi Sakae
Komachi*,
*c.*1758.
Ink, colour and gold
on paper,
177·6 x 97·2 cm
(70 x 38¼ in).
Museum of Fine Arts,
Boston

44
Utagawa Toyokuni,
*Ichikawa Danjuro VII
in the Shibaraku Role
of Kumai Taro*,
1807.
Colour woodblock,
38·7 x 40 cm
(15¼ x 15¾ in)

Entertainment always needs advertisement. A few rare signboards (*kanban*) for some *kabuki* performances survive, the earliest dating from 1758, acting as a poster and attracting the passing crowds to enter the theatre and enjoy the performances of leading actors (43). This signboard portrays two scenes from a drama. In the bottom half, the board tells one of the incidents befalling the poetess Ono no Komachi, who is threatened by the villain played by Danjuro IV, a member of one of the great theatrical dynasties, which survives today.

The sheer theatricality of the signboard prepares us for the dramatic work of such artists as Hiroshige, Kunisada, Kuniyoshi (*c.*1892–1953), Shunsho and especially Toyokuni (1769–1825; 44), whose portrayal of an actor striking a pose in an *otokodate* role (a role similar to that of Robin Hood – robbing the rich to help the poor) has just the bold simplicity of outline which so excited European artists. Such theatrical prints are brilliant records of individual performances, capturing the memorable moments when a climax in the dramatic action elicits a roar of applause from the fans as the action freezes for a minute or so. These prints would be passed from hand to hand in teahouses, thus serving an immediate purpose as 'fliers' to advertise actors or forthcoming performances, but coincidentally also preserving, like a fly in amber, the buzz and excitement of the *kabuki* stage. Single actor prints such as this were sold by hawkers to the audience.

One of the most important artists to portray the *kabuki* stage was Toshosai Sharaku, a mysterious figure appearing in 1794 and disappearing within a year without trace. In just nine months he produced 144 prints of actors appearing at the three *kabuki* theatres in Edo. He was particularly successful in capturing the grimaces and grotesque expressions which convey the actors' stage personae, and excelled at brutal close-up images, so cruel that it has been suggested that he was murdered by one of his sitters. Sharaku's powerful imagery is seen at its most effective in such noteworthy examples as the actor, Tanimura Torazo, in *The Loved Wife's Parti-Coloured Reins*, published in 1794 (45).

There were, of course, prints on other *ukiyo-e* subjects, many inspired by life in the chief centre of pleasure at Edo, the enclosed quarter of the Yoshiwara. On entering it the visitor was confronted with a complex hierarchy of merchants, waitresses, musicians, geishas and prostitutes. Off-duty actors and incognito samurai were often among the clients. The prints which record this society were many and various but included the depiction of such themes as Kunisada's *At the Dressing Table*, in which a woman muses on the aesthetic pleasures of the colour white, such as white chrysanthemums, white snow or just being a beauty with white skin.

Such prints of *bijin* – beautiful women – not only captivated their immediate purchasers, but also found their way back to Europe, and in particular Paris, where they would inspire the first great practitioner of the art of poster design, Jules Chéret (1836–1932), who towards the end of his career defined his aims:

The poster artist must be a psychologist; he must have gone through a hard school and become familiar with the logical and optical laws of his art. He must invent something that will attract and excite even the average man when the street scene passes before his eyes as he walks along the pavement or drives past in his car; and nothing, I believe, is better suited to this purpose than a simple, charming and yet captivating picture in bright, yet harmonious colours.

Several of these aims were also described in an article of 1901 on Japanese art and the poster, in which the critic Raymond Needham described the essential qualities a poster required for success:

Take any representative Japanese print – a book illustration, a broadsheet or a theatre bill – and it will be found to embody all that a good poster should. One dominant idea is presented graphically, beautifully, the detail does not weaken, but actually enforces the motif.

45
Toshusai Sharaku,
The Actor Tanimura Torazo,
as the Villain in The Loved
Wife's Parti-Coloured Reins,
1794.
Colour woodblock,
37 x 24·9 cm
(14½ x 9¾ in)

46
Jules Chéret,
La Diaphane,
1890.
Colour lithograph,
86 x 59 cm
(33⅞ x 23¼ in)

47
Georges Goursat ('Sem'),
Palais de Glace,
c.1910.
Colour lithograph,
30 x 46 cm (11¾ x 18 in)

There is not a superfluous line, the colour scheme of flat tints is fresh and striking but always harmonious. The composition gives an idea of balance and breadth, but affords no hint as to how these qualities have been obtained … The general effect is decorative in the highest degree, may be humorous and is certainly pervaded by the 'hidden soul of harmony'.

As a boy, Chéret was apprenticed to a lithographer, and then worked in London for seven years studying developments in the processes which enabled posters to be produced in a larger format. More than any other artist, he effected the change-over from the old typographical poster to the pictorial poster, in which female charms demonstrate the classic advertising dictum that sex sells. This is demonstrated in posters for beauty aids – one for soap and one for a face-powder *La Diaphane* (1890; 46), to which the great actress Sarah Bernhardt lent her name – an early example of the now familiar process of celebrity product endorsement, and an image that recalls the flat white make-up of the geisha.

When Chéret began designing posters, Napoleon III (r.1852–70) was demolishing the old narrow streets of Paris, and Baron Haussmann was building wide boulevards with large white buildings on either side. These walls provided perfect sites for the new flamboyant posters.

The citizens of Paris lived in public by frequenting cafés, and at the hour of the aperitif, half the population was sitting at little tables on the pavement watching the other half go by. Chéret's posters provided the perfect background to the comings and goings of Parisian life. Indeed, in an interview with the English critic, Charles Hiatt, Chéret maintained that for him, posters were not necessarily a good form of advertising but that they made excellent murals. It was his great achievement to take the visual language of popular folk art, add the delicate colours of the butterfly wings and Japanese prints he kept by him as he worked, and produce a new art form. His posters of the 1890s were aptly described by the contemporary critic, Crauzat, as 'a hooray of reds, a hallelujah of yellows and a primal scream of blues'.

Chéret loved to portray the constantly changing productions at popular music halls such as the Folies-Bergère, El Dorado and Olympia. At the time of the *belle époque* (1865–1914), dancers whirled across the stage in a tornado of sound, created by the most famous singers of their day, with loud orchestral accompaniment in the form of a noisy clash of cymbals. Another popular social activity was ice-skating (47), portrayed both by Chéret and Georges Goursat ('Sem'; 1863–1934). Sem was the chronicler of the social scene in Paris, Biarritz and Monte Carlo before the First World War.

48
Jules Chéret,
Pastilles Poncelet,
1896.
Colour lithograph,
127·3 x 92·4 cm
(50¹⁄₈ x 36³⁄₈ in)

49
Utagawa Toyokuni,
Two Actors in a Snow
Scene, One Dressed
as a Woman,
*c.*1814.
Colour woodblock,
37·4 x 50·8 cm
(14³⁄₄ x 20 in)

A number of Chéret's annual
Christmas seasonal posters were
entitled *étrennes* – literally, festive gifts –
which frequently included Japanese
toys, dolls, fans, masks, paper sparrows
and goldfish. These posters enlivened
the streets when shown on the
'Morrisy', round advertising columns
invented in the 1860s as a device for
displaying playbills, which can still be
seen today. Oscar Wilde, after a visit to
Paris in 1891, eulogized 'the charming
kiosks', which, 'when illuminated at
night from within, are as lovely as a
fantastic Chinese lantern, especially
when the transparent advertisements
are from the clever pencil of
M. Chéret.'

The public loved to collect Chéret
posters in proof state before the
letterpress was added, such as the
poster for *Pastilles Poncelet* (48),
in which the falling sleet forms a
wintery comparison with Toyokuni's
Snow Scene (49). Like Hokusai, Chéret
lived to a great age, producing 1,200
posters in the course of his long career.
According to a contemporary:

when he [Chéret] dealt with a stone
already impregnated with yellow,
blue or red ink, he projected a fine
shower of colour that … resulted
in gradations and ranges of tones
whose secret seemed impenetrable.
He did it with the dexterity of a
Japanese, while humming or chatting
with his charming French gaiety..

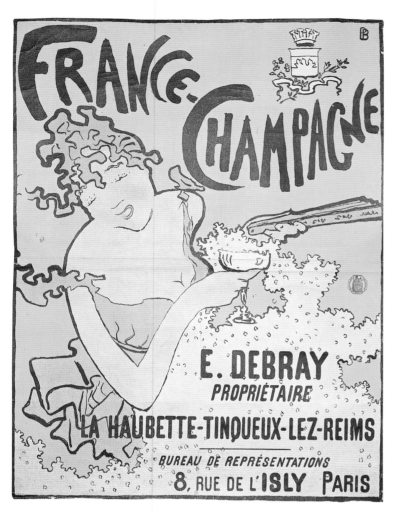

50
Pierre Bonnard,
France-Champagne,
1891.
Colour lithograph,
79·3 x 59·9 cm
(31⅛ x 23½ in)

51
Katsushika Hokusai,
Beneath the Wave off Kanagawa
(*The Great Wave*) from *Thirty-
Six Views of Mount Fuji*,
*c.*1830–2.
Colour woodblock,
25·7 x 37·9 cm
(10⅛ x 15 in)

While Chéret was the father of the poster, 'admired by policemen and people of taste alike', the great master of the discipline was Chéret's pupil, Henri de Toulouse-Lautrec (1864–1901). His friend, Gauzi, said that Lautrec considered the Japanese his 'brothers' as they were closer to his restricted size and beside them he looked normal. Interviewed in old age, Chéret hailed Lautrec as his successor and heir, saying, 'Lautrec is a master'. Lautrec's initial interest in the poster discipline was not aroused by Chéret's work, however, but by that of Pierre Bonnard (1867–1947) and his *France-Champagne*, a prize-winning entry in a poster competition advertising a wine merchant (50). Bonnard's poster is appropriately awash with the bubbles of its product, a frothy sea from which emerges the model, a chic Parisienne borrowed from Chéret, fan in one hand, glass in the other, who giggles her way onto a poster perfectly 'on message' and nicely calculated to achieve its aim and sell its product – champagne. As a composition, Bonnard's poster brilliantly mingles lessons absorbed both from Gauguin (for example, his use of fluent black lines set against a vivid yellow paper; see 135) and the Japanese print. From the most famous of all Japanese prints, Hokusai's *The Great Wave* (51), Bonnard borrows and satirizes the stylized spray and transforms it into the bubbly froth of the champagne.

Impressed by the success of the poster *France-Champagne*, Lautrec sought out Bonnard to discuss poster design. It was an art form which Lautrec came to love and which he would completely revolutionize, steeped as he was in the world of the Japanese print, from which he acquired various stylistic mannerisms – bold outlines, trimmed edges and the use of a diverse range of flat colour.

Lautrec's name will always be associated with that of the music hall in the Montmartre area of Paris, the Moulin Rouge (52). The worldwide fame of the Moulin Rouge began on 6 October 1889, when it gave birth to the cancan. The club had become badly run down under its previous manager, and was given a face-lift by an enterprising businessman who turned it into a glittering dream palace, with rooms decorated in Oriental and Moorish styles, where people could dance in an open courtyard under the gaze of a huge wooden elephant. The arms of the mill, which gave the cabaret its name, still keep turning today. The hall's great attraction was a dance quadrille from the nearby music hall, Elysée-Montmartre. Its wild dancers vied with each other in the spectacle of the cancan, culminating in a jump in the air, an ear-piercing shriek and the splits.

52
Henri de Toulouse-
Lautrec,
Moulin Rouge: La Goulue,
1891.
Colour lithograph,
191 x 117 cm
(75$^1_8$ x 46$^1_4$ in)

53
Keisai Eisen,
The Lonely Night House,
*c.*1848.
Colour woodcut,
36·5 x 25·5 cm
(14$^3_8$ x 10 in)

54
Henri de Toulouse-
Lautrec,
*Self-Portrait as a Sword
Hilt* (*Tsuba*), bookplate
for Maurice Guibert,
1894

The female dancers, notably La Goulue and Jane Avril, competed with each other, and also danced with the remarkable double-jointed male dancer, Valentin le Désossé, which means literally, the Boneless Wonder. He is portrayed in the foreground while La Goulue dominates the centre of the dance floor surrounded by an admiring circle of spectators depicted in silhouette. Similar compositions using a distant frieze of silhouettes can be seen in Japanese woodcuts, an example being *The Lonely Night House* by Keisai Eisen, which shows the shadowy figures of a courtesan's entourage on a spring evening (53).

Lautrec was so enamoured of Japanese prints that he was prepared to exchange one of his own works for a coveted example. He sent to Japan for special inks and brushes, and designed his own seal-like monogram, derived from a Japanese source, a *tsuba* or sword hilt (54), and loved to dress up in Japanese costume (55). His favoured subject matter – popular entertainers, dancers and dance halls, bars and restaurants, prostitutes and their activities – have many affinities with themes often to be seen in Japanese prints, as for example, *Debauchery* (56).

55
Toulouse-Lautrec in
ceremonial Japanese
samurai costume,
photographed by
Maurice Guibert,
1892

Lautrec owed a particular debt to Utamaro, and there are obvious parallels between his *Elles* album (1896), the lithographic products of Lautrec's stay in the brothels of Montmartre, and Utamaro's works produced in the 'Houses of Pleasure' in the Yoshiwara. Lautrec owned a copy of Utamaro's erotic work, *The Poem of the Pillow*, which he had acquired from the de Goncourt brothers (57).

Lautrec's technical debts to Japanese prints were extensive. As Berthe Morisot once observed:

the imaginative and total integration
of image and lettering into one
decorative and instructive whole in
his posters also owes much to
Japanese prototypes.

From them he also gained his assurance in posing single figures in bold silhouette against a neutral background, as, for example, in the famous poster *Ambassadeurs: Aristide Bruant dans son Cabaret*.

The poster entitled *Divan Japonais* was made for a café which was trans-formed in 1893 by decorations of lanterns and bamboo chairs in what was considered to be the Japanese style (58). In the design of the poster, Lautrec decided to adopt Japanese principles of composition, cropping off the image by truncating the body of the singer, Yvette Guilbert, who is recognizable only by her distinctive black gloves.

56
Henri de Toulouse-Lautrec,
Debauchery,
1894.
Lithograph,
23·5 x 32·2 cm
(9³⁄₈ x 12⁵⁄₈ in)

57
Kitagawa Utamaro,
Lovers from *The Poem*
of the Pillow,
1788.
Colour woodblock,
28·8 x 37·4 cm
(11¹⁄₄ x 14³⁄₄ in)

58
Henri de Toulouse-Lautrec,
Divan Japonais,
1893.
Colour lithograph,
81·5 x 62·3 cm
(32 x 24¹₂ in)

59
Kitagawa Utamaro,
*Servant on the Verandah
of the Restaurant
Nakataya,*
c.1794.
Colour woodblock

Years later Yvette Guilbert recalled the venue:

a little hall such as you may see in a provincial café, with a low ceiling and where at a pinch a hundred and fifty or two hundred people might be got in … a platform perched about five feet above the floor made it necessary to remember that I mustn't raise my arms incautiously or I should knock them against the ceiling. Oh! that ceiling where the heat from the gas footlights was such that our heads swam in a suffocating furnace!

Lautrec brilliantly conveys this feeling of claustrophobia by cutting off Guilbert's head completely, thus concentrating our visual attention upon the elegant seated figure of the dancer, Jane Avril. The flat patterning, asymmetric composition, elongated figures and bold outlines reveal the influence of the Japanese wood block, all elements to be found in Utamaro Kitagawa's depiction of a similar scene showing a servant on the verandah of the restaurant Nakataya (*c.*1794; 59). Although Lautrec greatly admired Jane Avril, who became a close friend, she complained that Lautrec's posters of her always made her look like a monster.

She may have been thinking of *Jane Avril au Jardin de Paris* (1893; 60), a work deriving its composition from Japanese prints, notably in the depiction of the double-bass player, whose face is half concealed by his hand that holds the instrument, which dominates the framing of the scene. It is rewarding to compare Lautrec's portrayal of the truncated hand with the bony knee of Hiroshige's oarsman in his *The Benten Ford Across the Oi River* of 1858 (61).

The notoriety that invariably surrounded the launch of Lautrec's posters put off many performers who still preferred to rely on Chéret for less innovative designs. One such figure was Loie Fuller, the most daring and original dancer of the 1890s. Her performances inspired poems from poets as diverse as Stephen Mallarmé, Arthur Symons and W B Yeats, while Chéret produced for her a poster printed in four colours of her famous *Fire Dance* in which she performed upon a stage of glass illuminated from all sides. A page of one of Whistler's sketchbooks vibrates with drawings inspired by her butterfly dance, which had a Japanese prototype. A fascinating contemporary of Fuller was Sadayakko, a Japanese actress (see also Chapter 7), who, with her company, was presented by Fuller at her theatre during the 1900 Paris exhibition.

62
William Nicholson,
Sadayakko,
c.1900–1.
Colour lithograph,
image: 24·6 x 23·7 cm
(9³₄ x 9³₈ in)

63
Eugène Grasset,
La Vitrioleuse,
1894.
Colour lithograph,
59·4 x 43 cm
(23³₈ x 17 in)

64
Jacques Villon,
Le Grillon,
1899.
Colour lithograph,
130 x 93 cm
(51¹₈ x 36⁵₈ in)

Sadayakko is seen here in a woodcut (62) by William Nicholson (1872–1949), one of the British poster artists known as the Beggarstaff Brothers.

Eugène Grasset (1841–1917), who would become a major French poster artist, began his career working under the architect Eugène Viollet-le-Duc (1814–79) on the restoration of the medieval walled city of Carcassonne in the south of France. He worked with great flair in an artistic discipline with similar problems to the poster, that of designing stained glass, and was also deeply influenced by the strong lines of Japanese prints. As a poster designer he met with mixed fortunes. In 1893 he interpreted the great actress Sarah Bernhardt as Joan of Arc. The Maid of Orléans was France's national heroine, and Grasset treated the subject with respectful dignity. The solemnity of the image did not meet with the unqualified approval of the actress, who wanted a more dramatic interpretation of her stage role, and demanded alterations which Grasset carried out with great reluctance, thus ending their collaboration. Grasset went on in 1899 to depict the terrifying image of a morphine addict injecting herself, and *La Vitrioleuse* preparing to throw vitriol at a target (63), which closely relate to the powerful close-up, large-scale heads of actors in performance by Toyokuni and particularly Sharaku (see 45).

EAST COAST
BY L·N·E·R

66
Aubrey Beardsley,
Poster advertising
children's books (detail),
1894.
Colour lithograph

67
Tom Purvis,
East Coast by LNER,
1925.
Colour lithograph,
100.6 x 126.5 cm
(39⅝ x 49¾ in)

65
Poster for Clement
bicycles,
*c.*1906.
Colour lithograph

The artist, Jacques Villon (1875–1963), who would become one of the first abstract painters, created in 1899 a memorable Art Nouveau poster, *Le Grillon* (64). A friend of both Théophile Alexandre Steinlen (1859–1923) and Lautrec, whom he met at the Moulin Rouge, Villon's work has splendid power and originality, and its calligraphy is highly reminiscent of Japanese prints, especially in the striking lettering which draws attention to the smart 'American Bar' at the restaurant.

Among the most amusing and socially interesting themes of the turn of the twentieth century were posters of bicycles and typewriters. Two anony-mous posters show intrepid Japanese girls, one actually wearing a kimono while cycling (65), while another uses a typewriter. For women, the bicycle, with its freedom of movement, of association and of dress, was a sign-ificant and liberating instrument. By featuring women, the manufacturer also implied to the contemporary viewer that the bicycle handled easily, and that 'femininity' was not lost, as some critics insinuated, but actually enhanced by riding a bicycle. Women were therefore not only portrayed, but idealized, in bicycle posters all over Europe and America.

AVBREY
BEARDSLEY

All these artists shared one thing in common. They owed and acknowled-ged a great debt to the art of Japan. As in every aspect of the graphic arts which he essayed, Aubrey Beardsley (1872–98) introduced into his posters novel qualities of remarkable originality and his indebtedness to the Japanese print is clearly revealed in his placing of the figure and the flat treatment of patterns on garments.

Beardsley's delight in being deliberately perverse could take many forms. In 1894, great controversy was aroused by his poster for a rarefied double bill of new plays, one by the young poet W B Yeats at the Avenue Theatre. The comic journal *Punch*, unable to resist a pun, chaffed in mock Cockney, 'ave a new poster', and went on to regret that 'your Japanese Rossetti girl is not a thing to be admired ...' Criticism was also levelled at Beardsley's poster for children's books where, indeed, the seated lady does seem a little *too* adult to be reading books for children (66). The tall upright format of the vertical panel on the left of both posters reflects Beardsley's love of Japanese art, and his study of 'pillar' prints – *hashira-e* – tall prints which could only be displayed in the formal alcove of the Japanese home like a hanging scroll painting, or on the side of a square wooden pillar.

The difficulties inherent in designing for such a tall and slim shape were just the type of challenge which Beardsley enjoyed. In an interview Beardsley claimed to prefer poster work to book illustration, remarking that although he personally had no great care for colour, he recognized that its use was essen-tial for posters. For him poster work:

pays well and it's interesting. I enjoy the colour. I myself only use flat tints, and work as if I was colouring a map, the effect aimed at being that pro-duced by a Japanese print.

With the greater ease of travel and more generous holidays of the twentieth century a growing demand arose for travel posters featuring in particular the attractions of seaside resorts. One of the last major figures to use Japanese-inspired themes in designing posters was the Scottish artist Tom Purvis (1888–1957). His poster for the London and North Eastern Railway with its vivid red parasol casting its protecting brown shade over two bathers wearing black costumes under a flawless azure blue sky (67), demonstrates the ongoing validity of a subject popular both in Japanese prints and advertising. Despite a lifetime's experience this is the dream we all have of the weather on Bank Holidays in England, the triumph of hope over experience, a wish to enter the always confident world of the poster where the sun always shines.

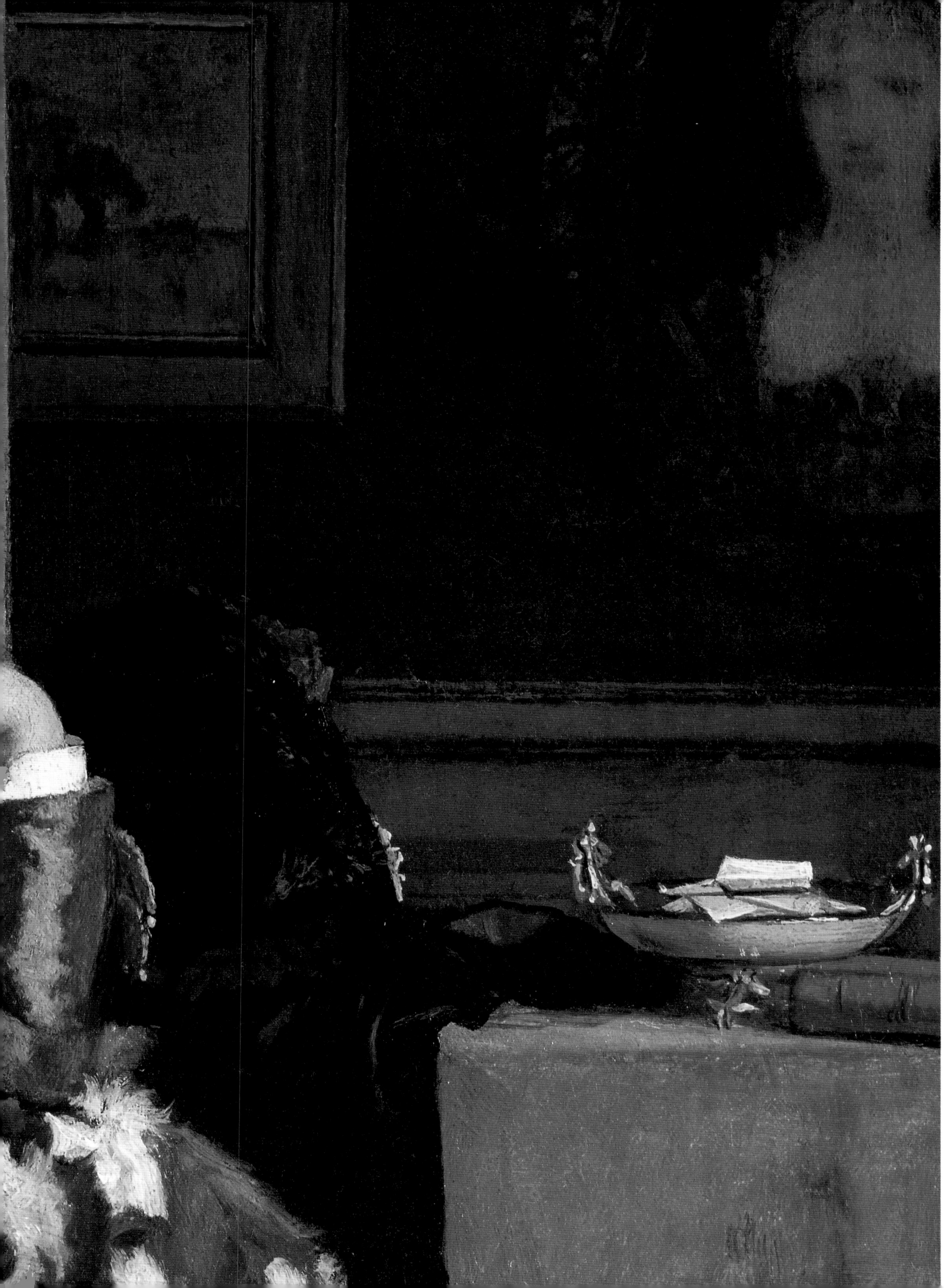

Chapter four: The Decorative Arts

Previous page
Alfred Stevens,
The Duchess (formerly
known as *The Blue
Dress*), *c.*1880
(detail of 80)

68
*The International
Exhibition: The Japanese
Court* engraving from the
Illustrated London News,
1862

*Avoid the European and cleave to
the Oriental.*
W J Loftie, 1876

*The very 'marks' on the bottom of a
piece of rare crockery are able to throw
me into a gibbering ecstasy; and I
could forsake a drowning relative to
help dispute about whether the stopper
of a departed Buon Retiro scent-bottle
was genuine or spurious. Many people
say that for a male person, bric-a-brac
hunting is about as robust a business
as making doll-clothes, or decorating
Japanese pots with decalomanie
butterflies would be ...*
Mark Twain, 1879–80

Although the shogunate regime of
Satsuma began to make overtures to
show goods in the 1851 exhibition in
the Crystal Palace, London, the times
were not propitious, and Japan was not
represented. By the time of the 1862
exhibition (68) a selection of Japanese
artefacts was made by the first British
diplomat in Japan, Sir Rutherford
Alcock. He had been the first
representative of the British Crown
in Edo since 1859 where he had collected 'a fair sample of the industrial
arts of the Japanese'.

The success of the exhibition was
marred by the untimely death of the
Prince Consort, but after the show
closed, both goods which had failed
to arrive in time and objects from the
display of prints, ceramics, textile
stencils and furniture were all bought
up by the Regent Street Oriental
Warehouse of Farmer and Rogers.
It was in this shop that Rossetti is
reputed to have introduced Whistler to
the manager Arthur Lasenby Liberty,
who was later to found his own famous
firm in 1875. Indeed Liberty's would
become the most important cross-
pollinating centre of the Aesthetic
Movement and Japonisme.

It was not until 1867 in Paris that
Japan officially participated in an
international exhibition. As was often
the case, the show was partly
motivated politically by the shogun
government which was on the brink
of collapse, but sought and found a
sympathetic supporter in France.

Japanese art also found its champions
in England. John C Robinson was an
immensely able administrator who
was largely responsible not only for
the Museum of Ornamental Art in
London, which eventually became the
Victoria and Albert Museum, but also
for making even the name South
Kensington, the area which still houses
the museum, virtually synonymous with
the decorative arts.

In 1855 he was laudatory in his
appraisal of the first Japanese
porcelain acquired before the
foundation of the museum in 1852:

*The Japanese porcelain is perhaps
distinguished by a purer taste in
design, the shapes of the pieces are
simpler and more elegant than the
Chinese, whilst in the painted
decoration, grotesque or fantastic
subjects are less affected; simple
renderings of natural flowers and
foliage, and elegant conventionalized
floral ornaments, being very frequent.
In colour, generally speaking, Japanese porcelain is fuller and richer in
effect than the Chinese.*

For its date this is a highly perceptive
appraisal of Japanese decoration and it
explains clearly the distinctive qualities
of the novel artefacts which both
Britain and the continent would so
greatly admire. This admiration would
soon reflect the truth of the old adage
that 'imitation is the sincerest form of
flattery' – however, some such
imitations would lead to extremely
strange and bizarre forms.

From the very beginning of the influx,
Japanese artefacts were copied all over
Britain and Europe – sometimes with
great sensitivity, sometimes with
appalling vulgarity or comic
misunderstanding of Japanese motifs.

This plagiarizing process is more
evident in the production of ceramics
than in any other discipline. The
reason for much of the great
popularity of Japanese wares lay in
their ability to present natural objects
in a completely novel manner. The
thought process was that by studying
and copying Japan, one could come to
a better understanding of one's own
place in nature. Throughout Europe,
wherever the ceramic disciplines of
pottery and porcelain flourished,
copying was rife and industrial
espionage thrived. Tracing the
resemblances and differences between
prototype and copy can lead to a
rewarding game of ceramic 'Snap',
providing immense entertainment for
the collector, dealer or art historian.
So successful, for example, were the
'Japanese' Royal Worcester Porcelain
pieces that a number of European
potteries copied them in large
numbers. Soon there stood on virtually
every 'what-not' or shelf throughout
the land, myriad vases and pots with
asymmetrical patterns of blossom, fans
and storks all proclaiming the stylistic
victory of Japanese design.

69
Katsushika Hokusai,
Various Types of Birds
from the *Manga* **vol. III,**
1815.
Colour woodblock,
17·5 x 11·5 cm (7 x 4½ in)

70
Félix Bracquemond,
Rooster Plate, **part of the**
faience 'service japonais'
commissioned by
Eugène Rousseau,
1867.
Glazed earthenware,
diameter: 24·5 cm (9⅝ in).
Private collection

The *Manga*, a particularly popular Japanese source from which Europeans borrowed motifs, has already been described (see Chapter 2). What exactly was in these fifteen volumes which made them so exciting? To turn the pages of the *Manga* today is to be transported back to two very different cities, the crowded streets of Edo – the capital of Japan – and Paris – the artistic centre of Europe – avid for visual novelty. The word *Manga* has been translated as 'drawing things just as they come', and the slim volumes do indeed provide a glorious hugger-mugger of random sketches, great landscapes, alternating with comic scenes in the bathhouse, some of which may well have influenced Degas. The architect and furniture designer, E W Godwin (1833–86), used illustrations from it of building methods and joinery. Exotic birds, fish, insects, animals and flowers provide an amazing cross-section of visual imagery (69). The possible decorative themes which can be used on pottery and porcelain are legion and sometimes conflict with European symbolism. Storks, for example, symbol of good luck and childbirth in Europe, represent happy old age in Japan, while the fox, a cunning villain in Europe, is regarded as a benevolent friend to the farmer whom he helps by eating the rodents that gobble up the grain.

In the winter of 1866–7 Félix Bracquemond designed a faience 'service japonais' made at one of the twin factories of Montereau and Creil to the commission of the glass-maker Eugène Rousseau (1827–91), with such motifs as cocks with flowing tail feathers (70), fish, plants and insects copied after Hokusai's drawings in the *Manga* and other Hokusai books. The service was a great success, was reissued twice and was also much imitated by other factories. Today it is regarded as being the most important example of the influence of Japonisme in French decorative art of the nineteenth century. More immediately, the service was put to practical use at the dinner evenings of the Club Jinglar, an exotic Japoniste rendezvous at which frock coats and cutlery were supplanted by kimonos and *hashi* (chopsticks).

In England similar Japoniste activities first began when a new company, Royal Worcester Porcelain, was founded in 1862, under the leadership of a dynamic art director Richard William Binns, who held the post with great distinction until he reluctantly retired in 1897.

About 1870 the factory began to experiment with the new 'Japanesque' style, using an 'ivory porcelain body' which gave the chief modeller, James Hadley (1837–1903), a chance to show his virtuosity. The wares sometimes included little modelled figures which, when recessed in panels in the sides of vases, proved very popular with the public. Binns was instrumental in getting Royal Worcester to exhibit at Paris in 1867 and Vienna in 1873. At both shows Binns was not only active in selling wares, but also amassed a large collection of Oriental ceramics, principally Japanese, but also Chinese and Korean, which were taken back to Worcester and shown to the factory workers to inspire them. Sadly this vast collection of over 10,000 pieces was sold off in 1900 after Binns' death.

A high point of Binns' life occurred in November 1872 when the works were honoured by a visit from the Iwakura Japanese mission touring the country to study the industrial might of the West. The delegation included the Junior Prime Minister, the Minister of Finance and the Assistant Minister of Foreign Affairs. After a morning passed watching fox hunting (no doubt baffling for the Japanese for whom the fox is a benevolent figure), they must have welcomed being conducted round the factory by Binns himself. They took careful notes of all the processes which he described, at one point asking him to 'speak a little slower as the secretary could not write the description given fast enough'.

71
James Hadley,
Royal Worcester,
Pilgrim Vase showing Japanese
craftsmen at work,
1872.
Porcelain, moulded in relief,
painted and gilded,
height: 26 cm (10¼ in).
Victoria and Albert Museum, London

72
Christopher Dresser,
W S Coleman (decoration),
Minton & Co.,
Vase with fish and prawn tug-of-war,
1867.
Porcelain,
height: 27 cm (10⅝ in).
Private collection

73
Christopher Dresser (design),
Minton & Co.,
Moonflask,
*c.*1875.
Porcelain, imitating
approx. height: 30.5 cm (12 in).
Japanese *cloisonné*.
Private collection

74
Edwin Martin (design),
Martin Brothers Pottery,
Vase,
1898.
Saltglazed stoneware,
height: 31·3 cm (12¼ in).
Private collection

Binns' words would indirectly have strange effects, for within a few years the extraordinary situation was reached that Worcester's copies of Japanese wares were actually being *re-copied* by the Japanese themselves, not to mention by many European potteries.

The Art Journal eulogized the display of Royal Worcester Porcelain in the Japanese taste at Vienna as:

unique in design, quaint, without losing a certain eccentric beauty … There are many vases of various shapes designed by Hadley; an octagonal pair decorated with the story of the silk worm in bronze and gold … and a series of six pilgrim or gourd vases having for subjects **The Potter at His Wheel, The Oven for Burning the Clay … The Painting of the Wares** *[71], and* **The Making of Saggers.**

At Vienna, Royal Worcester wares jointly gained the first prize with Minton & Co., a firm which actually employed one or two Japanese artists in the design team headed by W S Coleman (1829–1904). Coleman was a leading figure of the Aesthetic Movement, and was for a time in charge of Minton's 'Art Pottery Studio' in Kensington Gore, London.

The library of Minton's design studio included books of Japanese prints of birds and flowers from the early 1860s. Minton also produced a range of wares in porcelain and earthenware based not only on prints but also on such diverse sources as Japanese lacquer, ivories and bronzes (72).

At its most feeble, Japonisme appeared in the traditional forms of the Western potter, with a profusion of Japanese motifs – pine branches, prunus blossoms and storks. Direct imitation of Japanese pottery by English manufacturers was rare, Royal Worcester's ware being inspired by Japanese work in metals and ivories, while Minton's most virtuoso work was their porcelain decorated with gilding and inspired by Japanese gold and silver lacquer, seen to advantage in a magnificent moonflask by Christopher Dresser (1834–1904) dating from 1875 (73).

A very different creative team from the Royal Worcester factory or Minton's was provided by the first British studio potters, the Martin Brothers, who between 1873 and 1914 produced their highly distinctive saltglazed stoneware called Martinware at Fulham and on the banks of the Grand Union Canal at Southall, Middlesex.

 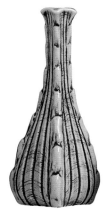   

There were four brothers involved in the team. Robert Wallace Martin (1843–1923) was the founder, sculptor and leader of the brotherhood, Edwin Bruce Martin (1860–1915) was the draughtsman, and Walter Fraser Martin (1857–1912) was the potter and chemist responsible for glazes and firing the kiln. The fourth brother was Charles Douglas Martin (1846–1910), the salesman and manager of the shop, whose business methods were, to say the least, rather unusual. He was always afraid of industrial espionage when visitors came to pry, and when some Japanese visited the shop he was quite sure that they wanted to copy key pieces and hustled them out as quickly as possible, much relieved that they left without taking any wares with them.

In 1874 Lady Laura Trevelyan gave the brothers a Japanese book with woodcut illustrations which whetted their taste for the style and led them to acquire books of Japanese designs well into the 1880s. Their 'canal bank' style was a predictable development from copying the typical Japanese motifs of nature. By the mid-1880s they had adopted a form of decoration based on the flowers, insects, reeds and grasses of the canal bank, and this was joined by the more grotesque motifs of extraordinary birds and fish. Edwin's designs now included a strong Japanese influence, with writhing dragons and sea monsters (74).

In 1900 Edwin, Walter and Charles visited the International Exhibition in Paris, making a beeline for the ceramic section to look at the work of Alexandre Bigot (1862–1927), Félix Auguste Delaherche (1857–1940), Lachenal and others. They enjoyed the work of the recently deceased potter, Jean Charles Cazin (1841–1901), and other examples of the stylized organic forms which were so popular in continental Art Nouveau. On their return they began to produce some of their finest work; vases and bowls inspired by the forms of marrows, gourds and melons, with remarkable surface textures which often reproduced the skins of fish or lizards, thus imitating the notion of bonding flora and fauna when embellishing an individual pot – a characteristic of Japanese decoration (75–79).

A keen artist-collector was the Belgian painter, Alfred Stevens (1823–1906), a friend of Baudelaire, Manet and Degas who specialized in portraits of elegant women in intimate boudoir scenes with titles such as *The Porcelain Collector* (1868). He developed an influential wealthy clientele ranging from the Vanderbilts of New York to the actress Sarah Bernhardt, who studied painting in his popular atelier for women, and was his sitter on a number of occasions. He frequently used his own luxurious home as a setting, for it was furnished with fine things. Indeed he was, as the great aesthete, Comte Robert de Montesquieu, once observed, one of the first to appreciate the brilliant and bizarre charms of Far-Eastern bibelots.

75–9
**Martin Brothers Pottery,
Vases,
1897–1914.
Saltglazed stoneware,
tallest height: 14 cm (5½ in).
Private collection**

80

Alfred Stevens,
The Duchess (formerly
known as *The Blue Dress*),
c.1880.
Oil on wood,
31·9 x 26 cm
(12½ x 10¼ in).
Stirling and Francine
Clark Art Institute,
Williamstown, MA

Stevens' fantastic *Salon Japonaise* was
described by Edmond de Goncourt in
the journal of Saturday 13 March
1875:

*Knowing that I am an amateur of
things Japanese, he opens up his
Japanese room. It is decorated with
two rolls of paper with a gold
background on which are two carts,
each carrying a gigantic bouquet of
flowers – the gift of a young man to
his fiancée. Japanese art is certainly
full of charming conventions! In order
to conceal the geometrical regularity
of the wheels the artist has broken up
his design by means of a cloud of dust,
a cloud of golden dust.*

In *The Duchess*, or *The Blue Dress*,
Alfred Stevens' pensive model sits
before a Japanese screen on which
we see Fuji's classic cone (80).

The portrait painter, James Tissot, in
the late 1870s designed a service of
cloisonné enamels, some of the most
attractive Japoniste constributions to
the decorative arts. A fine example
is the vase 'en gaine', *Children in a
Garden* (81). It is not known why in the
late 1870s he should embark on such a
new venture.

81
James Tissot,
Children in a Garden,
c.1882.
Cloisonné enamel
on copper,
height: 25 cm (9⅞).
Musée des Arts
Décoratifs, Paris

The process of making such *cloisonné*
wares was fraught with the nerve-
racking stress of keeping all the
dividing wires absolutely taut until
after the piece had been fired, as well
as other technical difficulties.
Fortunately new techniques for making
small-scale pieces were evolved by the
well-known French jeweller, Alexis
Falize (1811–98). Falize became
interested in the subject after seeing
Sir Rutherford Alcock's collection in
London in 1862. The exquisite quality
of Falize's *cloisonné* enamel jewellery
can be seen in his necklace and pair of
earring pendants (82), which utilize
motifs that Falize admitted tracing and
copying from Japanese print albums.

The widespread dissemination of
Japoniste sentiments was music to the
ear of the great impresario of both
Japonisme and Art Nouveau – Siegfried
Bing. He opened his Oriental Art
Boutique in Paris in 1875, where it
became a meeting place for the
exchange of ideas on Japan, which also
found an airing through Bing's journal
Le Japon Artistique, which ran for thirty-
six issues from 1888 to 1891 in French,
German and English editions (83).

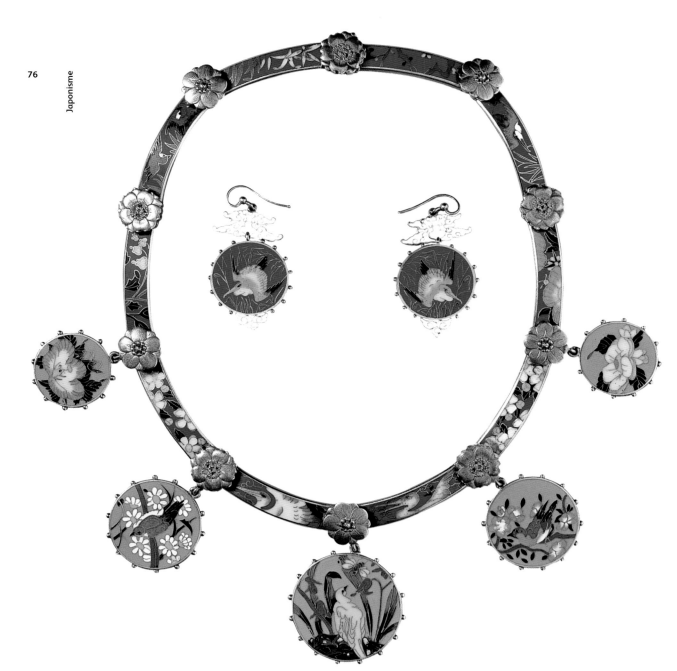

82
Alexis Falize,
Necklace and earring
pendants in the Japanese
style with joints disguised
by gold rosettes,
1867.
Cloisonné enamel,
diameter of largest
medallion: 3.5 cm (1³⁄₈ in).
Ashmolean Museum,
Oxford

83
Cover of Siegfried Bing's
journal *Le Japon
Artistique*, May 1888

In the issue of May 1888 Bing wrote:

The Japanese artist is convinced that nature contains the primordial elements of all things and, according to him, nothing exists in creation, be it only a blade of grass, that is not worthy of a place in the loftiest conception of art.

The intense study of the dynamic forces of nature was also the inspiration which motivated Emile Gallé (1846–1904) who produced some of the finest Art Nouveau furniture. Gallé, deeply influenced by Japanese prototypes and theories, was one of the greatest of all artists to work in the medium of glass. He first began at a small pottery works in 1874 experimenting with stoneware and porcelain, often embellished with dandelions, orchids and chrysanthemums using opaque glazes on simple, somewhat clumsy forms. On turning to glass-making in the 1880s Gallé used floral or insect motifs, and drew inspiration from many sources, notably Japanese art and nature. He was to produce many of the most beautiful of all Japoniste works of art in a material unfamiliar to the Japanese – glass.

LE JAPON

ARTISTIQUE

Documents d'Art

et d'Industrie

réunis par

S. BING

84
Emile Gallé,
**Vase made for the
Paris Exposition,**
*c.*1900.
Amber glass with etched
decoration,
height: 47 cm (18¹₂ in).
Victoria and Albert
Museum, London

85
Emile Gallé,
**Model of a crystal vase
with pine branches,**
1903.
Watercolour and
graphite,
49·5 x 32·2 cm
(19¹₂ x 12⁵₈ in).
Musée d'Orsay, Paris

Some of his most moving small-scale pieces are his *vases de tristesse* and *verreries parlantes* – small exquisite pieces, subtly textured and decorated to reflect the mood of the inscriptions with which they were etched. Such pieces were always intended to be handled, and to do so is a great privilege. Examples exist with quotations from Villon, Baudelaire and Victor Hugo – brief, terse phrases like a *haiku* that juxtapose the image on the glass and the poetry, the dual influence of Japonisme and the French literary tradition. A trained botanist, Gallé looked to plants and flowers for inspiration, as in this large vase, carved, etched and engraved with chrysanthemums (84).

For a really masterly example of Gallé's method of work, it is rewarding to turn to an original design for a pine-bough vase, the pine being a symbol of longevity (85). This is a telling exercise in turning a two-dimensional drawing into a three-dimensional object, just as the cone holds the seed of the future.

86
Daum Brothers,
Vase with poppy,
c.1900.
Glass,
height: 20·4 cm (8 in).
Bröhan Museum, Berlin

87
Eugène Rousseau,
Vase with carp,
c.1878.
Glass, encased and
engraved,
height: 17·8 cm (7 in).
Walters Art Museum,
Baltimore

88
Katsushika Hokusai,
Carp in a Pool,
c.1833.
Colour woodblock,
23·2 x 28·7 cm
(9³⁄₈ x 11¹⁄₄ in)

Gallé began the decorative application of glass to electric lighting, producing lamps in the form of flowers with light fittings concealed by half-open petals. After Gallé's death in 1904 the making of Art Nouveau glass continued to flourish in Nancy, for following in Emile Gallé's wake, like silver stars in a *pâte de verre* glass firmament, are the work of his followers, Victor Prouvé (1858–1943), who painted a famous portrait of Gallé, and the brothers Auguste (1853–1909) and Antonin Daum (1864–1930; 86). In Paris a spectacular glass was produced by Eugène Rousseau, who excelled at aquatic subjects (87). This vase recalls many Japanese treatments of the theme of carp moving though swirling waters, such as the woodcut by Hokusai (1833; 88).

Japan's influence began to be seen further and further afield. All over Europe in the late 1880s, from Cracow to Copenhagen, Japanese motifs triumphed, and irises and lizards, dragonflies and fish began to appear in any area not swamped already by asymmetric patterns. Nor was Europe the only continent to succumb to the charms of Japanese design. In Russia the Imperial Porcelain Manufacture at St Petersburg used the eagle motif from Hiroshige's *Eagle over Fukagawa* (89) to embellish the rim of a white porcelain jar (90). Another Russian piece using a Japanese theme is a vase decorated with a heron standing under blossom from the Imperial factory made in 1892.

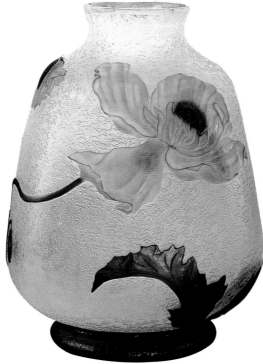

89
Utagawa Hiroshige,
Eagle Over Fukagawa from
One Hundred Views of Edo,
1857.
Colour woodblock,
33·8 x 23·1 cm
(13¼ x 9⅜ in)

90
Imperial Porcelain
Manufacture,
Jar with eagle decoration,
1913.
Porcelain,
height: 31·6 cm (12½ in).
The Hermitage,
St Petersburg

91
Arnold Krog for the Royal
Porcelain Factory,
Copehagen,
Vase,
1888.
Porcelain,
height: 35·7 cm (14 in).
Museum für Kunst und
Gewerbe, Hamburg

This motif is echoed by several manufacturers, notably at the Bing & Grondahl Copenhagen factory by Pietro Krohn who in 1888 designed an ambitious and original 'heron service'. A porcelain vase made in 1888 by Arnold Krog (1856–1931) of the Royal Porcelain Factory, Copenhagen, with underglaze painting of seagulls and waves echoes the conventional depiction of the waves of Hokusai and Hiroshige (91). Krog, an architect and painter with leanings towards the decorative arts, had visited England, Holland and France where he met Siegfried Bing who had just returned from the Far East laden with treasures.

Another major creative force involved with Japonisme was Théodore Deck (1823–91), an artist-potter and one of the most innovative figures in the ceramic business in France during the Second Empire. Born in Guebwiller, Alsace, he established himself in Paris in 1856 to make decorative earthenware and eventually became art director at Sèvres, but never lost touch with his native Alsace. Deck was an eclectic 'style cruncher', gathering images from both the Far East and his preferred Near East. Throughout his career Deck and his large design team experimented with stoneware, porcelain, tin-glazed earthenware and flambé glazes. Another of his factory's specialities were extensive tile panels derived from a wide range of Far Eastern design sources.

Surviving panels include decorations for a verandah depicted with gracefully drooping wisteria (a plant only recently introduced from Japan into Europe), flowering cherry blossoms, butterflies and two Mandarin ducks, symbolic of marital bliss. In the foreground are water lilies, one of the favourite subjects of the modern style, which anticipate by a decade the emergence at Giverny of Monet's magnificent visual celebration of the flower. Deck's most famous bathroom mural, an extensive series of variations on the always popular theme of cranes, was designed for the Villa Schlumberger for Deck's friend and patron, the textile manufacturer Jean Schlumberger (92). He was one of the new generation of wealthy factory owners who were also patrons of the arts. Such figures facilitated both the arts and local commerce by backing activities such as the weaving, textile and printing industries which flourished in Alsace, and also wallpaper-making which was the main industry of the town of Mulhouse.

As early as 1868 the Mulhouse firm of Scheurer, Rott & Co. was one of several enterprising manufacturers to see market possibilities in printing and exporting woollen fabrics to the Japanese market. They were the product of as many as sixteen rollers which each added a different colour or pattern to the fabric as it was threaded through the ingenious machines.

92
**Théodore Deck,
Bathroom tile scheme
from the Villa
Schlumberger,
1876.
Ceramic tiles.
Musée de Florival,
Guebwiller**

93
**Proof impression for
textile destined for
Japan,
mid-1860s.
Pigment on paper.
Musée de l'Impression
sur Étoffes, Mulhouse**

The fabric, plain at first, ended up covered with such familiar Japanese motifs as waves, branches, flowers (93) and inevitably Mount Fuji. The fabrics were inspired probably by Japanese silks which were greatly admired in Europe. Under this stimulus emerged a thriving two-way market between France and Japan. It seems therefore fitting that Lyon should own a textile called *A Chrysanthemum*, one of the symbols of imperial Japan, made in the mid-nineteenth century from satin, silk and strips of gold paper. Siebold brought it back from Japan after his second trip there and sold it in the 1880 sale of his collection at Munich, where it was acquired for the Lyon museum.

Surprisingly, although motifs such as stylized bird and flower forms were favourite themes of the fine and decorative artist, William Morris (1834–96), his only recorded remark on the subject of Japanese art and textiles is in a letter of October 1877 to his friend the dyer, Thomas Wardle, to say, 'I saw a piece of Japanese tapestry yesterday of silk very delicate in manufacture and fine in colour.'

Edmond de Goncourt, on the other hand, was not only interested in Japanese artefacts, but also collected a number of European textiles designed using Japanese themes. After his death on 16 July 1896 he left instructions that the collection should not be left to the cold maw of a museum to be gaped at by unfeeling passers-by, but dispersed at auction to give individual purchasers the same pleasures and pains of collecting and ownership which had been enjoyed by himself and his brother Jules. Ironically, Edmond's wishes would not be fully realized for at one of the resultant sales in 1897 some significant pieces were purchased for the Lyon Museum, notably an embroidery on tabby silk showing two old men looking symbolically at the setting sun, a symbol of eternity, leaving behind them pine trees, cranes and turtles, emblematic of longevity (94).

The weaving of silk, so associated with the city of Lyon since the Middle Ages, was celebrated by the opening of a major museum on the theme in 1890. The museum's real beginnings, however, can be traced back to the Great Exhibitions at London in 1851 and Paris in 1855, 1867, 1878 and 1889. At these events shrewd purchases for the future museum were made by one of its leading advocates, the economist, Natalis Rondot. From the start, wise and imaginative acquisitions were made that accentuated the new enthusiasm for Japanese silks.

94
*Cranes Flying Across the
Setting Sun, Watched by
Two Venerable Old Men,*
*c.*1850–60.
Japanese silk, painted
and embroidered with
silk and gold thread.
Musée des Tissus, Lyon

95
The Swallows,
1894.
Silk (detail).
Musée des Tissus, Lyon

96
Sortie de bal, or mantle
worn over ballgown,
created by Worth,
engraving from a
prospectus for the
Exposition Universelle
at Lyon,
1894

97
Edward Chandler Moore,
Tiffany & Co.,
Coffee pot, creamer and sugar bowl,
*c.*1877.
Silver, with various base metals applied,
tallest: 21·5 cm (8½ in).
Victoria and Albert Museum, London

98
Emile Auguste Reiber,
Christofle & Co.,
Vase and cover,
1867.
Copper inlaid with silver, on a gilt
bronze stand,
height: 30·5 cm (12 in).
Victoria and Albert Museum, London

In 1894 the great couturier Charles
Frederick Worth (1825–95) ordered
a fabric named *The Swallows* (95) and
used it to make an evening cloak for a
ball (96). It was also shown at an
important exhibition in Lyon and was
subsequently acquired by the museum
there. The motifs of swallows and waves
(used as a powerful background here)
often occur in Japanese art.

The jewellery manufacturer, Tiffany
& Co., was founded in 1834 by Charles
L Tiffany (d.1902), father of the
legendary Louis Comfort Tiffany
(1848–1933; see Chapter 9). In 1850
Charles opened a branch of the
business in Paris which from 1860
specialized in Japanese styles and
motifs. An intriguing example of the
Japoniste style is the coffee pot,
creamer and sugar bowl set made by
Edward Chandler Moore (1827–91),
Tiffany's leading independent designer
who had visited the Paris Great
Exhibition of 1867 (97). There he
became fascinated by Japanese sword
furniture, and mastered the technical
skills needed to make a varied palette
of coloured alloys from copper, gold
and silver. Moore, appointed director
of Tiffany's silver department in 1868,
was an avid collector of Japanese
metalwork. His knowledge of Japanese
technique enabled him to impart a
polychrome hammered surface on
this pitcher and other pieces which
resembled that possessed by Japanese
'crackle' pottery.

Siegfried Bing commented that in such pieces 'the borrowed elements were so ingeniously transposed to serve their new function as to become the equivalent of new discoveries', a point neatly demonstrated by the dragonfly on the creamer, which appears to have been borrowed directly from a page in Hokusai's *Quick Lessons in Simplified Drawing* (1812), demonstrating how to draw dragonflies (see 203). Perhaps fortunately, Britain could not compete in such stylistic struggles because its strict hallmarking laws forbade the mixture of precious with base metals, leaving Tiffany with little opposition to contend with and enabling him to create some of the most innovative metalwork of the century.

Tiffany's did not, however, have the field entirely to themselves. A vase and cover of 1867 (98) was designed by Emile Auguste Reiber (1826–1893), who was one of the most important of early Japonistes. The design for the inlaid silver on this vase may well have come from the *Useful Drawings for Art and Industry* of 1859 by Auguste Delâtré (1822–1907), which included eighteen engraved plates of Japanese birds, flowers, insects, marine life, samurai and landscapes by Hokusai.

Great department stores also helped to disperse Japanese artefacts. In his novel *Au Bonheur des dames* (1883), Émile Zola describes the world of a department store which he modelled on Parisian stores such as Le Louvre and Au Bon Marché. The owner of Zola's fictional shop had begun his business with:

a small bargain counter covered with faded bric-a-brac [which now] overflowed with old bronzes, old ivories, old lacquers … Few departments had had such modest beginnings, and now it had a turnover of thousands of francs a year, and stirred up all the Far East, where travellers ransacked temples and palaces. Four years had been enough to attract the entire artistic clientele of Paris.

In the decorative arts the cult of Japan continued to flourish even after it had lost its exotic novelty and when the whiplash lines of Art Nouveau reigned supreme. Japonisme survived because it offered a more lasting means of translating natural forms into a decorative style, a pursuit shared by potters, metalworkers, textile designers and above all by manufacturers, who all shared an eager enthusiasm to create variations, copies and imitations of Japanese novelties, which sold and sold and sold.

Previous page
Walter Crane,
Peacock Garden
wallpaper
(detail of 111)

99
E W Godwin,
Anglo-Japanese
Drawing Room
Furniture, **engraving**
from *Art Furniture*, **1877**

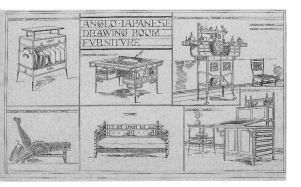

100
William Nesfield,
Folding screen of six
panels with twelve
Japanese paintings
of birds and flowers,
1867.
Ebonized wood with gilt
and fretted decoration
and painted panels of
Japanese paper,
height: 208 cm (82 in).
Victoria and Albert
Museum, London

Remember that the most beautiful
things in the world are the most
useless; peacocks and lilies for
example.
John Ruskin, 1851–3

The first trade agreement between
Great Britain and Japan was signed
in 1859. From that moment Japanese
goods began to flow into England, not
only via London but also through ports
such as Bristol, where Japanese prints
made one of their first recorded
appearances in England in 1862 on the
walls of the home of a talented young
Bristolian architect and writer, Edward
William Godwin. Godwin was an
eclectic genius, passionately interested
in subjects as various as the history
of costume, Greek art and stage
design. He drew constantly in a series
of small sketchbooks remarkable for
their clarity and precision. For such
a man, already deeply versed in
the European decorative tradition,
the discovery of Japanese art was
a novel and exciting aesthetic
revelation. He soon acquired not
only prints but fans and books,
and particularly prized two slim
volumes of Hokusai's *Manga* showing
Japanese techniques of construction,
joints and carpentry, which would
prove immensely influential on his
later career as a furniture designer.

101
E W Godwin,
William Watt,
Sideboard,
c.1885–8.
Ebonized mahogany
with painted decoration;
silver-plated handles
and fittings,
height: 184 cm
(74³⁄₈ in).
National Gallery of
Victoria, Melbourne

Thus in England as in France it was the arrival of a copy of the *Manga* which really triggered public interest in the art and artefacts of Japan. In England that interest would be primarily reflected in the decorative arts, in France in the fine and graphic arts.

From the *Manga* in the mid-1860s Godwin drew the inspiration for the design of his 'Anglo-Japanese' furniture, ebonized black sideboards and tables which reveal his profound understanding of Japanese concerns for space and volume, asymmetry, reticence and restraint (99). This appreciation led him to decorate his home in a restrained yet highly original manner, revolutionary for the high Victorian era. He painted the walls in plain colours, hanging on them a few Japanese prints, and placed some Persian carpets on the bare boards.

Godwin's early interests were also heightened by the display of Japanese lacquer, bronze and porcelain shown at the London International Exhibition held at South Kensington in 1862, which was collected by the British Minister in Japan, Sir Rutherford Alcock. After the exhibition closed, the firm of Farmer and Rogers sold off some of the exhibits and other goods that had failed to arrive in time.

The manager of this firm was Arthur Lasenby Liberty, who in 1875 was to establish his own firm. Liberty & Co. would become celebrated for its stocks of both Japanese and Art Nouveau artefacts.

As with any new fashion, enthusiasm for Japonisme spread by word of mouth. The Jewish painter, Simeon Solomon (1840–1905), wrote to his friend the poet, Swinburne, in 1863 and described the home of his friend the architect, William Eden Nesfield (1835–88):

His rooms are in Argyll Street near mine, and he has a very jolly collection of Persian, Indian, Greek and Japanese things that I should really like you to see … he is an intimate friend of Albert Moore.

The work of both Nesfield and Moore was greatly influenced by Japanese artefacts. A spectacular example of this influence at work is provided by a six-fold screen designed by Nesfield in 1867 as a wedding present for his business partner, the famous architect, Richard Norman Shaw (1831–1912), with whom he shared offices from 1863 to 1876 (100).

The screen displays a sophisticated knowledge of Japanese motifs. Twelve painted panels depict birds perched on blossoming branches of chrysanthemums, lilies, pinks, peonies and magnolias. They are surrounded by incised, ebonized wooden frames, separated at the top with strips of open fretwork and a band of gilded and carved Japanese motifs. The screen is elaborately inscribed with a four-line stanza:

All are Architects of Fate
Working on these walls of time
Some with massive deeds and great
Some with ornaments of Rhyme
Richard and Agnes Shaw AD 1867.

The gilded bands of asymmetric decoration are composed of the Japanese patterns *sayagata* (key fret motif), *uzumaki* (spirals), family crests known as *tomo-e* and the auspicious Asian symbol of the swastika, all handled with great technical flair.

The question as to where Nesfield and James Forsyth (who made the screen) had acquired such knowledge is an intriguing one. It can perhaps be partially explained by a study of *Grammar of Chinese Ornament* by Owen Jones (1809–74) which was published in a limited edition of 300 in 1867. The more unusual motifs of the screen could also have been borrowed from Japanese ceramics and textile stencils. Such goods were all obtainable at Farmer and Rogers's Oriental Warehouse in Regent Street.

102
Walter Crane,
Eleven, Twelve, Ring
the Bell from ***One, Two,***
Buckle My Shoe of the
'Six-Penny Toy' series,
1869

E W Godwin became one of the shop's most regular customers. As a practising architect he possessed a keen appreciation of the architectonic qualities of Japanese art. In 1867 he designed the famous sideboard which he had made for his mistress, the actress Ellen Terry.

Its rectilinear form and plain dark panels, covered with embossed leather, possess a simplicity remarkable for its date, when ornate over-decoration flourished in Victorian furniture design. At least ten of these sideboards were created, the example illustrated here, dating from 1885 to 1888, being probably the most elaborately decorated of them all (101). The upper cupboard doors are stencilled with gold chrysanthemums, the lower ones with geometric decorations.

Ellen Terry and Godwin had two children, a daughter, Edith Craig, and a son, Gordon Craig who would become a great theatrical designer. In her memoirs Ellen Terry recalled that in her children's nursery:

they were allowed no rubbishy picture books but from the first Japanese prints and fans lined the nursery walls while their English classic was Walter Crane.

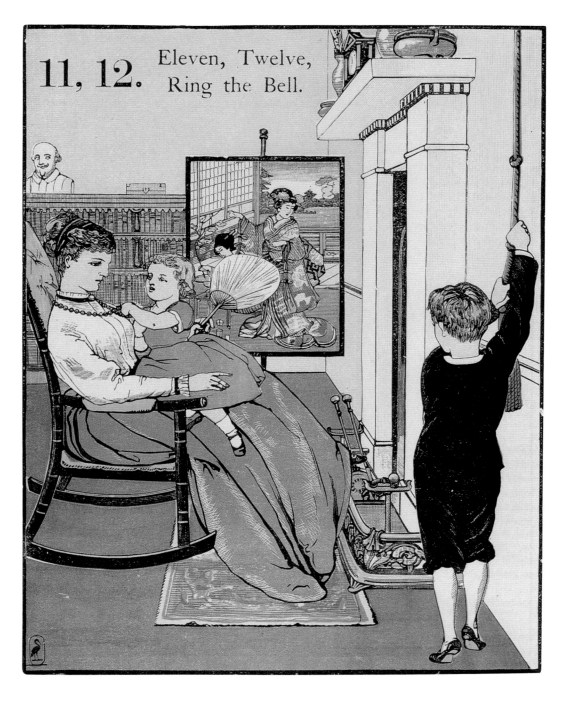

103
**E W Godwin and
William Watt,
frontispiece and title
page from** *Art Furniture*,
1877

104
**E W Godwin, attributed
to William Watt,
Gong and stand,
1877.
Oak, iron and bronze,
height: 82·6 cm
(32½ in).
Walker Art Gallery,
Liverpool**

Ellen Terry is referring to illustrations in a nursery rhyme book by Walter Crane (1845–1915), *One, Two, Buckle my Shoe* (1869) from the 'Six-Penny Toy' series. The illustration to *Eleven, Twelve, Ring the Bell* (102) shows an 'Aesthetic' interior: a mother is sitting on an Anglo-Japanese-style chair, holding a Japanese fan, and a screen is decorated with an enlarged Japanese print design. Walter Crane (1845–1915) was a great admirer of 'things Japanese', acknowledging 'Japanese colour prints' as 'an important factor' in the evolution of his style, and owning some prints by Toyokuni which had been given to him by a family friend returning from Japan in about 1867. Just to complete the picture, or, rather, the 'Japanese print', Godwin's friend Whistler gave both Ellen and the children kimonos.

Godwin always enjoyed a close association with Liberty's, which he described as an 'Anglo-Japanese Warehouse'. He bought from it his own household furnishings and also probably such items as the six carved ivory monkeys of Japanese make, closely resembling *netsukes*, which he used as handles on his 'Monkey' cabinet. This was made for his own use, probably by William Watt, in walnut inset with four Japanese boxwood plaques. Japanese carved wood panels were included in Liberty's stock, and by 1881 special designs and sizes could be ordered from Japan 'to any character of drawing'.

The use of actual Japanese materials in this new type of furniture may also help to explain the title 'Art Furniture', a term first used in 1868 by Charles Locke Eastlake in his influential book *Hints on Household Taste* to describe furniture made under the direct control of the designer rather than pieces produced by semi mass-production methods in factories.

In 1877 the furniture-maker, William Watt, published a catalogue entitled *Art Furniture Designed by Edward W Godwin F.S.A. and Manufactured by William Watt With Hints and Suggestions on Domestic Furniture and Decorations* (103). Godwin's frontispiece is the most Japanese of all his interior designs. He was keenly aware of new publications on the designs of Japan, and was fascinated by Aimé Humbert's *Le Japon illustré* (1870), a record of a year's stay in Japan in 1863–4. From an illustration in it Godwin designed a gong and stand probably made by William Watt (104). Gongs or bells were articles always in demand in large Victorian houses to summon people for meals. The gong's shape derives from the Japanese *torii*, freestanding gateways which are an imposing feature of Shinto shrines.

105
James Abbott McNeill
Whistler,
*Rose and Silver: The Princess
from the Land
of Porcelain*,
1863–4.
Oil on canvas,
199·9 x 116·1 cm
(78⅝ x 45¾ in).
Freer Gallery of Art,
Smithsonian Institution,
Washington, DC

A great friend of Godwin's and fellow enthusiast for Japanese art was the Gothic revival architect of Cardiff Castle, William Burges (1827–81). His review of the Japanese exhibits displayed in the 1862 Exhibition in *The Building News* positively glows with enthusiasm:

If the visitor wishes to see the real Middle Ages he must visit the Japanese Court, for at the present day the arts of the Middle Ages have deserted Europe and are only to be found in the East … these hitherto unknown barbarians appear to know all that the Middle Ages knew but in some respects are beyond them and us as well.

Some of Burges's own collection of Japanese prints survive in the Victoria and Albert Museum, pasted into five scrapbooks. To turn their pages is an exciting experience, enabling us to share vicariously with Burges and Godwin the thrill of seeing for the first time the exotic patterns and bold designs of Japan, which as a wallpaper designer Godwin particularly enjoyed. On a page in one of his sketchbooks we can study his careful drawings of Japanese crests or *mon*.

One evening in May 1863, Burges chaired a meeting of the Architectural Association on Japanese Art. A lecture on 'The Prevailing Ornament of China and Japan' was given by Christopher Dresser, a young man who was to play a remarkable role in the dissemination of knowledge of Japan.

Dresser, a fine example of the phenomenon of the Victorian polymath, first studied at the Government School of Design run by Sir Henry Cole in Kensington. There he encountered such major names in the design field as Richard Redgrave (1804–88), Matthew Digby Wyatt (1820–77), Gottfried Semper (1803–79) and, most notably, Owen Jones, then engaged upon his *Grammar of Ornament* (1856), a book to which Dresser contributed several designs. From South Kensington he went to Germany, becoming a Doctor of Philosophy at the University of Jena. All seemed set for an academic career and a fulfilled life of fellowships and publications. As a botanist, however, his knowledge of the infinite variety of natural patterns provided the basis for a highly successful career as a freelance designer. He was indeed a born eclectic, able to turn his hand to anything, and has left an amazingly varied design legacy. His first exposure to Japanese artefacts took place in the 1862 International Exhibition, at which he made more than eighty drawings. This was Dresser's first contact with international exhibitions, which would later loom very large in his creative activities.

At the 1867 Minton stand in Paris, for example, he introduced the effect of adapting enamel techniques on to porcelain. In a more light-hearted vein and with equal facility he could draw semi-humorous grotesques of bats, cats, cranes, ducks, beetles and other insects. From the mid- to late 1860s he designed for Wedgwood and Minton (see 72 and 73) and from the mid-1870s for Elkington & Co., the silverware manufacturers.

In 1876 he visited the Philadelphia Centennial Exhibition and also actually went to Japan for a short visit of four months as representative for the South Kensington Museum and agent for Tiffany & Co., New York, and to advise the Japanese on their export trade, visiting sixty-four potteries and dozens of manufacturers of different wares. He took hundreds of photographs, and on his return his own designs, particularly for pottery and metalwork, were radically altered, becoming far more abstract as a result of his greater understanding of Japanese materials and aesthetics.

In his 1882 publication, a still very readable and amusing study, *Japan, its Architecture, Art and Art Manufactures*, Dresser wrote:

I firmly believe that the introduction of the works of Japanese handicrafts-men into England has done as much to improve our national taste as even our schools of art and public museums … for these Japanese objects have got into our homes, and among them we live. I do not wish to destroy our art and substitute for it the Japanese style … we may borrow what is good from all peoples; but we must distil all we borrow through our own minds.

From the time of its very first arrival in Europe, Japanese art was greeted with enthusiasm for its novel approach to the applied arts – where applied arts were of equal importance as fine art in creating a Japanese aesthetic. This was of particular importance in Great Britain where John Ruskin (1819–1900) and William Morris had been concerned with re-creating medieval craft techniques of the Gothic era, and with spreading the gospel that the decorative arts were a vehicle of spiritual and aesthetic redemption for the common man.

This process, surprisingly, seems to have absolved Ruskin and Morris from making pronouncements of any type on the alien artefacts from Japan. It was left to the Pre-Raphaelite critic, W M Rossetti, to make one of the first major critical responses upon the subject after a visit to the 1862 Exhibition, when he remarked, 'the very best fine art practised at the present day in any corner of the globe, is the decorative art of Japan,' while his brother Dante Gabriel delighted in Japanese designs:

their enormous energy, their instinct for whatever savours of life and movement, their exquisite superiority to symmetry in decorative form, their magic of touch and impeccability of execution …

These views found support from the critic, Sidney Colvin, who, when criticizing the 'pseudo-Hellenic' style of paintings by Whistler's friend, Albert Moore, claimed that more perfect colour than Moore's could be found 'on a thousand fans, screens and painted hangings of Japan'. Predictably, Whistler also put his own individual spin on the received opinion of the difference between fine and applied art, declaring:

The painter must also make of the wall upon which his work is hung, the room containing it, the whole house, a Harmony, a Symphony, an Arrangement, as perfect as the picture or print which became a part of it.

Whistler's belief in his own axiom would be tested in the most controversial event in the history of Japonisme, *The Peacock Room* imbroglio. It begins in 1864 with the creation of arguably the most successful of Whistler's paintings using Japanese props, *Rose and Silver: The Princess from the Land of Porcelain* (105). The richly costumed figure of the princess wearing Japanese dress stands before a four-fold screen, behind which upon the wall hangs a *uchiwa* fan. Another fan with a design of irises is held in the princess's hand. The sumptuous colour and exotic background recall Rossetti's sensual female portraits.

The painting was exhibited at the Paris Salon and hung 'on the line', a good position which must have pleased Whistler, since it marked his first official recognition in France. Criticisms of the work varied from the caustic 'un pastiche chinois' to Gautier's alliterative observation concerning the blue-and-white Chinese carpet upon which 'the princess poses upon a pavement of porcelain'. After the first showing of *The Princess* in London at the International Exhibition of 1872, the painting was acquired by Frederick Richards Leyland (1831–92), a Liverpool shipping magnate and dilettante of music and the arts who played a major role in Whistler's life.

A great admirer of the work of Rossetti and Whistler, Leyland not only collected their paintings but also became fired by their enthusiasm for blue-and-white Chinese and Japanese porcelain, and, guided by the leading ceramic dealer, Murray Marks, he became one of a group of obsessive collectors.

One of the problems involved in collecting ceramics in large quantities is how to store and display your treasures. In the morning and billiard rooms at the home of fellow collector, Aleco Ionides, at 1 Holland Park, Leyland saw a remarkable quasi-Japanese installation devised by the architect, Thomas Jeckyll (1827–81). The fireplace in the morning room was especially remarkable for its serried rows of blue-and-white pots surmounting a cast-iron grate surround, devised by Jeckyll utilizing the shapes of Japanese *mon* (106).

As his collection grew, Leyland also began to dream of creating a similar 'palace of art' in his newly acquired and very grand town house, 49 Prince's Gate, Kensington. In one room, the dining room, he would unite Whistler's painting of *The Princess* with his porcelain collection in an imaginative and inspired setting. Leyland believed that a happy colour-contrast solution for the background to the display could be created by using the sumptuous red leather (then believed to be seventeenth-century Spanish, now thought to be eighteenth-century Dutch), which had already been used elsewhere in Ionides's house by Jeckyll. At one end of the room would hang the *Princess*, while facing her a prominent place was reserved for the *Three Girls*, another work commissioned by Leyland from Whistler, which sadly would never be completed.

In April 1876, Mrs Leyland passed on to Whistler a fateful enquiry:

Jeckyll writes what colour to do the doors and windows in the dining room … I wish you would give him your ideas.

These were ominous words in view of what was to follow: all was sweetness and light until the moment when *The Princess* was hauled into position, the blue-and-white porcelain arranged on the shelves, and Whistler was asked to comment on the effect by Leyland. Whistler felt that the red flowers on the leather, which were painted and not embossed, 'killed' the tones in his painting. Leyland gave permission for the flowers to be painted yellow and gold, and for the red border of the rug to be trimmed. Whistler was still not completely satisfied, and Leyland agreed to him adorning the wainscoting and cornice with a 'wave pattern'.

Business problems now intervened for Leyland. His fleet, the Leyland Line, was entering into the Atlantic trade, and he had to leave London to stay in Liverpool during the summer months of 1876, to supervise events. He left, assuming the decoration of the room to be virtually completed. But Whistler, in his patron's absence, was inspired to create a far more radical treatment of the room.

107
James Abbott McNeill Whistler,
Shutters from *Harmony in Blue and Gold: The Peacock Room*,
1876–7.
Oil paint and metal leaf on leather, canvas and wood.
Freer Gallery of Art, Smithsonian Institution, Washington, DC

108
James Abbott McNeill Whistler's room,
2 Lindsay Road, Chelsea,
1867–8

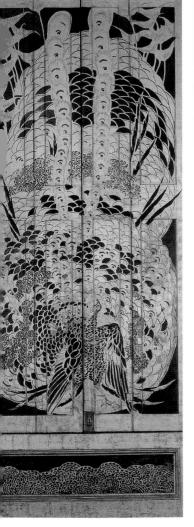

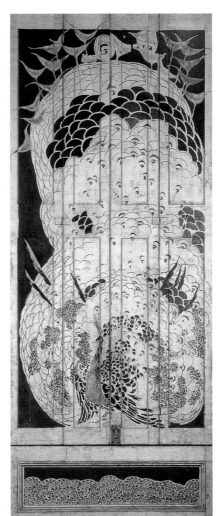

Whistler covered the ceiling of the room with 'Dutch metal', an imitation gold leaf, over which he painted a lush pattern based on peacock feathers. He gilded the walnut shelves and embellished the inner sides of the wooden shutters with four gorgeous peacocks whose vast sweeping trains derived from Japanese sources (107).

Exactly why peacocks should be so much on Whistler's mind must remain a mystery, although the birds have always been a popular subject in both the East and the West. It is worth being aware that the peacocks in Rossetti's back garden menagerie would have been all too audible to Whistler's ear, and that Whistler owned fifteen Japanese pictures of 'birds of many varieties and of the richest plumage'. An old photograph (108) tells us that at one time Whistler had three large Japanese paintings of peacocks hanging in his own rooms at 2 Lindsay Row, Chelsea. Such subjects were common throughout the Edo era, and birds were frequently depicted on screens by such artists as Ogata Korin (1658–1716), one of Japan's greatest decorative painters. Korin's birds provide a fascinating contrast with Whistler's – the former's shimmering yet perfectly restrained – Whistler's so animated and full of movement. While evidence of Whistler's contact with such a screen must remain conjectural, he may have seen a print by Hiroshige (109), which in its composition relates closely to the paintings on the shutters.

109
Utagawa Hiroshige,
Peacock and Peonies,
1833–5.
Colour woodblock,
38·7 x 17·1 cm
(15¹⁄₄ x 6³⁄₄ in)

It is pertinent to ask *why* Whistler should have selected the peacock as the dominant component in his decorative scheme for Leyland's room. The theme had in fact been in his mind for some time, for as early as 1873 he had suggested a decorative scheme involving peacocks for the dining room of Aubrey House, Campden Hill (also in London), belonging to the banker W C Alexander, who rejected it because of its expense. Clearly the concept remained at the back of Whistler's mind, and his interest was fostered by several factors. The Pre-Raphaelites, attracted by its sonorous colours, often used the bird in paintings, as for example in Rossetti's large peacock next to King David in his triptych in Llandaff Cathedral, while Edward Burne-Jones (1833–98), Arthur Hughes (1832–1915) and Frederick Lord Leighton (1830–96) painted peacocks in their easel pictures. Ceramic peacocks also abounded, Minton producing a life-size bird in 1876 (110).

In 1880 Walter Crane designed a mosaic frieze of peacocks in Leighton House, and later in 1889 the sumptuous wallpaper *Peacock Garden* (111). Whistler would certainly have been aware of two contemporary decorative room schemes using the peacock theme extensively. The best surviving example is happily still on public display in the Victoria and Albert Museum. Dating from 1869, it was originally called the Dutch Kitchen or Grill Room. It is now called the Poynter Room after its designer Sir Edward Poynter. In it a frieze of peacocks surmount the tiles, which include two large panels above the grill depicting the birds.

Another peacock scheme, at Frederick Lehmann's house at 15 Berkeley Square, was designed by the architect, George Aitchison (1825–1910), the peacock frieze being executed by Whistler's friend, Albert Moore, in 1872. Surviving sketches reveal Moore's peacocks modestly trailing their trains rather than flaunting them as do Whistler's (112).

110
Minton & Co.,
Ceramic peacock,
1876.
Glazed ceramic,
height: 154 cm
(60⅝ in).
Potteries Museum and
Art Gallery, Stoke-on-
Trent

111
Walter Crane,
Peacock Garden wallpaper (detail),
1889.
Victoria and Albert Museum, London

112
Albert Joseph Moore,
Cartoon for the Peacock Frieze at
15 Berkeley Square,
1841–93.
Charcoal and white chalk on brown paper,
46 x 154.9 cm
(18 x 61 in).
Victoria and Albert Museum, London

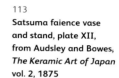

113
Satsuma faience vase
and stand, plate XII,
from Audsley and Bowes,
The Keramic Art of Japan
vol. 2, 1875

One of the best-known and most often cited Oriental sources for Whistler's peacock is to be found in George Ashdown Audsley and James Lord Bowes's *The Keramic Art of Japan* (1875). As an avid ceramic collector it is highly probable that Whistler saw this book, and was also influenced by the plate from it showing a large Satsuma faience vase with dragon handles and stand (113). Whistler almost certainly saw this vase, which belonged to a close friend of Leyland.

As the painting of the Peacock Room progressed, artistic circles in London buzzed with stories about the painter and his methods. Whistler, a brilliant publicist, held press conferences in the completed room. He actually issued a pamphlet, copies of which were distributed at Liberty's and several London shops, that audaciously welcomed the public to Leyland's house; he himself had not yet been allowed by the artist to judge the work for himself. When at last Leyland saw the room he was understandably irate at the complete reversal of his own preferred colour scheme, and the resultant disappearance of the red 'Spanish' leather under the brilliant blue and gold of Whistler's decorations. Leyland also disliked the creation of the peacocks on the shutters. When the shutters are drawn at night their sweeping trains swirl in cascades of golden feathers silhouetted against a background of gold leaf.

114
James Abbott McNeill
Whistler,
*Harmony in Blue and Gold:
The Peacock Room,*
1876–7.
Oil paint and metal leaf on
leather, canvas and wood,
Room dimensions:
4·2 x 10 x 6 m
(13 ft 9⅜ in x 32 ft 9¾
in x 19 ft 8¼ in).
Freer Gallery of Art,
Smithsonian Institution,
Washington, DC

115
James McNeill Whistler,
*Blue and Silver: Screen
with Old Battersea
Bridge,*
1871–2.
Distemper and gold paint
on brown paper laid on
canvas and stretched
on back of silk,
195 x 182 cm
(76¾ x 71⅝ in).
Hunterian Art Gallery,
University of Glasgow

These peacocks were not part of the original commission, however, and Leyland wrote:

The peacocks you have put on the back of the shutters may possibly be worth (as pictures) the £1,200 you charge for them but … I certainly do not require them and I can only suggest that you take them away and let new shutters be put up in their place.

What really rankled with Leyland was Whistler's arrogance in inviting the general public into Leyland's home without asking his permission.

As always, financial concerns exacerbated the situation. Whistler had in mind a fee of two thousand guineas, a sum he felt barely paid for the work. In Whistler's day a pound was worth twenty shillings sterling, and a guinea twenty-one shillings. Only tradesmen were paid in pounds, whereas gentlemen's fees were settled in guineas. The prickly artist felt deeply insulted, accepting payment of one thousand pounds with very bad grace. On the blank wall opposite *The Princess*, he painted two magnificent peacocks – one the patron, scrabbling under his claws a pile of silver coins, the disputed shillings, while the other bird, the artist, shrieks a proud defiance – providing a commentary on his relations with Leyland (114).

Godwin wrote one of the most vivid accounts of the room's final appearance:

The scene is wonderfully dramatic, so dramatic in fact as to make one fancy that a story might well be wrapped up in it. There is a haughty tremulous rage in one bird, the very feathers seeming to shake, a seeming secured partly by a shower of gold dots, and partly by force of drawing in the raised and recurved tail … the other bird, the one of the emerald eye which would make us tremble for the life of the raging cock if once roused to retaliate. There is, indeed, more of Aristophanes, more of the Greek satirist, here than of Japanese drawings on fans, or trays, or crapes. The birds are, in fact, human peacocks after all … not those of the ornithologist nor the peacocks of the zoo.

Godwin amusingly refers here to the play *The Birds* by Aristophanes implying that patron and artist are both inhabiting 'Cloud Cuckoo Land'.

It is to his eternal credit that Leyland kept the room as Whistler left it, and made no attempt to erase the visual satire from the walls. He continued filling the shelves with porcelain until his death, aged sixty, in 1892.

Whistler loved painting as night was falling, as did the Japanese artists whom he admired, whose favourite motif in Edo was painting the Sumida river at dusk or when fireworks lit up the night sky. He passed long hours contemplating the river either from his Chelsea window or skimming along the Thames at twilight in a skiff rowed by his faithful but abused follower, Walter Greaves, who once observed: 'To Mr Whistler a boat was always a tone, to us it was always a boat.' A painting which celebrates Whistler's love of the Thames at dusk took shape on a Japanese screen. In London, as in Paris, Japanese screens had become both fashionable and readily available by the 1870s. Whistler himself purchased a two-panelled screen depicting flowers and birds by a contemporary Japanese artist, a woman named Nampo Osawa. Whistler adapted the screen by using the back as a support for a composition of his own entitled *Blue and Silver: Screen with Old Battersea Bridge* (115). In this experiment, as in his Nocturnes, Whistler reveals his remarkable assimilation of Japanese aesthetic principles.

In a letter of 1868 to Henri Fantin-Latour (1836–1904), Whistler described his aims:

It seems to me that colour ought to be, as it were, embroidered on the canvas, that is to say the same colour ought to appear in the picture continually here and there, in the same way that a thread appears in an embroidery, and so should all the others, more or less according to their importance. Look how well the Japanese understand this.

After 1877 Whistler was never to see his masterpiece *The Peacock Room* again, although he had not yet finished with the predominant colours of the room, gold and silver. They make a spectacular reappearance in the room decor on which he collaborated with his friend E W Godwin at the 1878 Paris international exhibition. Their work took the form of a stand for the furniture-maker, William Watt, which prominently featured *The Butterfly Cabinet* surrounded by other pieces of furniture.

116
E W Godwin
Harmony in Yellow and Gold: The Butterfly Cabinet,
1877–8.
Oil on mahogany with yellow tiling, brass moulding and glass, height: 303 cm (119¼ in).
Hunterian Art Gallery, University of Glasgow

The cabinet was made in bright mahogany and painted in yellow and gold, which led Whistler to entitle it as a *Harmony in Yellow and Gold: The Butterfly Cabinet* (116), but was described by one critic as 'an agony in yellow', and the stand by another as the 'Primrose Room'.

One American visitor vividly described the effect:

yellow on yellow, gold on gold, everywhere. The peacock reappears, the eyes and the breast feathers of him, but whereas in Prince's Gate it was always blue on gold, or gold on blue, here the feather is all gold, boldly and softly laid on a gold-tinted wall ... The feet to the table legs are tipped with brass, and rest on a yellowish brown velvet rug. Chairs and sofas are covered with yellow, pure rich yellow velvet, darker in shade than the yellow of the wall, and edged with yellow fringe.

Today the originality of 'The Butterfly Suite', is only known to us by its central feature, *The Butterfly Cabinet*. The cabinet was originally designed as an overmantel for a fireplace of bright mahogany with a painted decoration of Japanese cloud motifs and butterflies in shades of yellow and gold. The lower part immediately after the exhibition was converted from a fireplace to a cupboard with doors painted by Whistler, the form in which it survives today.

When Whistler and Godwin visited the Paris exhibition in 1878 it is intriguing to speculate whether they were ever confronted by the saffron yellow cabinet (117) exhibited by Madame Duvinage, widow of Ferdinand Duvinage, who ran her husband's firm, Duvinage & Harinkouck, from after his death in 1874 until 1882. In her workshop she strove to emulate the virtuoso craftsmanship of the great *ébénistes*, the de luxe cabinet-makers of the eighteenth century. The overwhelmingly ornate surface of the cabinet is smothered in a rich jumble of stylistic borrowings from Japan of dragons, phoenixes, swallows, the inevitable butterflies and chrysanthemums. The approach was a very different one from that of Godwin and Whistler who both had a sensitive understanding of decoration and spatial proportion.

An alarming example of the Japonisme style, can be seen in the cabinet designed and manufactured by Gabriel Viardot in 1888 (118). There are relatively few purely Japanese elements apart from the panels, for the rest of the cabinet is a strange mixture of both Chinese and Vietnamese elements, perhaps reflecting the fact that Vietnam (formerly Indo-China) was then one of France's most important colonies.

117
Madame Duvinage,
Cabinet,
c.1878.
Rosewood, marquetry
of ivory, copper, brass,
pewter and bronze,
height: 130·4 cm (51³⁄₈ in).
Musée d'Orsay, Paris

118
Gabriel Viardot,
Cabinet,
1888.
Carved walnut with
gilt bronze mounts,
Height: 162·6 cm
(64 in).
Victoria and Albert
Museum, London

Nevertheless, the jury in the 1888 exhibition awarded Viardot a gold medal, praising particularly his 'Japanese furniture always extremely interesting for its tonality and perfect execution'. It provides an interesting comparison with the very different aim of Godwin's Anglo-Japanese works.

Japanese folding screens, like Japanese prints, provided a powerful visual stimulus for Western artists. Although lacquered screens were probably exported from Japan in quite large numbers from about 1630 to 1700, most were converted into furniture and very few survived intact. Like many of the most highly esteemed artefacts, screens possess both practical and aesthetic qualities. Uniquely adaptable into a variety of settings, screens function as freestanding partitions defining space, whether of an intimate or public nature. Folding screens vary from two to ten panels, but the most common format is a pair of six-panel screens. The design on a pair of screens may form a single composition when the screens are placed side by side, usually with complementary subjects such as landscapes of the spring and autumn. Themes linking screen with screen created exquisite visual conundrums as to which panel to emphasize by altering its position to make it more or less dominant, almost like a chime of bells.

119
**Attributed to Walter
Crane, Royal School of
Art Needlework,
Folding screen,
1875–6.
Wool thread on cotton
and silk,
151 x 59·7cm
(59¹₂ x 23¹₂ in).
Private collection**

It was not, however, until the last decades of the nineteenth century that Western artists embraced the screen's potential as a form of household decoration. There were some memorable 'variations on all too familiar themes', such as the four-panel screen depicting peacocks possibly designed by Walter Crane and executed by the Royal School of Art Needlework (119). Alongside a three-panel screen with Japanese motifs, this was made for the famous Centennial Exhibition of 1876, Philadelphia. Crane reinterpreted decorative themes from the Far East, especially in the aquatic border at the bottom of the composition. Encouraged not only by the Royal College, but also by the Morris circle's enthusiasm for embroidery, Anglo-Japanese screens continued to thrive throughout the 1880s.

In France one group of young artists in particular would be greatly concerned with the screen as a pictorial discipline, the group were called the Nabis, the Hebrew word for 'prophets', because of their proselytizing belief in promoting art as a form of decoration. In 1887 Édouard Dujardin hailed in *La Revue indépendante* the coming of a new art form which he named *cloisonnisme*, the pictorial equivalent of the recently established school of Symbolist literature, the creation of which he accredited to Louis Anquetin (1861–1932). Other members of the group included Paul Sérusier (1863–1927), a follower of Gauguin, Pierre Bonnard, Édouard Vuillard (1868–1940) and Maurice Denis (1870–1943).

Art as decoration was a sentiment which possessed a great appeal for Bonnard who, in his first interview, proclaimed: 'Painting must, above all, be decorative.' Bonnard became known as the 'Nabis très japonard' because of his love of Japanese prints. Of them he said, 'what I had before me was something fully alive and also extremely skilful.' The Japanese taught him that 'it was possible to translate light, form and character with nothing but colour, without resorting to shading'. Bonnard was the first of the group to take on the problems of a folding screen. In 1891, at the Salon des Indépendants, he exhibited four panel paintings showing women in a garden at different seasons of the year, each panel the same size but composed as a separate entity. While not strictly speaking a screen, this work prepared the way for one of Bonnard's most famous works, the four-fold panel *Nursemaids' Promenade* (120), a composition which floats effortlessly across all four panels, linked only by the boy's hoop and the line of waiting cabs at the top of the composition, which was also issued in lithographic form.

120
Pierre Bonnard,
*Nursemaids' Promenade
with Frieze of Carriages,*
1895.
Colour lithograph,
150 x 200 cm
(59 x 78³⁄₄ in)

122

Kitagawa Utamaro,
*Sankatsu and Hanhichi
With Their Baby*,
*c.*1790.
Colour woodcut,
62·2 x 14·9 cm
(24¹₂ x 6 in)

121

Pierre Bonnard,
Family Scene from an
album of *l'estampe
originale*,
1893.
Colour lithograph,
31·2 x 17·7 cm
(12¹₄ x 7 in)

Bonnard really loved Japanese prints. He delighted in their bright flat colours, and we may surmise especially the work of Kunisada and the domestic scenes of Utamaro so delightfully reflected in Bonnard's colour lithograph, *Family Scene* (121) of 1893. The work is inspired by the same ongoing human instinct to love and cherish childhood that is present in Utamaro's *Sankatsu and Hanhichi With Their Baby* (122) of a century earlier.

Bonnard's friend, Vuillard, is especially remembered today for his intimate easel paintings that capture the charm of scenes drawn from everyday life. He lived for much of his life in Montmartre among the ordered confusion of his mother's dressmaking shop, divided by screens which were in frequent use to provide privacy while garments were altered, while swatches of brightly checked fabrics were everywhere. His love of Japanese prints was to express itself not only by wearing a kimono and tacking prints to the wall, but also by owning a Japanese screen.

In the early 1890s Vuillard enjoyed several commissions for decorative panels for such patrons as Alexandre Natanson, the editor of *La Revue blanche* and his wife Thadée, the belle of the *belle époque*, who kept the gossip mills of the *beau monde* turning for years.

In the dining room of their luxurious new home he painted for them nine decorative panels of the Tuileries Gardens and the Bois de Boulogne. A great feature of this area are the well-ordered parks where children played among the trees under the watchful eyes of their nursemaids, who formed the unaware models for the later screen of 1894 painted in distemper on canvas, entitled *The Nursemaids*, *The Conversation* and *The Red Sunshade* (123). These everyday scenes of women gossiping on park benches while children play among the trees were organized on Japanese design principles, which build up large compositions by letting the eye rove from a single image to diptych to triptych to polyptych, the nearest analogy in Western art being provided by the individual panes which make up stained-glass windows.

Differing dates and locations are claimed as witnessing the beginnings of Art Nouveau, that most varied of all artistic styles. Details of its many manifestations were spread by a wide variety of international journals, a few of them being *L'Art moderne* (Brussels), *L'Art décoratif*, *Art et décoration* (Paris), and *Die Jugend*, *Simplicissimus* (Munich). One of the most influential of these journals was *L'Art nouveau*, edited by Siegfried Bing, a name already familiar from his patronage of Japanese art, who in December 1895 opened a gallery in Paris of the same name.

123
Édouard Vuillard,
The Nursemaids,
The Conversation
and *The Red Sunshade*,
1894.
Distemper on canvas,
213·5 x 308 cm
(84 x 121¼ in).
Musée d'Orsay, Paris

124
Emile Gallé
Dawn and Dusk Bed,
1904.
Wood marquetry.
Musée de L'École
de Nancy

In every land there was a desire for a new start for art with the abolition of the old divisions between the fine and decorative arts. The continuing influence of Japan is evident in the emphasis placed upon asymmetry and simple outlines, and the study of exotic birds and flowers.

Many artists in Europe and America would create screens in the exciting years of the Art Nouveau movement, when the decorative arts flourished dramatically. One such artist was the polymath Emile Gallé. Gallé first worked in glass (see Chapter 4), but in 1884 turned his attention to furniture, believing that the same decorative style, based on natural forms, should apply to all the furnishings of a house. He first became attracted to the subject by the colourful variety of grained woods he discovered in a lumber yard where he had gone to obtain wood for the base of a glass vase. The experience alerted him to the pictorial possibilities of marquetry, and it was this quality that intrigued him and that can be seen in much of his furniture, which uses applied floral decoration in various woods often signed 'Gallé' vertically in the Japanese manner.

With the consummate skill acquired from his work with glass and metals, Gallé went on to produce such masterpieces as the remarkable bed with a marquetry headboard depicting a giant moth whose wings are drawn over a star-filled sky. The theme of dusk is echoed by the foot of the bed with the colours of dawn (124). Many of Gallé's pieces of furniture are decorated with flowers, landscapes and quotations from his favourite poets. A work table (125), for example, bears the inscription, 'Work is Joy at the House of Gallé'. This optimistic and very Morrisian slogan was tested by the fact that at the time of his death in 1904 his works at Nancy were employing over 300 men. For Gallé the Japanese influence continued through his friendship with a Japanese botanist called Takashima who studied forestry at Nancy. Their discussions led to the ironic comment of a critic called E de Vogue who wrote about Gallé: 'Let us be grateful for the quirk of fate which caused a Japanese to be born in Nancy.'

At the 1900 Paris exhibition, the high watermark of Art Nouveau, the reactions of the artistic establishment took various forms. The vice president of the jury for the awards in the exhibition was the forward-thinking Sir George Donaldson, who wanted to familiarize English designers and manufacturers with the 'new art' of Europe.

**Emile Gallé,
Work table,
1899–1900.
Carved ash and walnut
with marquetry of
various woods,
height: 70 cm (27¹₂ in).
Victoria and Albert
Museum, London**

**Louis Majorelle,
Cabinet,
c.1900.
Mahogany and oak veneered
with kingwood and amboyna,
enriched with carving and
marquetry of pearl, amboyna
and sycamore.
Victoria and Albert Museum,
London**

Realizing that no public funds would be available to purchase controversial work he generously decided to present a number of pieces of furniture, pottery and metalwork to what is now the Victoria and Albert Museum. His gifts included an inlaid cabinet (126) by Louis Majorelle (1859–1926), another brilliant member of the Nancy School, and the Gallé work table already mentioned. Unfortunately, however, immense prejudice was easily whipped up against the new style, dubbed the 'cult of the ugly' and a 'strange decorative disease' by Walter Crane, then Principal of the Royal College of Art. Other critics preferred to call it the 'noodle' style, descriptive both of its Japanese borrowings and decorative effects. So great was the volume of criticism that the offending artefacts were quickly removed from public exhibition in the museum, when they were shown there in 1901. Today, ironically, they are treasured as major examples of the furniture of their time.

By the early twentieth century the always changing Western perception of what was truly inspirational in Japanese culture would be radically altered by the work of a new generation of architects and designers. They would be concerned not with the ornamental tradition, but with the Japanese sense of architectural proportion, and a new realization that everything in a Japanese house is determined by rule.

The Czech artist and writer, Emil Orlik (1870–1932), visited Japan several times between 1900 and 1921 and wrote two important essays on Japanese woodcuts, noting that:

The feeling for clear articulation in the Japanese colour woodcut impressed me the very first time I came across it. Horizontal lines always stand in an interesting relation to the verticals … Japanese painters … have even developed a grille-motif of posts or trees in the foreground, middle distance, or background to specify artistic effect.

These concepts would take memorable shape in both buildings and furniture, and the continuing contest between Anglo-Japanese and Japonisme would take new forms in Frank Lloyd Wright's America (see Chapter 9), and Charles Rennie Mackintosh's (1868–1928) Scotland, exemplified in an amazing large chair or very small semicircular settle (127) from the Willow Tea Room made in 1904 which vividly looks forward to the abstract tenets of the new twentieth century.

127
Charles Rennie Mackintosh,
Chair,
1904.
Ebonized oak,
re-upholstered with
horsehair,
height: 118·2 cm
(46¹₂ in).
Glasgow School of Art

Chapter six:

Fans, Parasols, Combs, Pins, Kimonos

Japonisme

Previous page
**The Duke and Duchess
of Connaught and their
children dressed in
Japanese costume and
taking part in a Japanese
tea ceremony,
c.1890**

*The story of the beautiful is already
complete – hewn in the marvels of the
Parthenon – and embroidered, with
birds, upon the fan of Hokusai at
the foot of Fujiyama.*
J A M Whistler, 1885

In his novel *Pierre and Jean*, written
between June and September 1887,
Guy de Maupassant once again used
a literary device at which he excelled
by letting his description of a room
crowded with Japanese bric-à-brac
establish a mood. A young widow,
Jean, wants to impress his fiancée, and
he and his mother decorate a room in
his new apartment with:

*Japanese lanterns. Mother and son
had put as much imagination into this
room as they were capable of. With its
bamboo furniture, oriental figures and
vases, gold sequined silks, transparent
blinds of glass beads like drops of
water, fans fixed to the wall to hold
back curtains; with its screens, swords,
masks, cranes made of real feathers,
and all its knick-knacks in porcelain,
wood, paper, ivory, mother-of-pearl
and bronze, this room had the
pretentious and mannered
appearance which unskilled hands
and untrained eyes bestow upon
objects requiring the utmost tact,
taste and artistic training.*

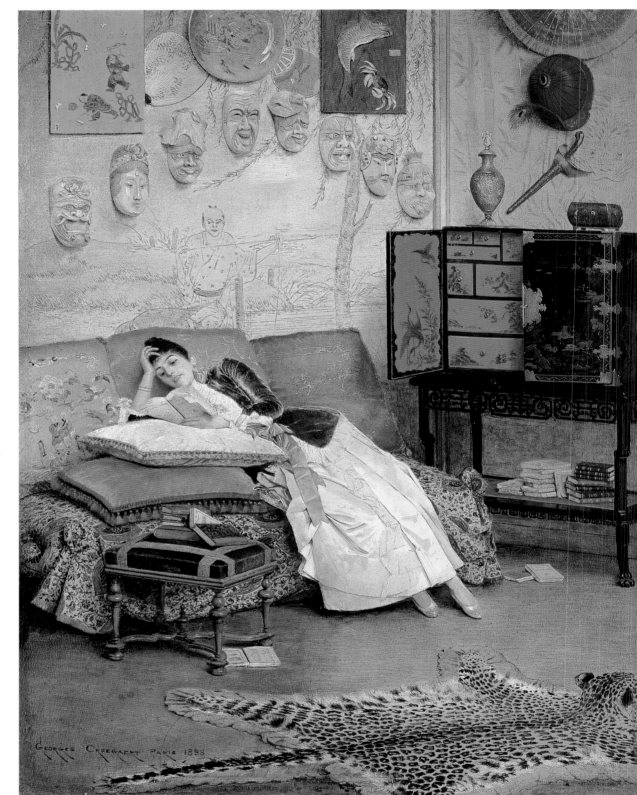

De Maupassant in this passage is subtly asking the question why the presence of Japanese artefacts could at one and the same time produce aesthetically pleasing and appallingly vulgar effects. In discovering why this is so we must look again at the importation of goods from Japan, and the standard of export wares deemed suitable for the barbarians in the outside world. By the 1880s acute artistic perceptions were becoming swamped by the popular mania for paper lanterns, fans and masks. Japanese motifs spread like a rash on everything from cheap trays to biscuit boxes. Fans, kimonos, screens and porcelain enlivened the 'artistic' rooms of the day, creating a decor of varying quality. An excellent example of a room of this type is provided by *The Reader* (1888; 128) by Georges Croegaert (1848–1923). In it we see a young Parisian lady who is, one may surmise, an avid reader of the extensive literature of Japonisme, and also a keen collector. Japanese objects jostle for our attention in her studio, including an awesome array of *noh* theatre masks, the obligatory fans and parasols, *kakemono* (hanging scrolls), lacquer panels and a valuable lacquer cabinet.

In the course of Japan's history both folding and fixed fans played a varied role. The importance of the fan went far beyond its practical use of keeping its bearer cool. Fans feature in a wide range of court and social activities; and were also used for the military purpose of making signals on the battlefield.

Fans figure largely in the disciplines of the theatre, dance and in the sumo wrestling ring, in which the referee, *gyoji*, controls the bout using a folding fan of a type known as a *gumpai uchiwa* (military fan). Today such fans can still be seen in use in the ceremonies, displays and bouts of the sumo ring. Fans were also created in large numbers for the 'fans' of famous *kabuki* actors by specialized artists such as Kunisada.

The growth of *ukiyo-e* woodblock printing during the Edo era provided a great stimulus to the development of fans of all types. Certain *ukiyo-e* print-makers were noted for their ability to create captivating fan shapes, notably Utamaro, whose *Women on the Ryogoku Bridge* (three sheets from a set of six; 129) shows women using a variety of both fixed *uchiwa* and folding *ogi* fans.

As Japanese fans began to be exported in large numbers in the 1860s, European artists began to experiment in painting on fan-shaped supports. Surprisingly, Whistler himself made no experiments in actually painting within the discipline of the fan shape, although fans do appear in his other work as background accessories, for example, a folding fan tucked behind a mirror frame, or a parasol in the grate, acting as a screen and indicating that the painting depicted a summer scene, as in the winter a fire would occupy the grate.

130
George Du Maurier,
Reading Without Tears,
from *Punch,*
February 1869

131
Simeon Solomon,
Lady with a Japanese Fan,
1865.
Watercolour,
41 x 35·5 cm
(16¼ x 14 in).
Grosvenor Museum,
Chester

A friend of Whistler from student days in Paris was the cartoonist, George Du Maurier (1834–96), who, in a cartoon for *Punch* dating from February 1869, showed his children seated on a sofa above which hang five *uchiwa* fans displayed very much like a military 'trophy' on the wall (130). Such casual displays of both fixed and folding fans were widely popular among aspiring followers of fashion at all social levels. The fan – cheap, frivolous, flirtatious and univer-sally available – became a badge of commitment to the arts for those of both high and low degree throughout the last quarter of the nineteenth century.

Close rivals to Whistler's *Symphony in White, No 2: The Little White Girl* (see 19), for the distinction of being the first paintings by a Western artist to depict a woman holding a Japanese fan, were two works by Simeon Solomon, who was an important figure in the nascent Aesthetic Movement. In one work, *Lady with a Japanese Fan* (131), Solomon's model sits posed against a background of *tatami* matting (Japanese floor covering) and a screen on which can just be discerned a stork. Behind her are Japanese Arita ware plates and two vases, one containing the obligatory aesthetic lily.

The painting, which dates from 1865, shows the model dressed in a Chinese robe but holding a Japanese fan, with a distinctive design of fans upon it. In another work of the same date the model is posed against a wall embellished with two *kakemono* paintings.

By the 1870s their cheapness and easy availability led to the visual triumph of fans in Europe and America. Curio shops selling both screens and fans abounded. Whether arranged symmetrically or casually in clusters, or attached to a screen, fans could enliven any room, arranged upon dado rails, or pinned to walls, and Whistler, as always, got in first with the idea of sticking fans to the ceiling. Nor was their more usual purpose forgotten, for as a writer in Oscar Wilde's journal, *The Woman's World*, observed in 1887, 'in the hot summers that have become the fashion, [we] fan ourselves, without regard to sex or condition, with Japanese fans.' As early as 1880, when George Du Maurier advised Frank Burnand to put 'Japanese sixpenny fans here and there on the walls' for the set of his play *The Colonel* satirizing Whistler, they had become an aesthetic cliché in England. In France, however, they still had a dramatic role to play.

132
Claude Monet,
La Japonaise,
1876.
Oil on canvas,
231·6 x 142·3 cm
(91⅛ x 56 in).
Museum of Fine Arts,
Boston

Artists used fans to decorate both their studios and their paintings, and Édouard Manet used a display of fans as an amusing visual ingredient in the portrait of Nina de Callias on a settee in a studio entitled *The Lady with the Fans* (1874). The sitter was a famous society hostess, renowned for her salons which, for more than fifteen years, were crowded with artists, musicans and writers. But while the fans in Manet's painting provide a striking background, they are eclipsed by the cascade of fifteen colourful fans which emblazon the wall of Claude Monet's studio in 1876. Before them stands his wife in a provocative pose clad in a *kabuki* actor's discarded robes. One fan, in particular, is of note, seen behind her left shoulder it portrays a 'tug of war' between a fish and a prawn, a theme also used by Christopher Dresser (see 72).

The painting *La Japonaise* (132), when first exhibited, met with both fierce criticism and great success, and would later gain iconic status. While the painting was in progress Monet wrote to his friend, Phillipe Burty (1830–90), saying that the *kabuki* actor's robes were 'superb to do'. But forty years later he was to describe the painting as 'une saleté' – a piece of filth – for reasons we can only guess at, but which may be connected with the embroidery of the figure of a warrior who seems to be fighting his way out of the woman's body.

133
Jean Louis Forain,
Dancer With a Rose,
*c.*1885–90.
Watercolour on linen.
Dixon Gallery and
Gardens, Memphis

Madame Monet is wearing a blonde wig, and clearly enjoying the fun of dressing up. The fan that she is holding is, however, not Japanese, but a red, white and blue tricolour fan of a type often used by Parisians at 14 July celebrations. The dancer's pose may owe something to Monet's friend, Théodore Duret, who had visited Japan, and wrote with knowledge of the entertainment at a famous Kyoto teahouse:

The Japanese dancer is covered from head to foot in a large, richly coloured robe whose lowest folds form a circle around her. She changes position very slightly while dancing … her dance is all in character; it consists, above all, of the movement of the head, the upper part of the body and the arms. Our dancers first danced singly [using] a fan or a parasol to mark or accentuate their pose.

The enormous demand in Europe and America for Japanese fans radically altered production methods. Mass-production techniques were brought in from the early 1860s when vast quantities of fans were exported in order to satisfy the ever-growing demand for 'something Japanese'. Before the floodgates really opened with the end of the Edo era in 1868 and the accession of the Meiji emperor, fans and prints provided a novel visual stimulus to a whole generation of European artists.

The mingling of diverse traditions provided a challenge which particularly appealed to Edgar Degas, who formed an extensive collection of Japanese prints, including at least fifteen drawings by Hiroshige, two triptychs by Utamaro, sixteen albums of miscellaneous prints, and various loose sheets by Hokusai, Utamaro, Shunsho and others, while a framed diptych of *Women at the Bath* by Kiyonaga once hung in his bedroom. The influence of this collection can be particularly clearly seen in the twenty-five paintings by Degas which took the form of fans. They were painted on two main occasions, three in the year 1868, and the remainder mainly around 1879, when he began enthusiastically to plan for the fourth Impressionist exhibition, where a room would be totally devoted to fan-shaped paintings. But although other artists were asked, in the end at the exhibition only five fans by Degas, four by Jean Louis Forain (1852–1931) and twelve by Camille Pissarro were shown on what proved to be the only occasion on which Degas exhibited this aspect of his art.

Degas's disciple, Jean Louis Forain, however, soon became a particularly successful creator of fan-shaped compositions. Forain was a man of great enthusiasms, a passionate admirer of Degas, a lover of ballet and of Japanese prints, several examples of which can be seen hanging on the walls of his home in a photograph taken in 1892 on the occasion of his marriage. Forain's *Dancer With a Rose* (133) demonstrates his abilities at their best.

Rather surprisingly, given the fan's intrinsic frivolity, it was the seriously minded Camille Pissarro who would create most fan-shaped compositions, exhibiting them in the fifth and eighth Impressionist exhibitions. In 1885 Pissarro grumbled that he 'had got to churn out fans because times are hard and for the moment one can only find a market for them, one mustn't count on paintings'. He experimented with the difficult shape to great advantage, creating such rural idylls as *Peasants Planting Pea Sticks* (1890; 134).

Paul Gauguin was also fascinated by the fan shape and owned an example by Pissarro, which he lent in 1879 to the fourth Impressionist exhibition mentioned above. Gauguin, always hard up, painted no fewer than thirty fans in his career probably because they sold well owing to their small size.

134
Camille Pissarro,
Peasants Planting Pea Sticks,
1890.
Gouache and black chalk
on grey paper,
39 x 60.2 cm (15³⁄₈ x 23³⁄₄ in).
Ashmolean Museum, Oxford

135
Paul Gauguin,
The Dramas of the Sea:
A Descent into the Maelstrom,
1889.
Lithograph on yellow paper,
17·5 x 27·6 cm
(7 x 10⁷⁄₈ in)

The most memorable of Gauguin's
fan-shaped compositions, *The Dramas
of the Sea: A Descent into the
Maelstrom* (135), is based upon
Sadahide's colour woodcut of
The Seaweed Gatherer (136). In a
lithograph on zinc, printed on yellow
paper from a series of eleven, Gauguin,
with brilliant inventiveness, has taken
the basic fan shape, turned it upside
down, and used its sloping sides to
suggest the giddying depths of the
whirlpool's sloping walls. The semicircle
at the top of the print has been used
to suggest the calmer waters of the
more distant sea. The boat and sailor
caught in the maelstrom suggest the
theme of Edgar Allan Poe's story,
A Descent into the Maelstrom (1841)
and the climax of Victor Hugo's *Toilers
of the Sea* (1867), while Gauguin has
borrowed from Sadahide the figure of
a man plummeting downwards threatened by the dark and angry waves and
the inevitable progress towards the
centre of the vortex of water.

136

Sadahide,
The Seaweed Gatherer.
Colour woodblock,
22·9 x 28·6 cm
(9 x 11¼ in)

115

The aesthetic artist and illustrator, Walter Crane, was given some prints by Toyokuni by a family friend who had returned from Japan, and subsequently he acknowledged 'Japanese colour prints' as 'an important factor' in the evolution of his bold linear style and flat and delicate colours. These are seen to advantage in his 'Shilling Series'. Crane provided a visual pun on the artist's name, and he used the bird as his signature in the same way that Whistler used the butterfly. The most extraordinary mixture of all Crane's 'exotic' images of the Middle and the Far East, particularly Japan, is provided by *Aladdin; or The Wonderful Lamp* (1875; 137). One page shows an Arabic princess dressed in a kimono and *geta* (Japanese sandals), attended by Japanese maids and servants holding a Japanese fan and parasol. Architectural details reveal Japanese motifs in the lacquer screens of the doors and in painted tiles. A vase with hydrangea is seen in the foreground arranged in the Japanese manner.

Fans, Parasols, Combs, Pins, Kimonos

Sales of fans in the 1870s went from strength to strength, but with an inevitable decline in quality. The brilliant colours which created such a violent contrast to the subtler shades of the natural pigments used by the early masters were due to the importation of Prussian Blue from the West, a new chemical pigment which was accompanied by a crude aniline red, a regrettable manifestation of Japanese interest in imported colours. In 1876 Whistler's friend, E W Godwin, who had long advocated 'a fitting disposition of Japanese fans as an alternative … decoration for dining room walls', now warned against 'the common paper fan of today … impregnated with the crudeness of the European's sense of colour'.

Despite these warnings the craze continued, and in their fixed form the cheap paper *uchiwa* were by the 1880s made literally in millions in Japan specifically for the export market. In 1891 the combined total of folding and rigid fans exported from Japan reached the astounding total of nearly sixteen million. As the caption for a *Punch* cartoon by Harry Furniss put it:

Twopence I gave for my sunshade,
A penny I gave for my fan,
Threepence I gave for my straw hat –
forrin made –
I'm a Japan-aesthetic young man.

137
**Edmund Evans, after
Walter Crane,
Aladdin; or The
Wonderful Lamp, from
the 'Shilling Series',
1875.
Colour woodblock,
27 x 23·5 cm
(10⅝ x 9⅜ in)**

The Grossmith brothers' classic novel of suburban life, *The Diary of a Nobody*, serialized in *Punch* in 1888 and published in book form in 1892, has a passage in which Carrie Pooter beautifies 'The Laurels, Upper Holloway' by tacking up a few fans, a fashion which was by then, to use the slang of the day, already 'old hat'. By the time Henry James wrote his *What Maisie Knew* in 1897, Mrs Beale gives Maisie a Japanese fan to hang up, but neither lady is sure where to put it. In 1894, Rudyard Kipling also turned to exotic associations of the fan to conjure up a 'decadent' milieu in his poem 'The "Mary Gloster"' when the dying sea captain says to his son:

*The things I knew was proper you
wouldn't thank me to give,
And the things I knew were rotten
you said was the way to live.
For you muddled with books and pictures, an 'china an' etchin's an' fans,
And your rooms at college was beastly
– more like a whore's than a man's...*

A craze began for amateurs painting fans. The materials for doing this appeared in the form of assembled fans void of decoration, and manuals on the art of composing and painting fans. Fan shapes were everywhere; mantelpieces groaned with Christmas cards with asymmetrical forms and fan-shaped vignettes with such popular themes as cherry blossom or sparrows. Fans were also put to commercial use, with free fans advertising shops and luxury goods. In *Fans of Japan* (1894) Charlotte M Salwey describes the way in which:

fans find their way into almost every drawing-room and boudoir in our Western Hemisphere, and are twisted up with wool and silk and tawdry materials, and repainted by the modern Goth. They are set in fireplaces and windows as summer screens, put to all sort of tortures, for letter racks and tidies, and devoted to uses for which they were never intended.

Their use as a symbol of status in society was vividly described in the rural classic, *Lark Rise to Candleford*, by Flora Thompson, an autobiographical account of English village life at the turn of the century, published in 1945, in which she describes:

the homes of ... newly married couples illustrated a new phase in the hamlet's history ... there were fancy touches hitherto unknown ... Japanese fans appeared above picture frames and window curtains were tied back with ribbon bows.

The parasol, like the fan, found an appropriately warm welcome when introduced into Europe in the 1860s. Its arrival on the fashionable scene created an instant vogue. Light and elegant, it could be used to protect an elaborate hairstyle, hide the modest bearer from unwelcome glances or, alternatively, prove an effective aid to coquetry, although its main use was to protect its users from the hot rays of the sun.

Parasols feature significantly in several major paintings of both the Aesthetic and Impressionist movements. For portrait and figure painters it provided a dramatic background for a beautiful face and delicate female complexion. As a compositional device it was elegantly used by Tissot in his portraits of his mistress Kathleen Newton.

In 1886, fashions, especially in Britain, became very elaborate; ribbon bows appeared near the handles while the sunshades themselves became 'daintily puffed veils at the end of sticks'. Carved animals and insects featured on the handles, which could be as big as billiard balls. By the end of the century ladies carried their parasols closed while gentlemen had the tightly rolled umbrella without which no English businessman's costume was complete.

The parasol briefly occupied a central place in the artistic concerns of Whistler, who was a friend of Sir Henry Cole, the first director of what is now the Victoria and Albert Museum. He obtained for Whistler in 1873 a commission to execute two mosaic panels to join thirty-five portraits of artists already installed in arcaded niches. Unlike the other designs, Whistler's would be of women and depict 'a Japanese art worker'. One of Whistler's own suggestions for this project depicted a woman decorating a parasol, while in a second pastel she is shown decorating a fan. However, Whistler failed to enlarge his drawings to the requisite size desired and the project was never realized.

Fortunately for posterity, some related drawings for this commission do survive, of which one of the finest is *The Japanese Dress* (138), a pastel which Whistler himself described as 'a very brilliant drawing and of beautiful colour – Gold – & blue & violet – in short a sparkling business altogether'.

Whistler also used parasols in several of his most 'Japanese' landscape studies of the early 1870s, such as *Battersea Reach from Lindsey House*. But his most important compositions using both parasols and fans as props were the *Six Projects* dating from 1868, commissioned by Leyland, Whistler's most important and difficult patron (see Chapter 5).

In the *Six Projects*, four of the six compositions are horizontal in format and show ladies in Tanagra-style classical draperies standing by the sea with Japanese fans and parasols. The paintings were all given different titles such as *Symphony in Blue and Pink*, which indicate the predominant colours of the picture. To establish the key colour notes a strip of fabric of the appropriate colour was inserted into the slats of the parasol or fan held by the model.

118

The paintings were designed to form a frieze in Leyland's music room, for he was an accomplished pianist and first suggested the word 'nocturne' to Whistler as a generic term for his night scenes. Although the projects were never completed, they mark a turning point in Whistler's career, enabling him to synthesize his various interests – Japonisme, classicism and the analogies between music and painting – into a coherent aesthetic of his own.

In addition to the main type of parasol, the *kinugasa*, there were also more elaborate parasols designed for the export trade, the *komori-gasa*. It is surprising that in Europe and America there do not seem to be any examples of parasols designed by artists, with one predictable exception, a parasol designed by Whistler for his great friend and taxing client, Lady Archibald Campbell, known as Lady Archie. It was well known that Whistler's monogram and the prominent pair of butterflies depicted on it immediately identified it as his signed work, and by implication hinted at an intimate relationship between the creator and the user. The design consisted of six pale green leaves enclosing seven darker leaves around a central flower. Washes of pale green and cream hint at the subtlety of the final effect.

Given our universal interest in weather, the parasol, sunshade and umbrella have surprisingly been relatively little studied. As a subject they are often shown in use in Japanese prints, Hiroshige, in particular, being fascinated by the way humans behave during the downpours of the rainy season or heavy falls of snow. In Hokusai's *Group With Umbrellas* (139) we possess one of his insights into human discomfort. This print may in part have inspired Édouard Manet's *Queue in Front of the Butcher's Shop* (1870–1; 140), a poignant memory of the siege of Paris when rats joined dogs and cats on the menu.

Renoir, most chauvinist of artists, had strong reservations about copying Japanese prints, complaining that:

Japanese prints are certainly very interesting, as Japanese prints – in other words as long as they stay in Japan. A people should not appropriate what belongs to another race; in so doing, they are apt to make stupid mistakes. There would soon be a kind of universal art, without any individual characteristics.

This prophetic disclaimer apart, Renoir seems to have at least looked at the same subject from the *Manga* when working on his major painting, *The Umbrellas* (c.1881–6; 141). It is one of his most puzzling pictures, perhaps because of a four-year gap which took place between working on both halves of the canvas – the half containing the umbrellas being left until last. Maybe he had just mislaid his umbrellas?

141
Pierre-Auguste Renoir,
The Umbrellas,
*c.*1881–6.
Oil on canvas,
180·3 x 114·9 cm
(71 x 45¼ in).
National Gallery, London

143
Ernst Ludwig Kirchner,
Girl Under Japanese
Umbrella,
*c.*1909.
Oil on canvas,
92·5 x 80·5 cm
(36³⁄₈ x 31⁵⁄₈ in).
Kunstsammlung
Nordrhein-Westfalen,
Dusseldorf

144
Vitaldi Babani,
Chrysanthemum Kimono,
*c.*1905.
Musée de la Mode et du
Costume, Paris

142
Front cover of *Vogue*
magazine, April 1917

In the twentieth century the parasol would continue to surface as a decorative accessory, as in the cover for American *Vogue* for April 1917, with its use of the Japanese motifs of trailing cherry-blossom branches before which posed the willowy figure of an American, rather than a Japanese, beauty (142). The parasol also found a powerful interpreter in the German Expressionist artist, Ernst Ludwig Kirchner (1880–1938), who used a parasol in his vibrant *Girl under Japanese Umbrella* (*c.*1909; 143).

Both fans and parasols featured in the studios of European artists at the height of the craze for Japonisme and so also did the kimono (literally meaning 'the thing worn'), a garment which dates back over three hundred years. During this time various techniques for dying and painting developed, including Yuzen, a starch-dying technique named after Yuzen Miyazaki (*fl.*1688–1704). Yuzen was a famous dye master who began to use rice-paste as the 'resist', a substance that is applied to part of the fabric to prevent it taking up the dye.

This technique started a revolution in the dying of freestyle designs, as dyers could easily depict landscapes, flowers, leaves and birds on silk textiles. The structure of a kimono as a cloak suspended from the shoulder provides a large area upon which to create a pictorial effect. Another nuance of the word kimono implied 'things to carry' and the make-up of the garment in crude but accurate terms can be compared to that of Western 'sandwich' men. Another more flattering analogy can be cited comparing the wearer with an easel and the garment with a blank canvas, upon which are created a design appropriate to each season, with such traditional motifs as cherry blossoms, chrysanthemums, bamboo, pine branches and running water. This example (144) of a kimono was from the shop on the Boulevard Haussmann in Paris founded by Vitaldi Babani in 1895, whose '*robes d'interieur japonaises*' were greatly sought after by fashionable ladies. His talent for publicity led to the opening of workshops and branches as far afield as Kyoto and Constantinople.

We gain a good idea of such works seen through European eyes through the paintings of the Amsterdam-based Impressionist artist, George Hendrik Breitner (1857–1923), who loved to paint women in kimonos.

145
George Hendrik Breitner,
Girl in Red Kimono,
*c.*1893.
Oil on canvas,
85 x 52·2 cm
(33½ x 20½ in).
Haags Gemeentemuseum,
The Hague

146
Pierre-Auguste Renoir,
Madame Hériot,
1882.
Oil on canvas,
65 x 54 cm
(25½ x 21¼ in).
Hamburg Kunsthalle

147
Miss Turner,
Gown,
*c.*1872.
White silk, printed and
embroidered with
chrysanthemums and fans.
The Kyoto Costume Institute

He created many 'variations on a theme' with models wearing either a white or a red kimono elaborately embroidered with cherry blossoms and birds (145).

In the studios of Europe and America, quite apart from its use as an exotic prop, the kimono was also to provide a vital ingredient in seductive aspects of the battle of the sexes, lending a new dimension to the phrase 'why not slip into something a little looser?' In the process the garment could suffer many modifications from its traditional form, for the Japanese use of a kimono with its tight, waist-encircling *obi* (sash) can be restricting rather than liberating. Nevertheless, in the 1880s the garment was utilized by fashionable European ladies as a *robe de chambre* because of its comfort. In the portrait of *Madame Hériot* (1882), Renoir, trained as a decorative porcelain painter, clearly delighted in the related task of painting the silk embroidery worn by the wife of the director of the Grands Magasins du Louvre, who sits comfortably installed in an armchair (146). She wears a kimono which has clearly been adapted to fit her, made up from silk produced in Japan in the last years of the Edo era. A very similar fabric was used in England *c.*1872 by Miss Turner, a court dressmaker, to create a dress with a bustle (147).

148
Amaryllis du Japon,
1890–1.
Colour lithograph,
129 x 93 cm
(50³⁄₄ x 36⁵⁄₈ in)

The voluptuous appeal of Japanese silks and kimonos also ensured that they featured frequently in the literature of Japonisme. J K Huysmans, who took such perverse delight in pinning down artistic styles, describes in an early working-class novel, *The Vatard Sisters* (1879), how his hero, Cyprien Tibaille, expresses a longing 'to embrace a woman dressed as a rich circus artiste, under a wintry, yellow-grey, snow-laden sky, in a room hung with Japanese silks …' Guy de Maupassant, who, as we have seen, had such a sharp eye for the more kitsch aspects of the fashion, describes in his most famous novel, *Bel Ami* (1885), how the 'hero', Duroy, an unprincipled social climber of boundless ambition, is excited by the sensual aspects of the garment:

Duroy sat and waited, waited for some time. At last a door opened and Madame de Marelle ran in, wearing a pink silk Japanese kimono embroidered with a gold landscape, blue flowers and white birds … he found her very attractive in her soft, brightly coloured kimono, less elegant than Mme Forestier in her white negligée, less endearing, less dainty, but more exciting, more seductive … What he wanted to do most with Mme Forestier was to lie at her feet or kiss the delicate lace of her bodice and breathe slowly the warm scented air between her breasts. With Madame de Marelle, he was conscious of a definite, animal, sensual desire, which made his hands tingle, to stroke the soft curves of her silk wrapper …

Scent, so powerfully evoked in this passage, was also advertised by a poster *Amaryllis du Japon* (1890–1), which one can easily imagine Duroy purchasing during one of his amorous campaigns (148).

A painting very close in mood to de Maupassant's novel was *The Japanese Woman* (149) painted in 1875 by Hans Makart (1840–84) who usually specialized in exotic themes from the Middle East. Makart may have been drawn to a Japanese theme by the popular success of the Japanese section of the International Exhibition held in Vienna (1873). Many splendid Japanese items were on view at this exhibition, and it is possible that the combs and kimono the model is wearing were acquired at that time. In the painting a very Rubenesque Austrian lady is posed semi-nude in a kimono while still retaining her Japanese hair pins. Her head and bust are shown against a bedraggled parasol made of feathers. She teases a bird by holding its nest which still contains eggs, thus arousing the ire of the rejected parent bird who complains at the window, creating a complex symbolic conundrum worthy of investigation by the famous Viennese doctor, Sigmund Freud.

149
Hans Makart,
The Japanese Woman,
1875.
Oil on panel,
141 x 92·5 cm
(55¹₂ x 36³₈ in).
Oberösterreichisches
Landesmuseum, Linz

Makart's friend, Gustav Klimt, was also a collector of Japanese art and owned an impressive collection of *noh* theatre costumes and kimonos. The Austrian art journal *Ver Sacrum* frequently published articles on such themes as 'The Spirit of Japanese Art' (Ernst Schurr, 1899), from which Klimt learnt much on the design of bold patterns derived from butterfly wings and peacock feathers. Photographs of Klimt's studios survive showing walls crowded with Chinese and Japanese scrolls, and samurai armour. Klimt enjoyed working in a smock (a kimono-like garment of his own design) made up in a Japanese-inspired textile by his friend the designer and architect Josef Hoffmann (1870–1955). Like Godwin and Hoffmann, Klimt was also fascinated by Japanese heraldic *mon*, filling several sketchbooks with drawings. Some of the *mon* were subsequently transformed in his paintings, which utilize abstract patterns recalling butterfly wings and peacock feathers. Klimt made much use of gold leaf in his backgrounds of brilliant colours, perhaps derived from seeing examples of screens of the *Rinpa* school founded by Ogata Korin, one of Japan's greatest decorative artists.

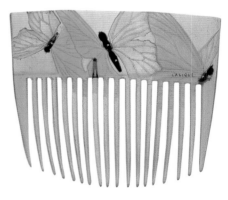

In 1905 Adolphe Stoclet, a Belgian millionaire, asked Hoffmann to design a palace in Brussels. Hoffmann commissioned Klimt to paint a frieze in the dining room (150). In it the figures of a man and a woman emerge from elaborate foregrounds and backgrounds made up of flakes of gold and semi-precious stones. The patterns vary from close-set studies of flowers in bloom to geometric triangles and rectangles. Although Klimt also deeply admired the Byzantine mosaics at Ravenna in Italy, the Japanese influence was important. Today these deeply sensual paintings are familiar as reproductions all over the world.

A Japanese theme which Klimt, a great womanizer, must have felt particularly attracted to was the 'search for the fashionable beauties of Kyoto or Edo'. This ongoing quest for ideal female beauty occupied print-makers, who struggled to cope with the bewildering frequency with which famous beauties changed fashions. When the hairstyle needed a change it was not uncommon for the engravers to set into the cherry plank small squares of a much harder wood onto which new hairstyles could be cut, thus prolonging the life of a block four or five times. The same beauty could be portrayed with an up-to-date, fashionable hairstyle, and such insets saved time and money.

152

René Lalique,
Drone With Umbels
hair comb,
*c.*1901–2.
Carved horn, gold and
enamel,
16 x 11·5 cm
(6¼ x 4½ in).
Calouste Gulbenkian
Museum, Lisbon

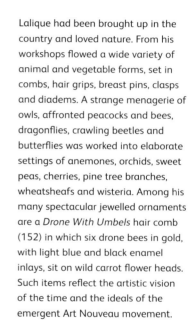

The chief accessories were the fan, comb and the hair pin (*kogai*), the latter being not only ornamental but also, depending on how many were worn, a mark of distinction and rank in the world of the geisha. Between 15-cm (6-in) and 30-cm (12-in) long, like a knitting needle, the top is surmounted with a gold, silver or copper knob which can take the form of amulets, flower buds, nuts or little bells. The ornamental hair comb, which was such a feature of Japanese women's dress, became a vital ingredient of the extremely high coiffures of the fashionable woman of the West. This set a challenge to many jewellers of the time, who also turned their attention to the manufacture of hat pins, which played a useful function at such outdoor pursuits as the races, regattas and garden parties then so popular.

Western jewellers, such as Henri Vever and René Lalique (1860–1945) in Paris and Louis Comfort Tiffany in New York, conscious of their own virtuosity, not only manufactured splendid pieces for practical wear, but also created *objets de vitrine* – stunningly beautiful display pieces. A splendid example of such a luxurious object is provided by Lalique's *Butterfly Combs* (151), carved on horn with gold and enamel, on which the insects jostle for our attention. These examples are carved in low relief to produce an impression of insects thronged in a swirling mass. One can imagine the consternation which greeted such a realistic effect of butterflies set against the elaborate hairstyles of the day.

Lalique had been brought up in the country and loved nature. From his workshops flowed a wide variety of animal and vegetable forms, set in combs, hair grips, breast pins, clasps and diadems. A strange menagerie of owls, affronted peacocks and bees, dragonflies, crawling beetles and butterflies was worked into elaborate settings of anemones, orchids, sweet peas, cherries, pine tree branches, wheatsheafs and wisteria. Among his many spectacular jewelled ornaments are a *Drone With Umbels* hair comb (152) in which six drone bees in gold, with light blue and black enamel inlays, sit on wild carrot flower heads. Such items reflect the artistic vision of the time and the ideals of the emergent Art Nouveau movement.

Kimonos, sunshades and Japanese ornamental accessories were also greatly in demand in the West as costumes at fancy dress balls, a popular fashionable diversion of the 1880s. In Henry Somm's paintings *Elegant Lady in a Japanese Garden*, and *A Procession of People in Japanese Costume* we get a glimpse of this type of 'dressing up' party. Even the British royal family took part in a variant of this type of entertainment known as a *tableau vivant*, as an engaging photograph of about 1890 of the Duke and Duchess of Connaught and their children in Japanese costume reveals (see pp.106–7).

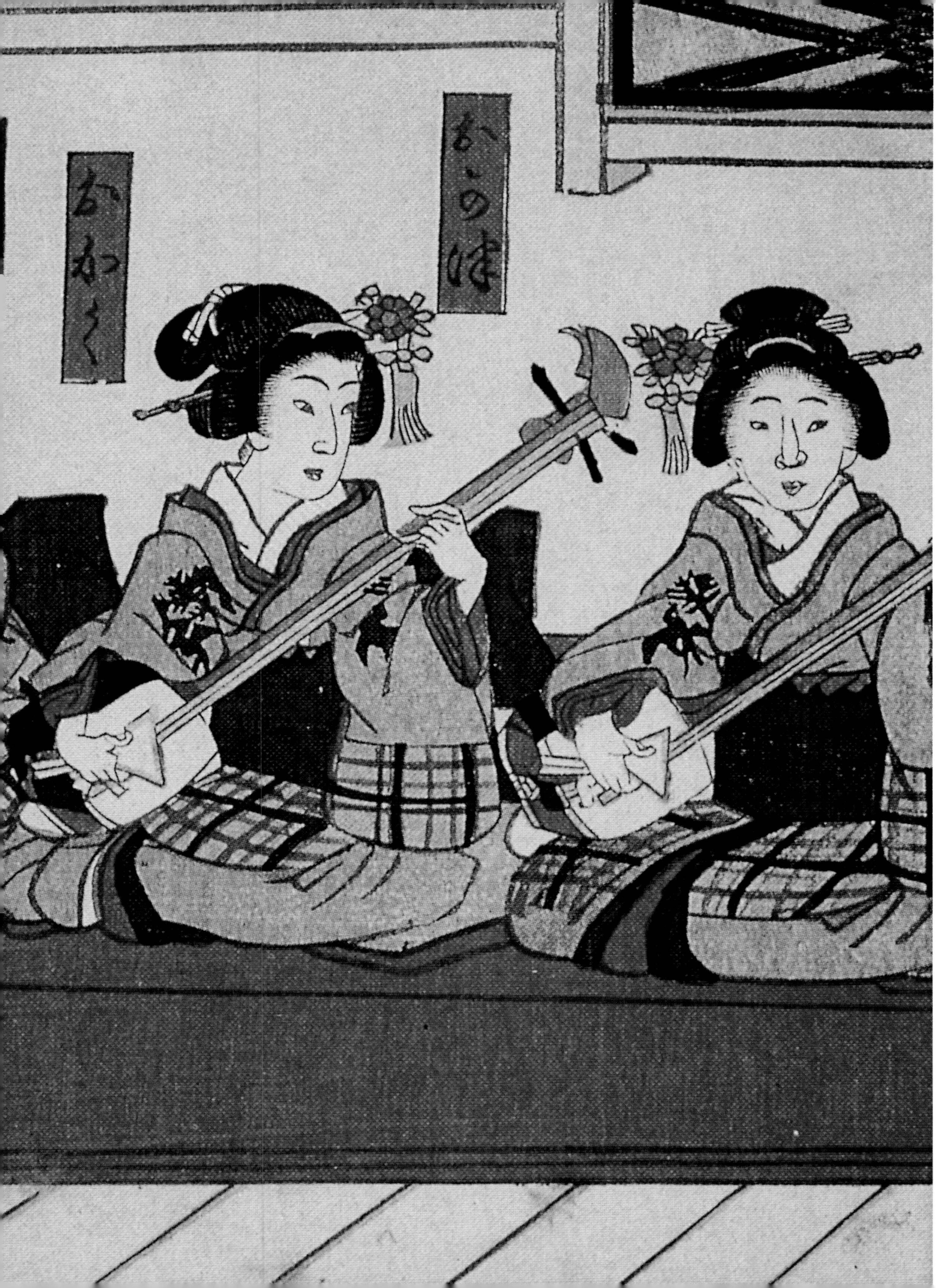

Chapter seven: The Novel, the Stage and the Opera

Previous page
**Baichoro Kunisada
and Oko Kunisada,
The Matsumotoro
Theatre in the Tokyo
Pleasure District**, 1870
(detail of 172)

153
**James Tissot,
Chrysanthemums,**
c.1874–5.
Oil on canvas,
118·6 x 76·2 cm
(46¾ x 30 in).
Clark Art Institute,
Williamstown, MA

'Japonaiserie forever'.
The de Goncourt Brothers, 1867

Everything is Japanese now.
Alexandre Dumas (fils), 1887

**Rog-a-by bebby off in Japan
You jus' a picture off of a fan.**
John Luther Long, 1900

Japonisme, generally considered as a phenomenon which only affected the visual and decorative arts, also influenced the novel, the stage and the opera. As a style, Japonisme coincided almost exactly with the Impressionist movement but also with the French school of naturalistic fiction which centred on Émile Zola, who vied with the de Goncourt brothers for recognition as a leader of the new 'realist' or naturalist school, and also as a collector of Japanese prints. He was once described by Edmond de Goncourt as being 'an engine greased for industrial labour', an analogy which refers to his role as the great chronicler of the lives of the working class and lower bourgeoisie. He preached the value of obtaining sociological insights by the accumulation and careful documentation of material facts.

Zola's passion for the meticulous recording of detail to achieve authencity led him, so it is said, to have been deliberately run over by a hansom cab in order to describe the experience exactly.

While not all of his followers would go to quite such drastic lengths, they nevertheless shared a belief that they should use every effort to obtain accurate descriptions for the backgrounds to their stories. Such 'realism' has been amusingly defined as 'truth to the observed forms of life (especially when they are gloomy)'.

Not all writers known as 'realists' relished the label. Gustave Flaubert, in particular, disliked being so categorized, describing himself as 'a rabid old Romantic – or a fossilized one, whichever you prefer'. Yet some of the greatest exponents of realist doctrines were his disciples, the de Goncourt brothers and Guy de Maupassant. De Maupassant loved clutter and enjoyed describing the details of a crowded room, or an artist's studio laden with Japanese gee-gaws, a device tellingly used in *Bel Ami*, written in 1885. In the novel the hero becomes nervous and apprehensive when his new mistress announces that she is coming to see his sleazy 'bed-sit' in a working-class quarter of Paris. He decides the room needs redecoration:

As soon as he had finished his newspaper work, he planned the rearrangement of his room to receive his mistress and conceal as far as possible the poverty of the flat. He had the idea of pinning on the walls small Japanese knick-knacks, and he laid out five francs on a whole collection of rolls of coloured crinkly paper, little fans and screens, with which he hid the worst stains on the wallpaper. On the window-panes he stuck transparent pictures, boats on rivers, flocks of birds against a background of red skies, women in brightly coloured costumes on balconies, and processions of little black dwarfs over snow-covered plains. His rooms, which were just big enough to hold a bed and chair, soon began to look like the inside of a Chinese lantern. He considered the result satisfactory and spent the evening sticking on the ceiling birds cut out of the coloured plates he had not yet used. After that he went to sleep, lulled by the whistles of the trains. Next day ... [his mistress] was charmed by the dazzling colour of the prints, exclaiming, 'What a delightful room!'

Vying with the popularity of Japanese artefacts was the craze for a flower – the chrysanthemum, which began even before the publication of Pierre Loti's best-selling novel, *Madame Chrysanthème*, firmly established the flower as a popular symbol of Japan. This popularity is reflected in one of the most beautiful works by James Tissot (153). The flower is referred to in Marcel Proust's *Remembrance of Things Past*, when his hero Charles Swann is captivated by the *demi-mondaine* Mme Odette de Crécy's apartment, with its:

huge Japanese lantern ... and a long rectangular box in which bloomed, as in a hothouse, a row of large chrysanthemums, at that time still uncommon, though by no means so large as the mammoth specimens which horticulturists have since succeeded in producing.

Swann was irritated by the sight of these flowers, fashionable in Paris throughout the late 1880s. Odette pins Charles down:

in one of the many mysterious little alcoves ... [she] installed behind his head and beneath his feet great cushions of Japanese silk which she pummelled and buffeted as though to prove that she was prodigal of these riches, regardless of their value ... she drew his attention now to the fiery-tongued dragons painted on a bowl or stitched on a screen ... or a toad carved in jade.

154
Katsukawa Shunsho,
Lovers on a Balcony from
the series *The Twelve
Hours of Lovemaking*,
*c.*1800.
Colour woodblock,
24·8 x 37·4 cm
(19³⁄₄ x 14³⁄₄ in)

In 1887 Alexandre Dumas (*fils*) enjoyed a huge success with his play, *Le Francillon*. One exchange in the play gained immense publicity. A guest at a fashionable dinner asks his hostess for the recipe of the salad they had eaten that evening, to which the hostess replies that she calls it a Japanese salad, as 'it must have a name, and everything is Japanese nowadays'.

These words 'everything is Japanese nowadays' rapidly became a widely used catchphrase. Later in Proust's novel the hero, Swann, while passing an evening at the Verdurins', is deeply bored by a fellow guest, Mme Cottard, who, despite having not yet seen *Le Francillon*, gushes unceasingly about it, saying, 'wherever I go I naturally find everybody talking about that wretched Japanese salad. In fact one is begin-ning to get just a little tired of hearing about it.' Remorselessly, Mme Cottard continued, swayed by the power of the catchphrase, which for the duration of the 1880s demonstrated that Japon-isme had become, as a contemporary critic remarked, 'no longer a fashion, it's an infatuation, a folly'. It was a craze, and one which had some inter-esting effects on literature of the time.

As the enthusiasm for Japanese art spread like a contagious virus across Europe, Edmond de Goncourt's annoyance grew. Anticipating Oscar Wilde twenty years later, he began to grumble that the subject had become vulgarized and over-popularized. On 29 October 1868 he protests:

The taste for things Chinese and Japanese! We were among the first to have this taste. It is now spreading to everything and everyone, even to idiots and middle-class women. Who has cultivated it, felt it, preached it, and converted others to it more than we; who was excited by the first volumes and had the courage to buy them?

In the first of our books En 18 .., [Eighteenth-Century French Painters] a description of a mantelpiece with Japanese ornaments brought us the honour of being called Baroque fools, people without taste, and caused Edmond Texier to demand that we be committed to Charenton [the lunatic asylum which had housed the Marquis de Sade].

But despite these groans, a recurring cry of all collectors, Edmond continued to acquire works at fever pitch. On 30 October 1874 with his friend, Burty:

we went to inspect the arrival of two shipments from Japan. We spent hours in the midst of those forms, those colours, those objects in bronze, porcelain, pottery, jade, ivory, wood and paper – all that intoxicating and haunting assemblage of art. We were there for hours, so many hours that it was four o'clock when I had lunch. After these debauches of art – the one this morning cost me more than 500 Francs – I am left worn out and shaking as after a night of gambling.

I came away with a dryness in the mouth which only the sea water from a dozen oysters could refresh. I bought some ancient albums, a bronze ... and the gown of a Japanese tragedian on whose black velvet there are gold dragons with enamel eyes clawing at each other in a field of pink peonies.

By 1883 de Goncourt's obsession with collecting Japanese art had reached new and worrying levels. On 29 December, reviewing the purchases he had made in the passage of the year, he wrote describing 'madness, a sexual passion for things Japanese. This year I have spent 300,000 francs on them – all the money I have made.'

On 17 July 1884 he writes of his envy of the dealer, Siegfried Bing, who 'will have seen almost all the art of China and Japan pass through his hands'. Bing was not only a dealer in Japanese art, he also edited the influential journal *Le Japon Artistique*, which was published in thirty-six issues from 1888 to 1891 in French, German and English (see 83). The periodical's influence continued long after it stopped publishing; Gustav Klimt, for example, buying a complete set in 1906. Bing also organized several exhibitions of Japanese prints, the most important being held at the École des Beaux-Arts in Paris in 1900; others were at the Fine Art Society in London in 1890, and Boston in 1894. Bing went on to become one of the great impresarios of the next new artistic movement, Art Nouveau.

On 28 December 1886 de Goncourt attended a party where he met another leading figure in the dissemination of knowledge of Japanese art, Tadamasa Hayashi (1851–1906), who first came to Paris in 1878 when he was employed at the Exposition Universelle as a translator. In 1884 he set up in Paris as a dealer and researcher. He was at the heart of Parisian cultural activities and became virtually the father of the study of Japanese art history in Europe, and thus a congenial spirit for Edmond de Goncourt.

A few days later, on 5 January 1887, Edmond gave a lunch party, one of the guests being the etcher, Félix Bracquemond, who earlier in the mid-1870s had first acquired a copy of Hokusai's *Manga*, and brought it to the attention of French artists and writers. After the lunch Edmond noted:

I have Bracquemond and the sculptor Rodin to lunch today. Rodin, who is full of fawnishness, asks to see my Japanese erotics, and is full of admiration before the women's drooping heads, the broken lines of their necks, the rigid extension of arms, the contractions of feet, all the voluptuous and frenetic reality of coitus, all the sculptural twining of bodies melted and interlocked in the spasm of pleasure [154].

155
Édouard Manet
Portrait of Émile Zola,
1867–8.
Oil on canvas,
146 x 114 cm
(57¹₂ x 44⁷₈ in).
Musée d'Orsay, Paris

Zola shared the de Goncourts' enthusiasm for erotic prints, and the staircase of his home was lined with the kind of print that he chose to call 'my furious fornications'. Zola always needed a new artistic cause to champion, and an ideal contentious issue presented itself in Édouard Manet's works, which in the 1860s had become synonymous with scandal and ridicule, leading Manet to erect his own 'pavilion' in a shed at the World's Fair held in Paris in 1867. There he showed fifty of his paintings, some of which were attacked for their resemblance to the popular imagery of crude penny-plain and twopence-coloured prints, which are still produced in France today in the town of Épinal in the Vosges. Zola defended Manet's work in a 23-page article published on 1 January 1867 in the *Revue du XXe siècle*, a eulogy written after visiting the artist in his studio. In this article (subsequently published as a book) Zola suggested, in defence of Manet's works, that it would be much more interesting to compare his bold simplified style of painting with Japanese prints, which resembled Manet's work 'in their strange elegance and their magnificent patches of colour'.

Zola's portrait by Manet (155), probably begun in the autumn of 1867, is full of both clear and coded references to the interests of both artist and sitter. These range from the Japanese screen seen on the left which became a familiar prop in Manet's studio, to 'short-hand' references to his principal artistic interests. These are represented by three prints pinned or stuck casually to a board at the top right of the painting, which refer both to Manet's love of the painter Velázquez (1599–1660) and a shared interest in the Japanese print, apparent in the woodcut of *The Sumo Wrestler Onaruto Nadaemon of Awa Province* by Kuniyaki II (1835–88). Manet's own work is represented by a graphic version of *Olympia* (1863), the painting which Zola had stoutly defended in his article, shown prominently displayed among the clutter of books and brushes on a small table. The eyes of all the figures in these three prints are directed towards the sitter Zola, as if to acknowledge the writer's role as defender of Manet's interests. Manet may have adopted this compositional device from one of the prints by Sadahide (1807–*c*.1873) depicting foreign visitors to Yokohama, such as the *Englishman Sorting Fabric for Trade at Yokohama* (156), whose thoughts have strayed to his wife so far away in reality, but symbolically present in the cartouche (for similar fabrics see 93–95).

Some years after painting his portrait of Zola, Manet painted a 'portrait' of the prostitute, Nana (157), in Zola's *L'Assommoir* of 1877. The geisha and the courtesan were favourite themes of the Japanese print, and Manet also clearly welcomed the opportunity to treat similar potentially popular subjects. In the painting Nana looks over her shoulder at a gentleman visitor, cut off by the edge of the picture in the Japanese manner. She gazes at us seductively with her back to her caller. On the wall behind her is the same screen decorated with cranes, which appears in Manet's earlier painting of Zola. Here the presence of the cranes in the screen provides both a visual and verbal pun, for the word *grue* ('crane') was also commonly used to describe a courtesan. Nana's small head, long neck and white slip, despite her plump stature, make a jocular visual reference to the 'crane'.

Such meticulous descriptions of squalid, yet erotic interiors captured the popular imagination, as would an incident which became one of the most famous of love stories. Everyone today is familiar with the story of Puccini's *Madame Butterfly*, Cio-Cio-San, and her desertion by Lieutenant Pinkerton. It was based upon a nineteenth-century true story of Yamamuru Tsuru. She attempted suicide after being deserted by an English merchant who had fathered her child and later returned to enrol his son in the American missionary school in Nagasaki. It was first published as *Madame Butterfly* in 1901 by John Luther Long.

This all-too-familiar story of love and betrayal when combined with the clash between the cultures of East and West is unforgettable. These tragic events are all wrapped up with the axiomatic assumption of Western superiority that falling in love with a white man entailed. This theme still continues to hold an extraordinary fascination for dramatists, film-makers and composers, producing such contemporary variants as the recent musical, *Miss Saigon*. Tales of betrayed trust and desertion move us, just as they did Giacomo Puccini when he wrote the music for his opera in 1904. To understand the background to *Madame Butterfly* it is rewarding to trace its antecedents, right back to the time when the English navigator, Will Adams, settled in Japan in 1600 and took a Japanese wife with whom he had two children. Ever since then, the relationship between Western men and Japanese women has inspired fantasy and speculation. But while the sexual mores of the two societies differed widely, not all male visitors to Japan abandoned their partners completely, for some married and settled down either temporarily or permanently in Japan.

Variations of these human dilemmas continued throughout the nineteenth century. One interesting story, little known in the West, can be studied in the life of Charles Wirgman, the war artist for the *Illustrated London News*.

Wirgman is remembered affectionately in Japan for his humour, manifest in his comic publication, *The Japan Punch*, published intermittently between 1862 and 1887 (158). *The Japan Punch* was very popular among Westerners in the treaty ports, as were such sketchbooks as *Artistic and Gastronomic Rambles in Japan from Kyoto to Tokyo by Tokaido* (1872). That there was also a tender side to Wirgman's personality is revealed in a number of watercolour sketches of such subjects as Japanese women, notably several sensitive studies of his wife, of whom unfortunately very little is known (see 174).

Ever since 1785, when Philip James de Loutherbourg had staged at Covent Garden in London the pantomime *Omai, or A Trip Round the World* in the wake of Captain Cook's explorations in the Pacific, the exotic East provided a popular theme for stage shows. For European composers the romantic East was also always a trump card to play from the time of Gluck's *Le Cinesi* (*The Chinese Ladies*), a lavish *chinoiserie* production staged in Vienna in 1754 with crystal and transparent decor in the Chinese style, to Giuseppe Scarlatti's *L'Isola disabita* (*The Desert Island*) in 1757. This slapstick farce with mock Chinese words, a Chinese beauty and a handsome Dutchman proved a huge success, not least because of the scenery, costumes and mockery of Chinese customs.

A century later, the visual enthusiasm for *chinoiserie* themes had given place to a demand for subjects presented with the wrappings of Japonisme fostered by a vast public demand for traveller's tales, poems and dramatic and musical celebrations of Japan. Musically the first Western celebration of a specifically Japanese theme took place as early as 1872 in Saint-Saëns's obscure but engaging third opera *La Princesse jaune* (*The Yellow Princess*), which was first performed at the Opéra Comique in Paris, but was not a success. This was perhaps because it had only two characters, and the exotic atmosphere is largely evoked by means of pentatonic melodies.

It may also have arisen because the piece was not, as is misleadingly suggested in the title, set in an exotic foreign land, but in the much more familiar locale of Holland, and was really a satire on the national passion for collecting all things Japanese. The story concerns the love between the heroine and her boring cousin, the pedantic Cornelius, who is completely obsessed with Japanese artefacts, and has unfortunately fallen in love with a girl portrayed upon a fan. Disillusionment sets in with a dream which reveals to Cornelius the restricted nature of Japanese life, and tells him that what he really needs is a beautiful Dutch girl. With such a fustian plot it is hardly surprising that the opera only received five performances and has rarely been revived.

Japonisme had very differing effects on different artists, and the same applied even more to composers and writers. In 1878 a Japanese fantasy by Ernest d'Hervelly opened to packed houses in Paris, while at the Opéra during the same year a 'Japanese ballet' proved equally successful. Both these events no doubt relied on spectacle but they show the potential which existed for musical extravaganzas.

It was at first within the covers of a successful novel that the artistic cross-pollination of Japan and Europe, first on the page and later on the stage, effectively took place. Its author was Pierre Loti, the *nom de plume* of Louis Marie Julien Viaud, a French naval officer who eventually left the French navy to specialize in stories of passionate but transient romance in exotic Oriental settings.

Published in 1888 as *Madame Chrysanthème*, the story takes the form of a diary kept by Pierre (the author), a naval officer on the *Triomphante*, forced to stay at Nagasaki from July to September while his ship underwent repairs. In its entries Loti describes the process by which officers of foreign navies were permitted to enter into temporary marriages with geishas, a convenience which could be easily terminated with the expiration of the husband's stay, an arrangement of which, as Loti ironically observes, the officers of the American, British and French navies enthusiastically availed themselves.

During his two months with his 'geisha' Chrysanthemum, Loti comes to know her intimately and becomes, in a detached way, more amused than charmed by her childlike, playful gaiety, 'a little creature made to laugh yet easily saddened'. He captures her personality in a passage describing a walk through Nagasaki with her friends:

All five of them hold hands, like little girls out for a walk … Seen from behind, they're very fetching, these dolls, with their hair so nicely done, and their tortoiseshell combs so prettily arranged … As with all Japanese women, the backs of their little necks are delicious … In the bazaars our girls make lots of purchases every evening. Like spoiled children they want everything – toys, combs, belts, flowers. And then they all give one another presents, with pretty, girlish little smiles. Bluebell, for example, chooses for Chrysanthemum an ingeniously conceived lantern in which shadow puppets, set in motion by a hidden mechanism, dance round and round the flame.

In return, Chrysanthemum gives Bluebell a magic fan which can show, according to your inclination, either butterflies flitting among cherry blossom or monsters from beyond the grave chasing one another among black clouds …

In the well-known teahouses, where we round off our evening, the little serving girls welcome us when we arrive with an air of respectful recognition as one of the groups who are living the high life in Nagasaki. There we chat brokenly, often losing the thread, in miniature gardens lit by lanterns, beside goldfish ponds with little bridges and little islands and little ruined towers.

Loti apologized to his readers for the style of this last sentence regretting that 'in describing this land one is tempted to use the word "little" six times in a line'.

An oil painting, *L'Ameya: The Sweet Stall* (1892; 159) by Robert Blum (1857–1903) records a shopping spree very similar to that described by Loti. Blum's painting first appeared as an illustration to *Japonica* by Sir Edwin Arnold accompanied by a commentary describing the virtuosity of the sweet stall owner who was able to use molten sugar just like a glass-blower to create edible toys.

159
Robert Blum,
L'Ameya: The Sweet Stall,
1892.
Oil on canvas,
63·7 x 78·9 cm
(25 x 31 in).
Metropolitan Museum of Art, New York

160
Felice Beato,
Game of Shuttlecock,
1868.
Hand-painted albumen print

Such popular genre subjects taken from street life as *Game of Shuttlecock* (160) were also the delight of the busy photographer, Felice Beato. Beato's photographs (and those of his many imitators) provide remarkable visual records of the childlike games beloved by Chrysanthemum and her friends, which Loti began to find juvenile rather than charming. Unable to suffer fools gladly and swiftly bored with the liaison, Loti leaves – his last illusions about the love affair being shattered by the sight of his discarded girlfriend happily counting her money and testing the coins with a hammer 'with the competence and dexterity of an old money lender'.

Loti retired from the French navy in 1883. He had not, however, yet finished with all his Japanese material. In 1883 he had attended a ball at Edo and used his memories of this event to describe a scene in *Japoneries d'automne* (*Autumnal Memories of Japan*, 1889):

They're a little too bedecked with gold braid, these numerous Japanese gentlemen – ministers, admirals, officers, officials of one kind and another – all in their party outfits … And then how oddly they wear their tailboards. No doubt their backs were not designed for this sort of thing. Impossible to say where the impression comes from, but I find all of them, always, in some elusive way bear a marked resemblance to monkeys.

Such crude racist analogies, which recall both the *singeries* of eighteenth-century French art and post-Darwinian prejudices (present elsewhere in Loti's work), were particularly disliked by the liberal-minded painter, Félix Régamey (1844–1907), who had visited Japan with Émile Guimet, founder of the great museum which bears his name in Paris. Régamey embarked on a protracted disagreement with Loti over the moral implications of his novel. Their arguments reached a climax after 1893, when the composer, André Messager wrote and conducted an opera based on Loti's tale. Régamey published his own version of the story in 1894, entitled *Le Cahier rose de Madame Chrysanthème* (*The Pink Notebook of Madame Chrysanthemum*), told by the heroine in the form of an intimate journal.

It was, however, the circus ring which was to inspire one of the most important and spectacular renditions of the theme. In November 1892 Henri de Toulouse-Lautrec visited a show entitled *Papa Chrysanthème* at The New Circus, an elegant establishment in the Rue Saint-Honoré. He made many strikingly Japanesque sketches, notably a large drawing in which the hair, hat and dress of the lady take on bizarre shapes, while the dancer bends her body backwards to create a sharply exaggerated curve.

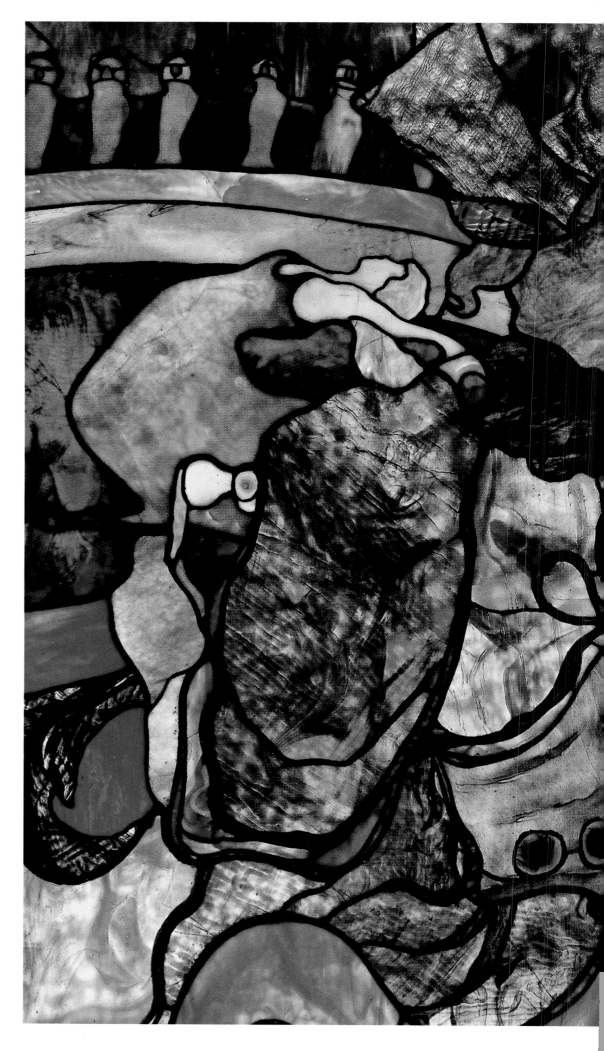

161
Henri de Toulouse-
Lautrec,
Tiffany & Co.,
At the Nouveau Cirque,
Papa Chrysanthème,
1895.
Marbled glass,
120 x 85 cm
(47¼ x 33½ in).
Musée d'Orsay, Paris

The broad handling of the subject
suggests that it was probably first
thought of as a design for a poster,
but the black outlines also suggest that
stained glass was a favoured option
from the beginning. The title yet again
cashed in on the success of Loti's
novel, which had made the very word
'chrysanthemum' synonymous with
both Japan and exoticism. This
particular variant of the oft-told tale
was a nautical fantasy of a prince who
returns to Japan with a European
fiancée, who presents herself at court
in a ceremonial dance in the centre of
the ring. In Toulouse-Lautrec's sketch
of the scene, an overdressed lady with
a huge hat gazes across the ring at the
spectacle, watched by five gentlemen
wearing evening dress – the 'stuffed
shirts' of the title, *Clowness and Five*
Stuffed Shirts, whose hairstyles have
a distinct resemblance to Oriental 'pig-
tails'. For this number the circus ring
was transformed into a pool, dotted
with water lilies and lotus leaves, and
dancers using diaphanous veils and
coloured electric lights in imitation of
Loie Fuller (a flooded ring is still used
to create a similar effect at the
Blackpool Tower circus).

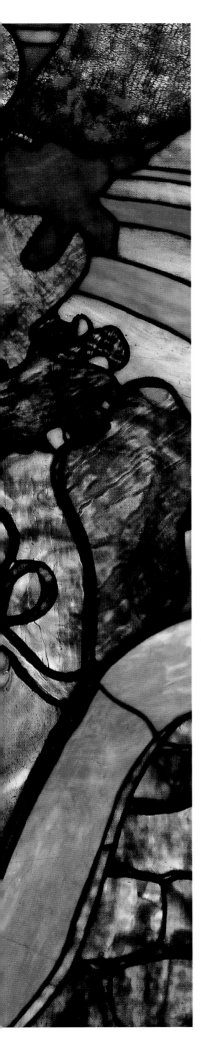

162
George Grossmith as Pooh-Bah in *The Mikado*, 1885

On a visit to New York in the early 1890s the entrepreneur, Siegfried Bing, discovered the art workshops of Louis Comfort Tiffany and was immensely impressed by the new forms of stained and decorative glass that Tiffany named 'favrile' glass. Here, he sensed, was a major attraction for his new salon dedicated to the novel themes of Art Nouveau. Impressed by the remarkable effects that could be obtained in this exciting new medium, he commissioned the Nabis group of artists – among them Bonnard, Vuillard, Denis, Sérusier and Félix Vallotton (1865–1925), together with Toulouse-Lautrec, to supply a series of cartoons for stained glass. For his contribution to the scheme Toulouse-Lautrec recalled his drawings of three years earlier of *Papa Chrysanthème* and realized how well his design, with its bold, broad lines, would adapt into the supportive 'leading' needed in a stained-glass composition (161). Tiffany's craftsmen brilliantly interpreted Lautrec's studies and the resultant glass panels formed the opening display in Bing's new salon. In a review of the show in *La Revue Blanche*, Jacques Émile Blanche singled out Lautrec, 'who has composed the loveliest, and the most modern, of decorative motifs out of a circus scene and a harlot's hat'. With its bold design, and extremely Japanese composition, the panel became one of the most remarkable examples of Japonisme's influence upon the decorative arts.

These themes would seem at first very far from the stock-in-trade of the famous British partnership between the composer Arthur Sullivan and librettist William Schwenck Gilbert, aided by the indispensable impresario, Richard D'Oyly Carte, who together created with reforming zeal a new genre of English operetta. In 1881 Aestheticism had provided Gilbert and Sullivan with the ideal contemporary subject to satirize in *Patience* in Bunthorne's song of confession: 'I do *not* long for all one sees that's Japanese.' Four years later, in 1885, the cult for Japan provided the perfect target for their greatest satirical partnership, which took the form of *The Mikado* or *The Town of Titipu*. By 1885 plentiful evidence existed for any theatrically aware impresario that virtually any show with a Japanese theme had a good chance of success. This was manifest in such musical extravaganzas as *The Japs* or *The Doomed Daimyo*, performed at Bristol on 31 August 1885 and at the Novelty Theatre in London, which was basically a conjuring show. Much more successful was *The Great Taykin*, a 'Japananza' in one act with music by George Grossmith, produced at Toole's Theatre under Toole's management on 30 April 1885 and withdrawn on 6 August after eighty-seven performances. Its female characters enjoyed such excruciating names as Kissi-Missi and Tickle-Ing.

The production of *The Mikado* on 14 March 1885 was a much more important event, which really ensured the popularity of Japanese art in England and America, by making gentle fun of it. Gilbert himself described the initial moment of inspiration for the piece, when:

an executioner's sword hanging on the wall of my library – the very sword carried by Mr Grossmith at his entrance in the first act – fell off the wall and suggested the broad idea upon which the libretto is based [162].

The libretto of *The Mikado* created the land of Titipu, a 'topsy-turvy' mirror of England, dressed 'à la japonaise'. In reality there was nothing Japanese in it except the Lord High Executioner's name Ko-Ko, which means pickles, and a single pseudo-Japanese tune in Sullivan's music, accompanying the entrance of the Mikado: 'Miya sama, miya sama, On n'm-ma-no mayé ni' etc. The tune is almost identical with the war song of the Imperial Army to which the troops went to battle in 1868 and saw the victory of the Meiji emperor over conservative warlords opposed to the opening up of Japan. Years later a Japanese visitor pulled Sullivan's leg by telling him that it was 'the foulest song ever sung in the lowest teahouse in Japan'. In reality the stirring words describe the waving of the imperial banner of silken brocade, as a signal for the chastisement of rebels.

164

Characters in The Mikado
sketched by the
illustrator 'Henry Stephen
'Hal' Ludlow (1851-1930).
The costumes include
those worn by the 'Three
Little Maids from School'
– Peep-Bo, Yum-Yum and
Pitti-Sing. At the bottom
left, the Lord High
Executioner, played by
George Grossmith,
brandishes his sword.

163

*Afternoon Tea at the
Japanese Village in
Knightsbridge* from
The Graphic,
13 March 1886

When Katisha threatens to reveal that Nanki-Poo is not a second trombone player but the son and heir of the Mikado, the other characters sing loudly to overpower her voice the Japanese words, 'O NI! bikkuri shakkuri to! oya! oya!' – a non-Japanese farrago of words which may be translated as 'You devil! with fright! with hiccups! hey! hey!'

The first lines of the operetta conjure up the popular enthusiasm for imported goods and things Japanese:

*If you want to know who we are
We are gentlemen of Japan
On many a vase and jar
On many a screen and fan ...*

A stickler for accuracy in his productions, Gilbert visited one of the popular attractions of the 1880s, what we would call today a 'theme park' in the form of a Japanese village run by a showman named Tannaker in Hyde Park, London, near the top of Sloane Street (163). A flyer for the show gives the entrance charge, one shilling for adults, and children six pence. It announces 'New and Novel Entertainments' at 1, 3, 5 and 8 p.m., and proclaims it to be the only Japanese village in Europe, warning the public that since its establishment, 'many wretched imitations have sprung up in provincial towns. Beware of impostors and imitators.'

The poster proclaims grand entertainments: '... streets of houses, shops, temples populated by Japanese men, women and children showing their everyday life', and Gilbert was delighted when he found in the teahouse an authentic Japanese girl. Despite the fact that her English was limited to 'Sixpence please' (the price of a cup of tea in Knightsbridge), she was able to instruct his 'three little maids from school' in the correct furling and unfurling of their fans to denote wrath, delight or homage.

The sets were created by Hawes Craven, a leading theatrical designer, who worked for most of Sir Henry Irving's productions. The costumes were by Wilhelm (William John Charles Pitcher; 1858–1925), the leading theatrical costume designer of the day. Wilhelm's designs for *The Mikado* show Gilbert's collaboration in their insistence on the accurate representation of Japanese dress (164). Gilbert boasted that the costumes worn by the principals were genuine and original Japanese ones of ancient date:

the magnificent gold-embroidered robe and petticoat of the Mikado was a faithful replica of the ancient official costume of the Japanese monarch; the strange-looking curled bag at the top of his head was intended to enclose the pigtail.

Such costumes can be seen in a poster by John Hassall (1868–1948) for a touring version of the show (165).

The Mikado (Mr. R. Temple).
Nanki-Pooh (Mr. Durward Lely).
Katisha (Miss Brandram).

Pooh-Bah (Mr. R. Barrington).
The "Three Little Maids from School" (Misses Sibyl Grey, L. Braham, and Jessie Bond).
Ko-Ko (Mr. G. Grossmith).

Ko-Ko (Mr. G. Grossmith).
Yum-Yum (Miss L. Braham).

Pish-Tush (Mr. F. Bovill).

Nanki-Pooh (Mr. Lely).

SKETCHES FROM "THE MIKADO" AT THE SAVOY THEATRE.

165
**John Hassall,
Poster for** *The Mikado,*
**D'Oyly Carte Opera
Company,
1905.
Colour lithograph,
50·8 x 31·8 cm
(20 x 12¹₂ in)**

Antique suits of armour were brought over from Japan only to be found useless because they would not fit any man taller than 1·4 m (4 ft 6 in). Later Gilbert enlisted a male dancer to teach the company proper Japanese deportment, posture and carriage. They were shown how to use fans and to apply Japanese make-up, and how to make the curious hissing sound which passes for laughter among high-born Japanese ladies. The supervision of costumes and of incidental dances was undertaken by a member of the staff of the Japanese Legation in London.

But although Gilbert strove his hardest for accuracy of dress, his private opinions about the Japanese craze are best summed up by the lines about:

*The idiot who praises with
enthusiastic tone,
All centuries but this and every
country but his own*

Over the whole production hung the long-standing problems of copyright wars between England and the United States of America. This complicated issue meant that any foreign author's work was fair game. Until 1891 printers and publishers did as they liked with the work of English authors; pirate productions abounded and no redress was available. As Arthur Sullivan remarked of the American judges, who decided against appeals to stop unauthorized performances: 'It seemed to be their opinion that a free and independent American citizen ought not to be robbed of his rights of robbing somebody else.'

The material for the costumes was supplied by the famous shop, Liberty's, who sent a team to Japan to study materials and designs and were rewarded by an advertisement for 'Liberty Art Fabrics' in the programme of the first performance in London on 14 March 1885. Liberty's also loyally refused to sell a duplicate set of fabric to an American named Duff, who was rushing to secure the American copyright by bringing out a pirated production of the piece in New York before the official production. Duff's agent went on to Paris, but Richard D'Oyly Carte (the long-suffering manager of the company) had already purchased every Japanese costume in the city, declaring, 'I don't mind how much money I spend to smash Duff!'

The subsequent secret rush to New York by the official company in order to open before the pirated version and secure American copyright led to intense public interest. During the winter of 1885–6, Madison Square Gardens housed a 'Mikado' village with demonstrations of silk weaving. The music of the show became immensely popular throughout Great Britain and her empire, and right across America wherever a military band went, selections from *The Mikado* were played. As the *Daily Telegraph* commented on the first night of *The Mikado* in 1885: 'We are all being more or less Japanned.'

The show ran initially for no fewer than 672 performances at the Savoy and 430 in New York between 1885 and 1886, and a number of touring companies spread not only the fame of Gilbert and Sullivan's operetta but also a taste for things Japanese both across America and around the world.

An amusing finale to the triumphant progress of *The Mikado* was provided in 1907 by the heralded arrival of Prince Fushimi on an official visit to England. Japan had just beaten Russia in the War of 1906 and politicians anxious to create a good impression on the imperial visitors, as so often happens, fell over backwards in threatening to ban performances of the piece. Questions were inevitably asked in the House of Commons, prompting a debate which sounds just like Gilbert at his best:

Mr Faber: Is it not a fact that the playing of the music of The Mikado on board ships of war and by regimental bands has been forbidden? (laughter) Is the Right Hon. Gentleman aware that the action of the Lord Chamberlain in this matter has made this country ridiculous in the eyes of the civilized world?
The Home Secretary: I strongly protest against the last remark of the Hon. member, and as regards the first question, it has nothing to do with <u>*my*</u> *department.*

A few years later, in January 1914, the first Japanese performance of *The Mikado* took place at the Imperial Theatre in Tokyo amidst the inevitable controversy, summarized in a leading Tokyo newspaper by an indignant 'old Fogey' who wrote:

an opera like this can only be a national disgrace. If, however, we reflect that this is the image of Japanese women held by Westerners, then this opera could be of some use to us in showing how Westerners think about Japan.

Another crisis for conservative lovers of Gilbert and Sullivan occurred in 1926, when the artist and aesthete, Charles Ricketts, was asked to design the costumes for a revival of *The Mikado* at the Princess Theatre in London. His superb designs were notable particularly for the way in which he stencilled the Japanese patterns on the costumes. Ricketts was delighted by the commission, particularly enjoying designing fantastic court dresses. He wrote:

The Geisha, Madam Butterfly, *and* **The Mikado** *have created a dreary pink dressing gown style quite unlike anything Japanese and I believe the public would be startled by the novelty of an entirely different presentment [166].*

Charles Ricketts,
Original design for *The Mikado*
from a souvenir of Richard
D'Oyly Carte's season of
Gilbert and Sullivan operas,
Princess Theatre, London,
1926.
Gouache over pencil

167
Dudley Hardy,
The Geisha,
1896.
Colour lithograph,
70 x 48 cm
(27¹₂ x 18⁴₅ in)

Startled the public certainly were and, as with any attempt in Great Britain to change a long-established and much-loved tradition, also scandalized. *The Globe* newspaper turned to verse to parody the fact that:

We've lost The Mikado; the scenes we all know
Poo Bah and Yum Yum and the schoolgirls must go,
With Katisha and also the cheerful Ko Ko.

The runaway success of *The Mikado* in 1885 created a demand for shows with an exotic Japanese subject, and in 1896 *The Geisha* (167) was staged by the great impresario, George Edwards, at the Gaiety Theatre, London, starring the inimitable Marie Lloyd, who sang the role of the English girl, Molly Seamore, visiting Japan. She foolishly puts on the dress of a geisha, and thus finds herself put up for public auction. She is bought by a Japanese aristocrat, who proposes to make the English girl his wife, but Mimosa San, a 'real' geisha, rescues the imprudent Molly. Marie Lloyd's interpretation of the hit song of the show was remarkable for its innuendo:

Ev'ry little Jappy chappies gone upon the Geisha
Trickiest little Geisha ever seen in Asia!
I've made things hum a bit, you know, since I became a Geisha
Japanese-y, free and easy Tea house girl!

168
Madame Sadayakko on front page of *Femina*, 1907

The show was immensely successful, earning in its tours of the United Kingdom, America, Australia and Canada over two million pounds in the money of the time. Two jolly songs, *The Amorous Goldfish* and *Chin Chin Chinaman*, and two lovely sets, *The Teahouse of Ten Thousand Joys* and *A Chrysanthemum Fête in the Palace Gardens*, helped to pull in the public wherever the show was staged. The success of such a male chauvinist plot is remarkable when it is remembered that these were the years of the New Woman and the emergent suffragette movement.

In London, as in Paris, a tremendous interest in Japanese costume began to influence fashion and make its mark upon the musical and dramatic stage. In 1900 the celebrated actress, Réjane, wore a kimono which caused a sensation and led to the opening of a shop selling similar garments under the trademark 'Kimonos Sadayakko'. Sadayakko was a famous geisha with dramatic talents who had once enjoyed the patronage of the Japanese Prime Minister. She first appeared in the West in San Francisco (1899) with an all-male troupe and rapidly gained superstar status. In New York in *The Geisha and the Knight* she created a sensation by the removal of layers of kimonos to persuade monks to admit her into a temple.

In the Paris Exposition of 1900 she performed at Loie Fuller's theatre in a free adaption of Dumas's *The Lady of the Camellias* (*La Dame aux Camélias*), set in sixteenth-century Japan. Sadayakko's likeness can be seen in a memorable woodcut by William Nicholson (see 62). He was one of the many artists to try to portray her personality, ranging from the Dutch Fauve painter, Kees van Dongen (1877–1968), the German, Max Slevogt (1868–1932), and the young Pablo Picasso (1881–1973), who took up a commission to design a poster for her, for which four sketches still exist. Auguste Rodin begged her to sit for him, but she told him quite truthfully that she had no time. Sadayacco subsequently signed a contract with the shop Au Mikado to advertise a range of beauty products and perfumes. Frequently in the public eye in the pages of the leading fashion journal *Femina* (168), she became known in Paris as a Madame Chrysanthème figure, 'a Madame Butterfly become very Parisienne', whose products formed a remarkable finale to the years of 'kimonomania'.

Kimonos featured spectacularly in several dramatic presentations in Paris, notably *The Seller of Smiles* in the *Théâtre Japonais* (1888), *The Dream* (1890), and especially, *Madame Chrysanthème*, which was staged on 30 January 1893, fixing a stereotype of the geisha, although it was not the only work to deal with such a theme.

'Desertion' plays entertained readers and audiences in America and the West well into the twentieth century with such titles as *A Flower of Yeddo*, *The Lady of the Weeping Willow Tree* and *A Japanese Marriage*. A number of popular novels with Japanese settings were also published in America between 1880 and 1905, one notable title being *Honda the Samurai: a Story of Modern Japan* (1890) by William Elliot Griffis, America's best-known early interpreter of Japan's recent history. It was, however, Edward H House, who taught for twenty years in Tokyo, and edited the *Tokyo Times*, who was one of the first to write novels describing love affairs between Japanese women and Western men, notably his *Yone Santo, A Child of Japan* (1888). In the late 1870s House had adopted a seventeen-year-old girl, Koto Aoki, who was on the point of suicide after her marriage failed, a moving parallel between an incident in the novel and House's own life.

The first woman novelist to write stories with a Japanese setting was Winnifred Eaton Babcock. Born in Montreal in 1879, the author was the daughter of a Chinese mother but took the pen-name of Onoto Watanna and adopted a Japanese viewpoint when writing a series of love stories set in Japan that featured women of mixed Japanese and Western ancestry.

Floral titles flowed effortlessly from her pen, *The Wooing of Wisteria* (1902) being followed by *The Love of Azalea* (1904), but neither of them match her earlier novel, *A Japanese Nightingale* (1901), in which the heroine Yuki is of mixed blood and a geisha whose mother was deserted by a Dutch naval officer at Nagasaki. The plot in *A Japanese Nightingale* relates the eventful love affair between a wealthy American and a girl with an American father and a Japanese mother. The protagonist of the novel is a performer, 'hostess' and a hired 'wife' but her fate is far less tragic than that of Madame Butterfly. The story of *Madame Butterfly*, dealing as it does with similar themes, far exceeds these works of popular fiction as a work of art.

The writer, Lafcadio Hearn, was in a very different league. Of Irish-Greek parentage, he was educated in England. As the result of an accident in boyhood he lost the sight of one eye, which both made his appearance a little alarming and made him 'a bit of a loner'. In 1869 he settled in Cincinnati, working as a journalist and incurring scandal by living openly with a mulatto woman. In 1890 he went to Japan where he settled for the last fourteen years of his life. He married a Japanese woman, Setsu, and had a son, Kazuo (169).

169
Lafcadio Hearn with his
wife and son, Kazuo, at
Kumamoto,
photographed in
1895

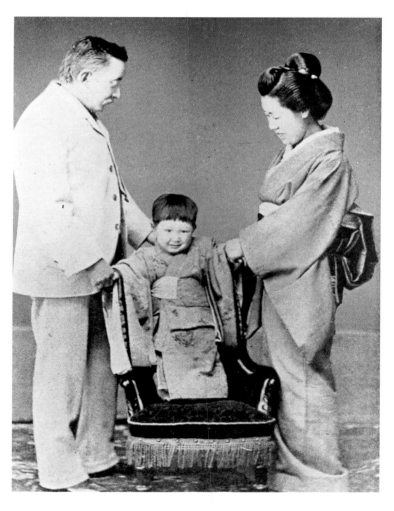

Hearn adopted Japanese dress, and although he never fully mastered the language, took the name of Yakumo Koizumi. From 1896 to 1903 he taught at Matsue and lectured on English literature at the Imperial University in Tokyo. To this day his work is underestimated in the West and he is remembered as a travel journalist, but in Japan he is revered as the first major writer from the West to interpret Japanese customs, mythology and landscapes sympathetically. He is famed particularly for his documentaries, notably *Glimpses of Unfamiliar Japan* (1894), *Out of the East* (1895) and *Japan: an Attempt at an Interpretation* (1904). Hearn had been unhappy and unsuccessful in the West and felt bitter at his failure, emotions that he purged in his exhilarated espousal of Japan and his belief in the moral and aesthetic superiority of Japanese culture.

The life of Madame Butterfly differed from its predecessors by the power of its simple story of seduction and unrequited love, based on a real incident. The story was written by John Luther Long, a successful Philadelphia lawyer and author. Besides *Madame Butterfly* he wrote the novels *Miss Cherry Blossom of Tokyo* (1895) and *The Fox Woman* (1899).

Long probably never visited Japan himself, but his sister had lived there as the wife of an American missionary in Nagasaki. She told Long about the tragic event in the true story of Madame Butterfly (Yamamuru Tsuru) and was able to confirm every incident in detail. Substituting an American naval officer for the English merchant, Long's story appeared in the *Century Magazine* in 1898 and was adapted for the stage in 1900 by the actor, manager and playwright, David Belasco.

Giacomo Puccini, the great Italian composer, once described himself as 'a passionate hunter of women, wild duck and libretti'. Soon after successfully launching *Tosca* in Rome in January 1900 he began to search for another story with exotic colour in order to inspire his established librettists, Illica and Giacosa, and his publisher, Ricordi. Puccini was consumed by a compelling personal motivation, the wish to vie with his great rival, the operatic composer, Pietro Mascagni. Mascagni had followed the sensational success of his *verismo* opera *Cavalleria Rusticana* with a tragic piece called *Iris*, with a Japanese setting, which was produced with great success in Rome in 1898 and Milan in 1899. The stage designs for the opera were remarkable, for the artist, Adolpho Hohenstein, had clearly done his homework, as the rod puppets in the first act were carefully based upon the Japanese *bunraku* puppet theatre.

Both the puppets and the geisha costumes produced a dramatic effect, added to by the musical novelties of the *koto* (a stringed instrument), bells, a tam-tam drum and gongs, all used in the travelling theatre scene in the first act, and the scene in the Yoshiwara in Edo in the second act.

The melodramatic plot of the opera tells the story of Iris (soprano), a beautiful young laundress, who is the only support of her blind father Il Cieco (bass). As dawn breaks over a small village near Mount Fuji, Iris awakes troubled by a nightmare, in which her doll had been attacked by serpents and monsters, a presager of ill omen. As the action develops, a performing troupe of actors, musicians and puppeteers arrives, and the young Osaka (tenor), a wealthy rake, and his friend, Kyoto (baritone), a brothel keeper, are attracted by Iris and attempt to abduct her. She continues to repulse Osaka, who helps Kyoto to imprison her in his brothel.

In a crowd scene Iris's voice is recognized by her father, who curses her and throws handfuls of mud at her as she tries to escape through the crowd. Shocked by his rejection, Iris jumps into the inflamed mob and is left for dead.

In the final act, set in the sewer below the brothel, some rag-pickers, thinking she is dead, rob Iris's body of her remaining finery. As she reflects on life the sun's rays warm her last moments and her soul ascends to heaven, in one of the most melodic moments in the work.

Consumed with envy at Mascagni's exotic Japanese theme, Puccini, while in London for the first British performance of *Tosca* at Covent Garden in June 1900, happened to see Belasco's play at the Duke of York's Theatre enticingly entitled *Madame Butterfly*, and with a glamorous leading lady, Blanche Bates. Although Puccini spoke almost no English, he rushed backstage on the opening night and, weeping copiously, asked him for the operatic rights to the play. Pinkerton's adage, 'it is easier to go to bed than talk', was a motto close to the heart of Puccini, who was himself a great womanizer. The heroine Cio-Cio-San's suicide by harakiri awoke all his dramatic instincts. Back in Italy, in order to create the right atmosphere, he undertook careful research of the exotic subject. He questioned artists and authorities on Japanese culture, transcribed melodies from records sent from Tokyo by his friend, the wife of the Japanese ambassador. When after some maddening delays he finally caught up with the performances by Sadayakko and her troupe in Milan, Puccini was deeply impressed by the gory finales of several *kabuki* plays in their repertoire.

171
Makino Yoshio,
The Darling of the Gods,
1903.
22.8 x 16.2 cm
(9 x 6²₅ in)

On a more lighthearted note Puccini's curiosity even extended to Gilbert and Sullivan's *The Mikado*, a vocal score of which was still to be seen at Puccini's hunting lodge, Torre del Lago, in recent years, with a pencilled Italian translation of two of the songs. Puccini also studied collections of Japanese songs. Almost half the first act alone is dedicated to building up an authentic Japanese atmosphere and echoes of genuine Japanese themes. In the second act he strengthened the percussion, using a tam-tam and Japanese bells, together with *campanelli a tastiere* (glockenspiels) and tubular bells.

The first night was held in La Scala, Milan on 17 February 1904. The evening was a legendary disaster, not even the haunting 'One Fine Day' pleasing the fickle Milanese audience, and the birdsong at dawn was greeted by the claque (supporters of Mascagni) with derisive farmyard imitations. Some judicious cuts were made and three months later, when presented in Brescia, the revised piece triumphed. The opera has grown in popularity ever since, forming links not only between music and drama and the East and the West, but also creating a spectacular example of the unexpected power of Japonisme to effect a marriage with the *verismo* world of Puccini and Italian opera, reflected in the spectacular posters by Rossi and Myerbach-Rheinfeld in the Ricordi archive (170).

The success of the American run of his play *Madame Butterfly* inspired Belasco to write another drama with a Japanese theme. In 1902 he produced *The Darling of the Gods* (171) with expensive authentic Japanese settings in its production, which he once again co-authored with John Luther Long.

Madame Butterfly and *The Mikado* have one quality in common which leads to their continuing success – they both provide immensely rewarding opportunities for costume and scenery designers. Recent years have seen such novelties as 'Black' Mikados and 'Mafia' Mikados set in Sicily, while at the Royal Albert Hall in London, the audience has enjoyed a performance of *Madame Butterfly* with the central amphitheatre set up as a Japanese raked garden in the first act and flooded in the second act.

It is perhaps appropriate to conclude these excursions into the dramatic presentation of the butterfly by enjoying its depiction in a print signed Baichoro Kunisada and Oko Kunisada of a Butterfly dance. Two geisha are shown playing the roles of butterfly maidens (172) at the Tokyo Matsumotoro Theatre in Edo in Horse year, while the stage musicians, also geisha, sit on a dais.

Japonisme

**Baichoro Kunisada
and Oko Kunisada,
*The Matsumotoro
Theatre in the Tokyo
Pleasure District*,
1870.
Colour woodblock,
36·5 x 25·4 cm
(14³⁄₈ x 10 in)**

**Dustjacket for Claude
Debussy's *La Mer*,
adapting a detail from
Hokusai's *The Great
Wave*,
1905.
35 x 54 cm
(13³⁄₄ x 21¹⁄₄ in)**

CLAUDE DEBUSSY

LA MER

There is also a direct link between classical orchestral music in the West and the Japanese print. Claude Debussy loved England, which he visited on several occasions. He began to compose the piano version of his composition, *La Mer* (*The Sea*), while staying at the island of Jersey from whence he wrote to his new publisher, 'The sea has been very good to me, and has shown me all her moods.' Debussy much admired Hokusai and suggested using a stylized detail of the famous print, *The Great Wave*, on the cover of the piano score, which was published in 1905. Later Debussy worked on the orchestral version of his score while staying at the Grand Hotel in Eastbourne in a room overlooking the sea. There, despite the distraction of a band playing selections from Gilbert and Sullivan, he finished the work. The orchestral score bore a reproduction of the crest of *The Wave* (173).

Today, a century later, Debussy's masterpiece continues to provide potent evidence of the creative force of Japonisme's marriage of East and West, a union which, although much disparaged, has inspired some great art and music.

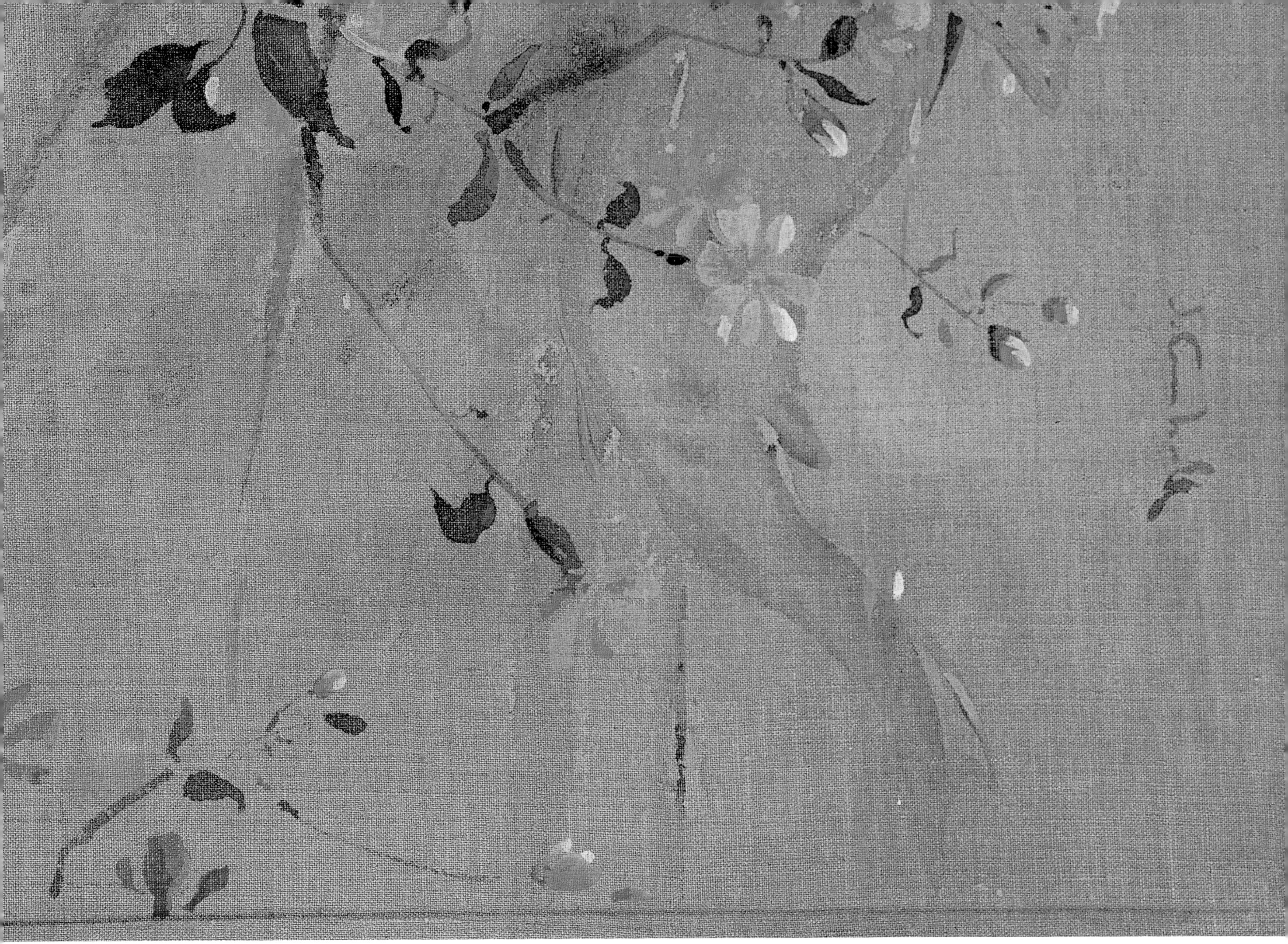

Chapter eight:
Visitors to Japan: Dream and Reality

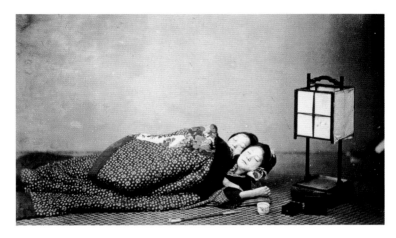

Previous page
Joseph Crawhall,
***A Trout Rising* (detail
of 184)**

174
Charles Wirgman,
***The Fortune Teller*,**
1873.
Watercolour on paper,
40·4 x 30·8 cm
(16 x 12¹⁄₈ in).
**Yokohama Museum
of Art**

175
Felice Beato,
***Sleeping Beauties*,**
1868.
**Hand-painted albumen
print**

*I no longer need to have Japanese
prints for I constantly tell myself
that I am in Japan here.*
Van Gogh, Arles, 1888

While Van Gogh found the imaginary
'land of Japan' he mentally
experienced at Arles an acceptable
alternative to actually visiting the
country, other artists, photographers,
collectors, writers and designers, for a
wide variety of reasons, needed the
stimulus of travel to Japan itself. All
shared the common motivation of
curiosity. They also possessed varying
reasons for the journey, from a wish to
expand the stock of a great shop and
other business endeavours to an
interest in comparative religion; from
a desire to provide a visual record of
every aspect of this strange land to a
wish to record the flora or fauna of the
country. Another potent factor was the
mysterious 'lure of the East', which still
remains today a major consideration in
our decisions about where to pass our
annual holidays. In the second half of
the nineteenth century this manifested
itself in the arrival of the first tourists
in Japan, who all had one thing in
common, a desire for pictorial
souvenirs as records of their stay. At
first such pictorial records could only
be created by the use of brush, pen
and the tools of the engraver.

One of the first artists to work within
these limits was the Londoner, Charles
Wirgman, who was only twenty-five
when he was sent to China in 1857 as
a war artist to cover the Opium Wars,
and then moved to Japan in 1861.
His vision of Japan comes down to
us today primarily via the engravings
after his drawings which appeared in
the *Illustrated London News*. These
vivid sketches became very influential
in forming the Victorian vision of
Japan. Like any skilled graphic
journalist, Wirgman's eye was constantly alert and he recorded vividly
such subjects as the temple of
Kamakura near the scene of the
murder of two British officers and
the subsequent execution of the
murderers, but also less disturbing
and more picturesque scenes, such as
The Fortune Teller (174).

While in China in 1860, Wirgman
met the photographer Felix Beato
(1830–1906), who was born in Venice
but trained in England and had
become one of the first war reporters
to use the new medium of
photography while working in Greece,
India, Egypt and the Crimea. In 1860
both men met while covering the
Opium Wars and the Anglo-French
military expedition which resulted
in the sack of the Summer Palace
in Peking. From China they travelled
independently to Japan where they
settled in Yokohama.

Beato arrived in 1863, and wrote an
entertaining article for the *Illustrated
London News* describing Wirgman's
house, which was packed with curious
Japanese visitors anxious to see
Wirgman painting in oils, a technique
not widely known in Japan. In 1862,
Wirgman, a jolly eccentric, founded the
humorous journal, *The Japan Punch*,
which appeared sporadically until 1887.
In 1863 he became one of the first
foreigners since Will Adams to marry
a Japanese woman (see Chapter 1).

In 1865 a business partnership was
formed entitled Beato & Wirgman,
Artists & Photographers, which lasted
until 1869. Beato covered the latest
news stories, including such major
events as the Battle of Shimonoseki in
1864 when the British navy shelled the
town in retaliation for earlier Japanese
retributive action in the Straits of
Shimonoseki. In a less belligerent spirit,
Beato also travelled the length and
breadth of Japan, capturing with his
camera the landscape and people,
subjects still virtually untouched by
Europeans. This work culminated in the
two-volume album, *Photographic Views
of Japan*, published in Yokohama in
1868, the first volume to record the
cities and landscapes of Japan in black
and white, including such classic views
as the Tokaido Road between
Yokohama and Fujiyama.

The second volume, *Native Types*,
comprised approximately 100 albumen
prints carefully hand-coloured by a
Japanese painter of such subjects as
Mother and Child and *Sleeping
Beauties* (175). In many of these prints
there are striking similarities in poses
and subject matter to *ukiyo-e* prints.
Indeed as in the West, the introduction
of photography was to prove a major
factor in the decline and fall of the
traditional woodblock print.

Beato's works were soon widely copied
by less skilful hands. The always
popular genre subject of two or three
young trainee geishas in rickshaws was
endlessly imitated for popular Western
taste. Described as 'Yokohama-shasin'
(Yokohama-photographs), they were
purchased in large quantities by
tourists. These were the type of prints
with which Carrie Pooter entertains the
guests in her home in Grossmith's
celebration of suburban life, *The Diary
of a Nobody*. Such photographs could
make the alien, but exciting, world of
Japan almost as familiar to the Pooters
in Upper Holloway, London, as aspects
of their own environment. Photographs,
created strictly for the export trade,
by their nature conveyed a sense of
the reality of daily life in the far-off
land of Japan.

Woodcuts, however, conceived as a popular art form in Japan, during their passage to Europe, 'suffered a sea change, into something rich and strange'. *Ukiyo-e* prints, still very cheap to buy, could give to their purchasers the exciting frisson imparted by the ownership of works of art. Their novelty could also encourage bolder spirits to venture to Japan and either make their own paintings, or form collections of Japanese works which eventually entered museums. From Bournemouth to Birmingham, Cracow to Cambridge and Maidstone to Mulhouse, both major and minor collections of Japanese works were assembled during the late nineteenth and early twentieth centuries.

An early visitor to Meiji-liberated Japan was the English painter, Frank Dillon (1823–1909). A topographical painter who had worked in Egypt, Dillon was a friend of the Pre-Raphaelite, George Price Boyce (1826–97), who is known to have been very interested in Japonisme. Dillon visited Japan in 1875 and on his return to England painted several interiors, including *The Stray Shuttlecock* (176), which were crowded with correct Japanese props – *samisen* (a stringed instrument resembling a zither), scrolls and sword racks – many items being left to what is now the Victoria and Albert Museum. His paintings possess a certain charm, but are very obviously painstaking, while not wholly accurate, re-creations of Japanese rooms, for there is far more on show than would be the case in reality.

The presence of *zori* (outdoor sandals) symbolizes summer, while the shuttle-cock represents the New Year, and therefore winter. In 1880 Dillon published *Drawings by Japanese Artists*, which included fifteen colour reproductions of Japanese paintings, and in the introduction a discussion of the use of decorative motifs such as flowers and birds, calligraphy and brush techniques.

For some liberated British women, the increasingly straightforward journey to Japan presented no real challenge, notably for the indefatigable botanical painter and illustrator, Marianne North (1830–90). She is remembered today by visitors to her memorial gallery in Kew Gardens, London, which displays 832 paintings arranged by her on the crowded walls. She visited Japan in 1876 and described in her journal her first glimpse of Fujiyama on 7 November of that year:

I watched the sun rise out of the sea and redden its top, as I have seen so well represented on so many handscreens and tea-trays ... we drove out into the country, and took funny cups of yellow tea in a bamboo tea-house, with five pretty girls rather over four feet high, in chignons with huge pins, blackened teeth, and no eyelashes, laughing at us all the while.

(The custom of blackening teeth with iron dissolved in vinegar mixed with powdered gall nuts goes back to the ninth century, as does the practice of shaving eyebrows and repainting them higher up the face.)

177
Marianne North,
Wisteria chinensis,
1875–7.
Oil on prepared paper
fixed to canvas,
30 x 45 cm
(11¾ x 17¾ in).
Marianne North Gallery,
Kew Gardens, London

158

Japonisme

During her all too brief stay, curtailed by an attack of rheumatic fever, she managed to paint a view of Fuji, seen through an arch of the climbing shrub *Wisteria chinensis* (177). Other paintings show the Hottomi Temple, Kyoto, among the pine trees and Japanese flowers. She enjoyed travelling about:

The railway went alongside the famous Tokaido road, and was full of interest. The rice and millet harvest was then going on, and the tiny sheaves were a sight to see. They piled them up against the trees and fences in the most neat and clever way, some of the small fan-leaved palm-trees looking as though they had straw petticoats on … At the last station one of the Japanese ministers got into our carriage in the costume of an English gentleman, chimney-pot hat included … and at Tokyo packed Miss C. and myself into two jinrickshas, a kind of grown-up perambulator, the outside painted all over with marvellous histories and dragons (like scenes out of the Revelation). They had men to guide them with all sorts of devices stamped on their backs, and long hanging sleeves. So we trotted off to the Tombs of the Shoguns.

Another redoubtable British lady traveller, Isabella Bird, visited Japan a year later in 1877, but found the experience already a little too tame. Like many other visitors in later years she reacted with suspicion to the industrial muscle of the new Japan, writing in her journal after spending just one day in the thriving commercial centre of Yokohama: 'I long to get away into the *real* Japan.' When she did manage to visit a small town called Yusowa, things were also unappealing as hundreds of people crowded round to enjoy the experience of seeing a Western lady eat lunch:

those behind being unable to see me, got ladders and climbed on to the adjacent roofs, where they remained till one of the roofs gave way with a crash.

A year earlier, in 1876, Émile Guimet, an industrialist from Lyon, landed at Yokohama accompanied by the painter Félix Régamey. Guimet, whose chief interest lay in the study of comparative religion, persuaded Régamey to accompany him as a 'human camera' to record religious rites and rituals. They had met up in the Philadelphia Centennial exhibition where an extensive display of Japanese items was on view, and then travelled on to Japan.

Régamey was already deeply interested in everything pertaining to Japan, which he had seen in the pages of the *Illustrated London News* (the journal for which he would later work himself), and he also made chromolithographic copies of prints by Hiroshige and Hokusai for a book on the poetess, Ono-no Komachi, by the Japanese enthusiast, Philippe Burty.

In three months of travels around Japan, Guimet and Régamey investigated the relationship between Buddhism and Shintoism. In temples and sanctuaries they observed the religious practices of the monks and studied the representations and gestures of the statues of gods, while also forming an important collection of ritualistic objects and ceramics. When they returned to France they collaborated on several books, notably *Promenades Japonais* (1878–80), a handsomely illustrated account of scenes of everyday life. They also contributed articles and illustrations to the Arts and Crafts journal, *Le Japon pratique*.

On his return to France, Guimet at first worked on setting up a museum in Lyon and then helped to arrange objects from the Far East in the 1878 exhibition at the Trocadéro in Paris, including forty paintings of religious subjects by Régamey.

In 1883 Guimet offered his extensive collection to the state, and subsequently the city of Paris donated a site for the building, which first opened in 1889 at the Place d'Iéna as a museum devoted to the religions of the world, and formed one of the attractions of the Exposition Universelle of that year. Subsequently the emphasis of the museum gradually became centred upon Asian art and an extensive library. Today the Musée Guimet, recently brilliantly modernized and rearranged, houses one of the finest Oriental collections in the world.

While great institutions such as the Musée Guimet will always gravitate to capital cities, local museums also play an important role in informing the public, a fact which often goes unrecognized. All over the West one can find many small collections of Japanese works often formed in the nineteenth century and left for the unexpected enjoyment of visitors. One of the most impressive small-scale collections of Japanese works in England is in the Maidstone Museum, Kent, where lived the Hon. Henry Marsham.

In the 1870s Marsham retired from the army in order to collect ceramics in Japan, which he bequeathed to Maidstone Museum in 1908, inspiring the Hon. Walter Samuel (son of Lord Bearsted, the founder of 'Shell' oil) to do the same with his excellent and varied collection of Japanese sword fittings, *netsuke, inro* (178), lacquer, books and prints which he left to Maidstone Museum on his death in 1924. Even more striking with its Japanese garden overlooking the sea is the Russell-Cotes Museum in Bournemouth, Dorset. In 1885–6 Sir Merton and Lady Russell-Cotes visited Japan and collected with immense enthusiasm. When they returned home Sir Merton recorded with pride that over 100 cases 'were filled by my wife and myself. Among the curios there were some rare and antique specimens of Japanese art.' The collection was initially displayed in the Royal Bath Hotel nearby during the construction of the Mikado Room with its ceiling depicting the Meiji emperor and empress.

Guimet's collecting activities were a part of his idealistic aims to make knowledge available to a wider public. For Régamey, a born romantic, the visit to Japan was the fulfilment of his wildest dreams, 'the age of gold, neither more nor less'. Everything enchanted him, from the tattooed rickshaw men to – inevitably – the geisha.

While Régamey romanticized Japan for many years after a brief visit of three months, other creative spirits dreamed of visiting Japan but avoided the actual journey. Foremost among such daydreamers was Oscar Wilde, who on his whistle-stop lecture tour of the United States of America in 1882, dreamt of new worlds still to be conquered. From San Francisco Wilde wrote home to say:

I feel an irresistible desire to wander, and go to Japan, where I will pass my youth, sitting under an almond tree, drinking amber tea out of a blue cup, and looking at a landscape without perspective …

To his friend and verbal sparring partner, Whistler, Wilde wrote with a more specific proposal: 'When will you come to Japan? Fancy the book, I to write it, you to illustrate it. We would be rich.'

Wilde wrote at the height of the aesthetic enthusiasm for the novel arts of Japan, although his own personal flirtation with Japanese art was not of very long duration. He did, however, write one poem in 1887, originally entitled 'Impression Japonaise':

*The white leaves float upon the air,
The red leaves flutter idly down,
Some fall upon her yellow gown,
And some upon her raven hair*

*She takes an amber lute and sings,
And as she sings a silver crane
Begins his scarlet neck to strain
And flap his burnished metal wings.*

*She takes a lute of amber bright,
And from the thicket where he lies
Her lover, with his almond eyes
Watches her movements with delight.*

While Japanese art still retained its capacity to surprise, Wilde responded to it with enthusiasm. He felt that there was a real kinship of attitudes between his own poetry and Japanese art, commenting on 'the influence which Eastern art is having on us in Europe, and the fascination of all Japanese work'.

Yet Wilde, always susceptible to the vagaries of fashion, soon sensed that the Occidental love for Japan would prove of limited duration. A close friend of his was the young Australian artist, Mortimer Menpes (1860–1938), Whistler's Australian assistant and biographer, who became godfather to Wilde's oldest son, Cyril. In 1887 Menpes visited Japan for eight months to learn 'all the methods of Japanese art'. On his return he exhibited 137 oils (179) and forty prints created in Japan, in the Dowdeswell Galleries, New Bond Street, London.

180
Kinkozan,
Vase.
Satsuma ware decorated
with gold and
polychrome enamels,
height: 25·1 cm (9⁷⁸ in).
Private collection

The exhibition was visited and reviewed by Wilde, who posed the question:

… do you really imagine that the Japanese people, as they are presented to us in art, have any existence? If you do, you have never understood Japanese art at all … One of our most charming painters went recently to the Land of the Chrysanthemum in the foolish hope of seeing the Japanese. All he saw, all he had the chance of painting, were a few lanterns and some fans. He was quite unable to discover the inhabitants, as his delightful exhibition … showed only too well. He did not know that the Japanese people are, as I have said, simply a mode of style, an exquisite fancy of art. And so, if you desire to see a Japanese effect, you will not behave like a tourist and go to Tokyo. On the contrary, you will stay at home and steep yourself in the work of certain Japanese artists and then, when you have absorbed the spirit of their style, and caught their imaginative manner of vision, you will … sit in the Park or stroll down Piccadilly, and if you cannot see an absolutely Japanese effect there, you will not see it anywhere …

As so often, Wilde is at his most profound when most paradoxical, here enraged by his disciple, Menpes, visiting Japan without his permission. It is impossible not to feel sorry for poor Menpes, who, characteristically, was also abused by Whistler. Undeterred, Menpes continued to be a passionate advocate of Japanese decoration, and his home, a house designed by the founder of the Century Guild, Arthur Heygate Mackmurdo (1851–1942), at 25 Cadogan Gardens, was described as a 'dream of Oriental beauty' with themed peony, camellia and chrysanthemum rooms. On a second visit to Japan in 1896, Menpes wrote:

I had taken with me very full plans and I gathered together the best artists and craftsmen that I could command … ceiling, doors, wallcoverings and windows were finished completely … by Japanese craftsmen. In two hundred packing cases their work was carried to London.

Menpes published his memories of Japan in *Japan, a Record in Colour* in 1901 with 100 colour illustrations. But in a few short years even Menpes had tired of the Japanese style and he sold the house in 1900, retiring to the sylvan delights of a Kentish fruit farm.

Wilde's satirical comments on Menpes's work provoked an outburst from Rudyard Kipling on his way to Japan in 1889:

Mister Oscar Wilde of the Nineteenth Century is a long-toothed liar. In an article … he, with his tongue in his brazen cheek, avers that there was no such a place as Japan – that it had been created by fans and picture books just as he himself had been created by pottery and fragments of coloured cloth. Never believe anything that Mister Oscar Wilde tells you.

Rudyard Kipling visited Japan in 1889 and again on his honeymoon in 1892. On his first visit he wrote a series of travel articles in the form of letters which he sent back to India for publication in the *Pioneer* newspaper in Allahabad. The eleventh letter includes descriptions of routine tourist excursions to potteries and workshops which are transformed by Kipling's humour, love of the grotesque and feeling for beauty.

For Kipling on that first visit, the experience of Japan was virtually love at first sight. His vivid reports on what he saw have been described 'the most graphic ever penned by a globetrotter', a description surely justified by this portrayal of a street in Tokyo after dark:

Half the town was out for a walk, and all the people's clothes were indigo, and so were the shadows, and most of the paper lanterns were drops of blood red. By the light of smoking oil-lamps people were selling flowers and shrubs – wicked little dwarf pines, stunted peach and plum trees, wisteria bushes clipped and twisted out of all likeness to wholesome plants, leaning and leering out of green-glaze pots … At a corner of a street, some rich men had got together and left unguarded all the gold, diamonds and rubies of the East, but when you came near you saw that this treasure was only a gathering of goldfish in glass globes – yellow, white and red fish, with from three to five forked tails apiece and eyes that bulged far beyond their heads.

A few days after his arrival Kipling visited a curio shop in Kobe to see its *netsuke* collections. *Netsuke* are small carved figures, designed to be used with the kimono, which is bound at the waist by a wide sash, the *obi*.

From the *obi* the *netsuke* is suspended and used as a 'toggle' from which to hang a wide variety of small boxes, *inro*, containing objects as varied as tobacco, ink pads, brushes, tea jars, seals, medicines and so on. Kipling greatly enjoyed:

the buttons and netsuke that … can be taken out and played with … the old man horribly embarrassed by a cuttle fish; the priest who makes a soldier pick up a deer for him and laughs to think that the brisket would be his and the burden his companions; or the dry, lean snake coiled in derision on a jawless skull mottled with the memories of corruption; or the Rabelaisian badger who stood on his head and made you blush though he was not half an inch long; or the little fat boy pounding his smaller brother, or the rabbit that had just made a joke, or – but there were scores of these notes, born of every mood of mirth, scorn and experience that sways the heart of man … [I] held half a dozen of them in my palm and winked at the shade of the dead carver!

On another occasion in Kyoto, Kipling visited a pottery, and a maker of *cloisonné* enamels. He recalled how:

the manager took us to see the potters [who] lived close to the kiln and had nothing pretty to look at.

It was different in the painting rooms which were reached by way of one or two Japanese gardens full of quaint flowers and the sound of the spring breezes. Here in a cabinet- like house sat the men, women, and the boys who painted the designs on the vases after the first firing. That all their arrangements were scrupulously neat is only saying that they were Japanese; that their surroundings were fair and proper is only saying that they were artists. A sprig of a cherry-blossom stood out defiantly against the black of the garden paling; a gnarled pine cut the blue of the sky with its spiky splinters as it lifted itself above the paling, and in a little pond the iris and the horsetail nodded to the wind. The workers when at fault had only to lift their eyes, and Nature herself would graciously supply the missing link of a design. Somewhere in dirty England men dream of craftsmen working under conditions which shall help and not stifle the half-formed thought. They even form Guilds … to bring about the desired end … Would they have their dream realized let them see how they make pottery in Japan … [180]

These references to the ideals of William Morris and the Guilds of the Arts and Crafts Movement came naturally to the pen of Kipling, who was the nephew of Burne-Jones. It is followed by one of Kipling's frequent expressions of regret that the virtuoso artistic abilities of the Japanese should be sacrificed to the pursuit of cheap export markets.

Such markets had arisen with the accession of the Meiji emperor in 1868 when great encouragement was given to plans to increase business overseas. The showcases to encourage export orders were provided by the prestigious world fairs held in America and Europe. The Satsuma pottery on show at such events was magnificent at its resplendent best, appallingly vulgar at its worst. Increased demand led to some of the major factories mass-producing Satsuma pottery of very poor quality to support the continuing existence of their master studios. Two distinct types of Satsuma evolved, the show pieces and the export wares. Kipling particularly disliked cheap Satsuma ware with a crackled white glaze, which he describes as having 'a golden smallpox upon it'. He pungently describes how:

the potters squat upon the floor making ormolu Satsuma for cheap shops at home. The barbarians want Satsuma and they shall have it, if it has to be made in Kyoto one piece per twenty minutes. So much for the baser forms of the craft.

The badness of the bad things I could describe at length: of the good I know only that they were desirable ... I saw others as good and as true as the eye could wish in blue, violet, imitation Imari, 'royal Keg' [Kutani] and half a dozen other varieties of the worked clay which ignorance debars me from naming.

Far from being ignorant, Kipling reveals a sophisticated discernment years ahead of his time, and a sensitive knowledge of the aesthetic sensibilities of Japanese taste and the dangers of over-elaboration.

After the pottery he visited the *cloisonné* enamel manufactory where he:

began to understand the cost of the ware when I saw a man working out a pattern of sprigs and butterflies on a plate about ten inches in diameter. With finest silver ribbon wire, set on edge, less than a sixteenth of an inch high, he followed the curves of the drawing at his side, pinching the wires into tendrils and the serrated outlines of leaves with infinite patience. A rough touch on the copper plate would have sent the pattern flying into a thousand disconnected threads.

Kipling was left with a mission – the resolve to save Japan from herself, saying, 'if they are left to themselves they will make *cloisonné* by machinery in another twenty years and build black factories instead of gardens'. This was the aesthetic dilemma of which Rudyard Kipling became so acutely aware during his visit to Kyoto in 1889 and so accurately described in the letters home.

On his second visit, his honeymoon trip, Kipling was less carefree, with less opportunity to enjoy parties at teahouses with pretty young girls, and he regrets that 'you cannot live on giggles'. Nevertheless the visit reveals Kipling's sensitivity to such great artefacts as the Daibutso in Kamakura, the great bronze figure of the Buddha. From his father, John Lockwood Kipling, an authority on Indian art and director of the museum at Lahore, Kipling had inherited a great empathy with depictions of the Buddha. At Kamakura he disliked the Western tourists' crass delight in being photographed sitting on the figure's lap. He read a naively worded notice deploring this practice put up by the priests at the shrine. and turned it into a poem with some memorable lines.

A tourist-show, a legend told,
A rusting hulk of bronze and gold,
So much, and scarce so much, ye hold
The Meaning of Kamakura?

But when the morning prayer is prayed,
Think, ere ye pass to strife and trade,
Is God in human image made
No nearer than Kamakura?

Yet spare us still the Western joke
When joss-sticks turn to scented smoke
The little sins of little folk
That worship at Kamakura

The grey-robed, gay-sashed butterflies
That flit beneath the Master's eyes.
He is beyond the Mysteries
But loves them at Kamakura

(181)

There were, of course, other English writers and artists of the 1880s and 1890s who visited Japan. But for some of them the experience did not quite live up to expectations. In Tennyson's poem the spell is broken when the Lady of Shalott looks out of the window at the real world, rather than observing its reflection in a mirror. So it was for the Scottish painters, Edward Atkinson Hornel (1864–1933) and George Henry (1858–1943), who visited Japan from 1893 to 1894. They were both members of the group 'the Glasgow Boys' from Scotland. Their visit was sponsored by the dealer Alexander Reid and collector, William Burrell, who were conscious of a growing Glaswegian interest in Japan and its culture. Before their departure Hornel stated that the reason for their visit was to go to see:

*a reed shaken by the wind, for those
acquainted even slightly with
Japanese art the words express
the spirit and motif of its dainty
achievements. Japanese art rivalling in
splendour the greatest art in Europe,
the influence of which is now
fortunately being felt in all the new
movements in Europe, engenders in
the artist the desire to see and study
the environment from which this great
art sprung, to become personally in
touch with the people, to live their life,
and to discover the source of their
inspiration.*

Unfortunately their visit was to prove a
less than ideal experience, for the spell
was broken for the two artists when
they too looked out of the window at
the real world of Japan, rather than
observing its reflection in the mirror of
the Japanese print. They both loathed
life in the missionary community where
they were billeted, complaining that:

*every second man you encounter
is a missionary, and your rest is
chronically broken by the
uncongenial clang of the church
bells, whose notes are as
unmelodious and distressing as the
music (so called) of the Japanese.*

They stayed at Nagasaki, Yokohama
and Tokyo, where they were disap-
pointed in an exhibition of works by
Japanese artists who had gone to
study painting in Paris and Munich,
and in Hornel's view had 'learned
their painting but lost their art!'

As these anecdotes show, artistic cross-
pollination could have its hazards, but
a work such as *Geishas in an Interior*
(182) has great charm despite Hornel's
very non-Japanese use of rich pigment.
Henry's watercolour paintings were
of course less opaque, and in a work
such as *The Koto Player* (183) he
successfully captures a memorable
musical moment.

For Henry the experience of visiting
Japan was a mixed blessing. A year
later, suffering from a bad case of
post-Japanese depression, he wrote to
Hornel, 'I have so little heart for these
d—d Japanese pictures that I am
seriously thinking of chucking the
whole thing up. I have not a bloody
cent.' He later recalled his visit to
Japan in less than enthusiastic terms:

*I painted landscapes there, both oils
and watercolour, and figures, from the
geishas, the most highly refined and
educated women in Japan; and in
both the same national feeling was
visible, the absence of any strong
contrast of colour. I had all my life
been trying for strong colour, tartan
landscape and vivid contrast.*

Their stay, which lasted nineteen
months was not, however, all doom
and gloom. Hornel certainly enjoyed
meeting his sitters, remarking:

*I love to remember them as a large
and happy family, clattering by in
the sunshine with smiling faces and
no thought of the morrow, to spend
the day mid plum or cherry blossom.*

182
Edward Atkinson Hornel,
Geishas in an Interior,
1894.
Oil on wood,
25 x 32 cm
(9$^7_8$ x 12$^5_8$ in).
Private collection

183
George Henry,
The Koto Player,
1903.
Watercolour,
67·9 x 45·1 cm
(26³⁄₄ x 17³⁄₄ in).
The Burrell Collection,
Glasgow

Hornel's 'welcome home' exhibition in Glasgow in April 1886 was a triumphant success with rave reviews and many sales. Henry continued for many years to relive the visual experience of Japan by working directly from the 'Yokohamashasin' photographs described earlier which he had bought in Japan. Both Henry and Hornel, like so many of the people discussed in this chapter, however short their visit to Japan, were never quite the same after the experience.

There were, of course, other poets and artists influenced by Japan, who never made the trip, notably another member of the 'Glasgow Boys' group, Joseph Crawhall, an exquisite animal artist. He excelled in such paintings as *A Trout Rising* (184). They successfully cross the border between Occidental and Oriental depictions of nature subjects to produce a highly successful blend of Caledonian and Japanese skills.

In the field of poetry there were other figures who came to know Japan solely via the medium of the Japanese print, including the now little-remembered figure of W E Henley, who wrote poems with such titles as *Ballade of a Toyokuni Colour Print*, and an evocation of the Thames – 'Under a stagnant sky' – which he dedicated to Whistler, whose work he consistently championed.

184
Joseph Crawhall,
A Trout Rising,
c.1907.
Watercolour,
25·7 x 36·8 cm
(10$\frac{1}{8}$ x 14$\frac{1}{2}$ in).
Hunterian Art Gallery,
Glasgow

185

Sir Alfred East,
The Entrance to the
Temple of Kiyomizu-dera,
Kyoto, With Pilgrims
Ascending,
*c.*1889–90.
Watercolour,
36·8 x 26·1 cm
(14¹₂ x 10¹₄ in).
Victoria and Albert
Museum, London

186
Self-portrait of
Gabriel Veyre,
1898

A literary figure who did travel widely in Japan was Sir Edwin Arnold, author in 1881 of the popular if prolix *The Light of Asia*, editor of the *Daily Telegraph* in 1873 and one of the several well-known Englishmen to marry a Japanese woman. His collection of travel essays, *Japonica*, is embellished with photographs showing some of his lady friends, playing the *samisen*, flower-arranging and when disrobed, posing by a bath tub.

Sir Alfred East (1849–1913) was born at Kettering, Northamptonshire, where the Alfred East Gallery houses a fine collection of his work. He studied at Glasgow and in Paris under Adolphe William Bouguereau (1825–1905) and was influenced by the Barbizon school. Success led to friendship with such figures as Arthur and Emma Liberty and Charles Holmes, who would become in 1893 the founder of the highly influential magazine *The Studio*, which was always sympathetic to Japanese themes.

The Libertys were the owners of the famous shop in London, which from its conception had been closely associated with the cult of Japan, and a visit there during a world tour was irresistible. In 1889 the four enthusiasts, East, the Libertys and Holmes set off on a journey which inspired a book, *Pictorial Records of Japan* (1911), illustrated with numerous oils and watercolours by East and photographs by Mrs Liberty.

An attractive example of East's powers can be seen in his oil painting of Kiyomizu-dera, the 'must see' favourite temple on everyone's visit to Kyoto (185). From the little rivulet's three channels you can choose to drink a pledge promising either Health, Wealth or Long Life. East captures brilliantly the remarkable way in which the wooden structure juts out from the mountainside. Both East's oils and Mrs Liberty's photographs created records similar to those made by many visitors to Japan, but the still camera used by professional and amateur photographers alike would soon have a rival – the movie camera.

Visitors to the Villa Lumière, a splendid Art Nouveau house in Lyon, can capture something of the excitement which surrounded the making of the very first films in 1895 by the Lumière brothers, Auguste and Louis. The first films were entitled *Workers Leaving the Lumière Factory*, *The Gardener and the Hose* and *Arrival of a Train*. They presaged a race to demonstrate the new discovery of cinematography around the world. The Lumière brothers needed an Opérateur Lumière for the difficult job of presenting the new medium to audiences across the world, and also making films of distant lands and showing them as the journey progressed. In this way the thrilling new experience of cinematography could be virtually self-financing and excite audiences with an extended global vision.

The right man proved to be the extrovert figure of Gabriel Veyre (186) a young chemistry student always keen to don local costume. He was the perfect man for the job, at ease with audiences in North or South America, China, Indochina and Japan, where between October 1898 and February 1899 he made ten films with titles such as *Geishas in a Jinricksha* (see 246), *Japanese Dances, Rain Dance of Spring* and *The Rice Harvest*. These, the first films made in Japan, added real movement to the frozen reality of the photograph, a realization of the Lumière brothers' dream that their new invention would 'open the world to the world'. A few years later the first Japanese costume films would familiarize audiences the world over with the reality of Japan and the stirring historical figures of the samurai. Whether you went to Japan, or stayed at home and dreamt of it – the reality of the moving camera and the cinema would permanently change the outside world's perceptions of Japan.

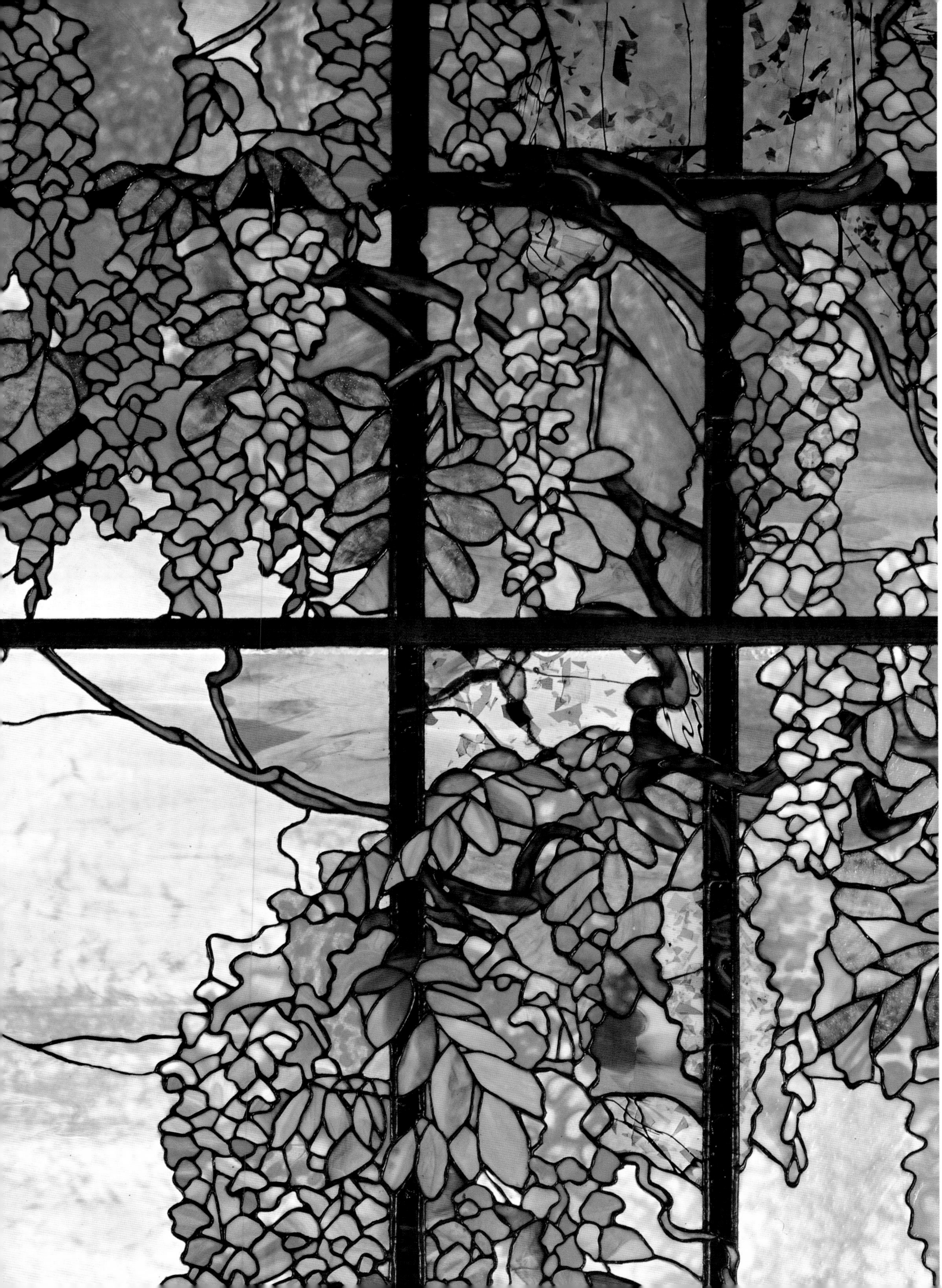

Chapter nine: The United States and Japan

Previous page
**Louis Comfort Tiffany,
Tiffany Glass & Decorating Co.,**
View of Oyster Bay window from
**the William C Skinner House,
New York**
(detail of 191)

187
**Taiso Yoshitoshi,
Commodore Matthew Perry
arrives in Japan,**
*c.*1876.
Colour woodblock

188
Japanese Parlour at
**William H Vanderbilt
House, New York,
photographed by
Christian Herter,
1883–4**

*I have never confided to you the
extent to which the Japanese print
per se has inspired me. I never got
over my first experience with it and
I shall never, probably, recover. I
hope I shan't.*
Frank Lloyd Wright 1954

When, in 1851, Herman Melville
published his massive prose epic,
Moby Dick, and launched the *Pequod*
and Captain Ahab in search of the
white whale in Japanese waters, he
evoked the mysterious beauty of the
endless unknown archipelagos which
protected the impenetrable land of
Japan from the outside world.

For Melville both the great white
whale in *Moby Dick* and Japan itself
possessed a powerful but enigmatic
beauty, still unexplored and unknown.
In the real world, however, the fateful
initial contact with Commodore Perry
(187) would set off an exchange of
ideas and artefacts that, after slow
beginnings, became a flood. In Japan
itself, a reciprocal passion for the
productions of America led in the
early summer of 1860 to a Japanese
delegation visiting America, on a
mission to ratify the treaty brought
about by Perry's visits.

The delegation visited several American
cities. In New York they drove through
crowded streets, watched by Walt
Whitman who described the event in
a poem originally entitled 'The Errand
Bearers', but changed to 'A Broadway
Pageant'. Its opening lines described
the scene when:

*Over the Western sea hither from
Nippon come,
Courteous, the swart-cheek'd two
sworded envoys,
Leaning back in their open barouches,
bare-headed, impassive,
Ride today through Manhattan.*

Many similar delegations would follow,
but although America had initially
opened up Japan, the terrible internal
struggles of the American Civil War
meant that interest in the new
discoveries in Japan was at first
restricted to a relatively small circle,
and the boom only really began in the
more peaceful decade of the 1870s,
which saw the celebration of the
centenary of the signing in
Philadelphia of the Declaration of
Independence in 1776. Fifty box-
carloads of materials were shipped
to Philadelphia to be displayed in the
Japanese stand at the Centennial,
the first Japanese-style building to
be erected on American soil.

The display proved extremely popular,
beginning an enthusiasm for Japanese
prints, screens, bronzes and other types
of metalwork, and the novelties of
kimonos, fans and parasols. As
knowledge of these artefacts spread
across America 'from sea to shining
sea', American tastes began to shift
from the dominance of European
culture to include a delight in things
Japanese. Attempting to trace the
influence of Japanese art is
complicated by the emergence at
precisely the same time, in the mid-
1870s, of the eclecticism so
characteristic of the Aesthetic
Movement. This led to such uneasy
bedfellows as the objects Charles Caryl
Coleman (1840–1928) used in his *Still
Life with Peach Blossom*. In this
painting the Japanese theme was
almost swamped by the ornate Turkish
carpet which jostles for attention with
a Japanese fan and peach blossom.

Such aesthetic problems were a
familiar occupational hazard for Oscar
Wilde, the 'Aesthete' and erstwhile
champion of Japonisme, during his
famous lecture tour. Enthusiasm for
Japanese artefacts, and for American
productions utilizing Japanese motifs,
developed dramatically, ensuring the
popularity of the cult for Japan in
America. During the winter of 1885–6,
Madison Square Gardens housed a
'Mikado' village with demonstrations
of silk weaving, and subsequently a
Japanese room appeared in virtually
every New York home of artistic
pretensions.

A particularly remarkable example
was the Japanese parlour (188) of the
William H Vanderbilt house on Fifth
Avenue. It was the creation of the
interior decorator and designer,
Christian Herter (1840–83), with
brilliant ornamental glass by John La
Farge (1835–1910) depicting a
fantastic peacock, 'a bird of Eastern
fairyland', red lacquer beams against a
bamboo frieze, walls hung with gold
brocade, and lacquered shelves and
cabinets galore to hold 'the rarest
objects of *bijouterie* and *vertu*'.

Gustave Herter (1830–98) and his half-
brother, Christian became well known
as eclectic interior designers. The
brothers were greatly taken by the
Japanese works shown at the 1876
Centennial in Philadelphia. During
the early 1870s Christian visited
England and was probably exposed
to the design ideas of E W Godwin.
In the early 1880s the brothers
created a number of pieces in the
Anglo-Japanese style with which the
name Herter became synonymous.
Several pieces of their furniture closely
echo Godwin's designs, but in a remarkable cabinet of 1880 Japanese
and Gothic decorative themes are
linked with superb effects to produce
an outstanding example of what might
be described as 'American-Japanese'
furniture.

189
Herter brothers,
Wardrobe,
*c.***1880–5.**
Ebonized cherry wood,
inlaid woods and brass,
height: 199·4 cm
(78¹₂ in).
The Metropolitan
Museum of Art, New York

190
Artus van Briggle, Harriet
Elizabeth Wilcox
Rockwood Pottery,
Vase,
1896.
Sage-green clay,
height 30·4 cm (12 in).
Museum of Fine Arts,
Houston

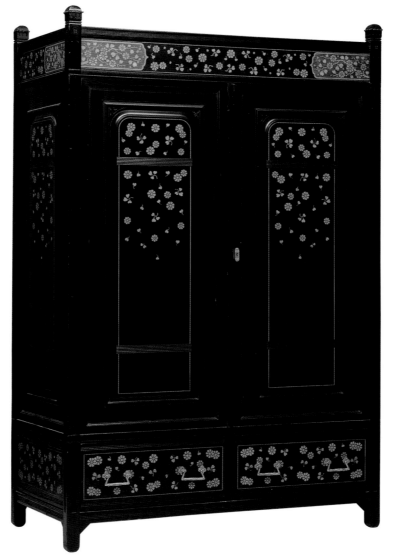

It is, however, surpassed by the restraint of the wardrobe (189), also of 1880, in which floral inlay of great distinction produces a work which ranks with the Nesfield screen (see 100). It was owned in the 1880s by the actress, Lillian Russell, who starred in Gilbert and Sullivan's *Patience*, in which Bunthorne, the 'Aesthetic Sham', confesses that he does 'not long for everything that's Japanese'. In spite of Bunthorne, the popularity of the new decorative vocabulary of Japonisme provided an incentive not just for American collectors but also for potters, glass-makers and textile and furniture designers.

The Rookwood Pottery, Cincinnati, was founded in 1880 by Maria Longworth Nichols, and in 1882 was given the ultimate 'aesthetic' accolade of a visit by Oscar Wilde. In 1887 Kataro Shirayamadani joined the company. He brought with him proficiency in the Japanese painting tradition, which led to the adoption by Rookwood of an instantly recognizable 'Orientalist' decorative style. The resultant productions of the pottery were stocked from the beginning by both Tiffany & Co. and Siegfried Bing. In 1900 the Victoria and Albert Museum bought from Bing a fine example of Rookwood ware, a vase decorated by Harriet Elizabeth Wilcox (*fl.*1880–1900). Another production of the Rookwood pottery was a vase in which the classic cone of Fuji is almost obscured by an arrangement of storks under a full moon (190).

In the ceramic painting craze which swept the country in the 1880s Japanese fans jostle for our attention with owls, peacock feathers, sprites and butterflies. Such collages of Aesthetic and Japoniste themes were also used extensively by the silver and jewellery businesses, Tiffany & Co., which were founded in 1834 in New York and in 1850 in Paris by Charles L Tiffany, the father of the legendary Louis Comfort Tiffany, an extravagant man with extravagant tastes who gradually took over both businesses in the 1860s and 1870s.

In the 1870s Louis Comfort Tiffany became particularly interested in the creation of glass which reproduced the appearance of ancient glass, and after years of experimentation patented an iridescent technique in 1880, the resulting vessels being decorated by trailing ivy leaves, lily pads, irises, dragonflies and peacock feathers. By good fortune, in 1879 Thomas Edison had invented the incandescent light-bulb at just the moment when over 300 tons of surplus material from the stained-glass workshops needed recycling.

In this way the Tiffany leaded lamp was born and took the world by storm. Similar motifs were used in the lamps and windows which have become so associated with the Tiffany name. The firm traded as Tiffany Glass & Decorating Co. from 1890 and opened furnaces in Corona, Long Island.

Tiffany's virtuoso powers as a designer of secular stained-glass windows and lamps are shown to immense advantage in his vast windows in Philadelphia and the American wing of the Metropolitan Museum of Art, New York, in which he uses one of the most Japanese of floral motifs, hanging branches of wisteria (191).

Apart from extensive travels in Europe and North Africa, Tiffany's life for nearly half a century was passed in New York, then, as now, one of the most assertive cultural centres, not only in the United States, but also the Western world. Its wealthy citizens provided a roll-call of money and power and imaginative customers for innovative designs. 'Cometh the hour, cometh the man': with hindsight it seems inevitable that Tiffany in 1879 should write, 'I have been thinking a great deal about decorative work, and I am going into it as a profession … I believe there is more in it than in painting pictures.'

Aged thirty-one, Tiffany was encouraged in this new career by Edward Chandler Moore, his father's chief designer, who had first become fascinated by Japanese art at the Exposition Universelle in Paris of 1867. Moore joined the firm in 1868, and, because no adequate training for silversmiths existed in New York, he established a programme at the Tiffany workshop. He freely used Japanese themes in the decoration of silver and jewellery. A characteristic work of the company at this time is provided by a fan brooch of green, white, red and yellow gold, set with opals, which gained international acclaim, as did a silver jug of 1878 decorated with irises, exhibited in Paris at the Exposition Universelle the same year.

191
Louis Comfort Tiffany,
Tiffany Glass
& Decorating Co.,
View of Oyster Bay
window from the
William C Skinner House,
New York,
c.1908.
Leaded favrile glass,
184·8 x 168·9 cm
(72³⁄₄ x 66¹⁄₂ in).
The Metropolitan
Museum of Art, New York

192
Louis Comfort Tiffany,
Tiffany Glass
& Decorating Co.,
Peacock Vase,
1893–6.
Favrile glass,
35·9 x 29·2 cm
(14¹⁄₈ x 11¹⁄₂ in).
The Metropolitan
Museum of Art, New York

193
William Merritt Chase,
*Shinnecock Studio
Interior*,
c.1892.
Pastel on paper,
40·6 x 50·8 cm
(16 x 20 in).
Private collection

From the 1870s Tiffany began to design the interiors of private and public buildings for such clients as the banker, J Pierpont Morgan, the railway tycoon, Cornelius Vanderbilt II, and the sugar magnate, Henry Osborne Havemeyer, for whose residence Tiffany created colourful glass mosaics and vases, one of which depicts the ubiquitous peacock theme (192).

While both the amateur and professional decorative artists of America found the visual cornucopia of ideas from Japan virtually inexhaustible, practitioners of the fine arts of painting and architecture looked to the lessons of the Japanese print not only for ideas but for discipline. A typical note was struck by the American Impressionist and friend of Claude Monet, Theodore Robinson (1852–96). His words can represent the thoughts of many American artists whose reactions to Japanese art were both muted and sensitive. He wrote:

My Japanese print points in a direction that I must try and take, an aim for refinement and a kind of precision seen in the best old as well as modern work. The opposite pole to the slap-dash, clumsy …

Robinson was writing in 1885, only thirty-five years after Hiroshige created *Fireworks over the Ryogoku Bridge, One Hundred Views of Edo* (1849–50), the print to which he is referring.

The mid-1880s were years in which the availability of the prints and the wide margins of profit realizable had created a great market opportunity for dealer and connoisseur alike, as de Goncourt recorded on 1 July 1893 after attending a dinner of Japanese enthusiasts at Véfours:

Bing talks today of the craze for Japanese prints among various American amateurs. He tells of selling a little packet of such prints for 30,000 francs to the wife of one of the richest Yankees, who in her small drawing room has an Utamaro facing the most beautiful Gainsborough in existence. And we admit to each other that the Americans, who are in the process of acquiring taste, will, when they have acquired it, leave no art object for sale in Europe but will buy up everything.

Bing and de Goncourt's admission was to prove prophetic, and from Boston to Chicago to San Francisco, major collections of prints were formed in those years, even more extensive than those still in Japan.

The three major American artists whose works were influenced by the print, Whistler in London, Mary Cassatt in Paris and Elihu Vedder (1836–1923) in Rome, could perhaps all be described like the painter John Singer Sargent (1856–1923) as 'American Express' Americans, who passed virtually all their lives as expatriates, coming to resemble characters far from home in a novel by Henry James, Edith Wharton or Frances Hodgson Burnett. That said, a key player in the process of making both Japonisme and Impressionist works popular in the United States of America was Mary Cassatt. Although most of her life was spent in France, her letters sped across the Atlantic to great purpose. She always retained close ties by correspondence with such influential long-standing American friends as the Potter Palmers and Mrs H O Havermeyer, the cheque-book and the force behind the acquisition of many major Impressionist paintings in the Metropolitan Museum of Art, New York, and the Art Institute of Chicago. Indeed late in her life Cassatt would declare, 'it has been one of the chief interests in my life to help fine things cross the Atlantic.'

Although Whistler and Cassatt will always be particularly associated with Japonisme, the genre was also practised to great effect by other American artists both well known and less familiar, including Winslow Homer (1836–1910), William Merritt Chase (1849–1916) and Maurice Prendergast (1859–1924).

The work of William Merritt Chase is still far too little known outside the United States. In *Shinnecock Studio Interior* (c.1892; 193), one of his most Japoniste paintings, Chase's daughter intently studies a volume of Japanese prints spread out upon the floor. From Chase too came one of the most sensual of all American versions of a woman wearing a kimono, a painting which vies with the work of Whistler in this genre. It shows the back of a semi-nude woman wearing a kimono seen from behind kneeling before a Japanese screen (194).

The Bostonian, Maurice Prendergast, was spiritually in tune with subjects from transient everyday life (the very definition of *ukiyo-e*). He loved to depict people enjoying themselves in such innocent pleasures as visiting Central Park in New York. He was born in Newfoundland, Canada, but the family moved to Boston in 1868 where he left school when very young. He never married and throughout his life was accompanied and supported by his brother Charles, a gifted frame-maker and also an artist. Prendergast made several long stays in Europe, the most important being a visit to Paris from 1891 to 1893, when he flirted with such sophisticated influences as the Nabis, Symbolist, Whistlerian, Art Nouveau and of course Japanese styles, developing from them his own highly innovative technique of watercolour painting.

194
William Merritt Chase,
Back of a Nude,
*c.*1885.
Pastel on paper,
45·7 x 33 cm
(18 x 13 in).
The Metropolitan
Museum of Art, NewYork

Two outstanding examples are
provided by *Umbrellas in the Rain,
Venice* and *Festival Night, Venice*
(195). The two works date from
eighteen months spent in Italy from
1898 to 1899, and although both
umbrellas and Japanese lanterns are
familiar props they are used here by
the artist with consummate skill and
to great effect.

To a greater or lesser extent these
American artists all returned to
America after foreign travel as
students. Almost inevitably in London
or Paris they saw collections of
Japanese prints, which created an
abiding interest in the subject. This
process often took place at exhibitions
all over Europe, beginning in London
with the Japanese exhibition held at
the Old Society of Watercolours in Pall
Mall in February 1854, and again in
1862. These were followed by exhibitions in Paris in 1867 and 1890,
Vienna in 1873, Philadelphia in 1876,
and Chicago in 1893. These were all
major exhibitions and there was a brisk
exchange of works not only in Paris but
also at The Hague and many other
centres. This growing accessibility of
prints at art dealers also took place all
over America. In 1890 for example
Almay's department store in Salem,
Massachusetts, opened a Japanese
section which led to further outlets
in Boston and Newport.

195
Maurice Prendergast,
Festival Night, Venice,
1898–9.
Gouache on paper,
27·8 x 38·2 (11 x 15 in).
Courtauld Institute of Art
Gallery, London

John La Farge,
Nocturne,
*c.*1885.
Watercolour, gouache
and charcoal on paper,
20·3 x 17·8 cm
(8 x 7 in).
The Metropolitan
Museum of Art, New York

Will Bradley,
The Serpentine Dancer,
1894.
Illustration for *The*
Studio

The moneyed ruling élite of railway tycoons and barons of industry and banking wanted spectacular results for the money they invested on furnishing their palatial homes. They acquired large decorative sculptures and paintings, and looked not to England and Aestheticism, but to Paris and the École des Beaux-Arts, the official French Academy, for inspiration. The term 'beaux-arts' is applied to works created by French-trained Americans, whose undisputed leader was the sculptor Augustus Saint Gaudens (1848–1907). His friend and colleague, John La Farge, already mentioned with the creation of the stained-glass window in Vanderbilt's *Japanese Parlour* (see p. 188), was trained as a painter. La Farge began collecting Japanese art at the start of his career, and later travelled to Japan in the 1880s and 1890s, painting many watercolours to illustrate his books on those journeys. In the late 1850s as a young student in Paris he had met Gautier, Baudelaire and the de Goncourts. La Farge was one of the most innovative minds in the American Aesthetic Movement, and demonstrated his lifelong debt to Japanese art in a watercolour, *Nocturne* (196). A typical polymath of the period, eminent as a landscape artist, collector and mural painter, he also became a stained-glass designer of great originality.

He began to experiment in this medium in 1875, after a visit to England in 1873 where he had studied the work of Morris & Co. La Farge was to take the art of stained glass in a different direction from medieval revivalism. His windows eschew painted glass, but use opalescent and streaked glass. In 1880 he established his own firm of interior decorators. In later years, after revisiting Japan, he returned to Japanese themes with new enthusiasm.

As we have seen in Chapter 3, the Japanese print played a major role in the design history of the poster throughout Europe. Americans from Henry James to Scott Fitzgerald and Gene Kelly have always loved Paris, and it is not surprising to find a school of American poster design which owes something to both Paris and Japan. This was true particularly in the case of Will Bradley (1868–1962). Often dismissed as being a mere Beardsley imitator, Bradley, like so many designers, was unable to resist the public's insatiable demand for peacock feather designs, of which he did several, most notably one for the Scribner publication, *The Modern Poster* of 1895–6. Bradley also produced one of the greatest designs depicting the virtuoso dancer Loie Fuller in one of her famous presentations *The Serpentine Dancer* (1894; 197) which recalls the swirling movement of the *kabuki* stage.

198
Edward Penfield,
Harper's March,
1897.
Colour lithograph,
35·6 x 48·3 cm
(14 x 19 in)

199
Charles Dana Gibson,
*Design for Wallpaper
Suitable for a Bachelor
Apartment* from *The
Weaker Sex*, 1903

The work of Edward Penfield (1866–1925) for *Harper*'s magazine in the 1890s shows again and again both his admiration for Japanese prints and the influence of Lautrec's posters, particularly in the marvellously controlled use of 'spatter' and the 'bleeding off' technique seen so clearly in some of his finest designs. In 1892 the decision was made to design a new cover for *Harper's* every month, reproducing them in a larger format as posters, a frequent feature in the life of many illustrators. Penfield designed each new monthly cover for the next six years. He was not averse to some direct 'cribbing' as, for example, *Harper's March* of 1897 (198) which compositionally is a straight 'rip off' from Bonnard's screen (see 120), showing a line of horse-driven cabs, using the same dramatic trimming of the image, borrowed directly from Japanese prototypes.

Charles Dana Gibson (1867–1944), like Chéret (see Chapter 3), was given the rare distinction of having a type of feminine beauty named after him – the Gibson Girl. She was fashionably dressed, incredibly poised and assured, and smiled but rarely laughed; the dream of American, or rather Anglo-Saxon, femininity.

Her charms were perhaps seen to most advantage in the remarkable *Design for Wallpaper Suitable for a Bachelor Apartment* (199). From 1894 to 1905 Gibson pictured her in a long series of drawings depicting her flirting and courting, playing croquet, set in the drawing-room, or promenading on the beach, all activities analogous to those of the geisha, although however strenuous the physical activity of a Gibson Girl, her bouffant hairstyle remained undisturbed. They played a distinct yet clearly related variation on the elaborate themes of the coiffeurs of the geishas, portrayed with their ornamental combs in the 'close-up' format adopted in the series of beautiful women by such an artist as Utamaro.

Japanese art not only played a highly important role as an influence on American artists, it was also a significant influence on American architects. In 1863 Sir Rutherford Alcock proclaimed that 'the Japanese have no architecture', a generalization which stuck and was often linked to the facetious judgement that 'Japanese gardening runs largely to gravel'.

As late as 1893, in virtually his only statement concerning Japan, William Morris declared that 'the Japanese have no architectural, and therefore no decorative instinct'. The events which gradually changed these ideas were the great International Exhibitions which introduced Japanese buildings and gardens to the West.

In the Philadelphia Centennial of 1876, a two-storey Japanese residence was much admired for its controlled use of space on a restricted site. This quality was emulated in the design of small detached houses on the Atlantic seaboard states, in such colonies as the fashionable Tuxedo Park in the Catskills. Another exhibition building to prove highly influential was shown by the Japanese at the World's Columbian Exposition in Chicago in 1893, a villa based upon the famous mid-eleventh-century Buddhist pavilion near Kyoto, known as the Hoo-den (Phoenix Hall; 200). The Chicago version had lightweight timber construction, deep roof overhangs, and a stress on horizontal lines. This was the first time that the young architect, Frank Lloyd Wright saw Japanese architecture, an experience which would prove of great significance for his work.

200
The Japanese Pavilion,
Hoo-den, or Phoenix Hall,
on Wooded Isle, at the
Columbian Exposition
of 1893, Chicago

201
**Frank Lloyd Wright,
Warren Hickox House,
Kankakee, Illinois,
1900**

202
Arthur Wesley Dow,
Japanese Colour Prints,
1896.
Colour lithograph,
64·7 x 49·5 cm
(25¹₂ x 19¹₂ in)

Two years later Wright's design for the Chauncey Williams residence in the Chicago suburb of River Forest, included short walls and and a tall steep roof like a farmhouse in a Hokusai print. By 1900 Wright was borrowing directly from Japanese architecture, as seen in a house he designed in Kanakee, Illinois (201) which made use of predominantly horizontal lines, low-pitched roofs with deep eaves and the gables pushed forward at the apex, windows integrated within the half-timber framework, living-rooms opening on to terraces, and low-key, inconspicuous entrances. All these disparate Japanese elements have been completely assimilated into Wright's own architectural vocabulary.

Wright loved not only Japanese architecture but also the Japanese print, an interest which began in 1889, a moment that he later described with the nostalgic passion of a first love affair. Years later in 1932, he confided in his autobiography:

Ever since I discovered the print Japan has appealed to me as the most romantic, artistic, nature inspired country on the earth … If Japanese prints were to be deducted from my education, I don't know what direction the whole might have taken.

Among the many exhibitions of Japanese prints which Wright visited, one of the most important was held in New York in 1896 with a striking poster (202) by the artist, Arthur Wesley Dow (1857–1922). Dow was the protégé of the colourful figure of Ernest Fenollosa (1853–1908), one of the foreign experts brought in to modernize Japan during the Meiji era. Fenollosa was to become the foremost authority on Japanese art, and eventually the first curator of Oriental Art at the Fine Arts Museum, Boston.

For several years in the 1890s and 1900s Wright attempted to branch out as an independent architect, while also establishing himself as a dealer in Japanese prints, two very different pursuits which ran successfully in tandem although with the occasional ups and downs. These were often caused by him using his print collection virtually as currency, as he did on his return from his first visit to Japan in 1905. He had left Walter Burley Griffin (1876–1937), the future architect of Canberra, Australia, in charge of the Oak Park office, and on his return, dissatisfied with Griffin's performance, Wright paid him off with Japanese prints! The two men never spoke again. On his first visit to Japan in 1905 Wright stayed in the first Imperial Hotel, built in 1890 and designed by a Japanese architect, Watanabe Yuzuru (1855–1930), near the Imperial Palace in downtown Tokyo.

Yuzuru had trained in Germany and created a grandiose Neoclassical design for the façade of a three-storey building which could cater for sixty guests in lavish comfort in a manner comparable with Brown's Hotel in London, the Ritz in Paris and the Waldorf Astoria in New York, and would become the social centre of Tokyo.

Wright made many further visits to Japan particularly during the years 1916–22, the lead-up to rebuilding the Imperial Hotel. Using what would be called today extensive networking, Wright eventually secured the contract, work on which began in 1919, delayed by the death of the Meiji emperor. The building was not completed until 1922, and survived both the Tokyo earthquake of 1923 and the bombing of World War II only for it to be demolished in 1968. It was partially reconstructed at the Meiji village in the Gumma Prefecture in 1976. C R Ashbee (1863–1942), the English architect, designer and romantic socialist, wrote of Wright in 1909, 'the spell of Japan is upon him … he feels the beauty and makes magic out of the horizontal line', an acute appraisal of much of Wright's work throughout his later career.

While very busy on architectural projects with the financial backing of the wealthy Spaulding brothers of Boston, Wright was able to acquire major examples of Japanese prints. On his return to America, after what would prove to be his final visit to Japan in July 1922, Wright made his last major transaction as a print dealer by selling a large collection to the Metropolitan Museum of Art.

Wright was always a great attraction on the lecture circuit, and from the printed versions of the talks which remain we can gain a good idea of his shifting interests in Japanese art. In a lecture of 1908, subsequently published as *The Japanese Print: An Interpretation* (1912), Wright declares that Japanese art:

is a thoroughly structural Art …
the first and supreme principle of
Japanese aesthetics consists in a
stringent simplification by
elimination of the insignificant.

As an exemplar of these words Wright was particularly fond of a little volume that illustrated 'diagrammatic studies of various plants, animals, nearly everything on earth' by Hokusai, entitled *Quick Lessons in Simplified Drawing* (1812–14; 203). It possesses a magical quality of simplification which Wright so admired, the discovery that everything can be broken down into circles, squares, rhombuses and triangles.

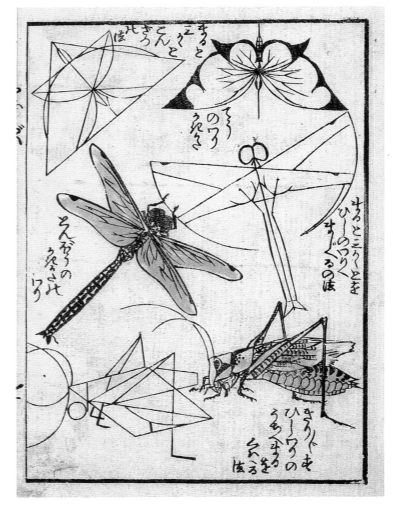

204
Greene and Greene,
The Tree of Life,
David B Gamble house,
Pasadena,
1907–9

Unfortunately, Wright was not always able to conduct his life with the serene simplicity that he admired, especially in the 1920s when his private life and career became a little 'blurred'. Whenever Wright was working in Japan at full stretch on the Imperial Hotel project making drawings for the builders, antique dealers besieged the lobby. His son, John, recalled:

Dad was buying so many works of Oriental art that vendors poured in every day and stood in line in the lobby of the hotel from morning until night. It kept him jumping from his stool at the drafting board to examine these antiques as they were presented to him.

Buying at such speed inevitably led to the acquisition of suspect works but, as in all stories unveiling forgery, it is not easy to ascertain exactly what transpired. Accusations were made that Wright had knowingly sold over-printed and revamped prints to innocent clients. The taint of the faked print led the closed community of Japanese print dealers to establish a vetting process, and not all Wright's works bore the association's seal of approval. Ironically, Wright had written to the Metropolitan Museum offering to lend a group of sixty well-executed 'vamps', 'true vampires convicted and generally admired as such', for an exhibition which would 'put the collector on his guard'.

After Wright ceased to visit Japan in 1922 the opportunity in the 1920s to play 'pass the parcel' with his 'mistakes' became very difficult. But throughout his life he continued to add to his own collection of Japanese art, and at his death at the age of ninety-one, he possessed about 6,000 prints, twenty large-scale folding screens and large quantities of textiles, ceramics and sculptures.

Today one of the most accessible of Wright's interiors is the living-room of the Francis Whittle House, Wayzata, Minnesota (1912–14), now installed at the Metropolitan Museum in New York, complete with its original textiles, Japanese prints on the walls and built-in furniture. Together they convey a magical feeling of uncluttered space so characteristic both of Wright's taste and of Japanese interiors. Another memorable Wright interior is the living-room of his own house at Taliesin, at Spring Green, Wisconsin. It provides a testimony to his strong perception of Japanese proportion and subtle understatement. Within it we glimpse Wright's 'sense of place', a demonstration of the abstract principles that E W Godwin had been among the first to perceive in Japanese art.

This unique fusion of carefully considered arrangements of furniture with ornament and ceramics can stand as a monument to the legacy of Japonisme to both the Arts and Crafts Movement and the Modernism of the twentieth century. Wright's work, the antithesis of the skyscraper, has a timeless validity.

The Greene Brothers, Charles Sumner (1868–1957) and Henry Mather (1870–1954), also owed the start of their successful careers as architects to seeing the Japanese displays at the Columbian Exposition, Chicago, in 1893 and in 1894 at the Midwinter Exposition, San Francisco. Working from their offices in Pasadena, they produced notable bungalows which in the light character of their building were distinctly Japanese in style. This is to be seen most impressively in their masterpiece for David B Gamble built in 1907–9, which now houses the Greene and Greene Library at 4, Westmoreland Place, Pasadena, California (204). Their successful buildings were amusingly described in the 1950s by the words of the founder of the Bay Region style, William Watson Wurster, 'Japanese houses are not best suited to Japan. They are more suitable for Honolulu and are best suited to California.'

An American who has done much since Lloyd Wright to make Japanese prints appreciated in America is a major figure from the world of popular musicals, novels and films. James Michener was the author of *Tales of the South Pacific* (1947), which achieved fame as the musical, *South Pacific*, and the drama, *Sayonara*. Some of his profits went to forming his great collection of prints now at the University of Honolulu in Hawaii. Michener's books on Japanese prints and on Hokusai's *Manga* provide a most readable and enjoyable introduction to Japanese prints. The position of Michener's collection, halfway across the Pacific in Honolulu, and a popular destination for Japanese visitors eager to practise their English, provides a symbolic and emotive link where West can meet East and East can meet West.

205
Katsushika Hokusai,
*Three Noblemen by
a Lake Under a Sickle
Moon,*
*c.*1830–49.
Colour woodblock,
50·6 x 22·7 cm
(20 x 9 in)

Leaving my brush behind
In Edo
I set forth on a new journey
Let me enjoy all the famous views
In paradise.
Hiroshige, on his deathbed, 1858

A garden in Japan is a representation
of the scenery of the country.
Sir Josiah Conder, 1893

In a series of prints of the 1830s
illustrating *The Imagery of Poets*,
Hokusai depicts a scene that
symbolizes an ultimate aim of Japan's
first great religion, Shinto. It expresses
man's delight in the beauties of
nature, be it a splendid tree, striking
rock, waterfall, cliff or vista. Entitled
Three Noblemen by a Lake Under a
Sickle Moon (205), it depicts the
minister, Minamoto no Toru (822–95),
son of Emperor Saga, portrayed with
two other noblemen in the extensive
landscape garden he created next to
his palace near Kyoto. The large lake
in the garden was dug out and in
imitation of Shiogama Bay, filled with
water transported all the way from the
coast. A poem by Toru which describes
'boats floating on the water in bright
moonlight, shaded by the pines' may
have inspired Hokusai's print.

Landscape was slow to emerge from
being a mere background accessory in
figure groups, until the appearance of
Hokusai and Hiroshige. In the 1840s
a new more powerful censorship had
virtually banned courtesan and *kabuki*
prints. As a result pictures of famous
views and great highways such as the
Tokaido road became much in demand
and Hiroshige in particular came to
dominate landscape art. Both artists
would produce popular imagery
showing heroes or poets enjoying a
famous view, as seen in Hiroshige and
Kunisada's *View of Tago Bay* (206)
which portrays Prince Genji and a
lady companion who listens while
he evolves his poem which compares
the garden with its two cones of
black sand with the distant classic
silhouette of Fuji.

Another example of the garden
emerging from the landscape and vice
versa is provided by Hokusai's *The Poet*
Abe no Nakamaro Gazing at the Moon
From a Terrace (207). The Japanese
nobleman, Abe no Nakamora
(698–770), when only sixteen
accompanied a delegation from Japan
to China to obtain the secrets of the
Japanese system of recording time.
Although warmly received by the
Chinese emperor he was refused
permission to return home. The rest
of his life was passed in China where
he eventually became a regional
governor. His life was always to be
passed in exile, yearning for his
homeland in Japan.

206
Hiroshige and Kunisada,
View of Tago Bay,
1857.
Colour woodblock,
each: 36·8 x 24·8 cm
(14^1$_2$ x 9^3$_4$ in)

207
Katsushika Hokusai,
*The Poet Abe no
Nakamora Gazing at the
Moon From a Terrace*,
1833–4.
Colour woodblock,
52·1 x 22·6 cm
(20¹₂ x 8⁷₈ in)

While attendants ply him with food the homesick poet muses:

When I look over Heaven's Plain
I wonder
Is that the same moon that rose
Over Mount Mikasa in Kasuga?

Shinto shrines fit into the landscape – the sacred plum and cherry blossom of spring, the azaleas and magnolias of summer and the maples of autumn. The most famous discussions of the art of gardening occur in Lady Murasaki Shikibu's classic Japanese novel *The Tale of Genji* written c.1001–15, reaching their apogee in the fictitious palace of the amorous Prince Genji, who gave all his lady friends a garden unit planted to suit their personal tastes. The author describes how in his own home Prince Genji effected:

great improvement in the
appearance of the grounds by a
judicious handling of knoll and lake
… finding it necessary to cut away
here a slope, there to dam a stream,
so that each occupant of the various
quarters might look out of her
windows upon a prospect that
pleased her best.

Several of the most basic principles in establishing a Japanese garden were first formulated during the Heian era (794–1185) in a gardener's treatise, the *Sakuteiki* (*Essay on Garden Making*) by the poet and courtier, Tachibana no Toshitsuna, a book still widely consulted today.

At that time the residences of noblemen and imperial palaces invariably included large gardens with a lake with islands, bridges and rocks. Discussions focused on the ever absorbing topic of how to use stones and water in their garden designs. By following these precepts, his designs developed into what are now known as stroll gardens and viewing gardens. Part of the garden at the Katsura Imperial Villa near Kyoto, completed in 1658, is a splendid example of the landscaped stroll garden (208).

The Way of Zen is a school of behaviour based upon an appreciation of the simplest acts of life, and involves the practice of seeking enlightenment through meditation, which could take the form, for example, of the simplest manual labour. This provided an ideal discipline for monks, whose labours with a rake we admire particularly in the Abbot's Garden at Ryoan-ji in Kyoto (209). Itinerant monks and poets were inspired by its teachings to practise beautiful calligraphy, the tea ceremony and garden design.

Some aspects of the art of Oriental gardening reached Europe from China in the eighteenth century, producing that strange Rococo amalgam, the Anglo-Chinese garden, of which Sir William Chambers' (1723–96) pagoda at Kew Gardens so engagingly reminds us. The Japanese garden was to be much more imitated than the Chinese in the West, particularly after the beginning of the Meiji era in 1868.

208
Garden and Tea Pavilion
at the Imperial Villa,
Katsura, Kyoto,
completed 1658

209
Saomi,
The Abbot's Garden at
Ryoan-ji, Kyoto,
1473

210
Sumiyoshi from *Meisho-e*
('Pictures of Famous
Places'),
*c.*1670–92.
Ink on paper,
21·5 x 32·2 cm
(8¹₂ x 12⁵₈ in).
British Library, London

Knowledge of Japanese gardens spread via such albums as *Meisho-e* ('Pictures of Famous Places'; 210), brought back by Engelbert Kaempfer, a German physician who was in Nagasaki with the Dutch East India Company from 1690 to 1692. This painting shows a garden with pine trees and a bridge over water at Sumiyoshi, and it was probably the work of a town painter producing souvenirs for travellers. Kaempfer brought back extensive quantities of such pictures of famous landmarks and seasonal events, and their vibrant colours and lively images were to play a major part in shaping the West's view of Japan and its culture. Kaempfer hoped to publish his collection of personal notes and illustrations but died before utilizing this example, and much of his library passed to Sir Hans Sloane, the catalyst whose collections brought the British Museum into being. Sloane published Kaempfer's manuscript, *The History of Japan*, translated into English, in 1727.

It is a wonder that Deshima (see Chapter 1), not much bigger than a running track, should have housed all the great collections of new plants and botanical specimens formed by the physicians of the VOC, often at great risk to their lives.

Their amazing discoveries provided European eyes with their first glimpse of exotic plants from Japan. How did someone as acquisitive as Engelbert Kaempfer or Philip von Siebold manage to amass and bring back so much? Shipping plants was facilitated by long Japanese experience in the transportation of mature trees and shrubs by carefully wrapping their roots in sacking.

After Siebold's dramatic flight from Nagasaki in 1829, narrowly avoiding death for spying, he returned to Holland where he received a hero's welcome and was nominated for a knighthood. His huge ethnographical collection of 5,000 items was bought for the Dutch state for 60,000 guilders while his fauna of 200 mammals, 900 birds and 5,000 invertebrates were kept at the Museum of Natural History in Leiden. The 2,000 plants and 12,000 dried specimens he had collected were acquired by the Hortus Botanicus, a great garden originally founded in 1587 'to expedite the instruction of all … who study medicine'.

The Leiden garden today possesses a peaceful inner garden dating from 1990 dedicated to the memory of Siebold, who himself planted several of the trees still growing in the original outer garden, notably a Japanese chestnut and a Japanese walnut. Siebold also commemorated his beloved 'wife' Kusumoto Otaksa in a romantic fashion by naming one of the most beautiful flowers he had brought back from Japan after her, the *Hydrangea otaksa* (211), commemorating it with a plate in his important book, *Flora Japonica* (1835–41). The Japanese garden of 1990 also uses elements of Japanese landscaping. The gravel symbolizes water and the rock composition opposite the pavilion symbolizes the mountains from which the water gushes downwards 'into' the gravel. The hills in the gravel sea are islands, the island closest to the rocks being the isle of the turtle, symbol of a long life. The island behind it is the crane island, wishing the visitor not only a long life but also a happy one. Most of the plants are 'Siebold' plants which he helped to introduce into Europe.

Excited by Siebold's discoveries, European botanists salivated at the thought of more unknown species of plants still to be discovered in Japan, although a steady stream of plants had filtered out via Deshima.

HYDRANGEA Otaksa

211

Hydrangea otaksa from
Philip von Siebold's
journal, *Flora Japonica*,
1835–41

212

Front cover of *Landscape
Gardening in Japan* by
Josiah Conder,
1893.
37 x 28 cm
(14¹₂ x 11 in)

Indeed the amazing influx of Japanese plants into European gardens began long before the 'official' opening-up of Japan. Trees introduced to Britain after the Meiji restoration of 1868 include the maples and magnolias, and most notably the Japanese cherries, especially the Sakura blossoms, the national flower beloved by the Japanese people and the very quintessence of Japanese spring – cherry blossom time. The name *Japonica*, which appears in numerous European novels and poems, is a plant which no one can seem to agree on exactly. Even the dictionary gives three possibilities: camellia, flowering quince and myrtle. It is amazing what a wide variety of plants in Western gardens have the species name *Japonica*, many of them recalling the plant explorers such as *kaempferii* (Kaempfer), *thunbergii* (Thunberg), *sieboldii* (Siebold) and *veitchii* (Veitch), whose lives and work would so alter the later appearance of gardens in the West.

A worthy successor to Siebold as a horticulturist was Josiah Conder (1852–1920), who worked for William Burges, the Gothic Revival architect, before settling in Japan in 1877. He was employed by the Ministry of Works to teach architecture at the Engineering College in Tokyo, and married a Japanese girl.

He designed the famous Deer Cry Pavilion, where throughout the 1880s fashionable dances were held with guests wearing Western style dress. In the early 1890s he wrote some important books, the first being *The Flowers of Japan, and the Art of Floral Arrangement* (1891), an early treatise in English on the subject of *ikebana* (also called *kado*), a traditional Japanese art of flower arrangement that has flourished since the sixteenth century. This art is said to have origins from the sixth century, when Buddhist priests offered up flowers before Buddha. The fundamental concept of Japanese flower arrangement is to express the three elements of heaven, earth and mankind in a balanced composition, using natural flowers. A wide-mouthed simple vase filled with water is used along with a metallic plate with thick needles pointing upwards on which the flowers are arranged. As a discipline *ikebana* has always appealed to British flower lovers, and *ikebana* societies continue to flourish. In 1893 Conder followed this work with a book, *Landscape Gardening in Japan* (212), which, along with a supplementary volume published the same year, greatly influenced landscape designers in Britain, Europe and America. In the supplement Conder proclaimed, 'a garden in Japan is a representation of the scenery of the country.'

213
Utagawa Hiroshige,
*Wisteria Blooms Over
water at Kameido*
from *One Hundred Views
of Edo*,
c.1857.
Colour woodblock,
35·3 x 24 cm
(13⁷₈ x 9¹₂ in)

Conder detailed the rigid set of rules which gave each feature in a garden its own special significance, whether it was a small hill representing a religious principle, or the use of raked gravel and cones of sand. The book describes ten or more ways of arranging a waterfall and innumerable permutations in the placing of stones, trees, bridges and islands to allow the eye to wander from feature to feature, or to be caught by some harmonious yet unexpected objects, such as stepping stones of carefully chosen shapes, promontories, hump-backed 'drum' bridges and hills of varying sizes which carry the eye effortlessly to the tallest tree on the largest hill, the focal point of the whole effect. Quite apart from the numerous illustrations, the sheer practicality of Conder's lavish, beautifully bound books contributed to a European vogue for Japanese gardens.

These publications enabled those unable actually to visit Japan to enjoy vicariously its botanical pleasures, not just by leafing through a volume of views of Japanese gardens but by making a garden of their own and choosing the shrubs and plants. The first Japanese gardens in Europe on the whole tended to be 'stroll gardens' rather than *karesansui* – a dry garden made of raked gravel.

One of the basic components of a 'stroll garden' is surprise, the garden gradually imparting its beauties to visitors as they stroll around and encounter unexpected features, turning a corner to find yet another vista, and after a rest the pleasure of setting forth upon a new journey. Conder also discusses the whole question of ornamental water gardens:

In one or another of its many forms of lake, river, stream, torrent, or cascade, water is an almost indispensable feature of Japanese gardens. Even in localities where no natural supply can be obtained, the idea of watery scenery is expressed in the design by the arrangement of surrounding hills, stones and plants. A sudden stretch of bare beaten earth or well raked sand, with isolated boulders scattered here or there will often indicate a lake or jutting rocks. In other cases, a meandering bed, spread with pebbles and crossed by a small bridge or stepping stones, will serve to convey the impression of a stream, which is further sustained by distributing water plants, rushes and rounded river boulders on its banks … It is essential that a garden should, above all things, look cool and refreshing in the summertime, and such a character is best maintained by the presence, or at least the idea of water.

Later chapters in Conder's book deal with the shape of garden lakes, garden cascades, garden rivers, garden islands … and duck ponds. Such gardens were often a curious hybrid, and one can readily believe the remark, 'How beautiful – we have nothing like this in Japan!' made by a senior Japanese diplomat on visiting the Japanese garden created in 1906 by Sir Frank Crisp at Friar Park, Henley-on-Thames.

The Impressionists also shared the profound Japanese preoccupation with water, most notably Claude Monet who, when an old man in his eighties, recalled his first purchase of Japanese prints in his home town of Le Havre. He would continue to collect throughout his life, both landscapes such as Hokusai's *Red Fuji* (see 39), and works relating to his garden such as *Wisteria Blooms Over Water at Kameido* (213) from Hiroshige's *One Hundred Views of Edo*. Hokusai and Hiroshige both tackled similar themes, among them the depiction of the effects of water in waterfalls, rivers, ponds, rainstorms and seascapes.

In 1883 Monet settled in Giverny and as he began to prosper, enjoyed creating a garden. The original garden (a neglected orchard) was gradually transformed by planting long archways of climbing plants and vividly coloured flowers and shrubs, and the apple trees were replaced with Japanese cherries, apricots and wisteria. Nearby he created a dazzling complement to the flower garden by diverting a tributary of the River Epte to make a large pond with rafts of water lilies. Inevitably Monet modified his ideas as the scheme progressed, developing a keen interest in the new hybrid water lilies which were then being introduced into France. To encourage their growth he dug out a series of beds and paths. He also loved to use other flowers and plants from Japan. Writing to his gardener in February 1900 from Giverny, Monet discussed the layout of his garden with a real plantsman's expertise and enthusiastic curiosity about the way a new planting would turn out:

Sowing: around 300 pots Poppies – 60 Sweet Peas – around 60 pots white Agrimony – 30 yellow Agrimony – blue Water-lilies in beds (green houses) – Dahlias – Iris Kaempferi … Don't forget the lily bulbs. Should the Japanese peonies arrive plant them immediately if weather permits.

It would be interesting to know whether Monet was aware of the advice in the *Sakuteiki* (*Essay on Garden Making*) that 'water takes its shape from the container into which it flows, with both good and bad results. Therefore you should always exercise the greatest care with the design of your ponds.' The eleventh-century author also advises on the best method of beginning a garden 'by positioning a particularly well-shaped stone and letting it dictate the arrangement of all other stones'. Wise though this advice is, there are no major or minor stones in the garden at Giverny, which it must be stressed is not an authentic Japanese garden. The ornaments, stones and lanterns found in true Japanese gardens were missing, and even the bridge (214), built heavier and flatter than the traditional full moon shape, was painted green, unlike the red of the bridges within Shinto shrines in Japanese temples. Although not entirely in the Japanese tradition, Monet's garden has many Japanese influences.

Claude Monet
The Water -Lily Pond (Japanese Bridge),
1899.
Oil on canvas,
88·3 x 93·1 cm (34¹₄ x 36⁵₈ in).
National Gallery, London

Utagawa Hiroshige,
Flowering Irises at Horikiri,
1857.
Colour woodblock,
37·2 x 24·8 cm
(14⁵⁄₈ x 9³⁄₄ in)

Its most important element was water,
and also Japanese plants such as huge
willows, wisteria, water lilies, azaleas,
bamboo and iris. This species of iris
(215) was introduced by Siebold into
Europe shortly before Hiroshige made
this print for the series *One Hundred
Views in Edo*. The water lilies would not
prove so malleable a subject as his
other sequence paintings of Rouen
Cathedral, haystacks, Waterloo Bridge
or the Houses of Parliament, for they
deliquesced, melted and demanded
more space, the freedom of the far
wider spectrum of a panorama. Monet
began to experiment with more
panoramic forms so that when the
canvases were butted together they
re-created the 360-degree illusionism
of the early nineteenth-century
panorama painters, producing the
effect that you, the viewer, were
virtually experiencing the same view
that the artist saw, whichever way you
turned. Monet may also have enjoyed
looking at painted Japanese six-fold
screens of landscape subjects imported
by dealers. He may also have seen a
full-scale reconstruction of the 'Room
of Cranes' in the Nishi-Hongan-ji
temple in Kyoto, which was shown in
London, Paris and Lyon. The transoms
were decorated with carvings of cranes,
but the sliding screens depicted
chrysanthemums, which may be
profitably compared to Monet's water
lilies, the subject which from 1899
began to dominate his work
completely.

216
Monet in his studio
*c.*1923

217
**Advertisement for Carters
Japanese Lanterns,**
*c.*1920

CARTERS JAPANESE LANTERNS

Direct from Japan, made of solid granite, and weighing from 5 cwt. to 1 ton.
Prices from 8 to 25 Guineas. Inspection invited.

As early as 1885 Judith Gautier translated a *haiku* by an unknown writer in a collection of Japanese poems which goes to the heart of Monet's vision:

*On the pool's surface
Waterplants are intertwined
A green carpet, spreading
No gaze can descend
Into the depth of my thoughts.*

These thoughts became his consuming passion and led him in 1914 to have a special studio built so he could work on the huge canvases of which he wrote:

These landscapes of water and reflections have become an obsession ... quite beyond my powers at my age, and yet I want to succeed in expressing what I feel. I've destroyed some ... I start others ... and I hope that something will come out of so much effort.

In the last twenty-five years of his life Monet continued to paint the surface of his water-lily pool and in the process came close to the precepts of Zen Buddhism, through his own long and contemplative communion with one aspect of nature. As the Belgian Symbolist poet, Émile Verhaeren, commented in 1901, when Monet painted nature, 'little by little he becomes alive in it ... The poet becomes the universe that he translates.'

The abstract painters of a later generation would claim Monet's paintings as their precursors and justification. A photograph (*c.*1923; 216) shows him at work on the water lilies in the studio. Monet died at the age of eighty-six in 1926. An epitaph on his tomb might well have been that on the grave of the poet, John Keats, 'Here lies one whose name was writ in water.'

Although the introduction of Japanese plants to Europe and North America was taken seriously by botanists and horticulturists, seekers after novelty in garden design often had little understanding of the fundamental ideas in the creation of a Japanese garden, and the cultural issues which its Shinto and Zen roots raised. A B Freeman Mitford, later Lord Redesdale, in his book *Tales of Old Japan* (1871), dismissed Japanese gardens, finding them 'all spick and span – intensely artificial and a monument to wasted labour', while Reginald Farrer, a Tokyo-based plant collector and writer, commented that he thought the Japanese hated plants because they 'butchered' them, referring to the severe pruning which is such a feature of Japanese horticulture. Such austerity was very alien to Western eyes, which found it far easier to appreciate the unexpected pleasures of the stroll gardens. Between 1880 and 1910 a number of Japanese stroll gardens were established in Britain and America.

218
Japanese Garden, Tatton
Park, Knutsford, Cheshire,
1910–13

219
Golden Brook, Japanese
Garden, Tatton Park,
Knutsford, Cheshire,
1910–13

Specialized shops soon arose to cater for the new demand for such virtually obligatory features in Japanese gardens as the stone lanterns which could weigh up to a ton (217). Hundreds of different varieties of Japanese moss also appeared both in special moss gardens or on stone lanterns, which were rarely furnished with the candles that in former times gave many gardens a strangely ghostly appearance at night.

Smooth recumbent rocks formed the stepping-stone journey through the garden, twisting obliquely to reveal views both near and far. In forming Japanese gardens massive boulders are a very highly valued commodity. Tall standing stones can act as the support for a short poem which can vary from the trite to far more profound texts. Such gardens, whether made at home or abroad, needed maintenance, and to this end Japanese gardeners were employed. Just as in the eighteenth century no ambitious large-scale landscape garden was deemed quite complete without a resident hermit, so in the late nineteenth and early twentieth centuries a Japanese gardener was deemed a vital ingredient of the scene to create and maintain gardens on correct philosophical principles. One of the most successful gardens was established in 1906 by the first Lord Wavertree at Tully near Kildare in Ireland, across the road from the Irish National Stud.

Designed by the Japanese gardener, Tassa Eida, its teahouse, stone lanterns, bonsai and a model village were made of lava from Fujiyama, imported from Japan. The path though the garden was designed as a symbol of man's pilgrimage through life, taking the visitor from the Gate of Oblivion along the Path of Childhood, up the Hill of Learning, across the Bridge of Matrimony and finally through the Gates of Eternity.

A permanent aspect of the great temporary international exhibitions through which Japan became known to the outside world were the Japanese gardens which were left behind after the close of the exhibitions, and the Japanese gardeners who were left behind to tend them, or establish new gardens based upon those seen in the exhibitions. In England one of the more notable of those gardens is at Tatton Park, near Knutsford, Cheshire (218), which was inspired by a visit by its owner, Alan de Tatton, to the Anglo-Japanese exhibition of 1910 at the White City, London. One of its best features is the Golden Brook (219), an informal garden lake with a Shinto temple at one end overlooking the gardens. After years of neglect it was completely restored in 2001.

220
**Isamu Noguchi,
Sunken Garden for
Beinecke Rare Book and
Manuscript Library, Yale
University, New Haven,
1960–4**

Careful restoration is also planned at Gunnersbury Park, London, built by Leopold de Rothschild in 1906, which typically for its time merged both Chinese and Japanese features, with palms and bamboos mingled with stone lanterns and a red-painted hump-backed wooden bridge over the water lily pool. Hot water was piped into this outdoor pool 'to bring on the water lilies', a process of pampering the flower that would have surprised even Monet.

Another particularly charming garden can be seen at Fanhams Hall near Ware, Hertfordshire. It was created between 1905 and 1933 by Herbert Goode, using stone lanterns, rocks and a variety of rare trees and shrubs imported from Japan. Goode was a porcelain importer, whose ceramic shop in Mayfair remains a key monument of the Aesthetic Move- ment. Goode's garden is an early Edwardian interpretation of a Japanese theme with a charming teahouse, which would have provided an ideal setting for Gwendoline to pass Cecily a cucumber sandwich in Oscar Wilde's *The Importance of Being Earnest*. Today, with an irony Wilde would surely relish, it is used as a centre for the study of the Japanese tea ceremony.

One famous garden that sadly has disappeared only in recent years was created by a great Victorian woman traveller, Ella Christie, whose later years were devoted to its creation at Cowden, Perthshire, at the marshy foot of the Ochil Hills in Scotland. The gardens were laid out in 1907 by Taki Honda, a female Japanese garden designer from Nagoya. A ditch was turned into a lake, weeping willows, azaleas and primulas were planted and a Shinto shrine was constructed from Japanese cedars. Groups of stones were arranged to symbolize the five virtues – patriotism, obedience, faith, loyalty to family life and obedience to parents. The last two precepts were not without bitter irony for Ella, for her father had tried to disinherit her, thus starting her travels. The gardens were maintained for over ten years by a Japanese gardener, Matsuo, who arrived as Head Gardener in 1925 and is buried in the local churchyard. In the 1960s the gardens were systematically vandalized, and the pavilions, bridges and ornaments destroyed. Today little is left except for a few mature shrubs and pines.

A characteristic American success story can be found in the career of the Japanese gardener, Takeo Shiota, who came to America in 1907 and laid out a successful contemporary 'Tea House' garden in fashionable Tuxedo Park near New York. His masterpiece, still easily accessible and well maintained, was the Brooklyn Botanic Garden designed in 1915 around the existing feature of a tiny lake, which Shiota embellished with a *Torii*, an island near the artificial cascade, and a viewing pavilion built over the water. A shrine, several bridges, a covered resting bench, imported stone lanterns and realistic metal statues of cranes added an amusing illusion to a garden which today is considered one of the finest of its kind in America.

The Nitobe Memorial Garden at the University of British Columbia in Vancouver, Canada, is one of the best traditional gardens in North America. Nestled in 0.8 hectares (2 acres) of native British Columbian forest, this Shinto-style enclosure includes a stroll garden which uses symbolism. The garden may be interpreted as a symbolic journey through life from infancy to teenage years, marriage and adulthood, thus achieving spiritual growth. The stone lanterns symbolize light dispelling darkness, and when placed at the junction of paths indicate choices in life – appropriate questions for a garden in a university.

Waterfalls illustrate both male and female traits of nature in the Shinto religion, the strength and masculinity of the waterfall contrasting with the calm feminine stream.

In more recent years the American-Japanese designer Isamu Noguchi (1904–88) who worked in the studio of Constantin Brancusi (1876–57) has created a garden at the UNESCO building in Paris and a memorable Zen garden, completely without plants, for contemplation at the Beinecke Library at Yale University (1960–4; 220). In the following year he completed gardens at the Chase Manhattan Bank and also the IBM headquarters in New York.

The immensely successful Anglo-Japanese exhibition of 1910 saw the re-creation to scale of Japanese buildings including a four-fifth actual size ceremonial gateway of a famous Buddist temple gateway in Kyoto known as the Chokushi Mon (Gate of the Imperial Messenger) dating from the latter part of the sixteenth century. After the exhibition the replica was removed to Kew and erected near William Chambers' eighteenth-century Chinese pagoda. The gateway was restored in November 1995, and is now complemented by a Japanese garden completed in October 1996. In 1991 the Kyoto Garden in Holland Park, London, was opened by the Crown Prince of Japan and the Prince of Wales near the site of a garden planted in the 1930s, which had almost disappeared.

221
Ron Herman,
Japanese Garden, Ellison
Residence, Woodside,
California, 1997

One of the most remarkable of all Japanese gardens ever erected outside Japan is in the process of being constructed today in Silicon Valley, California, where 'dot.com' millionaires grow weary of looking for unusual ways to spend their fortunes. An exception is the Oracle impresario, Larry Ellison, who has found an imaginative solution to the problem and is currently in the process of building the largest Japanese garden in America. In an interview in *Xpress Magazine* in May 2002 Ellison spoke of his first visit to Japan and love of Kyoto:

There were these wonderful gardens that were designed to promote intimacy between the viewer in the garden and the garden itself … when you spend time in a forest, and especially those wonderful, small reproductions of forests – those Japanese Zen gardens – it is a wonderfully reassuring and tranquil experience.

I always hear artists saying, 'I don't want to do that, it's been done before.' Well, the Japanese say 'I want to do exactly what has been done before, but just a little better.'

This motivation absorbed from Japan gives Ellison the determination to use as a model for the 9·3-hectare (23-acre) site, his favourite Japanese garden, Katsura Risky in Kyoto.

To achieve that result his gardener Shigeru Namba has restributed 81,000 cubic yards of earth dug out from the pond in the form of hills and islands. Over 500 trees have been added to about 700 existing natural trees, and 3,500 tons of boulders placed around the extensive pond. Stone lanterns and other hard-to-get Japanese materials have been brought from Japan.

The estate includes a large waterfall, a cascade, a pond and seven buildings, a round stone bridge and beautiful pathways with colourful trees and pink and yellow flowers leading to a serene courtyard where guests can see the main residence's north and south wings over the pond. The teahouse, which was reassembled in Woodside after being brought from Japan, stands peacefully in the deep forest. The moon pavilion, where a resident can enjoy watching the moon while soaking in the wooden bathtub, looks as though it is floating in the water. All the architectural structures are pavilions of varying dimensions, placed a few hundred metres apart around the five lakes which have been excavated, much to the concern of neighbours who were kept awake by the noise of lorries removing the smaller rocks and stones and returning with boulders (221).

When completed the garden complex will form a new chapter in the ongoing story of the West's fascinating variations on Japanese garden themes.

Previous page
James Abbott McNeill Whistler,
The Gold Scab: Eruption in Frilthy Lucre
(detail of 224)

222
Katsushika Hokusai,
Self-Portrait,
1843.
Ink on paper,
26·9 x 16·9 cm
(10⅝ x 6⅝ in).
Museum of Ethnology,
Leiden

The King of Hell being very old is retiring from business, so he has built a pretty country house and asks me to go and paint a kakemono for him. I am thus obliged to leave, and when I do so I shall carry my drawings with me. I am going to take a room at the corner of Hell Street and shall be happy to see you whenever you pass that way.
Reputed to be Hokusai's last letter, 1843, written with his last self-portrait, aged 83 (222)

I have one aim – the grotesque.
If I am not grotesque, I am nothing.
Aubrey Beardsley, 1896

What exactly was the Symbolist Movement and in what ways was it influenced by Japonisme? Unlike Impressionism, Symbolism was a loosely organized artistic movement which arose in the 1880s and 1890s, a group of painters closely allied with the Symbolist Movement in French literature, which began rather earlier. Proto-Symbolists included such names as the founder of the movement, Alfred de Vigny, author of a play on the tragic suicide of the seventeen-year-old poet Thomas Chatterton, and Charles Baudelaire, creator of the notorious cycle of poems *Les Fleurs du mal* (*The Flowers of Evil*).

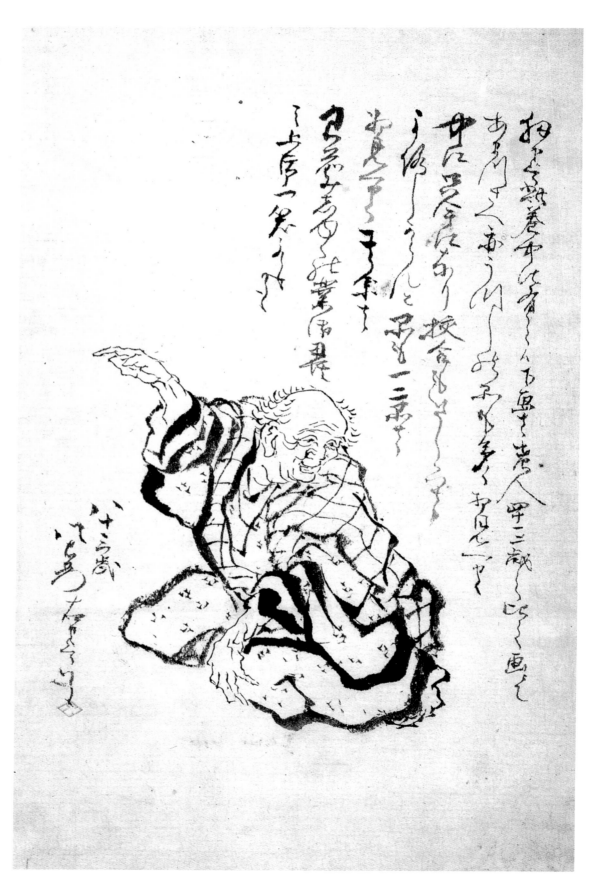

Later Symbolists included the poets Paul Verlaine and Stéphane Mallarmé, who coined the famous dictum, 'paint not the thing, but the effect which it produces', and embraced a manifesto which asserted:

We are tired of the everyday, the near at hand and the contemporaneous; we wish to be able to place the development of the symbol in any period, even in dreams (dreams being indistinguishable from life). We want to substitute for the battle of individuals the battle of feelings and ideas ...

Nothing could be further from the principle of realism as formulated by Gustave Courbet (1819–77), who declared that painting should only deal with 'real and existing things'. Symbolism on the contrary strove to give visual expression to the mystical and occult. For both artists and writers the choice of subject was of major importance, and this helps to explain the enthusiasm generated by the arrival of the arts of Japan with their novel scenes and themes.

As with other aspects of the arts already discussed, Hokusai's *Manga* contains many pages dealing with stories and superstitions, an extraordinary bran-tub of stimulating ideas which got the creative process going for Western eyes.

223
Katsushika Hokusai,
Yuten and the Ghost
from the *Manga* vol. XII,
1834.
Colour woodblock,
17·5 x 11·5 cm
(7 x 4¹₂ in)

For the Symbolists the morbid themes of Japanese mythology and the grotesque element in its folk tales such as *Yuten and the Ghost* had an especial appeal (223). The woodcut tells the story of Kasane, a woman cursed with the legacy of both a hideously ugly face and a large tract of land. She married the land-hungry Yoemon, a peasant who promptly murdered her. For years she haunted the countryside driving Yoemon's subsequent wives to their death. In despair Yoemon begged the priest Yuten, shown here, to exorcise Kasane's apparition.

To this day the Japanese are fascinated by such ghost stories, either when performed on the *kabuki* stage, enacted in traditional processions and festivals, or in the oral tradition of the spoken word.

One of the major tenets of the Symbolist Movement was a belief in the interrelationships, parallels and analogies between the arts of painting, music, poetry and prose. The painter Whistler also subscribed to this view, giving his paintings musical titles such as *Arrangement*, *Symphony* or *Nocturne*.

224
James Abbott McNeill
Whistler,
*The Gold Scab: Eruption
in Frilthy Lucre*
(*The Creditor*),
1879.
Oil on canvas,
186·7 x 139·7 cm
(73¹₂ x 55 in).
Fine Arts Museum of
San Francisco

225
Odilon Redon,
*The Siren Rising From the
Waves Clothed in Barbs*,
1888.
Lithograph,
27·5 x 17 cm
(10⁷₈ x 6³₄ in)

The story of Whistler's creation in 1876–7 of the *Harmony in Blue and Gold: the Peacock Room* for the shipping magnate F R Leyland and the consequent quarrel with his patron, symbolized in a mural by a pair of fighting peacocks, has been recounted above (see Chapter 5). It has become recognized as a key work in the story of both the Symbolist Movement and Japonisme. Whistler believed that Leyland subsequently drove him into bankruptcy, and painted in oils a caricature of Leyland entitled *The Gold Scab: Eruption in Frilthy Lucre* (224). It shows his victim with an engorged peacock's head playing the piano while perched on the gabled roof of Whistler's home, the White House, and erupting a shower of gold sovereigns from his frilly shirt. This horrifying creation is given a very Japoniste effect by the depiction of the peacock's erect crest and the great claw feet, an exercise in anthropomorphic comparison and abuse, one of the oldest weapons in the cartoonist's quiver. This theme would also be used by Symbolist artists, notably Odilon Redon (1840–1916) in his memorable *The Siren Rising From the Waves Clothed in Barbs* (225).

226
Gustave Moreau,
Two **Kabuki** *actors*
in Female Roles,
1869.
Watercolour and pencil,
26 x 21·1 cm
(10¹⁄₄ x 8¹⁄₄ in).
Musée Gustave Moreau,
Paris

The Symbolist poetry of Mallarmé and Verlaine (and in England the work of Swinburne) was labelled 'decadent' and associated with two of the most important French Symbolist painters, Redon and Gustave Moreau (1826–98). In 1869 the latter made one of his rare excursions into the watercolour medium when he visited the Japanese Exhibition in the Palace of Industry, where a *kabuki* company performed a traditional play. In it two actors fought a mimic battle, brilliantly recorded by Moreau (226).

The work of Moreau and Redon together with that of the mural painter, Puvis de Chavannes (1824–98) provided a focus for the movement. By its nature, however, Symbolism recognized no national barriers. There were always significant contributions from abroad by artists who admired Symbolist aims, ranging from Edvard Munch (1863–1944) to Edward Burne-Jones, and most strikingly, the young British illustrator, Aubrey Beardsley.

On a visit to Paris in 1892, Beardsley showed his portfolio to a sympathetic Puvis de Chavannes. It contained many examples of what he called his 'Japonesque' style in which the dramatic use of black areas was arrived at by experimenting with blots of Indian ink. Beardsley also used the asymmetric composition and the narrow upright format of the *kakemono*, a space which he found particularly congenial.

227
Aubrey Beardsley,
Vignette in *Bon-Mots*,
by Sydney Smith and
R Brindsley Sheridan,
1893.
5·1 x 5·7 cm
(2⅛ x 2¼ in)

228
Katsushika Hokusai,
Monsters from the
Manga vol. XII,
1834.
Colour woodblock,
17·5 x 11·5 cm
(7 x 4½ in)

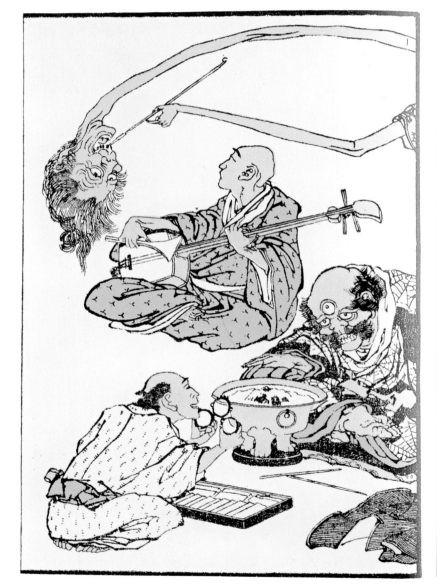

229
Aubrey Beardsley,
The Peacock Skirt from
Salomé by Oscar Wilde,
1894.
Ink drawing,
22·8 x 19·7 cm
(9 x 7³⁄₄ in).
Fogg Art Museum,
Harvard University,
Cambridge, MA

Beardsley made black the most exciting colour on the palette, and in his more straightforward drawings he abraded the surface of the black areas to obtain a richness of tone resembling a mezzotint effect. These experiments led him to become aware of the work of Redon, whose lithographs record his dreams by putting 'the logic of the visible world at the service of the invisible', and at the same time dallying with the supernatural.

It is possible that Beardsley saw examples of Redon's work either on his visit to Paris in 1892 or at the bookshop of Frederick Evans, from whom came the great commission for Beardsley of Malory's *Morte D'Arthur* and also a project for illustrations for a mini-anthology of aphorisms and wit entitled *Bon-Mots* (227). In creating over 200 drawings for *Bon-Mots*, Beardsley, the most original of artists, delved into the apparently inexhaustible resources of the *Manga* when seeking inspiration. Among the grotesque drawings that he made for this venture are several which have Japanese prototypes in the *Manga*, notably a creature with an immensely long neck (228), a geisha and two spiders with grotesque semi-human faces and wide-open eyes.

230
Kitagawa Utamaro,
The Outer Robe,
*c.*1797.
Colour woodblock,
37·3 x 25 cm
(14⁵⁄₈ x 9⁷⁄₈ in)

Another important early experience for Beardsley occurred in July 1891 when he and his sister visited Whistler's Peacock Room and illustrated a letter describing the experience with a watercolour sketch of *La Princesse du pays de la porcelaine* (see Chapter 5), the room's centrepiece, surrounded by little peacocks all flourishing their feathers. The experience much later reappeared in his work in the guise of *The Peacock Skirt* (229), an illustration for Wilde's *Salomé*, published in 1894. This was among the most famous and most Japanese of all Beardsley's works, and forms an intriguing comparison with Kitagawa Utamaro's *The Outer Robe* (230). Beardsley's *Salomé* illustrations formed a watershed both for the Aesthetic Movement and Japonisme. *The Peacock Skirt* was denounced by the critic of the *Saturday Review* as 'a derisive parody of Félicien Rops embroidered on to Japanese themes'. Rops (1833–98) was a brilliant but perverse artist who shared with Beardsley a taste for the erotic and macabre themes so beloved by the masters of the Japanese print.

By their very nature the Symbolists were a constantly fluctuating group with links to several other movements of the time, in particular the Nabis and followers of Synthetism who formed themselves around the compelling personality of Paul Gauguin.

Gauguin was a keen collector of Japanese prints, which he used to decorate his rooms in Brittany, the Pacific and Paris, where his studio contained 'a sort of frieze made by prints by Utamaro and Hokusai'. Prints appear in the background of several of his paintings, notably in *Still Life With a Japanese Print* (1879).

In *The Vision After the Sermon – Jacob Wrestling With the Angel* (1888; 231), Gauguin used a composition showing sumo wrestlers lifted directly from the *Manga* (232), a crib which aroused the ire of the Impressionist Camille Pissarro, who in February 1891 wrote to his son Lucien in London, specifically singling out Gauguin's painting for criticism:

I do not criticize Gauguin for having painted a vermilion background nor do I object to the two struggling warriors and the Breton peasant woman in the foreground ... What I do mind is that he swiped these ideas from the Japanese, the Byzantine painters and others.

The extent to which Gauguin 'swiped' from the Japanese is tellingly evident in several works, for he looked to Japan not only for inspiration on line and subject but also for bold colours.

Gauguin hoped in the South Seas to be able to live on ecstasy, calmness and art, and until the day he died, continued to value his Japanese collection, noting down in his intimate journal, *Before and After*, the contents of his home in the South Pacific:

In my hut there are all sorts of odds and ends that appear extraordinary because here they are unusual: Japanese prints, photographs of pictures by Manet, Puvis de Chavannes, Degas, Rembrandt, Raphael, Michel Angelo.

After his demise in 1903 the inventory of Gauguin's possessions included a Japanese book, a Japanese sword and forty-five prints tacked to the walls of his dwelling, many of which were undoubtedly Japanese.

The Nabis, a group of French painters active in the 1890s, derived their title from the Hebrew word meaning 'the prophets'. They were followers of Gauguin's expressive use of colour and, like him, admirers of the bold imagery and rich patterns and motifs of Japanese art. Paul Gauguin, in a letter to Émile Bernard (1868–1941) in December 1888, observed admiringly that the Japanese drew 'life outdoors and the sun without shadows', and resolved that he would do the same.

233
Émile Bernard,
Women Hanging Laundry,
from *Les Brettoneries*,
1889.
Zincograph with
hand-colouring,
24·7 x 31·7cm
(9³₄ x 12¹₂ in).
Indianapolis Museum of Art

Although Bonnard, Vuillard and Maurice Denis, the main theorist of the Nabis, all went their separate ways after their successful exhibition of 1899, one figure of the group stands out for works which demonstrate particularly Japanese qualities: Émile Bernard, who was aged twenty when he first met Gauguin during the summer of 1888 at Pont Aven. Both artists shared enthusiasms for medieval art, stained glass and Breton culture. Together they enjoyed experimenting with the techniques made possible with the new medium of zincography, an easy method of producing lithographic images. That winter Bernard conceived a series of seven prints which would form an examination of the life of Breton peasants at work and play, one of which was *Women Hanging Laundry* (233). Like Gauguin, Bernard collected Japanese prints and it is fascinating to see in the dominant figure on the left, the static pose of a *kabuki* actor.

The provision of images of ghosts, such a feature of the *kabuki* theatre, provided an important part of Hokusai's income. Public demand for his grotesque pictured imaginings led him to produce some of the most terrifying of all the monsters and ghost stories which abound in Japanese mythology.

He was not alone in creating in this lucrative field, as we can see in a book of ghost stories, *Once Upon a Time, or Stories of Strange Demons: The Former Wife's Return*, by Shun'ei and Shunsho. The illustrations for such ghost stories inspired several Symbolist painters, notably Odilon Redon and the Belgian, Félicien Rops. The influence of Japanese artefacts other than prints had a particular appeal for novelists and writers looking for copy in describing interiors, figures such as Philippe Burty who wrote a novel, *Grave Imprudence* (1880). The book's hero Brissot was a composite of Manet and Monet, and an early collector of Japanese prints. A sensual moment in the novel portrays Brissot painting Pauline, a Parisian model who is naked except for a Japanese red-orange robe, a clear reference to Monet's *La Japonaise* (see 132).

A writer who also trailed the Symbolist banner was Joris-Karl Huysmans. In Huysmans's notorious novel *Against Nature* (1884), his hero des Esseintes tries:

to rejuvenate the stereotyped forms of poetry, the sonnet for example, which he turned upside down, like those Japanese fish in coloured earthenware that are stood gills-down on their pedestals.

234
Ashinaga With a Fish,
18th century.
Ivory,
height: 15·1 (6 in).
Linden-Museum,
Stuttgart

235
Katsushika Hokusai,
[The Ghost] of Oiwa, from
One Hundred [Ghost] Tales,
1831.
Colour woodblock,
26·3 x 18·9 cm
(10³⁄₈ x 7¹⁄₂ in)

236
Utagawa Kuniyoshi,
*Takiyashi the Witch and the
Skeleton Spectre* from
Somai dairi
(*The Palace of Soma*),
c.1845.
Colour woodblock,
each panel: 37·3 x 25 cm
(14¹⁄₂ x 9⁷⁄₈ in)

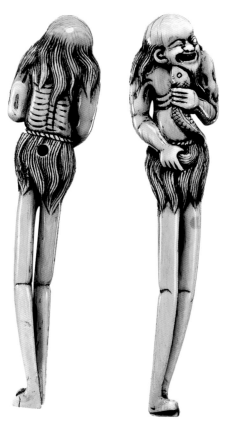

Elsewhere in the novel its hero des Esseintes 'enjoyed a perverted sense of pleasure in handling books whose covers, made of Japanese felt, were as white as curdled milk'. The extraordinary lifestyle of his hero is derived from 'those Japanese boxes that fit one inside the other', achieved by inserting a ship's cabin inside a real dining-room and setting off on imaginary voyages. In one of the most 'purple passages' in the novel, des Esseintes plans the decoration of the shell of a huge tortoise, so that as it moved it would set off the gleaming tints of his rich Oriental carpets:

From a collection of Japanese art he selected a drawing representing a huge bunch of flowers springing from a single slender stalk, took it to a jeweller's … and informed the astonished lapidary that the leaves and petals of each and every flower were to be executed in precious stones and mounted on the actual shell of the tortoise.

Needless to say the poor creature dies:

unable to bear the dazzling luxury imposed upon it, the glittering cape in which it had been clad, the precious stones which had been used to decorate its shell like a jewelled ciborium.

Such exotic European fantasies combined with the Japanese love of the grotesque and bizarre provoked exciting artistic cross-pollination, recorded in both the pages of Hokusai's *Manga* and such works as *Japan: Its Architecture, Art and Art Manufactures* by Christopher Dresser. He describes in it an ivory carving of two men violently disagreeing:

The one has long legs and short arms; the other has long arms and short legs. The tale goes that fish can only be caught in deep water, where the man with short legs could not stand. The man with long legs can get into the deep water, but, owing to his short arms, he cannot reach to the bottom and fish. The difficulty is overcome by the long legged man carrying the man with the long arms on his back. The two together can thus catch fish, but neither can do so alone. Hence the absurdity of these men quarrelling.

Such grotesque juxtapositions provided *netsuke* carvers with apposite subjects (234). *Netsuke* are the small carvings used as toggles to secure cord hanging from the *obi* or sashes. Another popular theme in Japanese folklore goes into the advantages and disadvantages of having a long neck, a subject which Hokusai depicts in the *Manga* (see 228). The lady on the right demonstrates that it can prove very useful if you want to smoke in bed.

Next to her an old woman remains seated but nevertheless gets her head into a better position for listening to the monk play the *samisen* while having a third arm helps with her pipe-smoking too. An enterprising oculist in the bottom of the left-hand sheet is quite unphased by a customer with three, instead of the more usual two, eyes.

Another popular symbolic theme both in Japan and the West was the use of skulls and skeletons, not only to signify *memento mori* (emblems of mortality) but also when animated to symbolize ghosts and apparitions. One of the most horrifying of all ghosts by Hokusai grins at us with a leer carefully calculated to make the most doubtful sceptic believe all too vividly in 'things that go bump in the night' (235).

A fine example of a print inspired by a theatrical production is provided by Kuniyoshi and entitled *Takiyashi and the Skeleton Spectre*, a triptych dating from *c.*1845 (236). This dramatic print shows a sorceress holding a scroll and conjuring up a skeleton spectre. She is Takiyasha, daughter of Taira Masakado (d.940), who attempted to become Emperor. After he was killed his castle was believed to be haunted by the ghost of his daughter.

237

James Ensor,
Chinoiseries,
1907.
Oil on canvas,
62 x 75 cm
(24³⁄₈ x 29¹⁄₂ in).
Museum Dhondt-
Dhaenens, Deurle

238
Félicien Rops,
Le Vice Suprême,
*c.*1884.
Etching and aquatint,
35·3 x 26·5 cm
(13⁷⁄₈ x 10¹⁄₂ in)

Such a theme has obvious parallels with the obsessive use of skeletons by the Belgian artists, James Ensor (1860–1949) and Félicien Rops (237 and 238). Death and the Devil are awesomely symbolized by piles of skulls and death's head moths, such as are seen in Hiroshige's *Taira Kiyomori Sees Strange Sights in his Garden* (239), which tells the story of the tyrant Kiyomori who, shortly before he died, was haunted by the spirits of all the people whose death he had caused. Hiroshige has brilliantly captured the delirium of the dying man as the snow-laden garden is revealed as being completely composed of a horrifying pile of skulls. This image strikingly parallels an illustration by the English artist, Sidney Sime (1867–1941), *The Gate of Knowledge* (240), which was published in the *Pall Mall Magazine* in June 1905. Sime lived a strange, lonely life, creating such skull-infested landscapes, which often accompanied the macabre short stories by his patron, the eccentric Irish peer Lord Dunsany. Today, sadly, their joint work is virtually forgotten, yet it embodies the very quintessence of the spookier side of Japonisme.

That most rigorous of dramatic disciplines, the *noh* play, intrigued one of the great poets of the twentieth century, William Butler Yeats. In 1916 he wrote an essay, *Certain Noble Plays of Japan*, which discussed the *noh* theatre.

He later wrote four *noh* plays, two being entitled *At the Hawk's Well* (1917) and *The Dreaming of the Bones* (1919). They formed a part of a series of 'four plays for dancers' using extreme simplicity of design and setting, the work of the illustrator Edmund Dulac (who also composed the music for the plays). In *The Dreaming of the Bones*, Yeats cleverly interwove the historic Irish symbols of nationalist struggle, seeking to convey his meaning by 'calling to the eye of the mind', deliberately stylizing his actors' movements and using masks.

The early twentieth century also produced artists whose work continued to show evidence of Japanese inspiration. One particularly interesting group of students became known as 'the Spooks' during their years at the Glasgow School of Art. Their 'spooky' works reveal a strange blend of Celtic romanticism filtered through Beardsley and Japan. The chief 'Spook' was Jessie M King (1875–1949). Her watercolour, '*I had never seen anyone so pale*' (241), illustrates Oscar Wilde's fairy story, *A Fisherman and his Soul* in *A House of Pomegranates*, and it succeeds in being both classically Japanese and thoroughly modern in its composition.

239
Utagawa Hiroshige,
Taira Kiyomori Sees
Strange Sights in
his Garden,
1843–5.
Colour woodblock,
36·8 x 76·2 cm,
(14$\frac{1}{2}$ x 30 in)

240
Sidney Sime,
The Gate of
Knowledge from
Pall Mall Magazine,
June 1905

241
Jessie M. King
'*I had never seen anyone
so pale*', pen, ink and
watercolour illustration
for *A House of
Pomegranates* by Oscar
Wilde, 1915

242
Edvard Munch,
The Scream,
1895.
Lithograph

'Illness, madness and death were the black angels that kept watch over my cradle', wrote the Norwegian artist Edvard Munch, whose mother and sister died while he was young, and whose father was a religious maniac. Munch made his first visit to Paris in 1885 and, while there, became interested in the Symbolists, Gauguin, and also the Japanese print. He gained mastery of painting and the graphic techniques of etching, lithography and notably the woodcut, at which he excelled. Certain images, in particular *The Scream* (1895; 242), recur again and again in different media. *The Kiss*, a supreme example of the use of the grain of the plank as background, reveals his knowledge of Japanese woodcuts, and the anguished intensity of his art is also in evidence in the themes of *Melancholy* (1896), *Despair* (1892), and *The Girl and Death* (1896).

After the horrors of the First World War different concerns would take precedence over Japonisme, although as Roger Fry (1866–34), High Priest of Modernism, observed:

It is partly due to Japanese influence that our own impressionists have made an attempt to get back to … ultra primitiveness of vision. Indeed they deliberately sought to de-conceptualize art.

In the 1900s a new interest in the art of Africa would overtake Japonisme. Yet, today Japanese aesthetics continue to affect the sensibilities of the West.

I·HAD·NEVER·SEEN·ANYONE·SO·PALE

Chapter twelve:

Coda: Floating World or Moving Image?

Previous page
Kokyo,
Japanese Destroyer
Squadron Outside Port
Arthur (detail of 246)

243
Henri Rivière,
The Painter in the Tower
from *The Thirty-Six Views*
of the Eiffel Tower,
1902.
Lithograph,
page: 17 x 20 cm
(6⅝ x 7⅞ in)

Put Oriental Art entirely out of
your heads.
John Ruskin, 1878

Japan has been infected by the
western culture virus, and is losing
its fondness for admiring the moon,
picnics for flower viewing, and
meditations at tea ceremonies
in the industrial smog.
Charlie Chaplin, 1935

As we have seen, the triumph of
Japonisme took place because it
was adopted more or less at the same
time by the most progressive artists
and designers in the closing years of
the nineteenth century. But, like all
fashionable vogues, its very popularity
soon led to it becoming distinctly
'outmoded'. Its influence still
continued, however, in the field
of book illustration, fashion and the
graphic arts. One of the minor marvels
of Japonisme is a series of prints by
Henri Rivière (1864–1951), entitled
The Thirty-Six Views of the Eiffel Tower,
compositions published in 1902 as
lithographs but first conceived as
woodcuts in the 1880s. Rivière first
encountered Japanese art through
seeing prints circulate at Rudolphe
Salis's famous cabaret, Le Chat Noir.
He became a habitué and joined the
staff working on the house journal and,
later, as stage director, ran the puppet
shadow theatre.

During his years at Le Chat Noir,
Rivière met the dealers in Japanese art,
Bing and Hayashi, and began to collect
prints himself. He also practised the
technique of cutting woodblocks,
mixing his own inks and using
Japanese paper on which to print. For
his act of homage to Hokusai's *Thirty-*
Six Views of Mount Fuji (*c.*1830–5),
however, Rivière used with great
sensitivity the medium of lithography
(243). Rivière's prints were published
not only as an explicit homage to
Hokusai's series but also as an ironic
comment on the permanence of the
controversial Eiffel Tower, built as a
'temporary' structure for the World
Exhibition of 1889, but which by 1902
had become a universally recognized
symbol of Paris. *The Eiffel Tower Under*
Construction, Seen From the Trocadéro
(244) reflects Rivière's special affinity
with the theme, while the shape of the
tower affectionately parodies the
flawless cone of the great volcano
and the Japanese woodcut technique
in the depiction of falling snow upon
the umbrellas of passers-by. All thirty-
six of Rivière's prints are not mere
pastiche but provide an informed
comment from a mid-point between
Eastern and Western art.

244
Henri Rivière,
*The Eiffel Tower Under
Construction, Seen From
the Trocadéro* from *The
Thirty-Six Views of the
Eiffel Tower,*
1902.
Lithograph,
page: 17 x 20 cm
(6⁵⁄₈ x 7⁷⁄₈ in)

Japonisme

245
Henri Rivière,
Celebrations on the Seine, 14 July from *Thirty-Six Views of the Eiffel Tower*,
1902.
Lithograph,
page: 17 x 20 cm
(6⅝ x 7⅞ in)

246
Kokyo,
Japanese Destroyer Squadron Outside Port Arthur,
1903.
Colour woodblock,
31·1 x 76·2 cm
(12¼ x 30 in)

Rivière shared with Hokusai a strong interest in the seasons, weather and the time of day and how these varying factors affect the human condition. These comparisons, or rather parallels, are strikingly conveyed in Rivière's depiction of the fireworks, Japanese lanterns and searchlights against the night sky in *Celebrations on the Seine, 14 July* (245). Rivière's lithograph showing the beams of intense light used in the celebratory display was published in 1902. Within a year searchlights would be depicted in military, not celebratory use, playing a part in one of the major events in the dreadnought race that involved the great powers at the turn of the century. Japan had become alarmed by the steady growth of the Russian presence in Manchuria, symbolized by the development of the Trans-Siberian Railway to Port Arthur, providing Russia with a supply route that could be used to take over Korea. This was seen as a territorial threat by Japan. Events escalated, a major incident taking place on 13 April 1903 when the Russian flagship was blown up by a Japanese destroyer. In Kokyo's print (246) the squadron ships are shown with their lights probing the night sky, revealing ships disabled by exploding torpedoes. Within a week of this event this triptych was for sale on the streets of Tokyo to a public avid for news. But the print marked the end of an era. New technology of mechanical photographic reproduction sounded the death knell of the popular woodblock print in both the East and the West.

Rivière's work, and the celebration in Paris of the Universal Exposition of 1900, marked the end of an era, but the old themes continued to work their magic. In 1905, Henri Matisse (1869–1954) painted a study of a woman beside water entitled *La Japonaise, Madame Matisse*. There is something reassuring, a sense of the continuity of artistic inspiration, that Matisse, the supreme decorative master of the twentieth century, should begin his career with a look back at the decorative art of the Japanese print.

In the world of high fashion, rather than that of avant-garde art, there was still inspiration to be gained from Japanese designs for fabrics. The old magical glamour continued to work when new fashionable dresses were worn by Sadayakko and reproduced in the pages of the fashion journal, *Femina* (see 168). Even the dislike of the young Picasso for Japanese subjects was overcome sufficiently for him to create four designs for a poster of her in a performance, although it does not seem to have been produced.

The needs of the fashion industry created a demand for Oriental themes far more wide-ranging in its borrowings than Japonisme. A list of the Oriental exhibitions held in Paris from 1900 to 1912 would take in every country in the East, creating vogue after vogue, crowned by a great Orientalist exhibition at the Grand Palais in 1909 which coincided with the triumphant arrival of the Ballets Russes. Although none of the new ballets had a Japanese subject, the great impresario Serge Diaghilev did start his career with a real appreciation of the subject. From 1899 to 1905 he ran a challenging magazine, *The World of Art*, published in St Petersburg in a large format and illustrated by black-and-white drawings. A large part of the February 1902 issue was devoted to the drawings of Hokusai and Hiroshige, somewhat incongruously accompanying long articles on Nietzsche, Dostoevsky and Tolstoy, followed by nine pages of drawings by Aubrey Beardsley, whom Diaghilev had met in Dieppe just before Beardsley died.

Although fashion was always changing, Japonisme would remain a constant factor to be reckoned with, whether on the catwalk, the potter's wheel or the cinema screen. In 1897, the Lumière brothers' representative, Gabriel Veyre, had made the first tentative short films in Japan of two or three minutes' duration.

Predictably, his first choice of subject for the new medium of film was *Geisha in a Jinrikisha* (247). Veyre also filmed such subjects as *Kendo Combat* (Japanese broad-stick fencing) and *Rain Dance of Spring*. Today in Kyoto, where many of the first Japanese films were made, the visitor can see a display in the city museum of a bank of videos showing excerpts from the period costume dramas which come so naturally to Japanese actors. The earliest clips date from the very turn of the nineteenth and twentieth centuries and they continue right up to present-day popular TV soap operas on period themes.

By 1925 the *kabuki*-orientated films of the early days of Japanese cinema had consciously changed into two genres that continue today, the *Jidai-geki* or period film set before 1868 (the year marking the beginning of the Meiji era), and the *gendai-geki* or film of contemporary life. The great success of Akira Kurosawa's films, such as *Rashomon* (1950) and *The Seven Samurai* (1954) owes much to these genres.

The Japanese cinema went through a much longer 'primitive' period than the cinemas of the West, for the perennial popularity of *kabuki* meant that the earliest Japanese films were versions of *kabuki* plays, of which there exist at least 350.

223

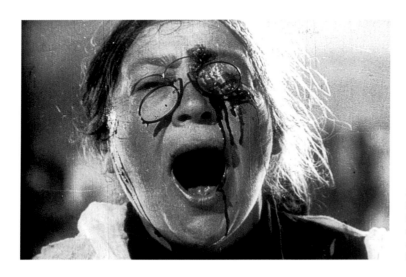

One *kabuki* convention – the use of *onnagata* professional female impersonators – was discarded in the 1920s, for it worked against any form of close-up photographic realism. However, another important convention was retained, that of the *benshi* – an actor-narrator who stands beside the stage (or screen) commentating on the action rather like the chorus in the Greek classical drama. As a result the introduction of sound in the 1930s was a much more gradual process in Japan than in the West.

The great Russian film director, Sergei Mikhailovich Eisenstein, first became interested in *kabuki* during the civil war when in 1920 he was sent back from active service at the front to study the Japanese language, the ideograms of which came to his mind later and played an important part in formulating his theories on montage and the swift flow of contrasting images. From this time Eisenstein began to collect Japanese prints, such as the close-up heads of *kabuki* actors by Sharaku (see 45). The convention of the frozen pose in an *otokodate* role had just the bold simplicity of outline which appealed to Eisenstein. In *Battleship Potemkin* in 1925 he elaborated his radically innovative theory of 'montage' (cutting) exemplified in one of the most famous film sequences ever made, the Odessa Steps.

In it Eisenstein combined close-ups of the action at decelerated camera speeds, and the frozen poses of such memorable subjects as the old lady wearing *pince-nez* which are broken by a bullet (248).

It was not, however, until August 1928, when the *kabuki* theatre visited Moscow, that Eisenstein enjoyed his first exciting experience of their acting, which he studied intently. His initial reaction was to compare the actors' performances with sportsmen:

The first association that occurs to us in our perception of the Kabuki is football, the most collective ensemble sport. Voice, rattle, mime, the narrator's cries, the folding sets, seem like innumerable backs, half-backs, goal-keepers forward passing the dramatic ball to one another and scoring a goal against the astonished audience.

The following year (1929) he published *Beyond the Shot (the Cinematographic Principle and Japanese Culture).*

In 1941, nearing the end of his career, Eisenstein was commissioned to make a large-scale historical epic glorifying the sixteenth-century tyrant *Ivan the Terrible*. One of the most moving scenes in the film shows the grief-stricken Ivan retired to a provincial palace where he is petitioned to return to Moscow by his people. They form a long winding procession glimpsed by Ivan through slits in the castle wall (249).

249
Eisenstein,
The masses arriving at
the mountain retreat of
Ivan, still from *Ivan the
Terrible Part I*, 1944.

250
Katsushika Hokusai,
*The Duke Huan Returning
His Army Home,
Following the Lead of an
Old Horse* from the
Manga,
1834.
Colour woodblock,
17·5 x 11·5 cm
(7 x 4½ in)

251
Akira Kurosawa,
still from *Rashomon*,
1950

The sequence has an eerie resemblance to a double-page plate in the *Manga* depicting the Duke of Huan returning home with his army, following in the footsteps of an old riderless horse (250). The eagle-like profile of Ivan the Terrible recalls the bird of prey in Hiroshige's *Eagle over Fukugawa* (see 89). Yet again a print by Hiroshige and the magical bran-tub of Hokusai's sketches of things 'just as they come' had provided a major Western artist with direct inspiration.

The Japanese film director, Akira Kurosawa, started his career in the bellicose 1930s as a propaganda film-maker. In 1945, the last year of the war, he produced a film based on a *kabuki* drama and began to work on *Rashomon* (251). The worldwide fame of the film began with its success at the Venice Film Festival in 1951, where it won the Golden Lion of Venice award for best foreign film. It is difficult, half a century later, to realize how cut off from the outside world post-war Japan appeared. The country was still separated from the rest of the world by the events of World War II and the shadow of the atomic bomb's 'mushroom cloud'. Nothing of any artistic significance had emerged from Japan for some decades. The West, still fascinated by the Japanese legend, fell upon Kurosawa's epic with an enthusiasm that closely recalls the excitement with which their ancestors greeted the *Manga* a century earlier.

The film, set in medieval Japan, tells a story which, like Robert Browning's poem *The Ring and the Book*, deals with a murder and rape from the differing viewpoints of the principal characters in the drama. All the versions are different but which is the true one? One sequence in the film, in which the bandit kisses the victim while her eyes remain wide open, brought much criticism from Japanese audiences who accused Kurosawa of making films directed at Western audiences, a question to which he had replied, 'exoticism on its own isn't enough. I didn't think of being internationally famous: I just wanted to make good films.' This he went on to do with *The Seven Samurai* of 1958, with compelling characters who tell the story of an élite cadre of brave and heroic mercenaries who are hired by a village to protect them from bandits. The mercenaries' bravery is contrasted with the cowardly conduct of the civilians who pay them for their defence. For the concluding scene in the film, the battle between the samurai and bandits, Kurosawa created a montage sequence that rivals the massacre in *Battleship Potemkin*.

The American director, John Sturges, saw *The Seven Samurai* and realized that its story was as exciting as a good Western, and remade the film in Hollywood as *The Magnificent Seven* in 1960.

252
**Akira Kurosawa,
still from *Ran*, 1985**

Such borrowings were by no means all one way and, in tracing the following chain of events, it is intriguing to discover that Shinobu Hashimoto, the scriptwriter of both *Rashomon* and *The Seven Samurai*, admitted that John Ford's *Stagecoach* (1939) was his favourite film.

The Magnificent Seven was just one of several Hollywood Westerns which reflect the influence of Japanese samurai films with their emphasis on violence, loyalty and heroic death. Their popular success when remade by Hollywood ultimately spawned the 'Spaghetti Western' – violent films of the American West, starring American actors and shot for economic reasons in Italy, Spain and Yugoslavia. A classic example of a film of this type was Sergio Leone's *A Fistful of Dollars*, a painstaking shot-by-shot copy of Kurosawa's *Yojimbo* of 1961. *Rashomon* also could not escape the copying process, being insensitively remade in a 1964 Hollywood Western, *The Outrage*, starring Paul Newman, and again as *Iron Maze* in 1991, a US/Japanese version set in Pittsburgh. Several other films that Kurosawa made as tributes to American genres were remade yet again in Hollywood with varying results.

Today when watching these plagiarisms we recall Pierre-Auguste Renoir's prophecy which he made of prints but is equally applicable to films:

Japanese prints are certainly very interesting as Japanese prints in other words as long as they stay in Japan … people should not appropriate what belongs to another race; in so doing they are apt to make stupid mistakes. There would be soon a kind of universal art, without any individual characteristics.

Two of Kurosawa's finest films have Shakespearean themes: *Throne of Blood* (1957), a version of *Macbeth*, and *Ran* (1985; 252), literally *Chaos*, a version of *King Lear*, transposed to medieval Japan and described by Kurosawa as 'Human deeds as viewed from heaven'. In *Ran*, Lear's daughters are replaced by three sons but the fool is retained. Chaos reigns in powerful stylized battle scenes as brother wages war upon brother. Kurosawa spent ten years raising the money for the film and was 75-years old when he made it. While admired in the West as a master, in Japan Kurosawa is still merely regarded as a commercial film-maker.

The continuing interrelationship between East and West in the field of the cinema, the great visual art form of today, could equally be found in other disciplines. In examining such exchanges we can put into proper perspective the questions raised by Japonisme of the late nineteenth century and the process of borrowing, plagiarism or reinterpretation which still continues today.

253
Christopher Dresser,
Climbing Kilns, from
*Traditional Arts and
Crafts of Japan*,
1882

254
Bernard Leach,
Vase decorated with
leaping fish,
c.1965.
Stoneware,
height: 36·1 cm (14⅛ in).
Private collection

Since Whistler's demise, butterflies had found a different resting place with an artist such as Redon adding his own delicate colours to their wings. They had lost none of the magical powers of inspiration for Redon, who only took up the use of colour in his late middle age. As a theme for poetry they appealed to the Imagist poets, on whom Japanese themes still continued to cast a spell. Poets such as Ezra Pound and Amy Lowell experimented with the Japanese verse forms, the *Tanka* and the *Haiku*, with powerful and prophetic effect:

*On a Temple Bell
A tiny butterfly is settled
Upon a massive temple bell
Asleep.*

*Perched upon the muzzle of a cannon
A yellow butterfly is slowly opening
and shutting its wings.*

'I think without doubt that the Japanese are the most pottery-minded people in the whole world,' wrote Bernard Leach in the introduction to an exhibition:

We were not folk potters, nor were we simple country folk, like those who had made the best English medieval pots (or their counterparts in the Far East) – we were artist potters and, as such, our horizons had begun to be all horizons.

Bernard Leach is here describing his years with the Japanese potter, Hamada, whose own terse précis of similar thoughts reads, 'beauty is not in the head or heart, but in the abdomen.' Together in England and Japan the two men did more than anyone else to prove that although Japonisme as a fashionable craze was over, the dual aesthetic disciplines of Britain and Japan had still much to contribute to each other.

Leach, like William Morris before him, was one of those protean figures who is almost more important for what he represents than for his actual productions. Born in China in 1887, Leach was educated in England, a circumstance which enabled him to write, 'having these two extremes of culture to draw upon caused me to return to Japan, where the synthesis of East and West has gone farthest.' Aged twenty-one, attracted by the writing of Lafcadio Hearn, he went out to Japan, and remained there and in Beijing for eleven years, studying stoneware and going through full-time training as a potter under Kenzan Ogata VI, before returning to England in 1920. With Hamada he set up some traditional Japanese climbing kilns (the first to be made in the Western hemisphere; 253) at St Ives in Cornwall, the famous artists' colony.

The Leach kiln consisted of several chambers. The heat from the fire passed through the first chamber and into the second where it ignited extra wood to boost its heat level. This happened in each chamber until the last, which contained ware for biscuit firing. In 1936 he built more kilns at Dartington Hall in Devon. Leach's practice was based on an attitude to the craftsman's role which echoed Morris's views, combined with a sensitivity to materials that came from the traditional Japanese potter's search for aesthetic purity of form. For some time he continued to produce stoneware in the Japanese manner (254) before turning his attention to the English slipware tradition. When he died in 1979 at the age of ninety-two he had done more to interest the public at large in pottery than any other man, by his work, teaching and books, in particular his guide to the practical and aesthetic experience of pottery, *A Potter's Book*. Leach had become, like Morris, a legend in his own lifetime. As he remarked in 1968:

all my life I have been a courier between East and West. I believe in the interplay and marriage of the two complementary branches of human culture as the prelude to the unity and maturity of man.

His views on what makes a good pot he once summarized as:

curves for beauty, angles for stability. A small foot for grace, a broad one for stability. Enduring forms are full of quiet assurance. Overstatement is worse than understatement. Technique is a means to an end. It is no end in itself.

In his last years Bernard Leach's failing eyesight shielded him from the electronic cybernetic age and such strange artistic phenomena as the arrival of 'Japan Animation' and 'Techno Orientalism'. In the eyes of the West, Japan became the new Cyburg, a theme closely identified with the name of Osamu Tezuka (1928–89), whose science fiction led to the glorification of the robot, now seen in many fields and perceived as an object of both fascination and fear. Robots now manifest themselves in the sinister science-fiction world of Pokemon, popular not only in Japan but globally.

A much more reassuring development of cultural affinities between the East and West was provided by the composer Benjamin Britten, who in 1957 made an extensive tour of the Far East to study the musical instru-ments of different lands and visited Japan, where he heard *samisen* recitals by geisha and a *gagaku* orchestra whose reverberating sounds led him to declare, 'Oh! To find some equivalent to those extraordinary noises the Japanese musicans made!'

256
**Cecil Beaton,
Front cover design of
Japanese, published by
Weidenfeld & Nicolson,
1959**

On his return to England, acting on the advice of his librettist William Plomer, Britten used a Japanese libretto based upon a *noh* play he admired, entitled *Sumida Gawa* (*Sumida River*), in one of his three Church Parables. The result was a haunting work entitled *Curlew River*. Britten also used Japanese instruments and themes in his music for the choreographer John Cranko's ballet *The Prince of the Pagodas*, also written in 1957.

The name of Cecil Beaton (1904–80) has become virtually synonymous with glamour and high fashion, but he also had an amazing eye for the landscape, people and customs of foreign lands, which he put to good use when touring China, Egypt and India in the 1940s as a war correspondent. In 1959 just over a century after Wirgman's first European *ad vivum* studies of the daily life of Japan, Beaton followed his lead and visited Japan, commissioned by the American magazine, *Harper's Bazaar*. Both his camera and his pen created some of his finest landscapes and also captured the dramatic essence of *noh* and *kabuki* performances.

On the streets his eye noted 'sandwich' men lounging at a street corner, 'their salad-bowl hats and striped cloaks advertising the latest film' (255), and also shrines, tea ceremonies and contemporary writers, such as the dramatist and dandy, Mishima, whose ritual suicide shocked the nation in the 1960s. For Beaton:

Japan is in some respects like England. Both are island nations; both have a terrible climate. Both have traditions they are proud of, traditions that can be a glory but also an anachronistic curse in a world where time never stands still.

Whether using the camera lens or a brush, Beaton's genius resulted in a highly personal interpretation of the country. On the cover of his book *Japanese* he portrayed such pictorial clichés as trailing wisteria, irises, rocks and water, lanterns, a geisha – all subjects which when treated by less skillful hands teeter on the edge of kitsch, but which Beaton could make into unforgettable images (256).

Katsushika Hokusai,
*A Sudden Gust of Wind
at Ejiri*, from the series
*Thirty-Six Views of
Mount Fuji*,
*c.*1830–2.
Colour woodblock,
25·7 x 38 cm
(10¹⁄₈ x 15 in)

Today it is just over 150 years since the arrival in Japan of Perry and the black ships in Edo (see Chapter 1). Although so long ago, the old magic continues to give inspiration, notably in the work of the Canadian artist, Jeff Wall (b.1946). Using the landscape just outside Vancouver in British Columbia, Wall creates a vibrant photographic collage based upon Hokusai's print *A Sudden Gust of Wind at Ejiri* from the series *Thirty-Six Views of Mount Fuji* (257, 258). In both pictures the wind playfully snatches at the paper hand-kerchiefs which have escaped from the kimono worn by the lady with a head-scarf. Free as air they fly skywards to join the dancing leaves and an escaped hat.

A wind from the East still continues to blow ...

258
Jeff Wall,
*A Sudden Gust of Wind
(after Hokusai)*,
1993.
Photographic
transparency and
illuminated display case,
250 x 397 x 34 cm
(98$\frac{1}{2}$ x 156$\frac{1}{4}$ x 13$\frac{3}{8}$ in).
Tate Collection, London

For Maureen

I would like to thank the following for their advice over the years: Stephen Calloway, Richard Dennis, Amanda Jane Doran, the late Albert Gallichan, Peter Rose and Peyton Skipwith. Catherine Haill of the Theatre Museum shared with me her knowledge of Gilbert and Sullivan, and Ann Leane her love of fans, while Tomoko Sato gave encouragement and the long-term loan of books. Joan Navarre pointed out the interesting literary phenomenon of earlier versions of the Madame Butterfly story by American writers. In Alsace, Beatrix and Michael Everett were admirable guides to the Théodore Deck Collection, Guebwiller. In Leiden, Chris and Nellie Smeenk introduced me to Matthi Forrer, who showed me the riches of the Ethnology Museum at a very busy time. At Phaidon Press, Bernard Dod faced the strain of editing yet another book by me with equanimity. His colleagues, Beulah Davies, Maya Gartner, Sophia Gibb and Susannah Stone also kindly coped with my aesthetic demands.

Bibliography

Adburgham, Alison. Liberty's: A Biography of a Shop. London, 1975
Alcock, Sir Rutherford. The Capital of the Tycoon. 2 vols. London, 1863
Applebaum, Stephen (ed.). The Complete Masters of the Poster. New York, 1990
Asleson, Robyn. Albert Moore. London, 2000
Aslin, Elizabeth. The Aesthetic Movement: Prelude to Art Nouveau. London, 1969
Aslin, Elizabeth. E W Godwin: Furniture and Interior Decoration. London, 1986
Baily, Leslie. The Gilbert and Sullivan Book. London, 1952
Baldry, A L. Albert Moore: His Life and Work. London, 1894
Beardsley, Aubrey. 'The Art of the Hoarding', in The New Review. July, 1894
Beardsley, Aubrey. The Letters of Aubrey Beardsley. Maas, Duncan and Good (eds). London, 1971
Beaton, Cecil. Japanese. London, 1959
Beckson, Karl E. Aesthetes and Decadents of the 1890s: An Anthology of British Poetry and Prose. New York, 1966
Beerbohm, Sir Max. Rossetti and His Circle. London, 1922
Blussé, Leonard, Willem Remmelink and Ivo Smits (eds). Bridging the Divide: 400 Years The Netherlands – Japan. Amsterdam, 2000
Budden, Julian. Puccini: His Life and Works. Oxford, 2002
Burty, Philippe. Japonisme. Paris, 1875
Calloway, Stephen. Charles Ricketts. London, 1979
Carner, M. Puccini: A Critical Biography. London, 1992
Carr, Mrs J. Comyns. Comyns Carr's Reminiscences. London, 1926
Chesneau, E. 'Le Japon a Paris', in Gazette des Beaux-Arts, 1879
Cook, Clarence. The House Beautiful: Essays on Beds and Tables, Stools and Candlesticks. New York, 1895
Cooper, Emmanuel. Bernard Leach: Life and Work. New Haven and London, 2003

Cooper, Nicholas. The Opulent Eye: Late Victorian and Edwardian Taste in Interior Design. London, 1976
Crane, Lucy. Art and the Formation of Taste. London, 1882
Crane, Walter. An Artist's Reminiscences. London, 1907
Crane, Walter. William Morris to Whistler. London, 1911
Crauzat, Ernest de. L'Oeuvre gravé et lithographié de Steinlen. Paris, 1913
Crawford, T S. A History of the Umbrella. London, 1970
Dalby, Liza Crihfield. Geisha. London, 2001
Dalby, Liza Crihfield. Kimono. London, 2000
Downer, Lesley. Madame Sadayakko: The Geisha who Seduced the West. London, 2003
Dresser, Dr Christopher. Japan, its Architecture, Art and Art Manufactures. London, 1882
Dresser, Dr Christopher. Traditional Arts and Crafts of Japan. London, 1882, reprinted London and New York, 1994
Eastlake, C L. Hints on Household Taste in Furniture, Upholstery and Other Details. London, 1867
Ellmann, Richard. Oscar Wilde. London, 1987
Ferriday, Peter. 'The Peacock Room', in Architectural Review, CXXV, 1959, pp 407–14
Fletcher, Ian. Romantic Mythologies. London, 1967
Fletcher, Ian. Walter Pater. London, 1959
Floyd, P. Seeking the Floating World: The Japanese Spirit in Turn of the Century France. Toyko, 1989
Franklin, Colin. The Private Presses. Aldershot, 1969
French, Calvin L. Shiba Kokan: Artist, Innovator, and Pioneer in the Westernization of Japan. New York, 1974
Fry, Roger. Vision and Design. London, 1920
Gaunt, William. The Aesthetic Adventure. London, 1945
Gillespie, John K. and Yoichi Sugiura. Traditional Japanese Culture and Modern Japan. Tokyo, 1993
Girouard, M. Sweetness and Light: The 'Queen Anne' Movement 1860–1900. Oxford, 1977
Golden, Arthur. Memoirs of a Geisha. London, 1997
de Goncourt, Edmond and Jules. The Goncourt Journals 1851–1896. A complete scholarly edition appeared between 1956–9 and various selections have since been published.
Goodman, Andrew. Gilbert and Sullivan's London. London, 2000
Grossmith, George and Weedon. The Diary of a Nobody. First published as a serial in Punch, 1888. First published as a book with Weedon's illustrations in London, 1892.
Haill, Catherine. Fun without Vulgarity. London, 1996
Halen, Widar. Christopher Dresser: A Pioneer of Modern Design. London, 1990
Hamilton, James. Arthur Rackham. London, 1990
Hamilton, Walter. The Aesthetic

Movement in England. London, 1882
Harbron, Dudley. The Conscious Stone: The Life of Edward William Godwin. London, 1949
Hardwick, Michael. Discovery of Japan. London, 1970
Hart-Davis, R (ed.). The Letters of Oscar Wilde. London, 1962
Hart-Davis, R (ed.). More Letters of Oscar Wilde. London, 1985
Haslam, Malcolm. The Martin Brothers: Potters. London, 1978
Haweis, Mrs H R. The Art of Beauty. London, 1878
Haweis, Mrs H R. The Art of Decoration. London, 1881
Haweis, Mrs H R. Beautiful Houses. London, 1882
Heneage, Simon and Henry Ford. Sidney Syme: Master of the Mysterious. London, 1980
Herries, Amanda. Japanese Gardens in Britain. Princes Risborough, 2001
Hiatt, Charles. Picture Posters. London, 1895
Hillier, Bevis. Posters. London, 1969
Hobbs, Richard. Odilon Redon. London, 1977
Holland, Merlin and Rupert Hart-Davis (eds). The Complete Letters of Oscar Wilde. London, 2000
Hornung, Clarence P (ed.). Will Bradley: His Graphic Art. New York, 1974
Hutt, Julia and Alexander, Hélène. Ogi: A History of the Japanese Fan. London, 1992
Huysmans, J-K. Against Nature. 1884. Robert Baldick (trans.), Harmondsworth, 1959
Jacquier, Phillippe and Marion Pranal. Gabriel Veyre, Opérateur Lumière. Arles, 1996
John, N (ed.). Madama Butterfly, English National Opera Guide, No. 26. London, 1984
Kouwenhoven, Arlette and Matthi Forrer. Siebold and Japan: His Life and Work. Leiden, 2000
Lambourne, Lionel. The Aesthetic Movement. London, 1996
Lane, Richard. Masters of the Japanese Print: Their World and their Work. London, 1962
Luckhurst, Kenneth W. The Story of Exhibitions. London, 1951
Meech, Julia. Frank Lloyd Wright and the Art of Japan: The Architect's Other Passion. New York and London, 2001
Meech, Julia. Rain and Snow: The Umbrella in Japanese Art. New York, 1993
Merrill, Linda. A Pot of Paint: Aesthetics on Trial in Whistler v. Ruskin. Washington, DC, and London, 1992
Merrill, Linda. The Peacock Room: A Cultural Biography. Washington, DC, and London, 1998
Michener, James A. The Floating World. London, 1955
Michener, James A. The Hokusai Sketch Books: Selections from the Manga. Tokyo and Rutland, VT, 1958
Milner, John. Symbolists and Decadents. London, 1971
Milner, John. The Studios of Paris: The Capital of Art in the Nineteenth Century. London and New Haven, 1988
Omoto, Keiko and Francis Macouin. Quand le Japon s'ouvrit au monde: Émile

Guimet et les arts d'Asie. Paris, 2001
Ono, Ayako. Japonisme in Britain. London, 2003
Page, Jesse. Japan: Its People and its Missions. London, 1896
Pennell, Elizabeth and Joseph. The Life of James McNeill Whistler. 2 vols. London and Philadelphia, 1908
Pevsner, Sir Nikolaus. Studies in Art, Architecture and Design: Vol II Victorian and After. London, 1968
Quennell, Peter (ed.). Marcel Proust, 1871–1922. A Centenary Volume. London, 1971
Rossetti, W M. 'Japanese Woodcuts', in The Reader. 31 October, 1863
Reade, Brian. Aubrey Beardsley. Woodbridge, 1987
Reade, Brian. Sexual Heretics: Male Homosexuality in English Literature from 1850–1900. London, 1970
Ricketts, Charles. Recollections of Oscar Wilde. London, 1932
Rothenstein, William. Men and Memories: Recollections of William Rothenstein. London, 1931
Salwey, Charlotte M. Fans of Japan. 1894
Sansom, William. Proust and His World. London, 1973
Screech, Timon. Sex and the Floating World: Erotic Images in Japan 1700–1820. London, 1999
Soros, Susan (ed.). E W Godwin: Aesthetic Movement Architect and Designer. New Haven and London, 1999
Spencer, Isobel. Walter Crane. London, 1975
Spencer, Robin. The Aesthetic Movement: Theory and Practice. London and New York, 1972
Sturgis, Matthew. Aubrey Beardsley: A Biography. London, 1999
Sutton, Denys. Nocturne: The Art of James McNeill Whistler. London, 1963
Swinburne, Algernon Charles. Poems and Ballads. London, 1866
Taylor, Hilary. James McNeill Whistler. London, 1978
Taylor, Ina. The Art of Kate Greenaway: A Nostalgic Portrait of Childhood. Exeter, 1991
Thiébaut, Philippe and Fumi Yosano. Les dessins de Gallé: Emile Gallé et ses ateliers. Tokyo, 1988
Watkins, Nicholas. Bonnard. London, 1994
Watson, Oliver. Studio Pottery. London, 1993
Whistler, J M. The Gentle Art of Making Enemies. London, 1890, reprinted New York, 1967
White, Colin. The Enchanted World of Jesse M King. Edinburgh, 1989
Wichmann, Siegfried. Japonisme: The Japanese Influence on Western Art Since 1858. London, 1981
Wordell, Charles B. Japan in American Fiction, 1880–1905. Bristol, 2001
Yamada, Chisaburoh F (ed.). Dialogue in Art: Japan and the West. London, 1976
Young, Andrew McLaren, Margaret F MacDonald, Robin Spencer and Hamish Miles. The Paintings of James McNeill Whistler. 2 vols. New Haven and London, 1980

Exhibition Catalogues

In recent years much of the most rewarding research into Japonisme has been published in the form of increasingly weighty exhibition catalogues.

Art Nouveau. Museum of Modern Art, New York, 1960
Becker, Vivienne. The Jewellery of Rene Lalique. Goldsmiths' Company, London, 1987
Burke, Doreen Bolger. In Pursuit of Beauty: Americans and the Aesthetic Movement. Metropolitan Museum of Art, New York, 1986
Bury, Shirley (ed.). Liberty's, 1875–1975. Victoria and Albert Museum, London, 1975
Catalogue of the Van Gogh Museum's Collection of Japanese Prints. Van Gogh Museum, Amsterdam, 1991
Ceramiques: Théodore Deck (1823–1891). Musée du Florival, Guebwiller. 1991
Chrighton, R A. The Floating World: Japanese Popular Prints, 1700–1900. Victoria and Albert Museum, London, 1973
Christie, Ian, and David Elliot (eds). Eisenstein at Ninety. Museum of Modern Art, Oxford, 1988
The Dawn of the Floating World 1650–1765: Early Ukiyo-e Treasures from the Museum of Fine Arts, Boston. Museum of Fine Arts, Boston, and Royal Academy of Arts, London, 2001
Dorment, Richard and Margaret F MacDonald. James McNeill Whistler. Tate Gallery, London, 1994
Druick, Douglas W and Peter Kort Zegers. Van Gogh and Gauguin: The Studio of the South. The Art Institute of Chicago and Van Gogh Museum, Amsterdam, 2002
Faulkner, Rupert. Hiroshige Fan Prints. Victoria and Albert Museum, London, 2001
Farrer, Anne (ed.). A Garden Bequest – Plants from Japan. The Japan Society, London, 2001
Farrington, Anthony. Trading Places; The East India Company and Asia 1600–1834. British Library, London, 2002
Forrer, Matthi. Hokusai: Prints and Drawings. Royal Academy of Arts, London, 1991
The Great Japan Exhibition: Art of the Edo Period 1600–1868. Royal Academy of Arts, London, 1981–2
Hamilton, Vivien. Joseph Crawhall 1861–1913. Glasgow Museums and Art Galleries and The Fine Art Society, London, 1990
Hayes Tucker, Paul. Monet in the '90s: The Series Paintings. Museum of Fine Arts, Boston, and Royal Academy of Arts, London, 1989
Ives, Colta Fella. The Great Wave: The Influence of Japanese Woodcuts on French Prints. Metropolitan Museum of Art, New York, 1974
Japan und Europa 1543–1929. Berliner Festspiele 1993
Japanese Amazement: Shiba Kokan 1747–1818. Artist under the Spell of the West. Historisch Museum, Amsterdam
Le Japonisme. Grand Palais, Paris, and National Museum of Western Art, Tokyo, 1988
Japonisme Mode. Palais Galliera, Paris, 1996
Jervis, Simon. Art and Design in Europe and America 1800–1900. Victoria and Albert Museum, London, 1987
Komanecky, Michael and Virginia Fabbri Butera. The Folding Image: Screens by Western Artists. National Gallery of Art, Washington, DC, and Yale University Art Gallery, New Haven, 1984
Mackenzie, John M. The Victorian Vision. Victoria and Albert Museum, London, 2001
Matyjaszkiewicz, Krystyna (ed.). James Tissot. Barbican Art Gallery, London, 1984
Musée des Tissus de Lyons, Guide des Collections. Lyon, 1988
Monet and Japan. National Gallery of Australia, Canberra, and Art Gallery of Western Australia, Perth, 2001
The New Painting: Impressionism 1874–1886. Fine Arts Museums, San Francisco, and National Gallery of Art, Washington, DC, 1986
Reade, Brian Edmund. Art Nouveau and Alphonse Mucha. Victoria and Albert Museum, London, 1963
Reade, Brian Edmund. Aubrey Beardsley. Victoria and Albert Museum, London, 1966
Rivière Henri. Les trente-six vues de la tour Eiffel. New Otani Art Museum, Tokyo, 1989
Sato, Tomoko and Toshio Watanabe (eds). Japan and Britain: An Aesthetic Dialogue 1850–1930. Barbican Art Gallery, London, and Setagaya Art Museum, Tokyo, 1991
Smith, Lawrence (ed.). Ukiyoe: Images of Unknown Japan. British Museum, London, 1988
Soros, Susan (ed.) E W Godwin. Bard Graduate Center for Studies in the Decorative Arts, New York, 1999.
Spencer, Robin. The Aesthetic Movement and the Cult of Japan. The Fine Art Society, London, 1972
Toulouse-Lautrec. Hayward Gallery, London, and Grand Palais, Paris, 1991–2
Wichmann, Siegfried (ed.). World Cultures and Modern Art: The Encounter of 19th and 20th century European Art and Music with Asia, Africa, Oceania, Afro- and Indo-America. Haus der Junst and Organisationskomitee für die Spiele der XX Olympiade, Munich, 1972
Yonemura, Ann. Yokohama: Prints from Nineteenth-Century Japan. Smithsonian Institution, Washington, DC, 1990

Picture Credits

Melbourne: 101
National Museum of Ethnology, Leiden: 13
Oberösterreichisches Landesmuseum, Linz: 149
RMN, Paris: photo Harry Bréjat: 59, 257, photo Christian Jean: 226, photo R-G Ojéda: 117, photo Jean Schormans: 123
Roland Grant Archive: 248, 249, 251, 252
Peter Rose and the Albert Gallichan Foundation: 72, 73, 179
The Royal Archives © H M Queen Elizabeth II: ch. op. 6
Potteries Musem and Art Gallery, Stoke-on-Trent: 110
Sterling and Francine Clark Art Institute, Williamstown: ch. op. 4, 80
Sotheby's Picture Library, London: 255
Suntory Museum, Osaka: 65
Tate Collection, London: 19, 258
Tokogawa Museum, Mito: 24
Van Gogh Museum, Amsterdam, Vincent van Gogh Foundation: 83
Victoria and Albert Museum, London: 9, ch. op. 3, 44, 49, 57, 71, 84, 97, 98, 118, 125, 126, 136, 154, 176, 206, 236, 239, 245
Werner Forman Archive, London: cover, 18
Yokohama Museum of Art, Yokohama: 174

Index

Figures in italics indicate illustrations.